IARIA

SENSORDEVICES 2017

The Eighth International Conference on Sensor Device Technologies and Applications

September 10 - 14, 2017

Rome, Italy

SENSORDEVICES 2017 Editors

Winfried Vonau, Kurt-Schwabe-Institut für Mess- und Sensortechnik e.V. Meinsberg, Germany
Paulo E. Cruvinel, Embrapa Instrumentation, Brazil
Irinela Chilibon, National Institute of Research and Development for Optoelectronics, Romania
Vítor Carvalho, Ph.D., IPCA & Algoritmi Research Centre, Portugal
Marios Sophocleous, University of Cyprus - Nicosia, Cyprus

Printed from e-media with permission by:

Curran Associates, Inc.
57 Morehouse Lane
Red Hook, NY 12571

Some format issues inherent in the e-media version may also appear in this print version.

Printed by Curran Associates, Inc. (2017)

International Academy, Research, and Industry Association (IARIA)
412 Derby Way
Wilmington, DE 19810

Phone: (408) 893-6407
Fax: (408) 527-6351

petre@iaria.org

Additional copies of this publication are available from:

Curran Associates, Inc.
57 Morehouse Lane
Red Hook, NY 12571 USA
Phone: 845-758-0400
Fax: 845-758-2633
Email: curran@proceedings.com
Web: www.proceedings.com

Table of Contents

SENSORDEVICES 2017

Forward

The Eighth International Conference on Sensor Device Technologies and Applications (SENSORDEVICES 2017), held between September 10-14, 2017 in Rome, Italy, continued a series of events focusing on sensor devices themselves, the technology-capturing style of sensors, special technologies, signal control and interfaces, and particularly sensors-oriented applications. The evolution of the nano-and microtechnologies, nanomaterials, and the new business services make the sensor device industry and research on sensor-themselves very challenging.

Most of the sensor-oriented research and industry initiatives are focusing on sensor networks, data security, exchange protocols, energy optimization, and features related to intermittent connections. Recently, the concept of Internet-of-things gathers attention, especially when integrating IPv4 and IIPv6 networks.

The conference had the following tracks:

- Sensor devices
- Photonics
- Sensors domain-oriented devices, technologies, and applications
- Healthcare Sensors and Systems
- Sensor device technologies
- Trends on sensing devices and applications
- Medical devices and sensors applications
- Gas sensors
- Ultrasonic and Piezosensors
- Printed sensors

We take here the opportunity to warmly thank all the members of the SENSORDEVICES 2017 technical program committee, as well as all the reviewers. The creation of such a high quality conference program would not have been possible without their involvement. We also kindly thank all the authors that dedicated much of their time and effort to contribute to SENSORDEVICES 2017. We truly believe that, thanks to all these efforts, the final conference program consisted of top quality contributions.

We also gratefully thank the members of the SENSORDEVICES 2017 organizing committee for their help in handling the logistics and for their work that made this professional meeting a success.

We hope that SENSORDEVICES 2017 was a successful international forum for the exchange of ideas and results between academia and industry and to promote further progress in the field of sensor devices. We also hope that Rome, Italy provided a pleasant environment during the conference and everyone found some time to enjoy the historic charm of the city.

SENSORDEVICES 2017 Chairs

SENSORDEVICES Steering Committee

Sergey Y. Yurish, International Frequency Sensor Association (IFSA), Spain
Hiroo Wakaumi, Tokyo Metropolitan College of Industrial Technology, Japan
Jeong-Woo Choi, Sogang University, Korea
Jerzy P. Lukaszewicz, Nicoulaus Copernicus University, Torun, Poland
Daniele Zonta, University of Strathclyde, UK
Eiji Higurashi, University of Tokyo, Japan
Jean Paul Salvestrini, GeorgiaTech Lorraine, USA
Giovanni Pau, Kore University of Enna, Italy

SENSORDEVICES Research/Industry Chairs

Winfried Vonau, Kurt-Schwabe-Institut für Mess- und Sensortechnik e.V. Meinsberg, Germany
Paulo E. Cruvinel, Embrapa Instrumentation, Brazil
Dan Wilson, Southern Research Station - Center for Bottomland Hardwoods Research, USA
Yanxia Hou, Institut Nanosciences et Cryogénie | CEA-Grenoble, France
Yoseph Bar-Cohen, Jet Propulsion Laboratory | NASA, USA
Yurong Jiang, Hewlett-Packard Labs, USA
Irinela Chilibon, National Institute of Research and Development for Optoelectronics, Romania

SENSORDEVICES 2017
Committee

SENSORDEVICES Steering Committee

Sergey Y. Yurish, International Frequency Sensor Association (IFSA), Spain
Hiroo Wakaumi, Tokyo Metropolitan College of Industrial Technology, Japan
Jeong-Woo Choi, Sogang University, Korea
Jerzy P. Lukaszewicz, Nicoulaus Copernicus University, Torun, Poland
Daniele Zonta, University of Strathclyde, UK
Eiji Higurashi, University of Tokyo, Japan
Jean Paul Salvestrini, GeorgiaTech Lorraine, USA
Giovanni Pau, Kore University of Enna, Italy

SENSORDEVICES Research/Industry Chairs

Winfried Vonau, Kurt-Schwabe-Institut für Mess- und Sensortechnik e.V. Meinsberg, Germany
Paulo E. Cruvinel, Embrapa Instrumentation, Brazil
Dan Wilson, Southern Research Station - Center for Bottomland Hardwoods Research, USA
Yanxia Hou, Institut Nanosciences et Cryogénie | CEA-Grenoble, France
Yoseph Bar-Cohen, Jet Propulsion Laboratory | NASA, USA
Yurong Jiang, Hewlett-Packard Labs, USA
Irinela Chilibon, National Institute of Research and Development for Optoelectronics, Romania

SENSORDEVICES 2017 Technical Program Committee

Ahmed N Abdalla, FTECK, UMP, Malaysia
Iyad Abuhadrous, Palestine Technical College, Palestine
Itziar G. Alonso González, University of Las Palmas de Gran Canaria (ULPGC), Spain
Fabrice Andrieux, Lancaster University, UK
Djamila Aouada, University of Luxembourg, Luxembourg
Francisco J. Arcega, University of Zaragoza, Spain
Ammar Aryan, Université de Caen Basse-Normandie, France
Yoseph Bar-Cohen, Jet Propulsion Laboratory | NASA, USA
Michal Borecki, Warsaw University of Technology, Poland
Manuel José Cabral dos Santos Reis, University of Trás-os-Montes e Alto Douro, Portugal
John Canning, University of Technology, Sydney, Australia
Vítor Carvalho, IPCA, Barcelos, Portugal & Algoritmi Research Centre, Guimarães, Portugal
Paula M. Castro Castro, University of A Coruña, Spain
Christophe Caucheteur, University of Mons, Belgium
Jean-Pierre Chanet, Irstea, France
Irinela Chilibon, National Institute of Research and Development for Optoelectronics, Romania
Congo Tak Shing Ching, National Chung Hsing University, Taiwan

Copyright Information

Gas Detection Using a Multi-sensor Device with Pump Control and VOC Sensor

Universal Pump Sensor Control

Sergej Johann, Reinhard Noske, Viktor Feller and Matthias Bartholmai
Focus area Analytical Sciences
Bundesanstalt für Materialforschung und Prüfung (BAM)
12200 Berlin, Germany
e-mail: Sergej.Johann@bam.de; Reinhard.Noske@bam.de; Viktor.Feller@bam.de; Matthias.Bartholmai@bam.de

Abstract— **This paper deals with the development and investigation of a volatile organic compound (VOC) system for different scenarios. The integrated multi-sensor unit can detect different gases through the integrated 3-fold VOC sensor, whereby a continuous measurement takes place. The system-integrated flow control, with pump and flow sensor, allows the gas molecules to be transported directly to the VOC sensor. The entire measurement is permanently stored on an integrated Secure Digital (SD) card. If the previously determined limit range is exceeded, an alarm is generated. Due to the combination of different components, numerous applications are possible. The system is the first step or a tool towards further developments in the field of gas sensors and is primarily used for the validation of chemically based gas sensors, and it is still largely extended by application-specific influences.**

Keywords-gas detection; VOC; pump control; multi sensor device.

I. Motivation

The environmental pollution caused by air pollution is becoming increasingly important nowadays. Cities and densely populated villages suffer from the enormous pollution, but also other critical points at which people gather. Pollution caused by VOC plays a significant role and is addressed by the VOC Solvents Emissions Directive [1][2]. In order to counteract the causes, sporadic measurements are carried out in order to detect the rate of pollution and to define the threshold values. Gas fluctuations and critical concentration peaks are often overlooked, which can lead to locally extreme environmental problems, although the specific causes can often not be determined immediately. A system which can be deployed in a mobile manner, and hence which can be deployed in a distributed manner, enables chances to monitor pollution in various significant scenarios, e.g., in the areas of agriculture, chemical industry, and traffic.

Innovation is the catalyst for the technology of the future. It is important to develop new and better technologies that can continuously monitor the environmental impact. In the recently at BAM developed Universal Pump Sensor Control (UPSC3) module, different components and sensors are fused. The combination of the individual components makes the UPSC3 module an excellent monitoring and reference system. Measurements over long periods are possible, for mixed gas loads or for certain gas measurements. This paper describes the UPSC3 sensor module, which can be used for different application scenarios due to its functionalities [3]. The system is part of a mobile sensor network of several sensor units, which can also be used as standalone system.

Section 3 describes the structure of the system and how it works, followed by initial tests and comparison with commercial sensors in section 4. The paper is rounded off with the application examples of the system and their advantages in section 5 and 6. Section 7 shows the work to be done to optimize the tool and the measurement process.

II. System Description

The system and the sensors are protected from mechanical effects by an aluminum housing, see Figure 1. An air duct is provided for sucking and discharging the gas mixture. The exhaust air channel directs the induced gas-air mixture back into the environment from the commercially available VOC sensor, the sensor used is based on metal oxide semiconductor sensor technology. In order to be able to use the system on a mobile basis, all interfaces, such as supply voltage, communication and memory card slot are routed sideways. Any battery with 12 V DC voltage can be connected to the system as a power supply. The manual adjustment of the values and the monitoring of the measurement is possible on the 2.8 "touch color display; the 3 x 4 keyboard also serves as a manual entry of the values (sensor selection, threshold value, temperature, etc.). Further connection possibilities are control signals for the opening and closing of the disk valve, by servo motor to regulate the gas supply at the calibration stations, as well as I/O pins for the control of external hardware (e.g., interrupt).

Figure 1. UPSC3 front view with screen and key pad.

The connections for the signals as well as power supply are on the side.

A. UPSC3 Schematics

The system is divided into 7 blocks and figure 2 shows the sections. The control of the individual components and the sensor evaluation is handled by a 16 MHz AVR 8-bit microcontroller. In doing so, the system has been kept universal, and several interfaces allow communication with different devices. From the RS232 interface with 8 V Transistor-Transistor logic (TTL) level to Universal Asynchronous Receiver Transmitter (UART) interface with 5 V TTL level to keep the possibility of the connection to the older devices. The I2C bus allows the system to communicate with other sensors or systems. Table 1 shows the functionality of the components in function groups.

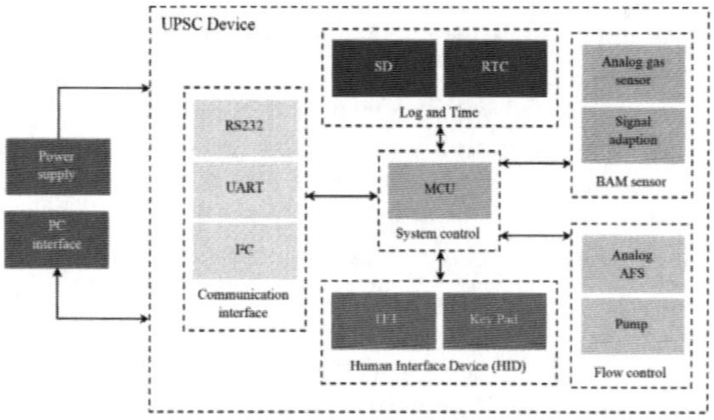

Figure 2. Schematics representation of the functional areas of the system.

TABLE I. COMPONENTS AND FUNCTIONS

Component	Group	Function
RS232	Communications Interface	Communication with PC (COM Port)
UART		Communication with PC (USB Port)
I2C		Communication with main device (Slave)
TFT	HID	Control the Device with touch screen Show the module and sensor data on TFT
KeyPad		Enter values
RTC	Log and Time	Current time
SD card		Save all measurement data into file Can be used for configuration file
AFS	Flow control	Current airflow
Pump		Control airflow
Gas sensor	BAM Sensor	Detects gas changes in the air
Signal adjustment		Control heater and signal adjustment
MCU	System control	Control components and calculate results

Table 1 describes the currently used modules of the system. Further components are planned, more in Section 7.

B. Modular design

Figure 3 shows the modular design of the system. This principle offers the user, as well as the developer a fast troubleshooting and the possibility of system expansion.

Figure 3. Modular design of the system

The UPSC3 system has been designed according to a modular principle. Components which do not represent a large disturbance for the measurement can be exchanged. This has the advantage that the user is also able to carry out repairs autonomously or to replace components. The modular components are:

- MCU (Micro Control Unit)
- Voltage regulators
- RTC
- All peripherals

C. Gas detection principle

Figure 4 shows the principle of the gas detection, whereby the air channels, the air flow sensor, and the pump play a decisive role in the gas detection.

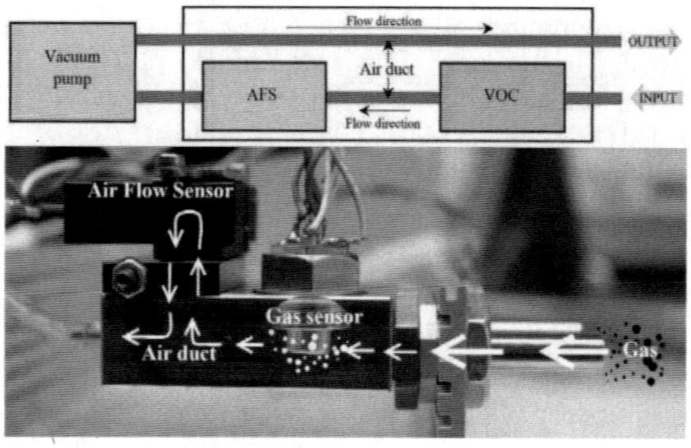

Figure 4. Gas sensor module with air flow sensor and air ducts

The transport of the gas mixture is carried out by the pump at a rate of 50 ml/min to 200 ml/min. The speed can be adjusted manually and is automatically adjusted by occurring loads or constriction of the air channels. The air flow meter quickly detects these fluctuations and initiates corresponding measures by means of the system. The gas mixture is then passed through the air channel system in which the VOC sensor is located, then the sucked air gas mixture is led back into the free environment.

The sensor layers located in the VOC sensor change their resistance as soon as the gas molecules settle on the layer surface or with the increasing concentration. The concentration cannot be determined unequivocally, but can estimate the danger level by increasing the initial value. In order to operate the VOC sensor and reactivate it more quickly during the measurement, the implemented heating element (Pt10), which is located in the immediate vicinity of the layers, is kept constant at a temperature. If temperature fluctuations occur, the system automatically adjusts the temperature. This has the advantage that the temperature changes in the surroundings can also be detected and compensated.

D. UPSC3 Flow chart sequence

Figure 5 shows the program sequence of the entire system. At the start of measurement, the sensors are read out in predefined sampling times and the current values are displayed on the TFT and stored on the SD card.

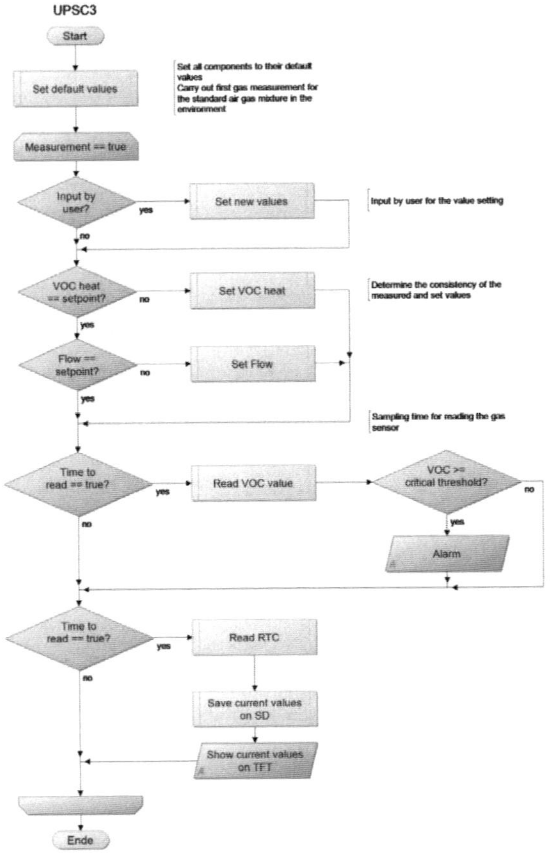

Figure 5. Main functions and the sequence of UPSC3

After the system is switched on, all components are initialized and the initial values are set. The measuring cycle is then started. The air flow and the VOC heater are set to the minimum values which are necessary to operate the system. During the measurement, interrupt-controlled inputs are monitored by the system. If an input is made, the measurement is stopped to perform the input. As soon as the input is finished, the set values are checked and compared with the current values. If the values deviate from one another, then a subsequent correction or adjustment of the values takes place.

Due to the relatively sluggish gas sensor, the values in the secondary clock are read out, displayed on the display and stored on the SD card. All sensor values are formed as a mean value from a 32-value ring memory. If the gas concentration exceeds the threshold values, these can be changed during operation, an alarm occurs in the form of a display or the threshold value can be exceeded by activating external hardware. All values are still stored on the SD card.

III. LABORATORY TESTS

Figure 6 shows a series of measurements in a closed room. The measurement took several hours to investigate the stability of the sensors and the system. The built-in UPSC3 VOC sensor and own signal processing (S1, S2, S3) is shown on the primary y axis, without the calculation of the resistance layers, only the analog voltage values however, the influence of gases can be explained, and the reference VOC sensor and signal processing (R1, R2, R3) is shown on the secondary y axis [4]. With the integrated pump and the flow sensor, conclusions can be drawn about the concentration of the gas. The reference is an identical VOC sensor, which is controlled by an evaluation tool kit developed by the manufacturer via USB [5]. Figure 6 shows not a direct comparison of the UPSC3 with the reference VOC sensor, this attempt should validate the control of the VOC sensor by the UPSC3 system and allows for classification of the sensor signals in regard to gas identification and quantification.

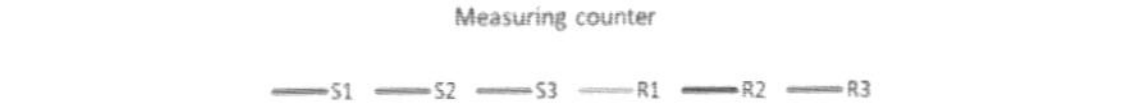

Figure 6. First measurements with UPSC3 and reference VOC

The experiment was carried out in three steps: Step 1 shows the initialization and the settling of the sensor layers after commissioning of the sensors. The heating element (Pt10) was brought to an operating temperature of 350 °C. Step 2 shows the detection of a gas, which is a 100 % essential oil called "exotic". The oil was held directly (1 cm) against the sensors, resulting in the deflections shown in Figure 6. In the last step, which is number 3, the operating temperature of the heating element was increased to 400 °C, which resulted in a change in the overall course of all layers. The influence of the temperature change in the direct connection of the Pt10 with the sensor layers.

IV. Applications

UPSC3 is primarily used to calibrate and validate new gas sensors, but its application is very wide. Figure 7 shows a large part of the application scenarios, ranging from indoor applications (laboratories), wide open areas (farms) and agglomerations (cities), as well as critical locations where a high concentration of gas poses a threat to humans (gas stations).

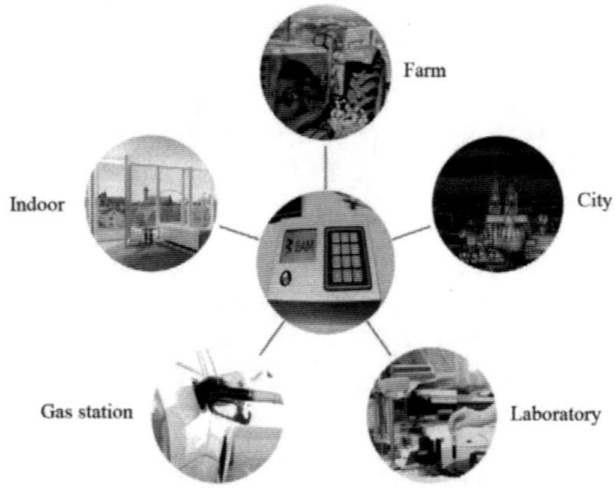

Figure 7. Application scenarios for the UPSC3 system

The module is primarily designed for the calibration of newly developed gas sensors. Other application scenarios are shown in Figure 7 but are not included in this paper.

V. Features and Benefits

- User-friendly
- Sampling and threshold monitoring
- Pattern recognition
- Standalone System (mobile)
- Robust aluminum housing
- Modular design
- Defective components are quickly interchangeable due to the modular design
- BAM multi sensor system device enables TCP/IP communication, too

VI. Conclusion

By the interaction of the pump with the air flow sensor and the VOC sensor, it is possible to develop a process which can determine the concentration of gases. By regulating the temperature, the temperature fluctuations of the environment can be compensated. Due to the small size and the possibility of the battery connection to the system, the mobility is given, the UPSC3 system could be carried along.

The detection of the gas takes place by the 3-fold VOC sensor, which can detect gases through its different layers. The pump supports and transports the air-gas mixture into the air ducts of the system. The detected values are displayed cyclically on the display and stored simultaneously on the SD card. If it is not possible to set the values directly on the system, configurations are also possible with a computer via the UART, RS232 or I2C.

The primary use of the system is to classify gas sensors under laboratory conditions that require control of external modules. The use in large areas is complicated by the lack of radio communication of the system.

VII. Outlook

In order to improve the system and make the measurements even more efficient, further sensors are planned for implementation. The sensors are placed directly in the air duct, the sensors will record the air humidity, as well as the temperature, so other parameters can be determined which are taken into account during the classification of the measurement. The validation of the system takes place primarily in a hermetically sealed desiccator, with selected gases being used to define the accuracy of the measuring system. Through this validation setup, a pattern recognition for different gases e.g., Benzene, will be developed. Remote control of the system via a web interface is also planned and partially implemented. The control system adopts a powerful mobile BAM control unit, which is also under development. For mobile use, an optimization of the power requirement is still planned.

References

[1] The Federal Environmental Agency. Volatile Organic Compounds (VOC) [Online]. Avalible from: http://www.umweltbundesamt.de/en/topics/health/environmental-impact-on-people/chemical-substances/volatile-organic-compounds-voc 2017.07.10

[2] The Official Journal of the European Communities. Directive 1999/13/EC

[3] L. Wander, A. Paul, K. Rurack et. al., " Compact sensor for online monitoring of nitroaromatics" Proceedings – 12. Kolloquium Prozessanalytik, pp. 11–61, November 2016.

[4] UST Umweltsensortechnik GmbH. UST Triplesensor® - The electronic nose [Online]. Avalible from: http://www.umweltsensortechnik.de/en/gas-sensors/ust-triplesensorR.html 2017.07.10

[5] S. Schütz, M. Gabriel, S. Paczkowski, M. Paczkowska, C. D. Kohl, M. Bauer, A. Weiß, O. Kiesewetter, M. May, A. Kraußer, T. Hertel, „Prduction optimization process on the basis of the information processing of the antenna of the Black Beetle beetle (Melanophila acuminata) for the detection of released organic volatiles from drying wood particles", fianl report, February 2012.

Discrimination between *Pseudogymnoascus destructans*, other Dermatophytes of Cave-dwelling Bats, and related innocuous Keratinophilic Fungi based on Electronic-nose/GC Signatures of VOC-Metabolites produced in Culture

Alphus Dan Wilson
Forest Insect and Disease Research
USDA Forest Service, Southern Hardwoods Laboratory
Stoneville, MS, USA
e-mail: dwilson02@fs.fed.us

Lisa Beth Forse
Center for Bottomland Hardwoods Research
USDA Forest Service, Southern Hardwoods Laboratory
Stoneville, MS, USA
e-mail: lfwilson@fs.fed.us

Abstract— **White-nose syndrome (WNS), caused by the fungal dermatophyte (*Pseudogymnoascus destructans*), is considered the most important disease affecting hibernating bats in North America. The identification of dermatophytic fungi, isolated from the skins of cave-dwelling bat species, is necessary to distinguish pathogenic (disease-causing) microbes from those that are innocuous. This distinction is an essential step for disease diagnoses, early detection of the presence of microbial pathogens prior to symptom development, and for discrimination between microbes that are present on the skins of hibernating bats. Early detection of *P. destructans* infections of bats prior to symptom development is essential to provide effective early treatments of WNS-diseased bats which significantly improves their chances of survival and recovery. Current diagnostic methods using quantitative polymerase chain reaction (qPCR) for the detection of the microbes on bats require invasive methods (skin swabs) that tend to arouse hibernating bats resulting in consumption of valuable fat reserves that reduce their chances of winter survival. Also, qPCR only indicates the presence and quantity of fungal inoculum on bat skin, but does not indicate that the fungus has infected the host or that a state of disease exists since substrate fungal DNA used for PCR comes from outside of the host (on the surface of the skin) rather than from within the host (in deep subdermal layers of the skin). Consequently, we are developing non-invasive methods for the early detection of WNS-disease and other microbes of bats based on their production of unique mixtures of volatile organic metabolites that may be detected using a dual-technology, electronic-nose/gas chromatography device for identifying and discriminating between the microbial metabolites produced in pure cultures. We determined that the Heracles II e-nose system was effective in discriminating keratinophilic fungal species using principal component analysis (PCA) of smellprints signatures coupled with discrimination index (DI) and gas chromatographic retention times (RTs) of major VOC GC-peaks produced in culture headspace.**

Keywords-electronic aroma detection; e-nose; fungal metabolites; volatile organic compounds; white-nose syndrome.

I. INTRODUCTION

A large diversity of microbes have been isolated from the skins of cave-dwelling bats [1][2]. The skin-swabbing of small mammalian trogloxenes (animals that are temporary cave residents and move freely in and out of caves), particularly insectivorous bats while in hibernation (i.e., in a state of torpor), is a common practice among animal pathologists and wildlife researchers interested in obtaining cultures and conducting diagnostic tests for determining the etiology of various dermatophytic diseases acquired by volant mammals. Bats are known to be attacked by relatively few fungal dermatophytes including *Pseudogymnoascus destructans* (Pd), causing deep-seated skin infections, and *Trichophyton redellii* (ringworm) that causes superficial skin infections [3]. Over the past decade, White-nose Syndrome (WNS), caused by the psychrophilic dermatophyte and pervasive fungal pathogen *P. destructans*, has emerged as the most important disease of cave-dwelling bats in North America, causing extensive mortality and regional population declines of hibernating bat species in the eastern, mid-western and southern United States as well as southeastern Canadian provinces [4]. WNS is known to significantly affect at least eight species of bats in North America including the big brown bat (*Eptesicus fuscus*), the gray bat (*Myotis grisescens*), the eastern small-footed bat (*M. leibii*), the little brown bat (*M. lucifugus*), the northern long-eared bat (*M. septentrionalis*), the Indiana bat (*M. sodalis*), the tricolored bat (*Perimyotis subflavus*), and the southeastern bat (*M. austroriparius*) [5]-[7]. The capability of clinical diagnosticians to detect and discriminate between the microbes growing on the skins of bats is a critical necessity for studying and identifying dermatophytic microbes involved in the complex interactions that occur on bat skins between fungal pathogens, innocuous microbes, and host defense responses that ultimately influence the final outcome of pathogenesis and disease development. To address this diagnostic capability, we are developing new noninvasive diagnostic tools and technologies to identify and discriminate between microbes that grow and multiply on the skins of bats in hibernation and outside of hibernacula.

Electronic-nose (e-nose) devices have been used extensively to identify microbial pathogens in culture which are causal agents of diseases in plants, animals, and humans [8][9]. Various types of e-nose devices, utilizing different operational mechanisms for chemical detection, are particularly useful and effective diagnostic tools for the discrimination of complex gaseous mixtures of volatile organic compounds (VOCs) that compose the most common metabolic products of microbes released into the headspace of microbial cultures [10][11]. Some important potential advantages of e-nose devices as diagnostic tools, particularly for hibernating bats, are noninvasive early detection of infectious diseases and causal agents (minimal disruption of bat torpor patterns and behavioral disturbances during hibernation), rapid real-time disease detection capabilities using portable e-nose devices, low-cost diagnostic testing, high precision of measurements, low incidence of false positive results, and complex VOC-mixture detections without identifying individual chemical species within diagnostic samples [12][13].

Soil-borne psychrophilic (cold-loving) fungi related to the Pd-pathogen include other *Pseudogymnoascus* species (such as *P. appendiculatus*, *P. roseus*, and *P. verrucosus*), and numerous *Geomyces* species. *Geomyces pannorum* var. *pannorum* is a nonaggressive pathogen that occasionally causes superficial human dermatophytic diseases [14][15]. Although these fungi are somewhat related genetically and metabolically, differences in specific metabolic pathways used by these microbes result in the production of different types, combinations and mixtures of VOCs produced and released into the headspace of microbial cultures. Consequently, unique complex VOC-mixtures, released into culture headspace, may be used as a basis for discriminating between microbial species when analyzed by specialized gas sensor arrays such as e-nose devices [8].

The objectives of this study were to 1) determine the capability of the Heracles II fast gas chromatograph (GC)/E-nose combination-technology instrument to discriminate between related keratinophilic fungi, including both pathogenic and innocuous species, isolated either from bat skin or from soils, a common reservoir of inoculum for fungal dermatophytes of bats, 2) document differences in gas chromatogram component peaks and patterns of VOC fungal metabolite mixtures released into the culture headspace of microbes tested, and 3) develop an aroma map indicating the relatedness and differences in fungal headspace VOC-metabolites of keratinophilic fungi based on 3-dimensional principal component analysis (PCA). The results from this study will be used to evaluate the efficacy of this dual-technology e-nose for discrimination of cultures of *P. destructans* and related fungi.

This paper is composed of an introduction to dermatophytic fungi of bats and the use of e-nose VOC-metabolite detection approaches in section 1, followed by experimental methods used for this work in section 2, describing the specific details of methods used in association with e-nose and GC runs and analytical procedures, followed by experimental results in section 3 providing details of research results and findings for e-nose analyses of fungal VOC metabolites from the headspace of microbial cultures, including sensor output responses to VOCs, PCA e-nose aroma maps of fungal dermatophytes, and associated data. Discussion and conclusions, based on the e-nose experimental results, are presented in section 4 to summarize the significance of findings and new discoveries resulting from this research.

II. MATERIALS AND METHODS

A. *Fungal Strains and Growth Conditions*

Eight genetically-related keratinophilic fungi were tested in this study including: *Pseudogymnoascus destructans* 20631-21 (PD6), the ATCC type strain originally isolated from a little brown bat (*Myotis lucifugus*) at Williams Hotel Mine, New York; *Pseudogymnoascus destructans* M-3902 (PD3) from West Virginia; *Pseudogymnoascus appendiculatus* UAMH-10509 (PA1) and *Pseudogymnoascus verrucosus* UAMH-10579 (PV1), both isolated from a *Sphagnum fuscum-Picea mariana* bog near Alberta, Canada; *Pseudogymnoascus roseus* 722101 (PR1), the type strain of the genus [16]; *Geomyces pannorum* CCF-340 (GP2), *Geomyces pannorum* CCF-338 (GP5), and *Geomyces pannorum* var. *pannorum* CMF-2582 (GP8) were obtained from the Center for Forest Mycology Research (CFMR; Madison, WI). All media were sterilized at 121°C under 15 PSI for 20 minutes. For long-term storage at −80°C, strains were grown and maintained in 24 hour darkness on Sabouraud dextrose agar (SDA) (4% dextrose, 1% Neopeptone, 2% agar), incubated at 14°C for 8 weeks. Asexual spores were collected by washing sporulating SDA cultures with 5 ml of 0.1% deoctylsulfosuccinate (DSS) in SD broth to which an equal volume of 50% glycerol was added to suspend hydrophobic conidia [17].

B. *Sample Preparation and Prerun Procedures*

All fungal strains tested were grown on SDA slants in 100 mL Kimax GL45 glass bottles with 40 mL SDA culture medium per bottle. Five glass-bottle cultures were prepared as replications for each strain. Three bottles of uninoculated SDA slants (SAB) served as controls. GL45 PBT open-top screw caps were fitted with Pyrex PTFE-faced silicone rubber septa. Agar slants were inoculated with 20 μl of frozen conidial spore suspension, spread with a sterile glass rod. Cultures were grown in darkness at 14°C for 4 weeks. To allow headspace VOCs to accumulate, cultures were moved to room temperature at 21°C in the dark for 18 hours prior to analysis on a weekly basis. The total quantity of VOCs accumulating in culture headspace over each weekly period were largely removed from bottle cultures for analysis each week so that the quantity of VOCs analyzed weekly indicated the quantity that had accumulated only over a one-week period.

C. *Instrument Configuration and Run Parameters*

The Heracles II GC/Electronic-nose system (Alpha MOS, Toulouse, France), composed of a dual-column (DB-5 and DB-1701 output) fast-gas chromatograph (GC) with flame-ionization detector (FID) and multiple e-nose sensors, was utilized for all culture VOC-headspace analyses. Fungal VOC-metabolites were manually injected using 15 ml of culture headspace per sample via 20 cc (Cadence Science Inc., Cranston, RI) glass syringe, trapped at 30 °C for 50 s before split-injection at 10 ml/min into DB-5 and DB-1701 GC columns following isothermal heating at 240 °C for 30 s at 57 kPa of pressure. Analyses were conducted at an initial oven temperature of 50 °C, ramping at 1 °C/s up to 80 °C, then accelerating the heating rate to 3 °C/s up to 250 °C for 21 s. Analyzer injection volume was set at 5000 µl at a speed of 125 µl/s, injection temperature of 200 °C at 10 kPa pressure, injection time 45 s, and venting at 30 ml/min. The two FID detector temperatures, for separate dual columns, were set at 260 °C. Retention times (RTs) of VOCs were recorded for each peak for both GC columns.

The e-nose analyzer component of the dual-technology Heracles II system utilizes a very large number of proprietary sensors in the sensor array. For data analyses involving statistical discrimination algorithms, only those sensors in the array that provided the largest output responses that added significantly to sample discriminations were utilized in data analyses, such as for PCA plots and derivations of aroma signatures or smellprint patterns that define the unique aroma fingerprints of VOC-metabolite mixtures contained within fungal headspace volatiles.

D. *Data Acquisition Parameters and Run Schedule*

Data acquisition rates for both GC data recording and e-nose data from the sensor array were collected every 0.01 s intervals (100 data points per second) set at a constant data-recording rate for the entire duration of each analysis run. Total run time for all analysis runs was 110 s. Both dual GC-columns and e-nose sensor arrays were purged with ultrapure air or blank samples between each sample analysis.

E. *Principal Component Analysis*

Three-dimensional principal component analysis (PCA) was performed on e-nose data using Heracles II software to compare the relatedness between aroma signature patterns derived from e-nose sensor array output responses to fungal VOC-metabolite mixtures in culture headspace. Distances between centers of data clusters (PCA mapping distance), derived from sensor array outputs of each fungal culture headspace (aroma classes or sample type), were determined on a PCA plot or aroma map by pairwise comparisons of aroma classes (sample types) in all possible combinations along with aroma Pattern Discrimination Index (PDI), expressed as a percentage, indicating the statistical level of discrimination (P-values) between each corresponding sample type compared based on aroma signature patterns (smellprints).

III. RESULTS

A. *Gas Chromatography VOC Peak Analyses*

Analyses of gaseous VOC-mixtures produced by individual fungi in culture headspace, based on gas chromatographic (GC) patterns on chromatograms, provided indications of differences in the types and quantities of volatile metabolites produced. Most of the fungi tested produced common metabolites with peaks at RTs of 16.50 s and 26.57 s in 3-week old cultures, although *P. destructans* strains did not produce the 26.57 peak until several months later in older cultures (Table I).

TABLE I. GAS CHROMATOGRAPHY PEAK RETENTION TIMES AND HEIGHTS FOR INDIVIDUAL FUNGAL VOCS PRESENT IN COMPLEX METABOLITE MIXTURES PRODUCED IN CULTURE HEADSPACE

	Peak height[a]					
	Peak RTs of VOCs					
Fungal species	**Strain**	**15.30**	**16.50**	**26.57**	**59.60**	**63.10**
P. appendiculatus	PA1	—	10,680	2,558	—	—
P. roseus	PR1	—	45,507	2,609	—	—
P. verrucosus	PV1	—	29,756	2,628	—	—
G. pannorum	GP2	—	7,361	2,650	—	—
G. pannorum	GP5	—	7,553	3,110	—	—
G. pannorum var. pannorum	GP8	5,542	12,438	—	3,467	—
P. destructans	PD3	—	81,246	PL	—	1,739
P. destructans	PD6	—	42,718	PL	—	1,981

a. Peak heights indicate relative heights of individual peaks, representing separate VOC-metabolites produced by each fungal strain at the indicated RTs (for DB-5 column) derived from GC-chromatographs in separate analyses of headspace from fungal cultures on SDA medium. Symbols PL = VOC peak was produced later (in older cultures).

The VOC-metabolite produced at RT=16.50 varied considerably in peak height for different fungi (up to 11-fold difference in quantities between *G. pannorum* and *P. destructans* strains, but variations in peak heights for the VOC-metabolite produced at RT=26.57 was quite consistent for all fungi tested with the exception of the *G. pannorum* var. *pannorum* strain that did not produce this metabolite. The unique production of two distinct metabolites at RT=15.30 and RT=59.60 only by the *G. pannorum* var. *pannorum* strain was considerably different from the other fungi, particularly *G. pannorum* strains that did not produce these particular VOC-metabolites at all. The two strains of *P. destructans* also produced a unique metabolite at RT=63.10 that was not produced by the other fungi.

B. *E-nose Signature Patterns of Headspace Volatiles*

Comparisons of differences in e-nose smellprint patterns, derived from multisensor e-nose array outputs of the Heracles II GC/Electronic-nose instrument, provided additional data for discriminating between fungal species based on differences in e-nose multisensor responses to unique VOC-metabolite mixtures produced in culture headspaces. The e-nose smellprints produced by the multisensor array in response to differences in VOC-metabolite mixtures were significantly different from that of SDA-medium alone that served as a control for comparisons to indicate the smellprint of background VOCs released from the common SDA culture medium itself (Figure 1, A-G).

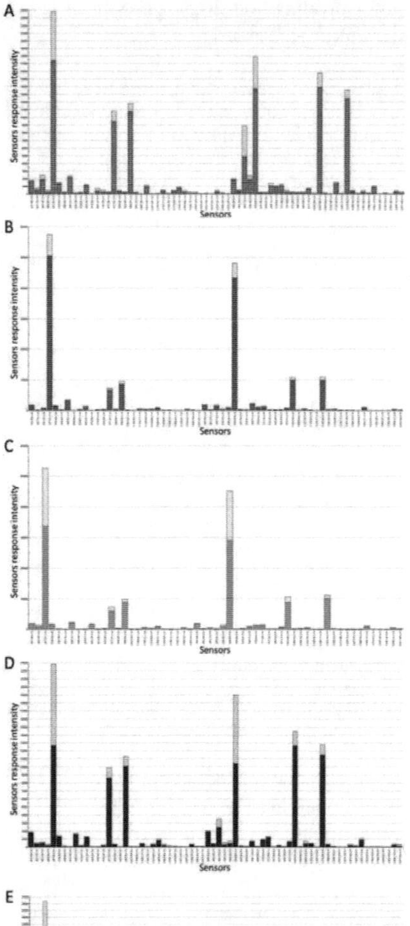

Figure 1. E-nose aroma signature patterns (smellprints) of complex headspace volatile mixtures, composed of fungal VOC metabolites from cultures of fungal dermatophytes and control: A) *P. appendiculatus*, B) *P. roseus*, C) *P. verrucosus*, D) *G. pannorum*, E) *G. pannorum* var. *pannorum*, F) *P. destructans*, and G) SDA medium control.

The sensor numbers, labeled on the x-axis, are listed in the same order for all sample types analyzed. All of the smellprints, produced as sensor responses to VOC headspace volatiles of fungi in culture, varied considerably in sensor response intensity, shown on the y-axis, and in overall smellprints compared with each other and with the SDA-control (Figure 1G). The smellprint pattern of *P. appendiculatus* differed quite drastically from the other *Pseudogymnoascus* species, including the WNS fungal pathogen (*P. destructans*), *P. roseus*, and *P. verrucosus* (Figure 1 A-C,F). The smellprint pattern of *P. appendiculatus* only superficially resembled that of *G. pannorum* strains, but differences in individual sensor intensity responses varied considerably (Figure 1 A,D).

The aroma signature patterns (smellprints) of culture headspace volatile metabolite mixtures of *P. roseus* and *P. verrucosus* were fairly closely related in appearance (Figure 1 B,C). However, the smellprint patterns of *G. pannorum* strains and the *G. pannorum* var. *pannorum* strain GP8 unexpectedly showed very little resemblance (relatively few sensor responses in common), but a very significant number of major and minor sensor responses were considerably different between these two sample types for the majority of sensors responding to VOC-metabolites within the e-nose sensor array (Figure 1 D,E). The smellprint pattern of *P. destructans* strains was uniquely different from those of other *Pseudogymnoascus* species and *Geomyces* species tested with relatively few major sensor responses and many minor sensor responses at low intensities (Figure 1 F).

C. Principal Component Analysis

The differences observed in sensor responses of the Heracles II e-nose sensor array to complex gaseous mixtures of volatile metabolites released into culture headspace were analyzed statistically using principal component analysis (PCA) to measure and quantify the differences between e-nose aroma signatures produced by individual fungi. Pairwise comparisons of e-nose aroma profiles, tested in all possible combinations to assess and measure these differences, indicated widely varying PCA mapping distances (between data clusters for individual fungal species) and statistical differences as measured using a percentage Pattern Discrimination Index (PDI) for each pairwise comparison (Table II). These analyses collectively included 36 distinct PCA-pairwise comparisons between individual strains of each fungal species and between the fungal strains and uninoculated SDA slant (SAB) controls.

All nine fungal strains tested showed high levels of significant differences from SDA-culture medium controls, both in terms of PCA mapping distances (range of 21,992-106,723 mapping units) and percentage PDI (range of 72.3-98.7%). PDI results provided precise numerical values (percentage indications) of differences between sample types in all possible combinations. The higher the value, the lower the relatedness between each paired combination.

TABLE II. PAIRWISE-COMPARISONS BETWEEN E-NOSE AROMA PROFILES OF CULTURE HEADSPACE VOC-METABOLITES OF FUNGAL DERMATOPHYTES AND SABOURAUD DEXTROSE AGAR CONTROL BASED ON 3-D PCA

Aroma class 1	Aroma class 2	PCA mapping distance[a]	PDI (%)[b]
PA1	PR1	43,728.52	91.98
	PV1	9,466.80	22.49
	GP2	16,164.98	64.55
	GP5	14,123.66	58.11
	GP8	21,517.88	76.88
	PD3	82,334.10	84.94
	PD6	28,688.58	46.70
	SAB	33,558.06	88.32
PR1	PV1	42,352.60	88.24
	GP2	58,469.24	97.89
	GP5	55,983.53	97.69
	GP8	62,777.83	98.26
	PD3	38,967.67	57.28
	PD6	17,424.10	25.88
	SAB	68,801.81	98.71
PV1	GP2	16,861.30	56.84
	GP5	14,904.61	50.69
	GP8	22,026.64	69.63
	PD3	81,088.75	83.76
	PD6	25,798.87	39.68
	SAB	29,460.40	78.39
GP2	GP5	4,006.78	24.00
	GP8	10,541.13	70.59
	PD3	97,246.99	89.50
	PD6	42,247.27	67.83
	SAB	22,116.79	93.74
GP5	GP8	12,396.70	76.75
	PD3	94,709.95	88.99
	PD6	40,020.94	65.42
	SAB	24,683.17	94.86
GP8	PD3	101,318.45	90.28
	PD6	46,643.56	72.09
	SAB	21,992.46	94.65
PD3	PD6	55,673.80	61.93
	SAB	106,723.11	89.36
PD6	SAB	51,724.00	72.25

a. PCA aroma mapping distances indicate actual plotting distances between centers of data clusters for each combination of sample types compared. b. Percentage values for aroma Pattern Discrimination Index (DPI) indicate the P-value of significant differences (expressed as a percentage) for each pairwise comparison between sample types being compared, based on PCA-statistical testing of aroma plot data.

The *P. appendiculatus* strain (PA1) PCA-mapping data cluster was most significantly different from *P. roseus* strain (PR1), *G. pannorum* var. *pannorum* strain (GP8), and *P. destructans* strain (PD3) based on mapping distance (between data clusters) and PDI (%). Strain PA1 of *P. appendiculatus* was considerably less different (more related) to *P. verrucosus* strain (PV1), but moderately different from *G. pannorum* strains (GP2 and GP5) as indicated by lower mapping distances and PDI values.

P. roseus strain PR1 showed a PCA mapping data cluster that had very high significant differences in aroma mapping distances and PDI values from strains GP2 and GP5 of *G. pannorum* and strain GP8 of *G. pannorum* var. *pannorum*, but much less differences with data clusters of strains PD3 and PD6 of *P. destructans*.

P. verrucosus strain PV1 displayed PCA mapping data clusters with highly significant differences in aroma mapping distances and PDI values when compared with *P. destructans* strain PD3, but only moderate differences with strains GP2 and GP5 of *G. pannorum*, strain GP8 of *G. pannorum* var. *pannorum*, and lower levels of significant differences with *P. destructans* strain PD6.

The PCA mapping data cluster of *G. pannorum* strain GP2 had low levels of differences in aroma mapping distances and PDI values when compared with data clusters of *G. pannorum* strain GP3, but differences in these two PCA statistical parameters were highly significant when compared with PCA data clusters of *P. destructans* strains PD3 and PD6 as well as *G. pannorum* var. *pannorum* strain GP8. Very similar results were observed for PCA comparisons of the mapping data cluster of *G. pannorum* strain GP5 with *P. destructans* strains PD3 and PD6 and *G. pannorum* var. *pannorum* strain GP8.

Construction of a 3-dimensional plot (aroma map) of all sample types tested using PCA provided a visual means of comparing the PCA mapping distances between data clusters of each sample type as well as an overall Discrimination Index (DI), indicating the relative overall strength or level of discrimination between all sample types included in the PCA test. Displayed DI values are validated by the Heracles II software (using green highlighting), indicating a passing PCA test at $P \leq 0.10$ level of significance when a successful discrimination between sample types is achieved.

The plotted aroma data cluster of *G. pannorum* var. *pannorum* strain GP8 was most obviously separated from the other fungi tested as indicated in the 3-dimensional PCA aroma map of fungal VOC-metabolite mixtures in culture headspace (Figure 2). The overall discrimination index (DI) was 67.0 for this 3-D PCA plot.

A most surprising result was the discovery that G. pannorum var. pannorum strain GP8 produced an aroma signature that was highly different from *G. pannorum* strains GP2 and GP5.

Mapping data clusters in the 3-D PCA plot of e-nose aroma signature data among *Pseudogymnoascus* species generally were well separated with only a few minor overlaps for some combinations between species. Data clusters for *P. destructans* strains were most distant (least related) with *P. appendiculatus* strain PA1, intermediately distant from (moderately related with) *P. verrucosus* strain PV1, and least distant from (most related to) *P. roseus* strain PR1.

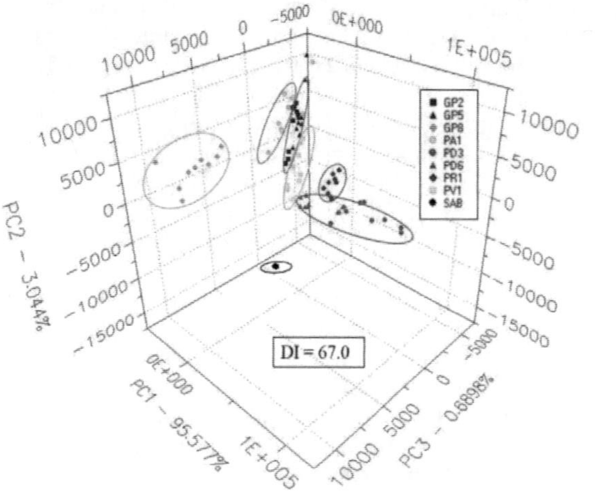

Figure 2. E-nose aroma map showing the chemical relatedness between fungal dermatophytes using Principal Component Analysis (PCA).

The percentages of total variance, accounting for the variability explained by each orthogonal principal component, are as follows: PC 1 = 95.6%; PC 2 = 3.0%; and PC 3 = 0.7%. Thus, most of the variability in the PCA was accounted for by PC 1 (x-axis), whereas PC 2 (y-axis) and PC 3 (z-axis) account for only a small proportion of the total variance.

IV. DISCUSSION AND CONCLUSIONS

Analyses of VOC-peak patterns from GC chromatograms of volatile metabolites produced in culture headspace indicated that most of the fungi tested produced metabolites at the same two RTs, suggesting the production of some common VOCs and the likely use of similar metabolic pathways by these genetically-related fungi. Differences in VOC peak heights at specific RTs provide evidence that different keratinophilic fungal species and strains may utilize slightly different metabolic pathways or have gene duplications within the genome that produce varying quantities of common VOC-metabolites in culture [18].

G. pannorum var. *pannorum* produced two unique VOC-metabolites that were different from those produced by all other related fungal species tested. Significant differences in VOC-metabolite mixtures (produced in culture headspace) in addition to pathogenicity differences, combined with PCA pairwise-comparisons and e-nose mapping data of VOC-metabolite mixtures, all suggest that *G. pannorum* (strains GP2 and GP5) and *G. pannorum* var. *pannorum* strain GP8 function metabolically as separate species and that *G. pannorum* var. *pannorum* perhaps should be elevated as a distinct new *Geomyces* species, rather than just a variety, or perhaps a new *Pseudogymnoascus* species. The taxonomy of *Geomyces* and *Pseudogymnoascus* species currently is in a state of flux and some researchers already consider *G. pannorum* var. *pannorum* to be a *Pseudogymnoascus* species based on more recent DNA-homology results from genetic studies.

The authors chose to compare the relatedness between smellprint patterns, derived from e-nose sensor array output responses to fungal VOC-metabolites, using the PCA method with PDI values because these e-nose analysis procedures are most useful for providing precise numerical values of differences with statistical levels of significance. The WNS-pathogen *P. destructans* was most closely related metabolically to *P. roseus* and *P. verrucosus*, and less related to *P. appendiculatus* based on 3-dimensional PCA mapping distance, PDI, and data clustering on the e-nose aroma map. These results were consistent with similar indications of relative genetic relatedness between these species based on genetic analyses using genomic DNA-homology tests [19]. The uniquely different mixtures of VOC-metabolites produced in culture headspace by strains of *P. destructans,* compared to its non-pathogenic cave-dwelling psychrophilic (cold-loving) and saprophytic relatives consisting of other *Pseudogymnoascus* and *Geomyces* species commonly in cave sediments, indicate that the Pd-pathogen has shifted its metabolic pathways toward pathogenic phenotypes and greater utilization of keratinogenic substrates. Recent evidence suggests that this shift in substrate specialization from saprobic to pathogenic phenotypes in *P. destructans* has occurred at the expense of reduced saprotrophic enzyme activity [20]. This data suggests that *P. destructans* has co-evolved over time with its bat hosts and moved away from the utilization of carbon sources in the environment, leading to its somewhat reduced capacity for saprotrophic growth. Although *P. destructans* is still considered a competent saprotroph that persists and sporulates in cave sediments (presumably due to its emergence from non-pathogenic ancestors), its reduced activity of urease and endoglucanase saprobic enzymes provide evidence that it may be shifting toward increasingly pathogenic activity [20][21].

Our results indicate that the Heracles II GC/e-nose dual-technology instrument was effective in discriminating between genetically-related species of *Pseudogymnoascus* and *Geomyces*, common keratinophilic fungi of bat skin, based on the production of unique VOC-metabolite mixtures in culture headspace. Furthermore, PCA provided indications of differences in metabolic relatedness between fungal species based on unique mixtures of fungal VOC-metabolites produced. This capability of e-nose devices to detect and discriminate between complex VOC-metabolites produced by pathogenic and non-pathogenic keratinophilic fungi of bats could potentially provide a new effective means for the noninvasive early detection and diagnosis of devastating wildlife diseases, such as WNS. A cheaper, more portable e-nose device potentially could be useful for both rapid diagnosis of the disease in living bats and for determining the cause of death post-mortem [22][23]. The WNS-epizootic has already killed over six million hibernating bats in North American since the disease was first detected and identified in New York State in 2006 [1][24][25]. Consequently, there is a need for a rapid, noninvasive method for early WNS disease detection at the geographical advancing front of the epizootic in order to allow for the application of very early, more effective WNS-control applications, particularly prior to the appearance of WNS-disease symptoms, as newly approved treatments are developed and become available.

ACKNOWLEDGMENT

The authors thank Charisse Oberle for assistance in running Heracles II GC fast-gas/e-nose analyses of headspace volatiles from fungal cultures.

REFERENCES

[1] K. J. Vanderwolf, D. F. McAlpine, D. Malloch, and G. J. Forbes, "Ectomycota associated with hibernating bats in eastern Canadian caves prior to the emergence of White-nose Syndrome," Northeastern Naturalist, 2013, 20, pp 115–130, doi: 10.1656/045.020.0109.

[2] L. J. A. N. Johnson, et al., "Psychrophilic and psychrotolerant fungi on bats and the presence of *Geomyces* spp. on bat wings prior to the arrival of white nose syndrome," App Environ Microbiol, 2013, 78, pp 5465–5471, doi:10.1128/AEM.01429-13

[3] J. M. Lorch, et al., "The fungus *Trichophyton redellii* sp. nov. causes skin infections that resemble white-nose syndrome of hibernating bats," J. Wildl. Dis., 2015, 51, pp 36-47.

[4] US Fish and Wildlife Service, "White-nose syndrome map 2017," USFWS, Hadley, Massachusetts, [Online]. Available from: whitenosesyndrome.org/resources/map. Accessed May 2017.

[5] D. S. Blehert, et al., "Bat white-nose syndrome: an emerging fungal pathogen?" Science, 2009, 323, pp 227, doi:10.1126/science.1163874.

[6] G. R. Turner and D. M. Reeder, "Update of white-nose syndrome in bats," Bat Research News, 2009, 50, pp 47–53.

[7] F. Courtin, W. B. Stone, G. Risatti, K. Gilbert, and H. J. Van Kruiningen, "Pathologic findings and liver elements in hibernating bats with white-nose syndrome," Vet. Pathol., 2010, 47, pp 214–219, doi:10.1177/0300985809358614.

[8] A. D. Wilson, D. G. Lester, and C. S. Oberle, "Development of conductive polymer analysis for the rapid detection and identification of phytopathogenic microbes," Phytopathology, 2004, 94, pp 419–431.

[9] A. D. Wilson and M. Baietto, "Advances in electronic nose technologies developed for biomedical applications," Sensors, 2011, 11, pp 1105-1176.

[10] A. D. Wilson, and M. Baietto, "Applications and advances in electronic-nose technologies," Sensors, 2009, 9, pp 5099-5148.

[11] A. D. Wilson, "Diverse applications of electronic-nose technologies in agriculture and forestry," Sensors, 2013, 13, pp 2295–2348.

[12] A. D. Wilson, "Advances in electronic-nose technologies for the detection of volatile biomarker metabolites in the human breath," Metabolites, 2015, 5, pp 140-163.

[13] A. D. Wilson, "Recent progress in the design and clinical development of electronic nose technologies," Nanobiosensors in Disease Diagnosis, 2016, 5, pp 15-27.

[14] C. Gianni, G. Caretta, and C. Romano, "Skin infection due to *Geomyces pannorum* var. *pannorum*," Mycoses, 2003, 46, pp 430–43, doi:10.1046/j.1439-0507.2003.00897.

[15] H. Zelenková, "*Geomyces pannorum* as a possible causative agent of dermatomycosis and onychomycosis in two patients," Acta Dermatovenerol Croat, 2006, 14, pp 21–25.

[16] R. S. Currah, "Taxonomy of the Onygenales: *Arthrodermataceae*, *Gymnoascaceae*, *Myxotrichaceae* and *Onygenaceae*," Mycotaxon, 1985, 24, 1–216.

[17] H. T. Reynolds and H. A. Barton, "Comparison of the white-nose syndrome agent *Pseudogymnoascus destructans* to cave-dwelling relatives suggests reduced saprotrophic enzyme activity," PLoS ONE, 2014, 9, e86437.

[18] H. T. Reynolds, H. A. Barton, and J. C. Slot, "Phylogenomic analysis supports a recent change in nitrate assimilation in the white-nose syndrome pathogen, *Pseudogymnoascus destructans*," Fungal Ecology, 2016, 23, pp 20-29.

[19] A. M. Minnis and D. L. Lindner, "Phylogenetic evaluation of *Geomyces* and allies reveals no close relatives of *Pseudomgymnoascus destructans*, comb. nov., in bat hibernacula of Eastern North America," Fungal Biology, 2013, 117, pp 638-649.

[20] H. T. Reynolds and H. A. Barton, "Comparison of the white-nose syndrome agent *Pseudogymnoascus destructans* to cave-dwelling relatives suggests reduced saprotrophic enzyme activity," PLoS ONE, 2014, 9, e86437.

[21] H. T. Reynolds, T. Ingersoll, and H. A. Barton, "Modeling the environmental growth of *Pseudogymnoascus destructans* and its impact on the white-nose syndrome epidemic," J. Wildl. Dis., 2015, 51, pp 318-331.

[22] A. D. Wilson, "Biomarker metabolite signatures pave the way for electronic-nose applications in early clinical disease diagnoses," Current Metabolomics, 2017, 5, pp 90-101.

[23] A. D. Wilson, "Electronic-nose applications in forensic science and for analysis of volatile biomarkers in the human breath," Journal of Forensic Science and Criminology, 2014, 1(S103), pp 1-21.

[24] A. Gargas, M. T. Trest, M. Christensen, T. J. Volk, and D. S. Blehart, "*Geomyces destructans* sp. nov. associated with bat white-nose syndrome," Mycotaxon, 2009, 108, pp 147-154.

[25] J. M. Lorch, et al., "Experimental infection of bats with *Geomyces destructans* causes white-nose syndrome," Nature, 2011, 480, pp 376-378.

FBG/Intensity Based Hybrid Fiber Optic Sensor for Simultaneous Measurement of Strain and Temperature

Seong-Yong Jeong, Sang-Jin Choi, and Jae-Kyung Pan
Dept. of Electrical Eng. and Smart Grid Research Center
Chonbuk National University, Jeonju-si, Jeonbuk, 54896 Korea
e-mail: jsy50541@jbnu.ac.kr, sang_jin@jbnu.ac.kr, pan@jbnu.ac.kr

Abstract—**We propose and experimentally demonstrate a hybrid fiber optic sensor (FOS) using fiber Bragg gratings (FBGs) and intensity based FOS for measuring the temperature and the strain simultaneously. Experimental results showed the simultaneous measurement performance of the strain and the temperature for the proposed FOS, which are in good agreement with those measured using commercial sensors. The proposed hybrid FOS has the advantages of low cost, simple structure, and remote multipoint sensing characteristics.**

Keywords- Hybrid FOS; simultaneous measurement; intensity based FOS; strain free FBGs

I. INTRODUCTION

Techniques for simultaneously measuring the strain and the temperature using fiber optic sensor (FOS) have been developed and considerable interested in the concomitant use of different forms [1]. Various discrimination methods to measure the strain and the temperature separately using fiber Bragg grating (FBG) have been reported [2]. FOSs for measuring the strain and the temperature simultaneously can be classified into hybrid FOS and integrated FOS. The hybrid FOSs are the combined FBG and long period grating (LPG) method [3] and the FBG/Fabry-Perot (F-P) cavity method [4]. The integrated FOSs are the combination of three sensors which consists of a polarimetric sensor, photonic crystal fiber, and FBG [5] and the combination of Mach-Zehnder interferometers and temperature insensitive photonic crystal fiber [6].

Recently, we had reported an intensity based FOS, which consists of general FBGs and intensity based FOS head for measuring the only strain [7]. In this paper, we propose and experimentally demonstrate a hybrid FOS using strain free FBGs instead of the general FBGs for measuring the strain and the temperature simultaneously, based on our previous work [7].

II. THE PROPOSED HYBRID FOS STRUCTURE

The proposed hybrid FOS for measuring the strain and the temperature simultaneously is shown in Figure 1, which consists of strain free FBGs and an intensity based FOS. The light from broadband light source (BLS) enters through hybrid FOS via ports ① and ② of an optical circulator (OC). The reflected spectra by strain free FBGs return to PD via an OC and a tunable F-P filter. The tunable F-P filter transmission spectrum is changed by the applied sawtooth wave. The overlapping power of $I_{FBG}(\lambda)$ and $I_{FP}(\lambda)$, $P(\lambda)$, can be expressed as follows:

$$P(\lambda) = \int_{-\infty}^{+\infty} I_{FBG}(\lambda) \times I_{FP}(\lambda + \lambda')\, d\lambda' \qquad (1)$$

where $I_{FBG}(\lambda)$ is the FBG reflection spectrum and $I_{FP}(\lambda)$ is the F-P filter transmission spectrum. To measure the temperature using FBG Bragg wavelength shift, we propose an adequate signal processing algorithm, which is shown in LabVIEW program of figure 1. The separated signals are detected as sharp peaks corresponding to FBGs Bragg wavelengths. They determine the corresponding tunable F-P filter driving voltages, which use to determine the Bragg wavelengths.

To measure the strain using the intensity based FOS, we used our previous FOS structure [7]. When the optical power of reflection spectrum from FBG_1 and FBG_2 are $P_1(\lambda)$ and $P_2(\lambda)$, respectively, the measurement parameter X can be expressed as follows [7]:

$$X = \frac{\int P_2(\lambda)\, d\lambda}{\int P_1(\lambda)\, d\lambda} = \beta \cdot H^2 \qquad (2)$$

where H is the transfer function and β is the calibration factor. The calibration factor, β, is determined when an intensity based FOS head has no loss. The transfer function, H, in (2) can be obtained from β and X. When the strain is applied to intensity based FOS head, the optical fiber bending loss corresponding to the applied strain occurs. The occurred optical power loss makes to change X and H. The applied strain can be obtained by using the H. Based on the above FBG Bragg wavelength detection algorithm and the intensity

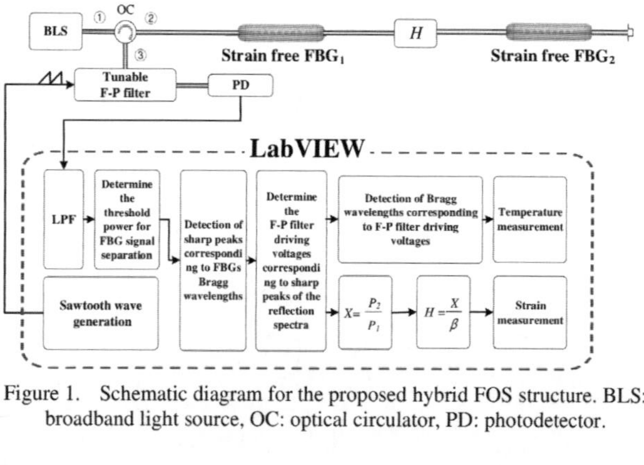

Figure 1. Schematic diagram for the proposed hybrid FOS structure. BLS: broadband light source, OC: optical circulator, PD: photodetector.

based FOS operating principle, the proposed hybrid FOS structure could have the ability of measuring the temperature and the strain simultaneously.

III. Experimental Results

To show the performance of the proposed hybrid FOS, we implemented a proposed hybrid FOS in Figure 1 using an intensity based FOS and two strain free FBGs. Two strain FBGs, FBG_1 and FBG_2, have a full width at half maximum (FWHM) of 0.1 nm, a gauge factor of 9.7 pm/℃, and Bragg wavelengths of 1553.1 nm and 1553.8 nm, respectively.

Firstly, to show the temperature measurement performance for the proposed FOS, we measured the temperature with the signal processing unit in Figure 1 and compared with the commercial FOS (I-MON 512E, Ibsen Photonics). Figure 2 shows the measured wavelength according to the temperature with the proposed FOS and the commercial FOS. As shown in Figure 2, the measured results of the proposed FOS have a good agreement with those of the commercial FOS. The FBG_1 and FBG_2 average errors for the proposed FOS from the reference curve based on the specification of strain free FBGs were 0.013 nm and 0.011 nm comparing with the commercial FOS errors 0.032 nm and 0.001 nm, which showed the same error range.

Secondly, to show the strain measurement performance for the proposed FOS, we measured the strain with the intensity based FOS in Figure 1 using a universal testing machine (5982 INSTRON). Figure 3 shows the measured strain by using the intensity based FOS comparing with those of the extensometer. The %strain determined by using H^2 has a good agreement with the measured %strain using an extensometer. To get the relationship between the two measured results, linear curve fitting was used, which showed the RMSE value of 0.002 and R-square value of 0.9956. The average difference of between %strain of the extensometer and one of the intensity based FOS were 0.003 %strain and standard deviation were 0.002 %strain. Also, we measured the H^2 in Figure 1 according to the varying temperature from -10 to 50 °C with step of 10 °C five times to confirm the temperature influence of the intensity based FOS. The standard deviations of the measured temperature at each temperature are less than 0.789E-04, which means little temperature influence of the proposed intensity based FOS.

From the above experimental results in Figures 2 and 3, we may consider that the proposed hybrid FOS has the ability measuring the strain and the temperature simultaneously.

IV. Conclusions

We have proposed and experimentally demonstrated a hybrid FOS structure using the intensity based FOS and the strain free FBGs. To demonstrate performance, we measured the temperature and the strain, which are compared with the commercial sensors. The average errors for the measured temperature and strain showed acceptable range of errors comparing with those of the commercial sensors. Also, we confirmed that the proposed intensity based FOS has little temperature influence. Further work under development is focusing on applying our proposed hybrid FOS with the measuring the strain and the temperature simultaneously for structure health monitoring.

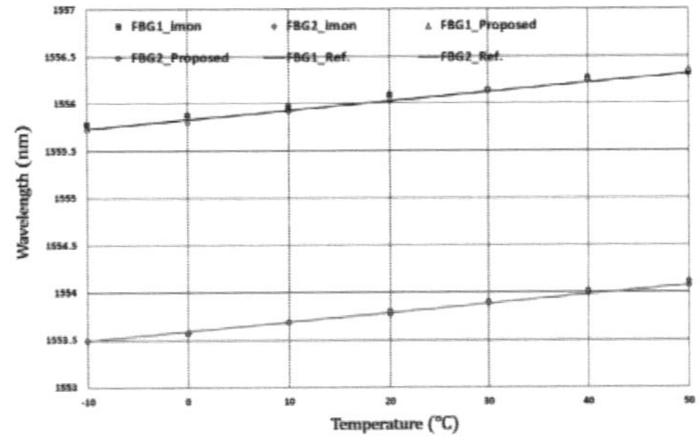

Figure 2. Measured Bragg wavelength FBGs vs the temperature with the proposed FOS and the commercial FOS.

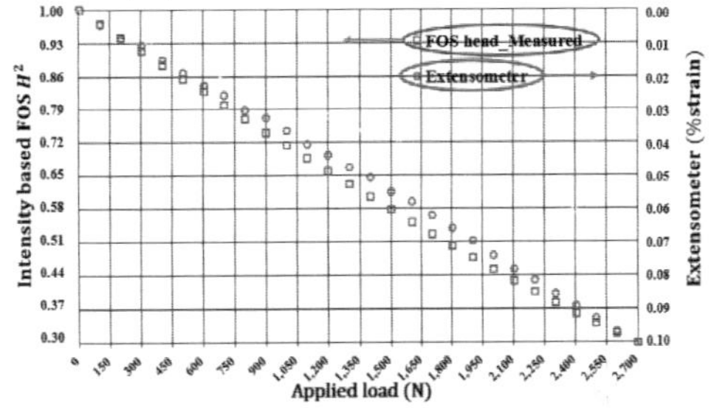

Figure 3. Measured the squared transfer function, H^2, and %strain according to applied load

Acknowledgment

This research was supported by Basic Science Research Program through the National Research Foundation of Korea (NRF) funded by the Ministry of Education (2016R1D1A1A09917117).

References

[1] A. Othonos and K. Kalli, Fiber Bragg Gratings: Fundamentals and Applications in Telecommunications and Sensing, Artech House, pp. 330-331, 1999, ISBN:0-89006-344-3.

[2] Y. Zhao and Y. Liao, "Discrimination methods and demodulation techniques for fiber Bragg grating sensors," Optics and Lasers in Engineering, vol. 41, pp. 1–18, July 2004, doi:10. 1016/SO143-8166(02)00117-3.

[3] C. Berrettoni, C. Trono, V. Vignoli, and F. Baldini, "Fibre tip sensor with embedded FBG-LPG for temperature and refractive index determination by means of the simpler measurement of the FBG characteristics," Journal of sensors, vol. 2015, pp. 1-8, Mar. 2015, doi: 10.1155/2015/491391.

[4] Q. Lin, et al., "High integrated FP/FBG sensor for simultaneous measurement of high temperature and strain," IEEE photonics technology letters, vol. 26, pp. 1715-1717, Sep. 2014, doi:10.1109/LPT.2014.2331359.

[5] M. Ramakrishnan, G. Rajan, Y. Semenova, and G. Farrell, "Hybrid fiber optic sensor system for measuring the strain, temperature, and thermal strain of composite materials," IEEE Sensors Journal, vol. 14, pp. 2571-2578, Aug. 2014, doi:10.1109/JSEN.2014.2306892.

[6] M. Najari, A. M. Javan, and N. Amiri, "Hybrid all-fiber sensor for simultaneous strain and temperature measurements based on Mach-Zehnder interferometer," Optik, vol. 126, pp. 2022-2025, Oct. 2015, doi: 10.1016/j.ijleo.2015.05.066.

[7] S. J. Choi, Y. C. Kim, M. H. Song, and J. K. Pan, "A self-referencing intensity-based fiber optic sensor with multipoint sensing characteristics," Sensors, vol. 14, pp. 12803-12815, July 2014, doi:10.3390/s140712803.

Chalcogenide Glass-based Chemosensors

Winfried Vonau, Ute Enseleit, Monika Berthold
Kurt-Schwabe-Institut für Mess- und Sensortechnik e.V. Meinsberg
Waldheim, Germany
e-mails: {vonau, enseleit, mberthold}@ksi-meinsberg.de

Claudia Feller, Uwe Partsch, Stefan Körner
Fraunhofer Institut für Keramische Technologien und Systeme
Dresden, Germany
e-mails: {claudia.feller, uwe.partsch, stefan.koerner}@ikts.fraunhofer.de

Abstract **– A number of chalcogenide glasses for the fabrication of potentiometric electrodes selective for heavy metal ions were melted and characterized. The focus was directed on the detection of Cu^{2+} and Pb^{2+} ions. In addition to the preparation of conventional rod electrodes, the purpose of the research was the realisation of corresponding planar electrodes in thick film technology. Until now, for measurements, only rod-electrodes were available. Miniaturized electrodes were achieved for the case of copper ion determination, whereupon several glass compositions were tested. The sintering behavior of the investigated lead ion selective glasses hitherto did not allow the fabrication by the thick film process. The requirement to add AgI to the initial mix is associated with light sensitivity of corresponding sensors.**

Keywords-determination of heavy metals; potentiometric sensor; chalcogenide glasses; thick film technology; copper; lead.

I. INTRODUCTION

Commonly used analytical procedures to detect heavy metals are Atom Absorption Spectroscopy (AAS), Optical Emission Spectrometry using Inductive Coupled Plasma (ICP-OES), Polarography and Ion Chromatography (IC) [1-4]. However, the devices needed are highly complex and require experienced operators. Measurements to be taken directly on-site are not possible by means of these methods. Other disadvantages are their high operational and equipment costs. A substantially more cost-effective alternative delivers the use of Ion Selective Electrodes (ISE) that allow continuous measurements in liquids [5]. Because of a simple experimental setup and a miniaturized sensor membrane, ion selective potentiometry is becoming increasingly important for the determination of ion activities and integrated sensor arrays [6]. For heavy metal ions, selective membranes chalcogenide glasses represent promising base materials. In the 1970s, Trachtenberg and Baker [7] introduced Ion-Selected Electrodes (ISEs) based on Chalcogenide Glasses (CG) to determine Fe^{3+} and Cu^{2+} ions.

At the end of the 1980s, Vlasov *et al.* [8]-[13] developed a systematic synthesis and carried out physical and electrochemical investigations at new CG-materials for the detection of Fe^{3+}, Cu^{2+}, Cd^{2+}, Pb^{2+}, Ag^{+} and Sn^{2+} ions in solutions. Further research results of CG for the analysis of liquids were presented by Vassiliev and Boycheva [14] in the year 2005. Conde Garrido investigated CG based on Ag-Ge-Se for the development of ISEs [15].

For the fabrication of such materials, in general, the required chemical compounds are heated in evacuated quartz ampoules and quenched, subsequently. In the process of making conventional potentiometric ISEs, the CG-bulk material is removed from the ampoules, cut into thin slices, mounted in a waterproof rod-shaped body and afterwards contacted. Pollrich [16] und Kloock [17] describe the fabrication of glasses. With regard to on-site analysis, currently, miniaturization of such as ISEs is at the core of research. During the on-site analysis, measurements can be carried out fast and easy at the sampling location with only reasonable effort and without equipped laboratory tests. Thus, quantitative and semi-quantitative statements about pollutant contents, e.g., in water, soil and solid waste, can be made. Therefore, especially small and robust sensors are required. For the miniaturization, several thin-film technologies are in use to deposit the CG-bulk material as thin membrane on, e.g., potentiometric or field effect based sensor structures. In the 1980s, Vlasov *et al.* [18] carried out first experiments to realize thin Cu^{2+}-ion sensensitive CG-membranes by means of Radio Frequency (RF) Co-Sputtering on Ion Sensitive Field Effect Transistors (ISFETs). Further procedures to produce thin film sensors for heavy metal analysis in liquids are RF Magneton Sputtering, Sputtering in combination with Ion Implementation, Evaporating, Flash Evaporating with Photo Doping as well as Electrochemical Deposition. All mentioned physical procedures have problems with respect to a stoichiometric deposition of thin CG-membranes based on multi-component mixtures. However, maintaining of the stoichiometry is of importance for the functionality of the CG-based ISEs. A method that realizes the stoichiometric deposition of glass membranes is Pulsed Laser Deposition (PLD). It was used by Schöning and Kloock [19]-[22]. In the PLD process, CG is rapidly removed from the bulk material and deposited on a transducer structure with remaining stoichiometry. Significant disadvantages of the procedure are high equipment costs and enormous amount of time for the realization of the CG-thin film membrane.

The rest of the paper is structured as follows. In Section II, advantages of thick-film (TF)-technology as possible fabrication method of CG electrodes are highlighted. Section III contains the description of all experiments in connection with fabrication and characterization of the electrodes. In Section IV, the achieved results are presented and discussed. We conclude in Section V.

II. OBJECTIVE

The goal of this work is the development of a cost-effective process for the manufacture of miniaturised CG-ISEs. This is given by thick-film (TF)-technology. Sensors for the determination of heavy metals fabricated by means of this technology would have the decisive advantage over those prepared with physical processes (like, e.g., PLD), namely, that they can be produced cost-effectively in small quantities.

The great potential that is offered by TF-technology, regarding market and technology, can be utilised for the development of electrochemical sensors. Advantages of a ceramic-TF based heavy metal sensor are its mechanical robustness, high chemical resistance and tightness, as well as the associated low susceptibility to cross influences. Thus, the aim is to create a TF-sensor for heavy metal ions, e.g., to be used in environmental analysis. In this paper, Cu^{2+} and Pb^{2+} ions are the focus of interest. One challenge is the material and process development for the realisation of CG-membranes in TF-technology on ceramic substrates. From CG-bulk material, a submicron powder has to be produced for the realisation of a sinterable TF-paste. This requires fundamental tests of the sintering behaviour of chalcogenide glasses under inert conditions.

III. EXPERIMENTS

Ag, Pb, Cu, As, S, As_2S_3, As_2S_5, As_2Se_3 and AgI, as well as PbS powders have been used for the fabrication of the glasses and Cu, Pb, K, Ca and Na nitrates for the preparation of the calibration solutions, in each case in a purity >99.99 wt.-% obtained from Alfa Aesar GmbH Co. KG and Sigma-Aldrich Chemie GmbH. For melting the CG, the individual glass components were inserted in a cylindrical quartz ampoule. This was filled with nitrogen in a reaction chamber, evacuated ($<10^{-3}$ mbar) and hermetically sealed. The powder containing body was transferred in a quartz glass reactor, which then was placed in a tube furnace (B180, max. temperature: 1300°C, see Figure 1).

Figure 1. Tube furnace with laboratory stirrer

For the slow movement of the ampoule during the heat-up phase with 100-110 K/h until temperatures of 1000-1100°C and a melting process duration of 8-9h, a stirrer was used. Immediately after the melting process, the ampoule was quenched in cold water and destroyed for the collection of the glass. In particular, following heavy metal ion selective CG-glass systems of different stoichiometry were melted: CuAsS, CuAsSe, CuAgAsSe (Cu^{2+} sensitive) and PbAgIAsS (Pb^{2+} sensitive)

Surface, structure, qualitative and quantitative composition as well as thermal expansion coefficient of the glasses and pastes that were later prepared for the screen printing process were characterised by means of following methods: Scanning Electron Microscopy (SEM) with Energy Dispersive X-ray Spectrometer (EDX), Microwave Digestion of the glasses with MARS 6 (CEM GmbH) and determination of the elements with Atom Absorbtion Spectralphotometer novAA400, X-ray Diffraction (XRD) by means of D8 advance from Bruker, Dilatometry and other thermoanalytic methods using several equipment from NETZSCH-Gerätebau GmbH.

As mentioned above, for the specific purpose of evaluation of TF-technology as manufacturing procedure for CG-glass electrodes, the determination of the sintering behaviour under inert conditions is important, for which several thermoanalytical investigations by means of Thermomechanical Analysis (TMA) were performed.

For orienting measurements of the electrochemical functionality of the glasses, initially the conventional electrode design, according to Figure 2a, was realised. Therefore, glass disks (thickness: 2mm) split by a diamond saw and embedded in epoxy resin were mounted in a liquid-tight polymer-pipe and encapsulated with epoxy resin. The electrical contact was realised by means of conductive silver lacquer via Ag or Cu wires. Later, impedance measurements were carried out to determine the internal electrode resistances using a GAMRY Electrochemical Measurement System. The determination of response times and slopes of the electrodes was performed in calibration solutions in the measuring range of 10^{-2} M-10^{-7} M Cu^{2+} and Pb^{2+} with a 0.1 M KNO_3 amount to adjust the ionic strength. The cross-sensitivity of the glasses was determined in the calibration solutions specified above by adding of 10^{-3} M interfering cation in each case. After having examined the electrode functions of the sensors, the CG that was found particularly appropriate (sensitivity: >25 mV/pX, X = Cu^{2+}, Pb^{2+}; measuring range: $>10^{-5}$ M; lower detection limit: $<10^{-5}$ M, pH-range: pH = 2- 7; response time: < 3 min) was chosen for the later fabrication of the TF-electrodes (Figure 2b). Therefore, the CG–bulk materials are milled to glass powder and brought into an organic vehicle, which is added to achieve screen printability. Afterwards, the pastes were processed on a three roll mill to make sure the particles were finely-dispersed. The pastes have been screen printed on Al_2O_3 substrates over a metallised layer (Au). The CG layers were fired according to the sintering temperature of the respective glass.

Potentiometric measurements with conventionally produced rod-shaped CG-electrodes, as well as with prepared TF-sensors were carried out by means of the multiple channel measuring instrument KM 3000 of Sensortechnik Meinsberg GmbH usually in connection with a saturated silver/ silver chloride reference electrode. On a specific occasion, the influence of light on the electrode potential of individual electrodes was determined, too.

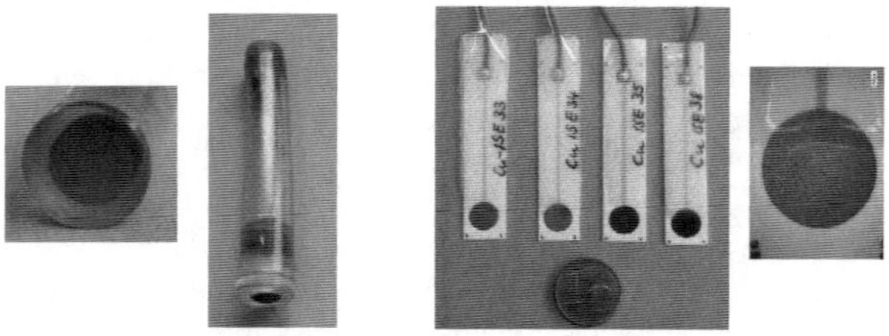

a b

Figure 2. Heavy metal ion sensitive chalcogenide glass electrodes (a rod-shaped electrode, b thick film electrode)

IV. RESULTS AND DISCUSSION

The results presented below relate to the relevant material science tests and to the investigations in connection with the use of the electrodes.

In Figure 3, an EDX measurement of a Cu^{2+} ion selective glass suitable for the thick-film process is presented; it shows a uniform distribution of the elements within the selective material. However, from AAS analyses, it can be concluded that there is a slight stoichiometric difference between weighed crystalline starting mixture and glass.

In particular, pulverisation of bulk glasses necessary for the preparation of TF-pastes causes sometimes unwanted partial recrystallisation for materials without silver. This becomes clear in the XRD diagrams of the relevant copper and lead ion selective materials shown in Figure 4.

Knowledge of the sintering behaviour of the glass powder is of great importance for the realisation of glass-based TF-sensors. By means of TMA, the shrinkage was measured of glass powder compacts (of cylindrical shape). During sintering, the glass powder should compress without crystallisation.

Figure 3. EDX-recordings of distribution of the elements copper, silver, arsenic, selenic in a chalcogenide glass with the composition: $Cu_{12.5}Ag_{12.5}As_{37.5}Se_{37.5}$

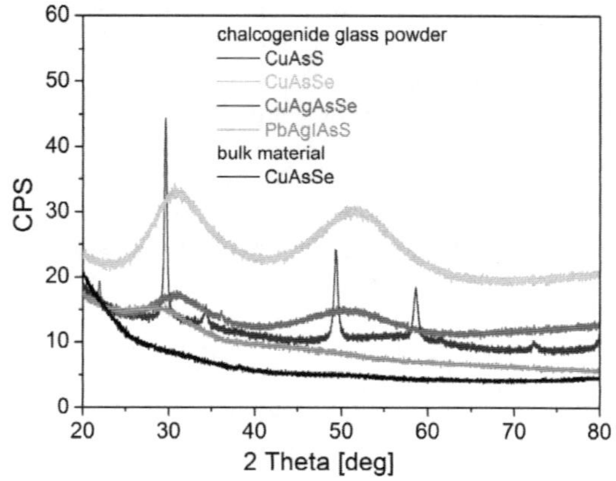

Figure 4. X-ray diffraction diagrams of Cu^{2+} and Pb^{2+} sensitive chalcogenide glasses

As a result of all orienting investigations on CG-bulk material and on CG-powder including Differential Thermal Analysis (DTA), Thermogravimetry (TG) and sintering behaviour, it could be concluded that all proposed systems of copper ion selective CG with copper contents >10 at.-% should be suitable for paste preparation. Due to phase formation/crystallisation of the investigated lead selective glass (see Figure 5) at 190°C, it should be sintered at temperatures <190°C what is possible in air and nitrogen, in principle. Using a heating rate of 10 K/min, an end of the sintering would be expected at 355°C. This corresponds to sufficient material shrinkages of 17% (see Figure 6).

Assuming a sintering temperature of 180°C that is relevant in the present case to prevent crystallisation, it would lead to shrinkage of only 4%; then, the glass is not sufficiently compressed. The available lead ion selective CG is, therefore, unsuited for the TF-process.

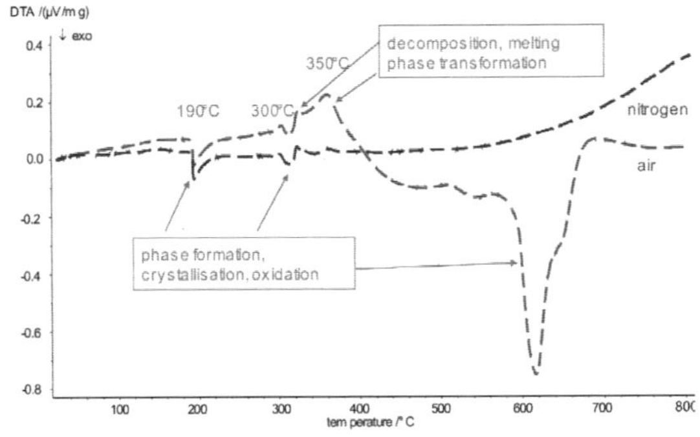

Figure 5. DTA investigations for a chalcogenide glass system PbAgIAsS

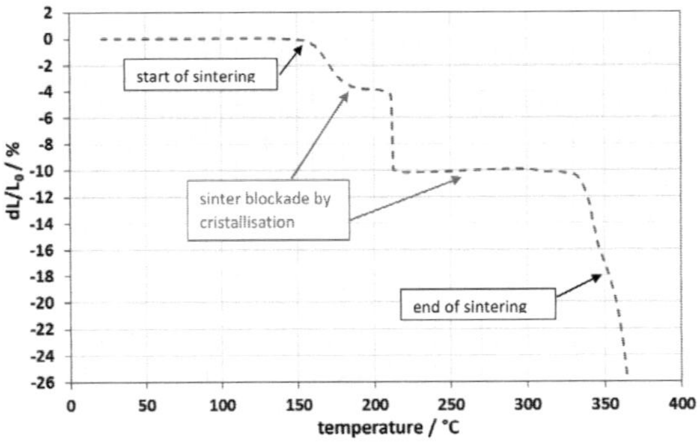

Figure 6: Linear shrinkage vs. temperature of PbAgIAsS-powder compact

For impedance measurements carried out with all rod-shaped and TF-electrodes, a 3-electrode arrangement was chosen, consisting of CG-working electrode, platinum-sheet counter electrode and saturated silver/ silver chloride reference electrode. The internal resistances are presented in Figure 7. Since conventional ion-meters have input resistances of about 10^{13} Ω, no measurement problems are expected.

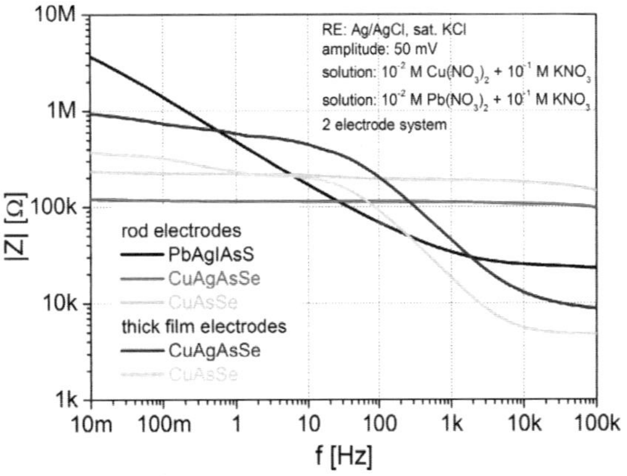

Figure 7. Impedance measurements with chalcogenide glass electrodes

Rod-shaped and TF-electrodes based on the glass systems CuAsS, CuAsSe and CuAgAsSe have been used for the potentiometric determination of Cu^{2+} ions. Lead analyses were performed only by means of rod-shaped sensors. It was ascertained that glass compositions with Ag content and the use of Se instead of S resulted in improved properties concerning the lower detection limit of the corresponding electrodes. The slopes of the measuring chains in the linear measurement range from 10^{-2} M- 10^{-8} M $Cu(NO_3)_2$, 0.1 KNO_3 with 28.7 ± 0.5 mV/pCu^{2+} were in good agreement with the Nernst equation for bivalent ions. The calibration curve of a corresponding TF-electrode is shown in Figure 8. The electrode sensitivities of lead selective rod-shaped electrodes obtained in calibration solutions of 10^{-2} M- 10^{-8} M $Pb(NO_3)_2$, 0.1 M KNO_3 had with 28.6 ± 0.5 mV/pPb^{2+} similar values. Furthermore, an extreme influence of light on the electrode potential of these (silver iodide containing) electrodes (see Figure 9) was detected. Strong responses of the potential of a corresponding electrode located in a black box under the influence of light with varying intensity were observed. This circumstance should be considered for practical measurements.

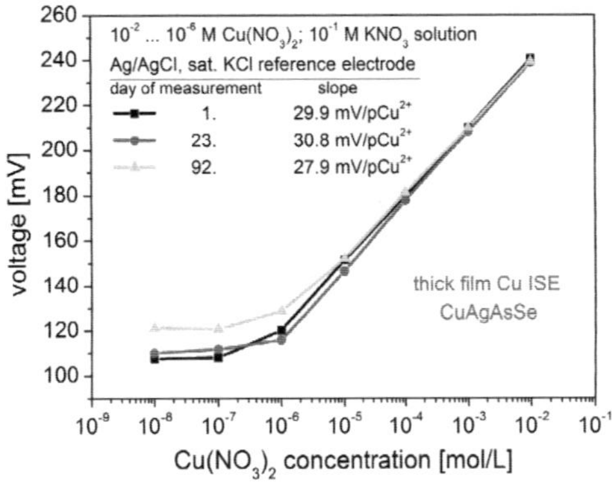

Figure 8. Calibration curve of a copper electrode in thick film technology

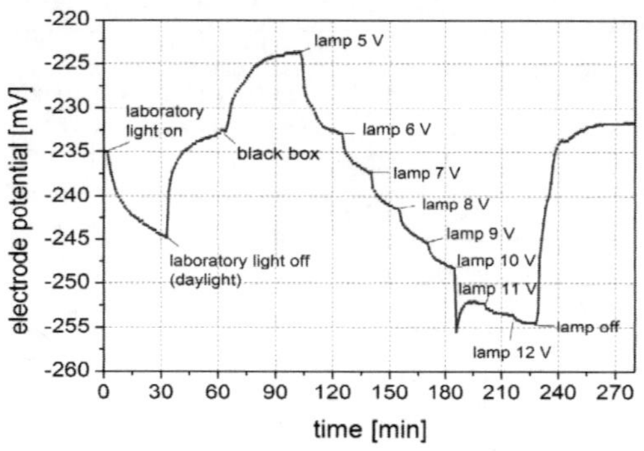

Figure 9. Light sensitivity of a lead ion selective chalcogenide glass electrode with AgI as component of the membrane

Finally, for the favoured copper ion selective TF-electrode the selectivity coefficients were determined according to the method of mixed solutions (see Table 1).

TABLE 1. SELECTIVITY COEFFICIENTS OF A Cu^{2+} CG-ISE

cation	$K^{pot}_{A,B}$
Cd^{2+}	$3.5 \cdot 10^{-4}$
Pb^{2+}	$5.0 \cdot 10^{-4}$
Na^{+}	$4.5 \cdot 10^{-1}$
Ca^{2+}	$3.0 \cdot 10^{-4}$

V. CONCLUSION

CGs of different stoichiometric compositions were melted. They were characterised by a number of physico-chemical methods with the aim to fabricate copper and lead ISEs in TF-technology. The focus was on the material systems CuAgS, CuAsSe, CuAgAsSe and PbAgIAsS. In a first step, rod-shaped electrodes were fabricated in conventional manner from these glasses. While the material properties of the lead selective glasses did not allow a preparation of processable TF-pastes, corresponding screen printedcopper selective electrodes could be realised. Their measuring performances were comparable with those known from rod-shaped electrodes. By an optimisation of the glass composition, the electrode properties were improved.

ACKNOWLEDGEMENT

The financial support by the German Federal Ministry of Economics and Technology in the context of the AiF project (grant number KF2218321KM4) is acknowledged.

REFERENCES

[1] C. J. Koester, B. K. Esser, and S. L. Simonich, "Environmental analysis", Analytical Chemistry, vol. 75, pp. 2813-2829, 2003.

[2] C. H. Hamann and W. Vielstich, Electrochemistry. Wiley-VCH. Weinheim, 1998.

[3] G. Harsanyi, Sensors in biomedical applications. Technomic Publishing Company. Lancaster, 2000.

[4] C. J. Koester and A. Moulik, "Trends in environmental analysis", Analytical Chemistry, vol. 77, pp. 3737-3754, 2005.

[5] K. Cammann and H. Galster, Working with ion sensitive electrodes. Springer-Verlag Berlin, 1996.

[6] J. Bobacka, A. Ivaska, and A. Lewenstam, „Potentiometric ion sensors", Chem. Rev., vol. 108, pp. 329-351, 2008.

[7] C. Baker and I. Trachtenberg, "Ion Selective Electrochemical Sensors-Fe^{3+}, Cu^{2+}", Journal of the Electrochemical Society, vol. 118, pp. 571-576, 1971.

[8] Y. G. Vlasov and E. A. Bychkov, "Ion-selective chalcogenide glass electrodes", Ion-Selective Electrode Rev., vol. 9, pp. 5-93, 1987.

[9] Y. G. Vlasov, E. A. Bychkov, and A. M. Medvedev, "Copper ion-selective chalcogenide glass electrodes: Analytical characteristics and sensing mechanism", Analytica Chimica Acta, vol. 185, pp. 137-158, 1986.

[10] Y. G. Vlasov and E. A. Bychkov, "Electrochemical ion-selective sensors based on chalcogenide glasses", Sensors and Actuators, vol. 12, pp. 275-283, 1987.

[11] Y. G. Vlasov and E. A. Bychkov, "Sodium ion-selective chalcogenide glass electrodes", Analytical Letters, vol. 22, pp. 1125-1144, 1989.

[12] Y. G. Vlasov, E. A. Bychkov, and B. L. Seleznev, "Silver ion sensors based on Ag-As-Se-Te glasses II. Surface studies and tracer measurements of ion response", Sensors and Actuators B: Chemical, vol. 2, pp. 43-49, 1990.

[13] Y. G. Vlasov, E. A. Bychkov, and A. V. Legin, "Chalcogenide glass chemical sensors: Research and analytical applications", Talanta, vol. 41, pp. 1059-1063, 1994.

[14] V. S. Vassilev and S. V. Boycheva, "Chemical sensors with chalcogenide glassy membranes", Talanta, vol. 67, pp. 20-27, 2005.

[15] J. M. Conde Garrido, F. Macoretta, M. A. Urena, and B. Arcondo, "Application of Ag-Ge-Se based chalcogenide glasses on ion-selective electrodes", J. Cryst. Solids., vol. 355, pp. 2079-2082, 2009.

[16] S. Pollrich, Chalcogenide glasses as ion sensitive membranes for potentiometric sensors. Hochschule Mittweida (FH), Fachbereich Mathematik/Physik/Informatik, Diplomarbeit, 2004.

[17] J. P. Kloock, Fabrication and characterisation of sensor membranes of chalcogenide glass films for heavy metal sensors in liquids. TU Ilmenau Universitätsbibliothek, Auflage 1, 2009, mv-Verlag, ISBN: 978-3-939473-43-5.

[18] Y. G. Vlasov, "Sensor R&D in the former Soviet Union", Sensors and Actuators B, vol. 15-16, pp. 6-15, 1993.

[19] M. J. Schöning et al., "Innovative thin film techniques for microfabricating electrochemical sensors", Biocybernetics and Biomedical Engineering, vol. 21, pp. 107-119, 2001.

[20] J. P. Kloock, Y. G. Mourzina, J. Schubert, Y. Ermolenko, and M. J. Schöning, "Pulsed laser deposition: A tool for fabricating thin-film microsensors", Biomedizinische Technik, vol. 49, pp. 1032-1033, 2004.

[21] J. Schubert et al., "Chalcogenide-based thin film sensors prepared by pulsed laser deposition technique", Applied Physics A: Materials Science and Processing, vol. 69, 803-805, 1999.

[22] M. J. Schöning et al., "Can pulsed laser deposition serve as an advanced technique in fabricating chemical sensors?", Sensors and Actuators B: Chemical, vol. 78, pp. 273-278, 2001.

SAW Temperature Sensors with Stable and Robust Electrical Response Versus Environmental Parameters

Marianne Sagnard*†, Thierry Laroche† and Sylvain Ballandras†
* Femto-ST - Time and frequency department
† Frec'n'sys SAS
emails: marianne.sagnard@frecnsys.fr, thierry.laroche@frecnsys.fr, sylvain.ballandras@frecnsys.fr

Abstract—**Surface acoustic wave (SAW) devices are often used to monitor environmental parameters. In order to ensure the continuity of the frequency response versus these parameters - namely, to remove the effects of directivity, transducers working out of the Bragg conditions are studied. Then, it is shown that the multimodal nature of the acoustic cavity can be exploited to design monolithic temperature SAW sensors.**

Keywords-Surface acoustic wave; SAW; resonators; sensors; temperature; Bragg band; directivity; three strips per wavelength.

I. Introduction

Physical quantities, such as temperature or pressure need to be monitored in various industry sectors for safety reasons and/or to ensure the good functioning of the facilities. One major issue is that some sensors are inserted in harsh environments and in places where human intervention is not possible. For instance, they could be located in rotary environment (airplane turbines), oven where they face high temperatures (steel industry), or they could also be subject to high magnetic field. Consequently, passive wireless sensors were developed. These sensors make use of piezoelectricity and surface acoustic waves (SAW) to allow remote measurements based on time or frequency [1], [2].

Classically, one of the most common configurations for SAW sensors is made of several resonators. These devices allow for frequency differential measurements by taking into account the behavior of each resonator regarding the quantity of interest [3], [4] (the frequency difference between the minima of the reflexion terms S_{11} is determined). However, two difficulties come up. The first one is a significant issue : how do different resonators interact and age in a different way along time? Secondly, these systems usually work at the Bragg conditions [5]; meaning that electrodes composing the transducer are deposited on the surface of a piezoelectric material so that the resonator is synchronous. Then, directivity properties can be affected by environmental changes and consequently, electrical response can be distorted, leading to the appearance of contributions at the beginning and at the end of Bragg band, to frequency jumps and finally, to wrong measurement interpretations.

The solutions to design SAW wireless and battery-free sensors proposed in this paper aim at resolving the two previous considerations. At first, the stability of the frequency response is ensured thanks to the geometry of the device, which directly impacts the sensitivity of the device to directivity. This assertion is pointed out through different cases. Namely, resonators are usually designed so that they are composed of mirrors to create an acoustic cavity and of a finite transducer whose mechanical period is twice smaller than the electrical period [6]. These resonators work inside the Bragg band and are subject to the previous constraints (risk of frequency jumps when the directivity evolves, interaction between the different resonators composing the structure). Thus, the idea is to modify the design of the transducers in order to make them work out of the Bragg band. The mirrors remain unchanged [7]. Therefore, several SAW structures using langasite (LGS) (YXlt)/48.5/26.7° cut and working out of the Bragg conditions are designed to create acoustic cavity with a prevailing mode. It is shown that resonators that meet the spectral purity requirements can be designed.

Next, the intrinsic multimodal nature of the cavity is used to design a monolithic sensor. By this way, the sensor is free from the aging of each system independently and from the interaction between them. A structure with more than three resonances in the Industrial - Scientific - Medical (ISM) band is designed to bring to light that a differential measurement can be conducted directly between the different modes of the system.

These different elements are pointed out using langasite once again. This choice was made for two reasons. Firstly, LGS was chosen due to the stability of its constants (piezoelectric, elastic,etc.) at high temperatures. It is consequently a good material for high temperature applications. Then, surface acoustic waves on LGS exhibit a low velocity, which allows the shrinking of sensoe dimensions for a given operating frequency.

Finally, experimental measurements are carried out on Quartz devices to emphasize the possibility to measure temperature from 25°C to at minimum 130°C with a single resonator sensor and to show the good calculation/test correlation. Quartz was selected for experimental validations thanks to its well-known material constants and because it is quite easy to process compared to materials like langasite.

Consequently, section II details the directivity effects and proposes a method to remove them. Next, section III is devoted to the design of a monolithic SAW sensor by exploiting the multimodal nature of the specific acoustic cavity described in this work. Last part (section IV) concludes draws conclusions on this study.

II. Stability of the Frequency Response of a SAW Device

A. *Preliminary assessments*

The stability of the frequency response of SAW sensors is a crucial issue in measurement. It has been noticed that the electrical response can be distorted and that frequency jumps can appear when parameters like temperature or pressure vary. This is pointed out on Figure 1, which shows the evolution of the frequency response of a resonator working at the Bragg condition when temperature varies from 25 to 300°C. A decrease in conductance with temperature is clearly observed. A change in the shape of the curve at the resonance is also noticed when temperature increases. The appearance of a second peak on the curve can lead to wrong measurement interpretation. For instance, if we pay attention to the peaks at 383.2 MHz on Figure 1, we can't establish the value of the temperature.

This phenomenon is due to the modification of directivity properties as shown in Figure 2. Indeed, directivity d expresses the energy distribution in the cavity created by the two Bragg mirrors. If $d = 0^o$, the energy is concentrated at the beginning of the stopband. On the contrary, if $d = 90^o$, the energy is mostly located at its end. As a consequence, when directivity evolves, as shown Figure 2, the shape of the sensor response is modified. This can be seen on Figure 1 : the device is designed to work at the beginning of the Bragg band. But, when temperature (so d) changes, the energy tends to move in the Bragg band. As the band is narrow in this device, this lead to the splitting of the peak.

Moreover, the reflection coefficient r is deeply linked to directivity as explained in [8]. It is well known by men of the art that the control of reflection coefficient is a critical criteria to design SAW systems. The collapse of r and the modifications of d with temperature (Figure 2) also induce the decrease of insertion losses when heat rises.

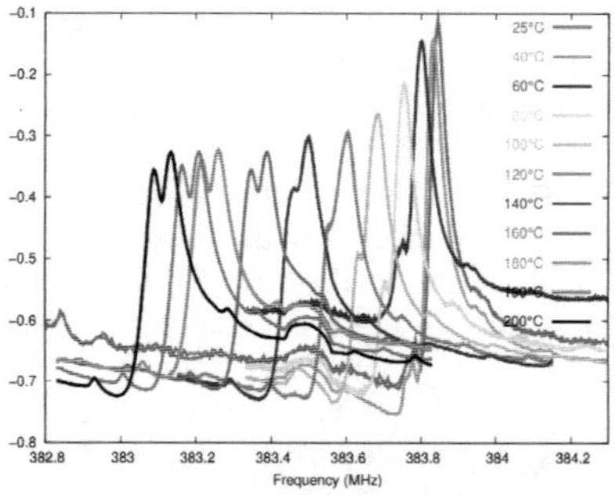

Figure 1. Evolution of the electrical response of a resonator on langasite (YXlt)/48.5/26.7° on a temperature range from 25 to 300°C to reveal directivity effects

B. Spectral quality of a three strips per wavelength resonator

To exhibit that a structure working out of the Bragg band can be used to remove the influence of directivity on the system, the behavior of a wave propagating under an infinite grating of platinum made of three strips per wavelength λ is studied (transducer Figure 4. Once again, a langasite (YXlt)/48.5/26.7° cut substrate is selected to put forward that contrary to the results of section II-A and despite the existence of two phase/frequency conditions involving the synchronism of the design, either the beginning or the end of the Bragg band is inhibited. That is to say, directivity has a negligible effect on the response of the structure.

The observations to be drawn from the results represented on Figure 3 are :

- the large frequency gap between the first and the second contributions (about 8 MHz) that can be noticed when looking at the x-axis of Figures 3a and 3b;
- the very low electromechanical coupling (near to zero for all the temperatures considered on Figure 3) of the second resonance (high frequencies).

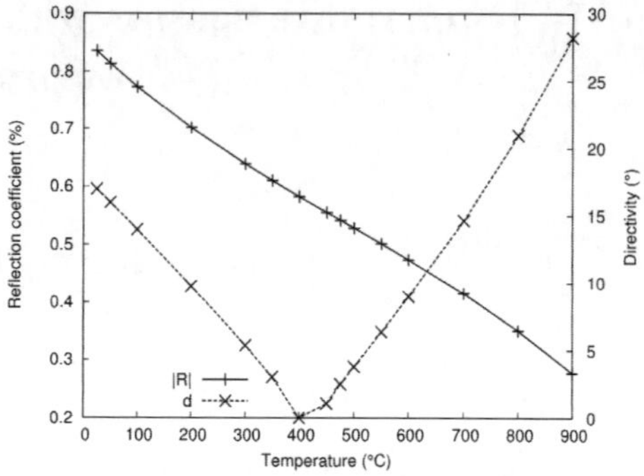

Figure 2. Theoretical estimation of the evolution of directivity and Rayleigh wave reflection properties under platinum electrode grating on langasite (YXlt)/48.5/26.7° cut

The mechanical coupling can be deduced from these graphs considering the frequency gap between the resonance (maximum of admittance) and the antiresonance (zero of admittance, which is also the maximum of impedance). On these figures, susceptance and reactance are considered instead of admittance and impedance because the behavior of the structure is simulated by taking no losses into account.

These two assessments can be compared to the results of Figure 1 : as the two modes are well separated, a splitting of the principle mode in two is no more possible. Moreover, the very low coupling of the second resonance induces that this mode will not perturb the first one.

This first result, obtained considering an infinite grating of electrodes, demonstrates that benefits are brought by working out of the Bragg conditions, especially the possibility to cancel the effects of directivity. As a consequence, a resonator can now be designed according to the previous results and following the pattern described on Figure 4.

The design of this kind of structures involves new criteria and depends on the parameter to promote (coupling factor, low cavity modes, etc.). The operating point is selected according to the specifications. Regarding these considerations, three cases are considered. Table I recaps their dimensions. The frequency response functions of these structures are plotted from Figure 5 to Figure 7. In first instance, the device is designed so that the resonant frequency (synchronous frequency) is on the edge of the bandgap. The second case presents a synchronous frequency between the beginning and the middle of the bandgap. Finally, this frequency is located in the center of the bandgap. We can notice that the use of one or another location solution involves a trade-off between design criteria. For example, the first case shows a good dynamic on the reflection coefficient S_{11} (y-axis of Figures 5a, 6a, 7a) but, the best ratio of cavity peaks on principal peak appears in the third case, as for the best coupling factor than can be determined on Figures 5b, 6b, 7b by considering the distance between the maximum of conductance and its zero.

Finally, despite a low coupling factor (about 0.1% whereas a similar structure working in the Bragg band has got a coupling factor of about 0.25%) a resonator with a frequency response function that meets the spectral purity requirements has been successfully designed.

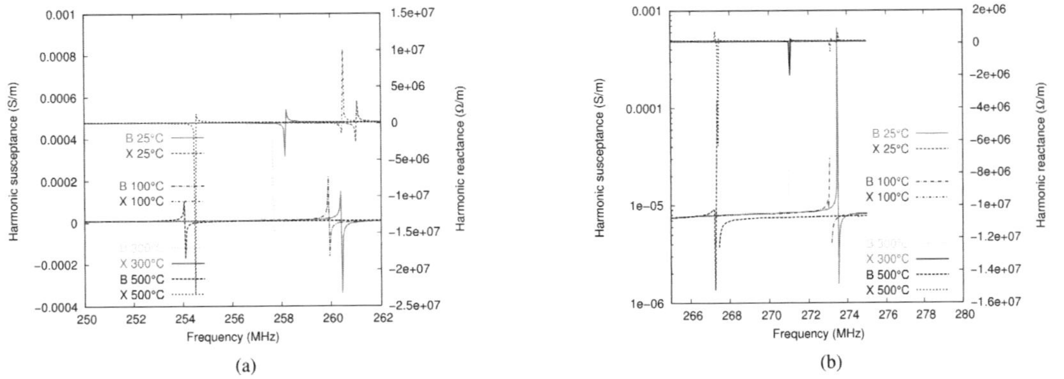

Figure 3. Rayleigh wave admittance on langasite (YXlt)/48.5/26.7° cut propagating under a platinum grating (harmonic analysis) for three electrodes per wavelength. (a) main contribution at "low" frequencies, (b) marginal contribution at high frequencies

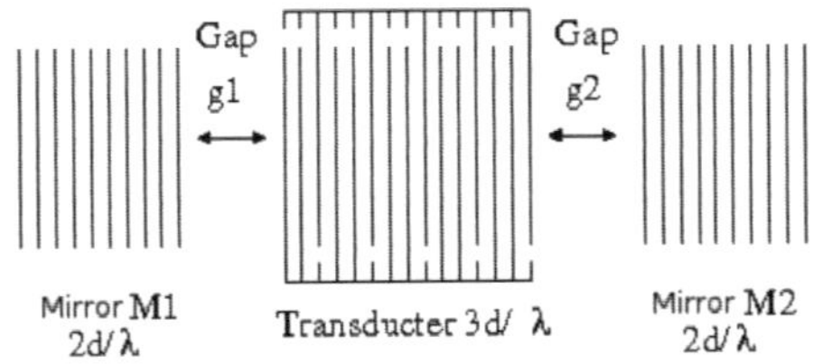

Figure 4. Schematic of a three strips per wavelength resonator

TABLE I. DESIGN TECHNOLOGICAL PARAMETERS OF THE THREE SIMULATED DEVICES

Parameters	*Device Figure 5*	*Device Figure 6*	*Device Figure 7*
number of electrodes (transducter: IDT)	900	900	900
IDT mechanical period (μm)	1.97	1.968	1.965
a/p (IDT)	0.5	0.5	0.5
h/λ (IDT)	2.369%	2.371%	2.375%
number of electrodes in a mirror	150	150	150
Mirror period (μm)	2.924	2.924	2.924
a/p (mirrors)	0.53	0.53	0.53
h/λ (mirrors)	2.394	2.394	2.394
Gap g1 (μm) / (g2=0μm)	1.15	1.8	1.8
acoustic opening (μm)	300	300	300
electrode height (nm)	140	140	140

C. Remarks on designs

Three remarks can be added to the previous results. Indeed, computations showed that the nearer your are from the pure periodical excitation (alternating of +V/-V), the more the secondary frequency contribution appears and the more losses at the synchronous frequency are intensified. For instance, a device with an excitation of floating/-V/+V/-V/floating/+V/-V/+V will have a better spectral purity that a device with +V/-V/+V/+V/-V/+V/-V excitation. To put it in a nutshell, the response of the SAW device is better if the excitation pattern is far from the +V/-V pattern.

Then, the design of resonators pointed out the possibility to obtain purified designs with a prevailing mode in spite of the multimodal character of the cavity.

Moreover, this kind of structure is easier to manufacture than a three electrodes per λ system (larger strips to reach the same frequency). Thanks to these two advantages, a $5/2\lambda$ electrodes structure would be preferred than the $3/\lambda$ electrodes system, which was presented at the beginning of the paper.

III. MULTIPLE MODE RESONATORS

Now that the possibility to remove the influence of the directivity on a SAW system response while keeping a good spectral purity as been demonstrated, we will focus our attentions on the possibility to design a monolithic temperature sensor to free the system from the problematics presented during the introduction. Consequently, the multimodal character of the cavity is exploited.

A. Demonstration of the possibility to design a monolithic SAW sensor

In the previous section, a single gap was taken into account in order to simplify the optimization of the electrical response. Now, two gaps are considered, as depicted on Figure 4. They are defined so that several resonances can exist in the wanted frequency range. To sum up, an acoustic cavity is created between the two Bragg mirrors. A transducer takes place inside this cavity that benefits from the energy of the cavity and interrogates it thanks to direct and inverse piezoelectric effects.

Such a configuration is an effective way to design a temperature sensor using only one resonator by putting several resonances in the ISM band. Indeed, the small variations of the frequency difference between the peaks can be measured. A SAW component is consequently designed. Its dimensions are determined to obtain two main modes well separated and with a maximum frequency interval between these two resonances. A langasite substrate is still used and electrodes are made of platinum. The structure of this component is summarized in table II and its frequency response at ambient is given Figure 8.

The frequency difference Δf between two resonances (f_b and f_a) can be numerically evaluated. Indeed, an harmonic analysis performed on a periodic and infinite electrodes grating reveals a phase velocity v_φ of about 2585 m/s. Considering the values given in table II, we can deduce the total length of the resonator: $L_c \simeq 915\lambda_{ac}$ with λ_{ac} the wavelength of the transducer. As a consequence:

$$\Delta f = f_b - f_a = \frac{v_\varphi}{2L_c} \simeq 236\text{KHz with } f_b > f_a \quad (1)$$

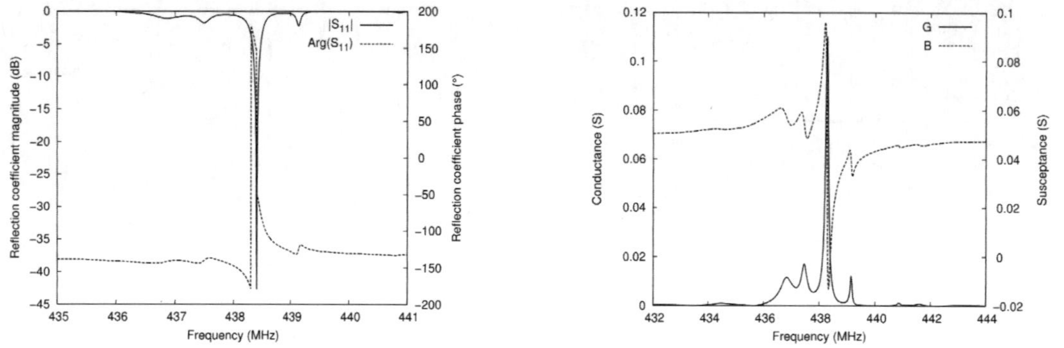

(a) (b)

Figure 5. Electric response of a resonator that works on the edge of the bandgap - (a) reflection coefficient s_{11}, (b) admittance Y

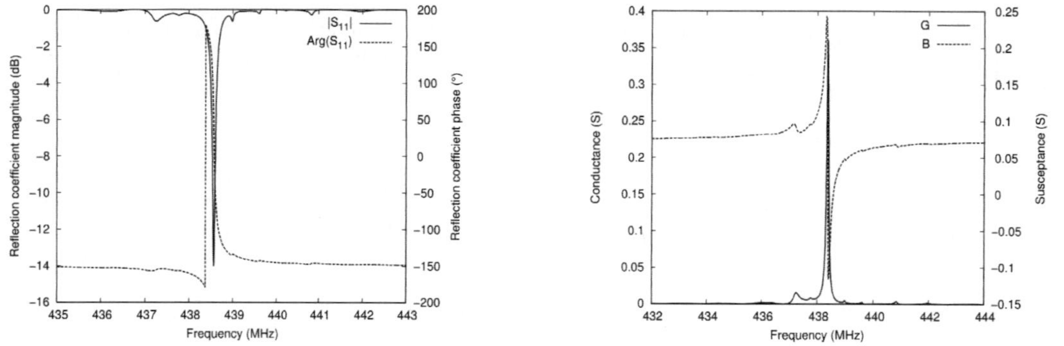

(a) (b)

Figure 6. Electric response of a resonator that works between the beginning and the middle of the bandgap - (a) reflection coefficient s_{11}, (b) admittance Y

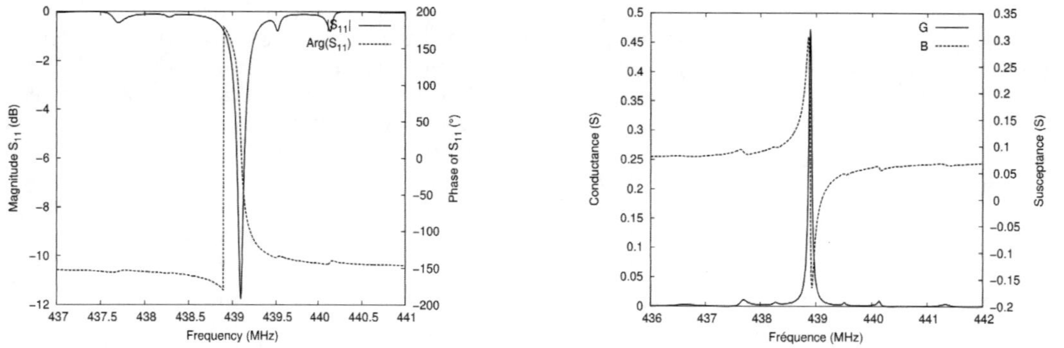

(a) (b)

Figure 7. Electric response of a resonator that works in the middle of the bandgap - (a) reflection coefficient s_{11}, (b) admittance Y

The previous equation is not entirely exact. Indeed, the total length of the device is considered to take into account the probability density of the presence of a mode. But, if the mirrors were perfect, only the acoustic cavity should be taken into account. However, it can be used as a first approximation to size the resonator. Then, this frequency difference evolves along temperature as follows:

$$\Delta(\Delta f) = \frac{\partial(\Delta f)}{\partial v_\varphi} dv_\varphi + \frac{\partial(\Delta f)}{\partial L_c} dL_c \quad (2)$$

$$= \Delta f_0 \times \left(\frac{\Delta v_\varphi}{v_0} - \frac{\Delta L_c}{L_0}\right) \quad (3)$$

with $\Delta(\Delta f)$ that expresses the variation of the frequency gap between two temperatures ; Δf_0 (resp. v_0, resp. L_0) is the frequency gap (resp. the wave velocity, resp. the length of the cavity) at the initial temperature. Terms in (2) correspond to the total exact differential of Δf.

Moreover, the variations of the wave velocity and of the length of the cavity versus temperature have been established by Bechmann and al. [9]. They are here expressed at the second order :

$$\frac{\Delta v_\varphi}{v_0} = CTV_1(T - T_0) + CTV_2(T - T_0)^2 \quad (4)$$

$$\frac{\Delta L_c}{L_0} = \alpha_1^{(1)}(T - T_0) + \alpha_1^{(2)}(T - T_0)^2 \quad (5)$$

Finally, as $CTV_2 \ll CTV_1$, the variation with the temperature of the frequency difference can be approximated by:

$$\frac{\Delta(\Delta f)}{\Delta f_0} = (CTV_1 - \alpha)(T - T_0) \quad (6)$$

The CTV and the first order dilatation coefficient α for the (YXlt)/48.5/26.7° cut of Langasite were determined by Bungo and al. [10]. It has been shown that $CTV_1 = -12.6ppm.K^{-1}$, $CTV_2 = 73.9ppb.K^{-1}$ and $\alpha = 5ppm.K^{-1}$. As a consequence, the calculation (as described in this section) of the frequency gap of this device between 100°C and 200°C is assumed to be 2.175 kHz if the initial frequency difference is 680 kHz. This is consistent with the results of the numerical simulations, which give a Δf of 2 kHz (Figure 9). Otherwise, in this LGS crystal cut, reflection and conduction losses rise fast with temperature, so the design has to be improved: both variation of the frequency gap at these temperatures and losses due to the fall of reflection and transducer coefficients can be seen. Nevertheless, despite the high losses due to the increase of temperature, the good correlation between expected frequency variations and simulation results have shown the interest of our approach to measure temperature: a monolithic SAW sensor has been designed.

TABLE II. DESIGN TECHNOLOGICAL PARAMETERS OF A FOUR PEAKS RESONATOR

Parameters	*Device*
number of wavelengths (transducter: IDT)	100
IDT mechanical period (μm)	1.989
number of electrodes in a mirror	200
Mirrors mechanical period (μm)	2.973
a/p (IDT & mirrors)	0.5
h (nm)	118
acoustic aperture (μm)	300
Left gap (μm)	994.5
Right gap (μm)	1990

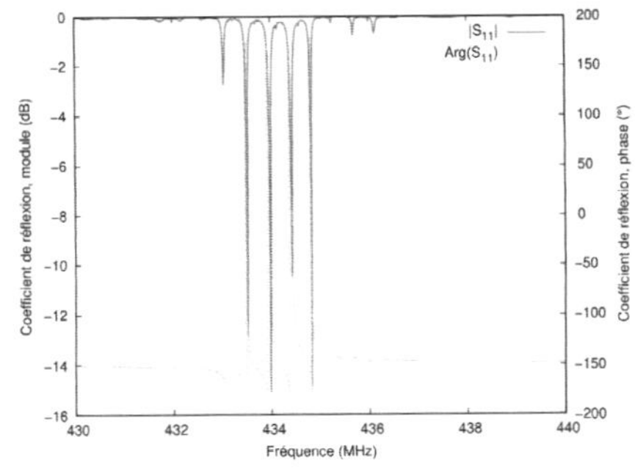

Figure 8. Reflexion coefficient s_{11} of a multiple mode resonator designed on langasite in the ISM band associated to the structure described table II

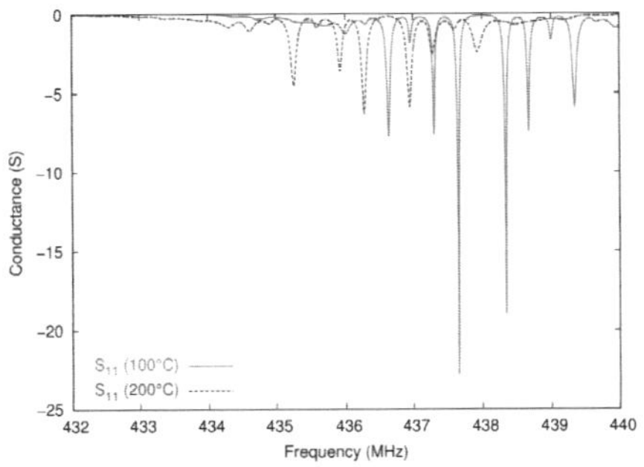

Figure 9. Frequency response of the device described table II designed on Langasite (YXlt)/46.5/26.7° with platinum electrodes for two different temperatures.

B. Experimental results

Finally, a monolithic temperature SAW sensor is manufactured to validate the previous results. A Quartz substrate and aluminum electrodes are used. The transducers are made of three strips per wavelength and three resonances in the ISM band are expected. The evolution of the frequency gaps is studied from 25°C to 130°C. The measures are done thanks to a wafer probe whose chuck heats in this temperature range.

Figure 10 shows the frequency response of this device for different temperatures. The frequencies are normalized. The shift of the three resonances due to temperature changes can be clearly observed on this graph. Furthermore, if we have a look at Figure 11, we can study the evolution of the frequency gap between the first and the last resonances along temperature. A decline of the normalized frequency difference with temperature can clearly be observed. Indeed, the frequency gap evolution under a temperature change can be approximated by the following law :

$$\frac{\Delta(\Delta f)}{\Delta f_0} = CTF_1(T - T_0) + CTF_2(T - T_0)^2 \quad (7)$$

with $CTF_1 = -102$ppm/°C and $CTF_2 = 226.5$ppb/°C.

These results are consistent with the previous theoretical analysis: a structure composed of an only transducer made of a three electrodes per wavelength pattern was designed. The response of this resonator shows three resonances whose frequency difference of one peak to another decreases when temperature increases.

As a consequence, after a set of calibrations, this device is ready for use as a monolithic temperature sensor, which won't be subject to inconvenience such as frequency jumps due to a change in directivity. Moreover, as a monolithic sensor, it will not be subject to different aging between the different structures.

IV. CONCLUSION

Finally, this paper described a new design for surface acoustic wave devices to mitigate the effects of the splitting of the mode due to directivity effects and to raise the issue of the badly known interaction between the resonators forming the sensor.

As a consequence, a structure on LGS whose transducer works out of the Bragg band is proposed. By this way, the shape of its response function is no more impacted by the

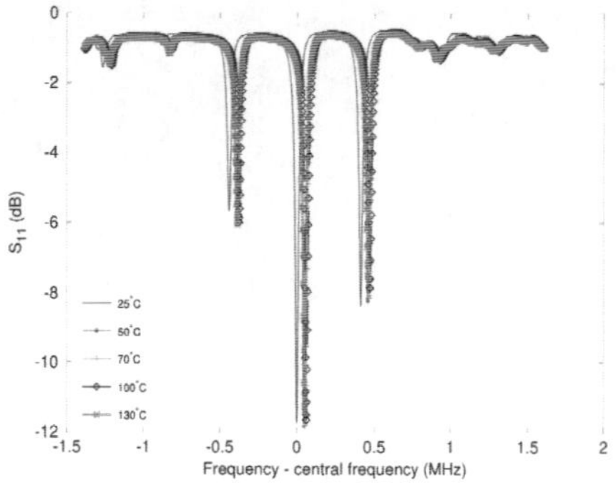

Figure 10. Reflexion coefficient s_{11} of a multiple mode resonator on Quartz substrate with aluminum electrodes. This figure shows the behavior of the three resonances when temperature varies for 25°C to 130^oC

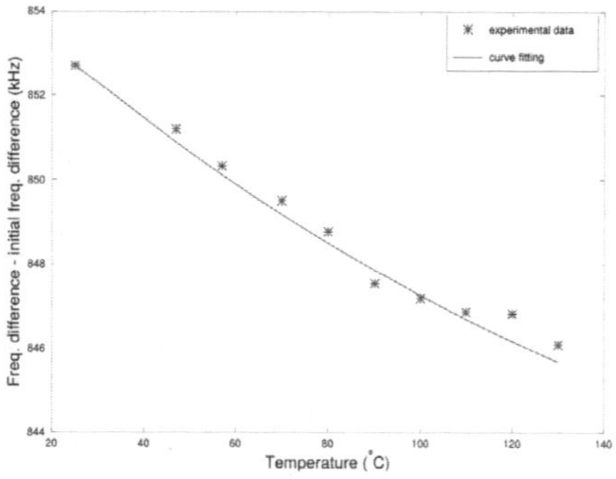

Figure 11. Evolution of the frequency gap between the first and the third resonance with temperature.

directivity while keeping a good spectral purity, which is required for resonators and sources.

Furthermore, the intrinsic multimodal character of the acoustic cavity is turned to its advantage. Indeed, a single resonator with three main resonances was designed so that differential measurements can be conducted to monitor environmental parameters. To validate this theoretical model, a three strips per wavelength structure was realized on a Quartz substrate. The possibility to monitor the evolution of temperature between 25 and 130°C was demonstrated.

Further works will highlight the good agreement between theoretical and experimental results on LGS.

Acknowledgment

We are grateful to the DGA and to the ANRT for their financial backings.

References

[1] L. M. Reindl and I. M. Shrena, "Wireless measurement of temperature using surface acoustic waves sensors," IEEE Transactions on Ultrasonics, Ferroelectrics, and Frequency Control, vol. 51, no. 11, Nov 2004, pp. 1457–1463.

[2] M. P. da Cunha, A. Maskay, R. J. Lad, T. Coyle, and G. Harkay, "Langasite 2.45 GHz ISM band SAW resonator for harsh environment wireless applications," in 2016 IEEE International Ultrasonics Symposium (IUS), Sept 2016, pp. 1–4.

[3] W. Buff, M. Rusko, E. Goroll, J. Ehrenpfordt, and T. Vandahl, "Universal pressure and temperature SAW sensor for wireless applications," in 1997 IEEE Ultrasonics Symposium Proceedings. An International Symposium (Cat. No.97CH36118), vol. 1, Oct 1997, pp. 359–362 vol.1.

[4] H. Tan, X. Chen, J. Ma, and Y. Tan, "A design of substation temperature online monitoring system based on SAW temperature sensor," in 2016 IEEE International Conference on High Voltage Engineering and Application (ICHVE), Sept 2016, pp. 1–4.

[5] M. Born et al., Principles of Optics: Electromagnetic Theory of Propagation, Interference and Diffraction of Light, 7th ed. Cambridge University Press, 1999.

[6] F. Sidek, N. A. Ramli, A. N. Nordin, and I. Voiculescu, "Design and fabrication of Surface Acoustic Wave resonators on Lithium Niobate," in 2010 IEEE Student Conference on Research and Development (SCOReD), Dec 2010, pp. 343–347.

[7] P. Ventura, P. Dufilie, and S. Boret, "The effect of the fabrication process in propagation and reflectivity in an IDT," in 1996 IEEE Ultrasonics Symposium. Proceedings, vol. 1, Nov 1996, pp. 281–284 vol.1.

[8] P. Ventura and J. M. Hode, "A new accurate analysis of periodic IDTs built on unconventional orientation on quartz," in 1997 IEEE Ultrasonics Symposium Proceedings. An International Symposium (Cat. No.97CH36118), vol. 1, Oct 1997, pp. 139–142 vol.1.

[9] R. Bechmann, A. D. Ballato, and T. J. Lukaszek, "Higher-Order Temperature Coefficients of the Elastic Stiffinesses and Compliances of Alpha-Quartz," Proceedings of the IRE, vol. 50, no. 8, Aug 1962, pp. 1812–1822.

[10] A. Bungo et al., "Analysis of Surface Acoustic Wave Properties of the Rotated Y -cut Langasite Substrate," Japanese Journal of Applied Physics, vol. 38, no. 5S, 1999, p. 3239. [Online]. Available: http://stacks.iop.org/1347-4065/38/i=5S/a=3239

Capillary Sensor with UV-Forced Degradation and Fluorescence Reading of Diesel and Biodiesel Fuel Chemical Stability

Michal Borecki
Institute of Microelectronics and Optoelectronics
Warsaw University of Technology
Warsaw, Poland
email: borecki@imio.pw.edu.pl

Michael L. Korwin-Pawlowski
Département d'informatique et d'ingénierie
Université du Québec en Outaouais
Gatineau, Québec, Canada
email: michael.korwin-pawlowski@uqo.ca

Mateusz Gęca
Institute of Electron Technology
Warsaw, Poland
email: mati.geca@gmail.com

Przemysław Prus
Blue Oak Inventions
Wroclaw, Poland
email: pprus@boinv.com

Abstract-**There are many standards set by national organizations and fuel producers to test and guarantee the diesel fuel stability under storage conditions. Traditional techniques for measuring fuel stability utilize oxygen–assisted degradation of heated sample submit the fuel sample to a relatively high pressure of air, temperature of the sample or a long time of examination. For example, American Society for Testing and Materials (ASTM) D4625 requires a time of up to 24 weeks of fuel exposition to air atmosphere heated up to 43°C. The degradation is evidenced by the appearance of resins and sediments. There are many different theories describing the mechanism of degradation of diesel fuels, as there are various factors that initiate and maintain the process. The stability of modern diesel fuel is mainly due to the reduction of the oxidation processes, the result of the presence of unsaturated components and components with oxygen as organic components and cetane index improvers. Therefore, the diesel fuel stability is related with the fuel composition. As a consequence of all that, fast and low-cost sensing of the stability of diesel and biodiesel fuel is important. The present paper concentrates on the construction of the capillary sensor which enables fast examination of fuel stability as a characteristic of fuel itself not of the gas atmosphere. Therefore, the fuel sample under examination is enclosed in a vessel and the degradation factor is assumed to be the UV radiation. The fuel samples used to develop the method are compositions of a classical mixture of petroleum products and the most widely used cetane improver (2-ethyl hexyl nitrate). The result is a sensor set-up based on two UV light emitting diodes, one used to stimulate degradation, the second used for signal reading.**

Keywords-biodiesel fuel stability; diesel fuel degradation; cetane index improvers; capillary sensor; LED excited fluorescence.

I. INTRODUCTION

Diesel fuel stability may be affected by a large number of parameters which can be categorized to describe the effects of oxidation, thermal and storage conditions [1]. The estimated life of a diesel fuel is determined according to the accelerated oxidation stability test ASTM D2274. This test is performed with fuel of 350 mL volume is to be kept at 95 °C in the presence of oxygen for 16 hours, which approximately corresponds to one year's storage at 25 °C. This test measures the ratio of the mass of settled gum and sediment to the mass of the diesel fuel sample. However, this method may not provide a prediction of the quantity of insoluble matter that will form in field storage conditions over any given period of time [2], as for example, microorganisms present in diesel fuel may be also the result of its storage [3]. Therefore, the chemical and biological stability of diesel fuel is under examination.

The storage conditions can be described as exposure to air and/or light at the environment temperature. The diesel fuel storage issue seems to be nowadays recognized as an issue even by fuel producers, who recommend the maximum time of diesel fuel storage in function of temperature conditions [4], for example 6-12 months at an ambient temperature higher than 30 °C. There are some other factors that accelerate diesel fuel ageing: contact with zinc or copper, as these metals will quickly react with diesel fuel to form unstable compounds; presence of water, which allows the growth of fungus and bacteria producing organic acids, which make the fuel unstable; exposure to high temperatures; exposure to dust and dirt, which contain trace elements that can destabilize the fuel; fuel composition as some components in diesel fuel naturally age quickly.

A. Modern diesel fuels

Classical petro-diesel fuels were made from stable components of straight run distillate products of crude oil (alkanes). The minimum cetane number of such diesel fuel was 40, but it has been determined that such fuel may be kept in storage for prolonged periods. Modern diesel fuels are the composition of petro-diesel products, bio-diesel products with an addition of improvers [5]. Modern petro-diesel fuels include stable components (alkanes) and cracked material, which contains olefins (alkenes) characterized by a double bond chemical and aromatic content. Bio-diesel components include fatty acids esters that are also characterized by the presence of double bonds. As the minimum cetane number of modern diesel fuel is 51, the cetane number boost of fuel composition is required. Most popular is the application of cetane number boosters in the form of 2-ethyl hexyl nitrate (2-EHN) or di-tertiary-butyl peroxide (DTBP). Both substances include oxygen and are reactive. Cetane boosters decompose rapidly and form free radicals when exposed to temperatures above 100 °C. These radicals increase the rate of main fuel components decomposition, therefore the ignition delay is negatively affected [6]. The use of cetane boosters in diesel fuel of high quality increases the engine durability [7]. On the other hand, cetane boosters are a potential source of oxygen for oxidation of hydrocarbons. For hydrocarbons that are characterized by double bonds the oxidation products are waxy solids and gums. Therefore, doses of cetane number boosters to diesel fuels have to be carefully calculated. The reduction of cetane number booster's concentration is possible when hydro-treating of fuel products is applied. But, the cetane number improving method using mainly cetane boosters is preferred due to its low cost [8]. The 2-EHN is the most popular cetane index additive. The ASTM D 4046 standard test method is used for determining the amount of alkyl nitrate added to diesel fuel.

B. *Optical sensors for diesel fuel stability testing*

The optical testing of fuel parameters is performed in laboratory and in-situ conditions of working engine [9]. The optical sensors implemented in a working engine (ICOS - Internal Combustion Optical Sensor) – are infrared sensors of air to fuel ratio, CO_2 concentration, and gas temperature. The optical sensors of diesel fuel used in the laboratory enable a wide range of examination. The sequence of visible effects of diesel fuel instability may be described as fuel clouding, fuel clouding disappearance, formation of fuel sediments at the fuel-environment contact area (vessel walls and fuel surface), changes in fuel color (loss of color or darkening) and sediments presence on the bottom of vessel [10].

The fuel components concertation may be examined with IR spectroscopy and UV excitation methods including synchronous reading fluorescence and time resolved fluorescence [11][12]. Despite spectroscopic method drawback of costs of examination of oils in quartz cuvettes including costs of cuvettes and reagents for sample dilution, dedicated components of sensors are under development [13-15].

The examination of diesel fuel fit for use may be performed with capillary measurement methods. These method include measurement of characteristic points of local sample heating of fuel positioned in a capillary and measurement of the dynamical rise of fuel in a inclined capillary [16][17]. Also, for these methods dedicated components have been developed [18][19].

The oxidation stability of oils with spectroscopy measurements in VIS and UV bands were reported in the case of baru oil [20]. The obtained results show that UV absorption from 230 nm to 270 nm during thermal aging increases non-uniformly, while VIS absorption at 475 nm decreases almost linearly down to a threshold value. The fluorescence intensity excited at 405 nm and measured in the range from 450 nm to 750 nm may be a pointer of thermal oil degradation. In particular, the emitted signal at 500 nm that represents oxidation products increases almost linearly and then saturates during thermal aging over a dozen hours at 110 °C.

Nevertheless, for their routine daily work, the fuel distributors still demand the development of new rapid and low-cost sensors for reliable determination of fuel stability.

The rest of this paper is organized as follows. Section II describes the sensor construction development including sensor head with optrode as well as optoelectronics system set-up. Section III addresses the experimental results of the fluorescent signal analysis. Section IV goes into short conclusions.

II. SENSOR CONSTRUCTION

The idea of rapid sensor of diesel fuel stability bases on forced UV degradation of fuels placed in a capillary vessel. In this case, the sample volume is reduced and the surface of sample increases in comparison to the standard cuvette set-up. The inner diameter of the capillary is 700 µm while the diagonal of the cuvette is 1.41 cm. Therefore, UV radiation that is intended to stimulate the sample's degradation penetrates the fuel sample volume more uniformly in the capillary than in the cuvette. Moreover, the use of capillary reduces significantly the costs of the measurement, because the cost of a single CV7087Q capillary is lower than the cost of the quartz cuvette, and is even lower than the cost of a cleaning and washing process of quartz cuvette.

A. *Light sources for the sensor*

For practical applications one has to consider the light emitted diodes as a source of radiation. For excitation of fluorescence and degradation, two LEDs were used. The UVTOP265 LED emitted 250 µW at 265 nm and was equipped with a ball lens, provided good coupling of radiation to the fiber. It was connected to the set-up with Thorlabs SMA adapters and a SM1 tube. The M365F1 LED equipped with a SMA fiber connector providing about 5mW into a 550 nm diameter fiber was directly implemented into the set-up. This LED is characterized by a residual radiation in the band of 400-460 nm. The LEDs were controlled with a Thorlabs DC2100 High-Power, 1-Channel Driver. Due to LEDs working points set at their maximum ratings, the examination was performed of the stability of radiated power of M3651F1 LED with direct fiber coupling to Maya 2000 pro spectrometer. The M365F1 LED is characterized by an increase of the coupled-to-fiber power when it is driven constantly with the current of 300 mA. Interestingly, the coupled power does not depend on the temperature of the LED as it increases even after LED's resting for 5 minutes and a sequential reboot as presented in Figure 1.

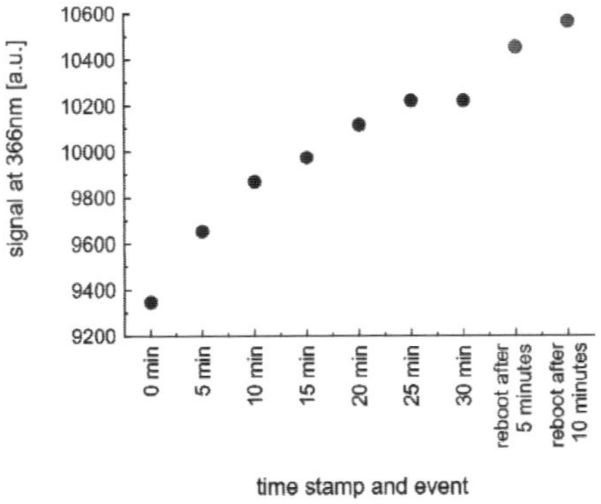

Figure 1. M365F1 LED optical power at 366nm coupled into optical fiber in function of time and event.

The fiber-coupled signal of the UVTOP265 LED constantly driven for 30 minutes at maximum current equal to 30 mA recorded using the sensor head with an empty capillary (see Fig. 4) versus time of measurement is presented in Figure 2.

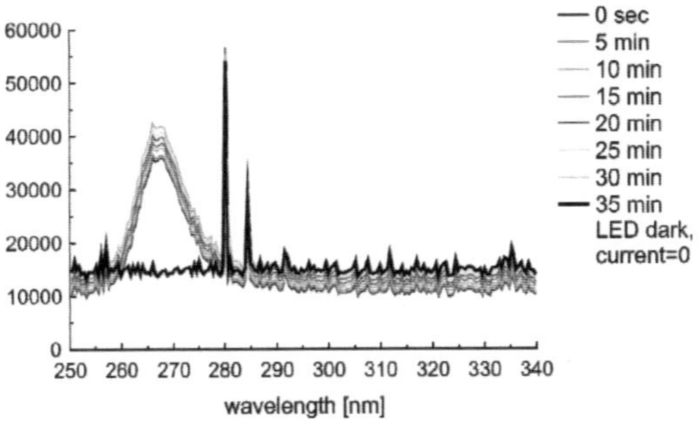

Figure 2. UVTOP265 LED optical power coupled into optical fiber in function of time.

The conditions described above were the worst case examination from the detection unit point of view, as the received signal was only scattered at the smooth glass surface of the capillary and the received signal was close to the sensitivity of the used spectrometer. Thus, spectral characteristics showed fluctuation due to high sensitivity set on the spectrophotometer. The examination of mid-range stability UVTOP265 LED showed similar results as for high power M365F1 LED. The signal peak present at 280nm represents spectrophotometer error. This signal of error varies versus time as presented in Figure 3.

The experimental results show that 10 % of variation of maximum signal intensity is to be expected, but signal changes are not uniform, and also at some signal sampling rate spectrophotometers are characterized by middle-time drift. Therefore, spectral examination requires optical power stabilization of the source or/and mathematical signal correction. Unfortunately, both solutions require source signal monitoring with additional sensing modules.

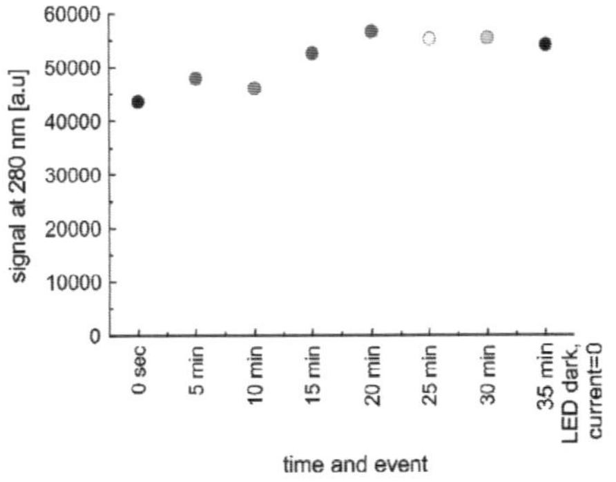

Figure 3. Spectrophotometer imperfection signal at 280nm in function of time and event.

Therefore, a sensor set-up with one and two UV sources was examined. In the case of one UV source, the source performs functions for both fuel degradation and fluorescence excitation. In the case of the set-up with two UV sources the mentioned functions are separated. In both cases, the sensor head enables the observation of the excited fluorescence in the sample of liquid positioned in a capillary vessel using optical fibers as probes.

B. Sensor set-up with one UV source

The sensor head of set-up with one UV source presented in Figure 4 consists of only two optical fibers.

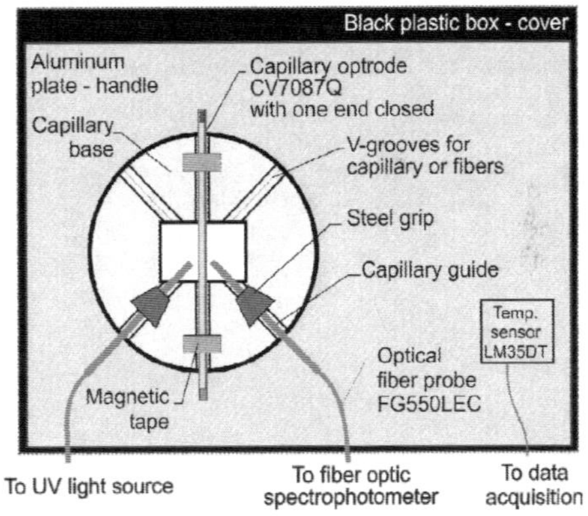

Figure 4. Scheme of the capillary sensor head with two optical fibers.

The head is coupled to the optoelectronic sensor set-up according to the scheme presented in Figure 5.

The set-up is divided into two functional units, optical and optoelectronic, working in a conjugated manner.

The optical unit consists of the head, the optical fiber divider and the monochromator. The set-up element causing the highest optical signal damping is the DMC1-02 monochromator, the attenuation of which is about 1:1000 at analyzed wavelengths. But, the set-up using the monochromator enables tuning of the LED's optical signal with proper accuracy.

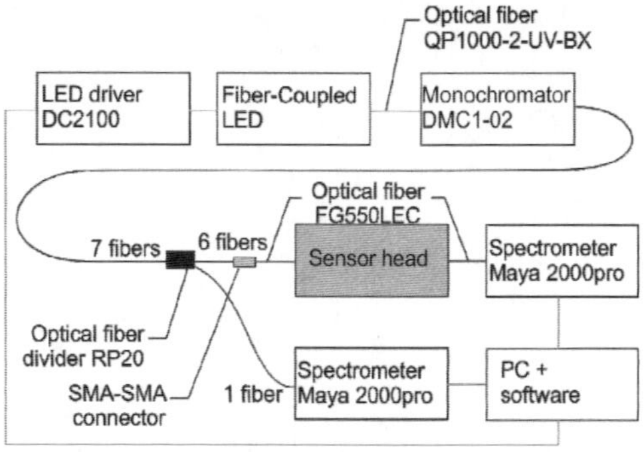

Figure 5. Scheme of the capillary sensor set-up with one LED.

The set-up is optically powered by a LED controlled with the hardware D2100 driver that is triggered from a PC with the use of software. The fiber optic divider 1:7 is used to produce a reference signal and monitor light source parameters with Maya 2000pro spectrometer connected to the PC. The head output is connected to Maya 2000pro spectrometer which is connected to PC. Both spectrometers are controlled by the PC with Ocean Optics software that enables sequential writing of data recorded for the fluorescence and source signals.

C. Sensor set-up with two UV source.

The sensor's head with two UV sources is presented in Figure 6.

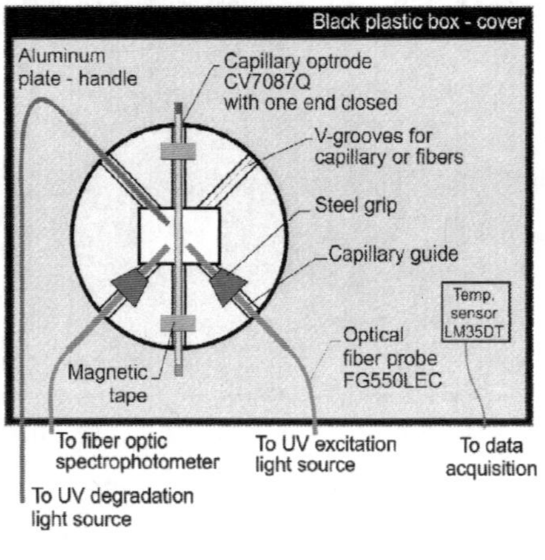

Figure 6. Scheme of the capillary sensor head with two UV sources and three optical fibers.

To make allowance for UV degradation and fluorescence excitation signals an additional optical fiber was placed in head. The system set-up scheme was changed by the addition of a LED block for UV degradation of the sample as presented in Figure 7.

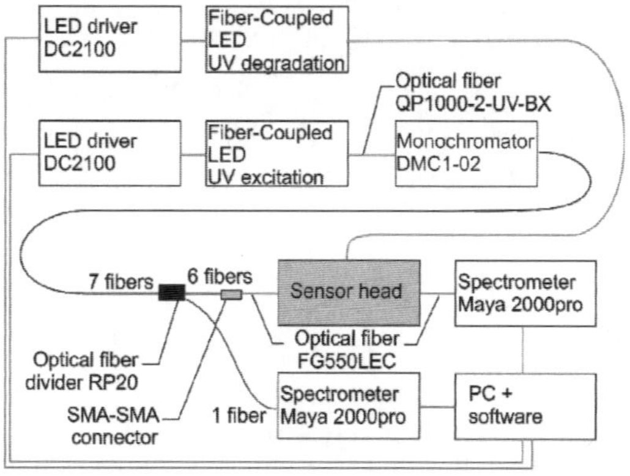

Figure 7. Scheme of the capillary sensor set-up with two LED-s.

The hardware of the detection units was not modified. The changes of the degradation signal may be observed with the spectrometer during the degradation as a reflected signal from capillary walls. This LED output is directly coupled to the head to avoid any power losses. Also the scheme of system control was changed as the LED drivers for UV degradation and UV fluorescence excitation were switched alternately.

III. Experimental Results

In this section, there are presented the experimental procedures and the results of examination of different diesel and biodiesel fuels.

The measurement procedure consists of a few steps. Step 1: At the initial configuration of the set-up the selected diode is mounted. Step 2: the background signal of for the empty optrode is measured. Step 3: optrode is directly filled from the tank and the outer optrode walls are wiped. Step 4: the signal of fluorescence is measured with the use of UV ageing procedure. Step 5: the spectra were calculated as the difference between the fluorescence and the background signals.

The operation of the sensor was examined with fuels provided by the Automotive Industry Institute in Warsaw. The fuels were mixtures of petrodiesel with additives including 2-EHN – one with as bio-component 7% of fatty acids methyl esters (FAME) (CN=59.1) considered as the standard fuel, and the second with 7% of hydrogenated vegetable oil (HVO) (CN=59.2) considered as premium fuel.

A. Set-up with one UV LED

First examination included measurements of the fluorescence of fresh fuels excited with a UVTOP265 LED or a M365F1 LED. Results presented in Figure 8 show similar shapes of characteristics, while the maxima of excited spectra for different excitation are at slightly different wavelengths. Taking into account LEDs currents, and therefore powers, the excitation efficiency at 265 nm is much greater than at 366 nm. The signal of biological fluorescence at 675 nm is readable for excitation at 366 nm.

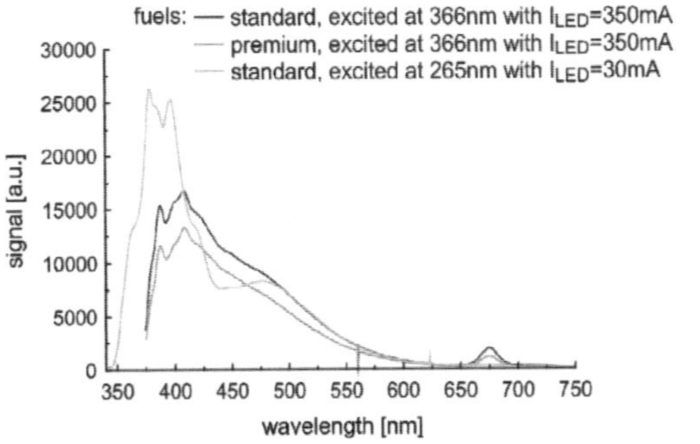

Figure 8. Spectra of fresh fuels excited with 366nm wavelength.

The visible fluorescence emitted signal is caused by the presence of the 2-EHN cetane booster. According to diesel fuel producers' classification, and evidenced by the emission spectra signals recorded at 366 nm excitation, the premium fuel is characterized by a lower concentration of cetane booster than is the case for the standard fuel.

The results of standard fuel degradation with the use of set-up from Figures 4 and 5 and with the use of one M365F1 LED are presented in Figure 9.

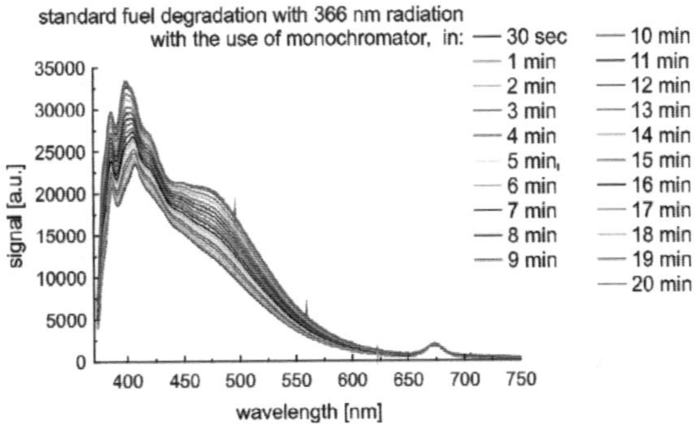

Figure 9. Spectra of fuels degradated and examinated with the use of one M365F1 LED coupled to the set-up and with the use of monochromator.

The fuel degradation is evidenced as the increase of the fluorescence signal. The wavelength position of the peak located about 404 nm shifts during measurement. Fortunately at wavelengths of 475 nm the signal increase is almost monotonic. The constant increase of the signal is adequate to measure the initial stages of fuel degradation. At that stage the degradation is evidenced by the constant presence and the value of the signal of the emitted biological fluorescence at 675 nm.

When the UVTOP265 LED is used in one-LED set-up the monochromator can be removed, as the excited spectra of 2-EHN and gums are positioned at a range where there is no residual emission of LED radiation. The direct spectra of degradation results of standard diesel fuel with the use of UVTOP265 are presented in Figure 10.

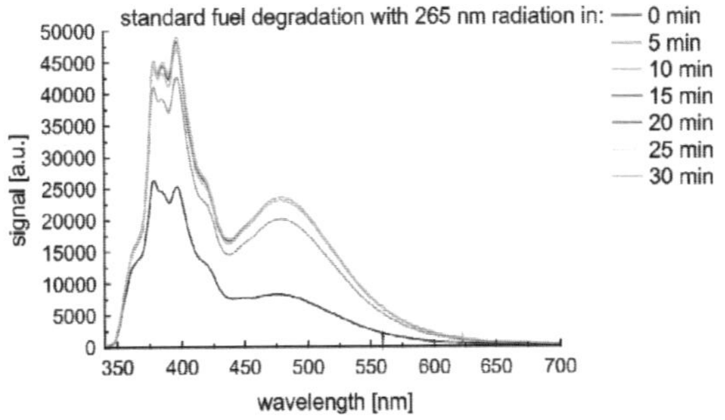

Figure 10. Spectra of fuels degradated and examinated with the use of one UVTOP265 LED directly coupled to set-up - without monochromator using.

The degradation of standard fuels is evidenced as the significant increase of fluorescence signal, which saturates after 10 minutes. The measured speed of the degradation varies. For example, the characteristics faster saturate at 380 nm than at 395 nm peak. But, what is most interesting, the peak wavelengths are stable, when fuel is excited with 265 nm, contrary to excitation results performed at 366 nm.

B. Set-up with two UV LEDs

The set-up with two UV LEDs used of two M365F1 LEDs as their expected stable operational life time is much greater than of UVTOP265 LED. The direct results of fuel aging and fluorescence reading are presented in Figure 11.

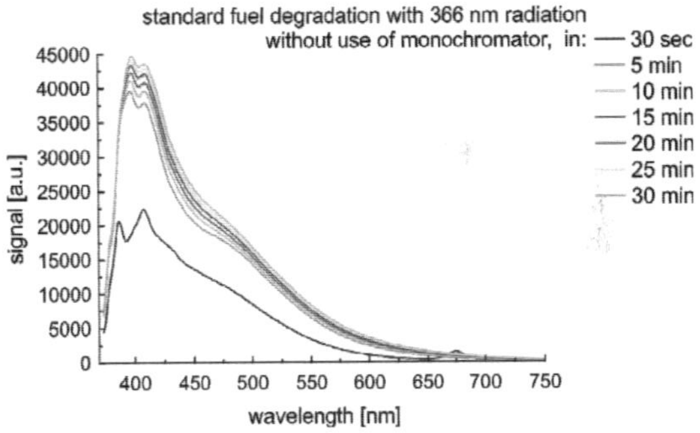

Figure 11. Spectra of fuels degradated and examinated with the use of two M365F1 LEDs.

Four signs of fuel aging are now presented. The first sign adequate for initial aging is the increase of fluorescence excited signal emitted by 2-EHN. The second sign is the disappearance of the emitted peak of biological contamination that happens faster than at 5 minutes of aging. The third sign is the shift of 2-EHN local emitted maxima. The last sign is the change of the relation of 2-EHN local maxima amplitudes.

V. Conclusions

We proposed a sensor for diesel fuel stability testing based on the examination of fluorescence. The key of the method is placing the sample of the fuel in a capillary optrode and using UV radiation for accelerated ageing.

The analysis of the sensor construction showed that 366nm, as well as 265 nm wavelength radiation is sufficient for simulation of initial and middle states of fuel degradation. The conclusion for sensor examination with one LED source is quite obvious; the monochromator decreases significantly the speed of fuel aging. But, the spectra of 366 nm emitted wavelength LED requires positioning at some distance of an optical filter or monochromator to enable proper florescence reading. Therefore, two constructions are proposed. One, with UVTOP265 LED does not require additional optical filtering of signal. The second, with two M365F1 LEDs – one coupled with a monochromator and used for fluorescence reading, – the second directly coupled to the sensor head and used for high power UV fuel degradation. Finally, the power emitted by the LEDs used has to be constantly monitored and its variations taken into account in calculations of aging spectra. The spectral response of the spectrophotometer has to be checked for calibration.

The proposed instrumentation can be further improved by changing the spectrophotometers for dedicated photodetecting devices. It may be a valuable added module to the capillary sensor system for diesel fuel fit-for- use examinations or as an independent device used at petrol station points of use.

Acknowledgment

This work was partially supported by the NCN grant "Oxide nanostructures for electronic, optoelectronic and photovoltaic applications", 2012/06/A/ST7/00398.

References

[1] S. Jain and M. P. Sharma, "Stability of biodiesel and its blends: A review," Renewable and Sustainable Energy Reviews, vol. 14, 2010, pp. 667–678.

[2] J. Czarnocka and M. Odziemkowska, "Diesel fuel degradation during storage process," Chemik, vol. 69, 2015, pp. 771-776.

[3] C.N. Lyles, et al. "Impact of Organosulfur Content on Diesel Fuel Stability and Implications for Carbon Steel Corrosion," Environ. Sci. Technol., vol. 47, 2013, pp. 6052-6062.

[4] BP Australia Limited, "Long Term Storage of Diesel," BP Fuel News, vol. ADF1403.doc, 2005, pp. 1-3.

[5] Technical Committee of Petroleum Additive Manufactures in Europe, "Fuel Additives: Use and Benefits," ATC Document, vol. 113, 2013, pp. 1-68.

[6] M. Nandi and D.Jacobs , "Cetane Response of Di-tertiary-butyl Peroxide in Different Diesel Fuels," SAE Technical Paper 952368, 1995, pp. 952368:1-18.

[7] A. Kulinowski, T. Henly, and T. Stocky, "The Effect of 2-Ethylhexyl Nitrate Cetane Improver on Engine Durability," SAE Technical Paper 981364, 1998, pp. 1-9.

[8] T. Herold, "Next Generation Derivered Cetane Analysis: High Precision Enables Refineries to Operate Close to Specifications and Increase Profitability," Petro Industry News, vol. 15, 2014, pp. 6-7.

[9] R. Vanhaelst, et al, "Optical infrared-sensor inside the cylinder to determine the EGR- and residual gas rate in diesel engine," Combustion Engines, vol. 52, 2103, pp. 3-11.

[10] M. Borecki and M.L. Korwin-Pawlowski, "Capillary Sensor with UV-VIS Reading of Effects of Diesel and Biodiesel Fuel Degradation in Storage," Sensors & Transducers, vol. 205, 2016, pp. 1-9.

[11] S. G. Wakeham, "Synchronous fluorescence spectroscopy and its application to indigenous and petroleum-derived hydrocarbons in lacustrine sediments," Environ. Sci. Technol., vol. 11, 1977, pp. 272–276.

[12] M. Wlodarski, A. Bombalska, M. Mularczyk-Oliwa; M. Kaliszewski, and K. Kopczyński, "Fluorimetric techniques in analysis and classification of fuels," Proc. SPIE vol. 8703, 2012, pp. 87030B.

[13] A. Kociubiński, M. Borecki, M. Duk, M. Sochacki, and M. L. Korwin-Pawlowski, "3D photodetecting structure with adjustable sensitivity ratio in UV – VIS range," Microelectronic Engineering, vol. 154, 2016, pp. 48–52.

[14] M. Borecki, et al., "Large-area transparent in visible range silicon carbide photodiode," Proc. SPIE, vol. 8903, 2013, pp. 89030H.

[15] M. Borecki, J. Szmidt, P. Wrzosek, and M. Beblowska, "Optical fiber switch for sensor networks: design principles," Proc. SPIE, vol. 6347, 2006, pp. 63471Q.

[16] M. Borecki, et al., "Fiber Optic Capillary Sensor with Smart Optode for Rapid Testing of the Quality of Diesel and Biodiesel Fuel," IJASM, vol. 7, 2014, pp. 57–67.

[17] M. Borecki, et al., "Dynamical Capillary Rise Photonic Sensor for Testing of Diesel and Biodiesel Fuel," Sensors & Transducers Journal, vol. 193, 2015, pp. 11-22.

[18] A. Baranowska, P. Miluski, M. Kochanowicz, J. Zmojda, and D. Dorosz, "Capillary optical fibre with Sm3+ doped ribbon core," Proc. SPIE, vol. 9662, 2015, pp. 96620Z.

[19] M. Geca, M. Borecki, M. L. Korwin-Pawlowski, and A. Kociubiński, "Local liquid sample heating: integration and isolation of a micro-heater," Proc. SPIE, vol. 9662, 2015, pp. 96620E.

[20] V.D. Silva, et al., "Oxidative Stability of Baru (Dipteryx alata Vogel) Oil Monitored by Fluorescence and Absorption Spectroscopy," Journal of Spectroscopy, vol. 2015, 2015, pp. 803705.

An Autonomous Time Synchronization Sensor Device Using a Chip Scale Atomic Clock for Earthquake Observation and Structural Health Monitoring

Narito Kurata
Faculty of Industrial Technology
Tsukuba University of Technology
Tsukuba City, Ibaraki, Japan
e-mail: kurata@home.email.ne.jp

Abstract - **This article describes the research and development directed toward an autonomous time-synchronized sensor device equipped with a chip scale atomic clock (CSAC) that records highly accurate time information. The R & D project presented herein aims to achieve earthquake observation to prepare for disasters and structural health monitoring to improve the efficiency of maintenance and management of buildings and civil engineering structures. For these reasons, it is necessary to install sensors in a wide area at a high density and to measure the data with accurately synchronized time information. It is recommended that the sensor device itself maintains accurate time information without relying on the network or a Global Positioning System (GPS) signal. Therefore, in this study, a sensor device that autonomously maintains accurate time information using an ultra-high precision, ultra-low power consuming, and ultra-small (and therefore, loadable on a board) atomic clock, known as CSAC, was developed. In this article, first, the concepts of autonomous time synchronization and CSACs are described, and the mechanism for assigning ultra-high precision time information to the sensor data by using a CSAC is explained. Next, the performance of the improved sensor device is demonstrated and the results of the vibration table test, which was conducted to examine the performance, are presented.**

Keywords-Time Synchronization; Chip Scale Atomic Clock; Earthquake Observation; Structural Health Monitoring; MEMS

I. INTRODUCTION

Previously, a sensor based on wireless sensor networks and microelectromechanical systems (MEMS) was developed for structural health monitoring and applied to a high-rise building as an Internet of Things (IoT) device [1]-[3]. In the corresponding research, the sensor device was installed at a high density inside the building, and a method to accurately detect the stability of the building and the damage caused to it after an earthquake, was demonstrated. However, in order to compare and analyze the data measured by several sensors, they must be time-synchronized [4]-[6]. In this work, time synchronization was achieved by transmitting and receiving wireless packets among the sensors [3]. Although a wireless sensor network enables time synchronization among the sensors installed inside a single building, it is not capable of achieving the same in multiple buildings, large-scale structures such as a bridge, or a wide urban space. Alternatively, a global positioning system (GPS) is available for outdoors; however, it cannot be used underground or in tunnels. To obtain measured data from any sensor installed anywhere using time synchronization, it is desirable that each sensor maintains accurate time information autonomously without relying on the networks or GPS signals. Therefore, by employing a chip scale atomic clock (CSAC), which is an ultra-high precision clock with considerably less delay than quartz oscillators [7]-[9], a sensor device that records accurate time information autonomously was developed [10][11].

In Section III, the concepts of autonomous time synchronization and CSACs are described, and a mechanism to assign ultra-high precision time information to sensor data using a CSAC is presented.

In Section IV, the sensor device, which was developed as a prototype, and the improvements made to the sensor are explained in detail.

In Section V, the construction of an autonomous time synchronization sensing system with the sensor device is discussed.

In Section VI, a vibration table test is performed for the improved sensor device, which is equipped with a MEMS acceleration sensor, and its amplitude performance is examined based on a comparison with the results obtained by a comparative servo-type acceleration sensor. Multiple sensor devices are installed on the vibration table and allowed to vibrate simultaneously in order to confirm that time synchronization is realized among the sensors within 0.001 s for a 100 Hz measurement sampling. In addition, the output of one displacement sensor is branched in order to connect to eight improved sensor devices via external analog sensor input interfaces, and a test is conducted to prove that the measured results are in agreement.

Furthermore, to apply this technology for earthquake observation, the logic for detecting the occurrence of an earthquake according to a set threshold and saving only the data of the earthquake event is presented. Its function is illustrated using a vibration table test.

Based on these test results, the performance of the developed autonomous time-synchronized sensor device is confirmed, and it is shown that this device can be applied for earthquake observation and structural health monitoring.

II. STATE OF THE ART

The time synchronization function is essential for sensor devices used in earthquake observation and structural health monitoring. In this research, a prototype sensor module that autonomously maintains accurate time information by applying an ultra-high precision clock, CSAC, was made to improve practical applications. Even if a huge number of sensors are installed, if accurate time information can be autonomously assigned to the measurement data of each sensor, time synchronization of the data of the sensors can be established just only by collecting data with arbitrary means and rearranging the data based on the time information.

For time synchronization sensing, many studies such as Global Positioning System (GPS) using radio clocks and satellites, and Network Time Protocol (NTP) [5] for achieving time synchronization on the Internet have been conducted so far. Some studies have realized highly accurate time synchronization with a simple mechanism by utilizing the characteristics of wireless sensor networks with small propagation delays. For example, various time synchronization protocols such as Reference Broadcast Synchronization (RBS), Timing-sync Protocol for Sensor Networks (TPSN), and Flooding Time Synchronization Protocol (FTSP) have been studied [4][8][12]-[14]. However, although these time synchronization techniques are still used today, as described in the Introduction, they are not ideal for sensor devices used in earthquake observation and structural health monitoring. As shown in this research, if each sensor gives accurate time information autonomously to the measurement data, even if a huge number of sensors are installed in an arbitrary environment, it is possible to create data groups with secured time synchronization and use them for comparison and analysis.

III. AUTONOMOUS TIME SYNCHRONIZATION AND CSACS

In order to obtain a collection of sensor data with stable time synchronization, even when GPS signals are not available, wireless data transmission is unstable, or there is no wired network connection, the most idealistic condition is that each sensor maintains accurate time information autonomously. If accurate time information (time stamp) can be provided to the data measured by each sensor, a collection of sensor data with time synchronization can be obtained. Therefore, in this study, a CSAC with a high-precision time-keeping performance and considerably less delay than quartz oscillators was used [7]-[9] to develop a sensor that can autonomously maintain accurate time information.

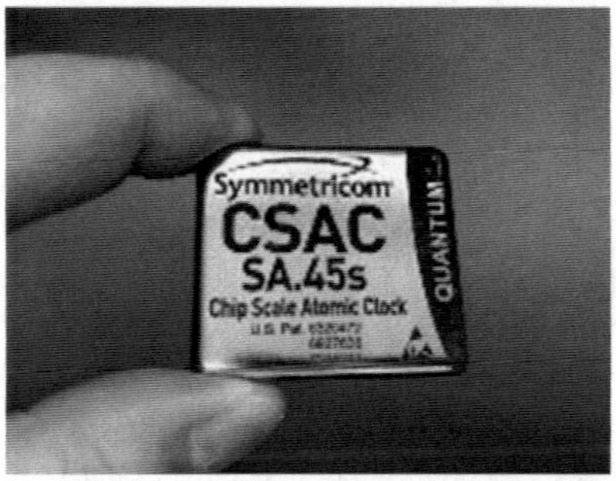

Figure 1. Chip Scale Atomic Clock (CSAC).

TABLE I. CSAC SPECIFICATIONS

Model	SA.45s
RF output	10 MHz
1 PPS output	Rise/fall time: < 10 ns Pulse width: 100 μs
Power consumption	< 120 mW
Outside dimensions (mm)	40 × 35 × 12
Frequency accuracy	$\pm 5 \times 10^{-11}$
Aging	$< 9 \times 10^{-10}$/month

TABLE II. VARIOUS CLOCKS AND OSCILLATORS

	Cesium atomic clock	Rubidium atomic clock	CSAC	Quartz oscillator
Time until it has a 1-s delay	50,000 years	1,000 years	1,000 years	1 day
Size	0.1 m^3	1,000 cm^3	1 cm^3	10 mm^3
Power consumption	50 W	Several tens of W	30 mW	10 μW

A CSAC is a clock that realizes ultra-high precision time measurement of several tens of picoseconds (5×10^{-11} s) with low power consumption. Owing to its ultra-small size, it can also be loaded on a board (see Figure 1, Table I and II). The development of CSACs began with the support of the Defense Advanced Research Projects Agency (DARPA) in the United States in 2001, and commercial products were launched in 2011. Its applications include countermeasures for disturbance of GPS positioning caused by jammed signals, high-precision positioning for smartphones and other devices, and incorporation in cloud servers. Owing to its increasing popularity, further reduction in price and a smaller unit design are expected. By installing a CSAC in each sensor device and loading a mechanism to assign highly accurate time stamps to the sampling data, a group of sensor data with autonomously secured time synchronization can be obtained. To collect the measured data with accurate time stamps, any technology, such as 3G, Wi-Fi, or Ethernet can be used.

IV. DEVELOPMENT AND IMPROVEMENT OF SENSOR DEVICE EQUIPPED WITH CSAC

A sensor device usually consists of the following: CPU for controlling the measurement, sensor, filter, analog-to-digital (A/D) converter, storage, and network interface. A crystal oscillator is used as the CPU. If a CSAC is installed in it and used for measurement, then a time delay will occur while correcting the CPU, because the timing accuracy of the CSAC is very high. Therefore, in order to directly assign the timing information provided by the CSAC to the data measured by a sensor using hardware, a mechanism equipped with a dedicated integrated circuit, field-programmable gate array (FPGA), was developed and a prototype of the sensor device was produced [10][11]. Since an FPGA is programmable, a logic for earthquake detection using the measured data can be incorporated, by assigning it the time measurement information provided by the CSAC.

From Figure 2, it can be seen that the sensor device consists of a main control unit, sensor unit, and wireless communication unit. The main board is equipped with a CSAC, FPGA, GPS, CPU, storage, and network interface. The main control unit controls the measurement made by the sensor while generating time stamps based on the ultra-high precision timing information given by the CSAC. The measured data is stored in the storage and then transmitted to the network via Ethernet or wireless communication. The measured data to be saved is of two types: data to be measured on a steady basis and data of extracted events such as earthquakes. To handle data of the latter type, the logic to detect the beginning and end of an earthquake is incorporated in the FPGA, and data of only the earthquake events are promptly transmitted to the network after the earthquake. For initialization and adjustment of time information, it is equipped with a GPS. The sensor unit obtains measurements based on the commands given by the main control unit. The sensor unit is equipped with tri-axial MEMS acceleration sensor, external analog sensor input interface, temperature sensor, anti-aliasing filter, and A/D converter.

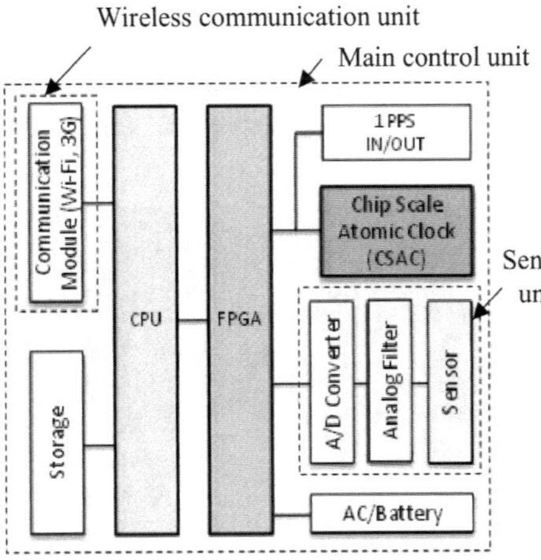

Figure 2. Design of Sensor Device Equipped with CSAC.

TABLE III. SPECIFICATIONS OF MEMS ACCELERATION SENSOR

Model	LIS344ALH
Measurement direction	3
Maximum acceleration (± G)	2
Outside dimensions (mm)	4 × 4 × 1.5
Consumption current (mA)	0.68
Stand-by power consumption (μA)	1
Detection sensitivity	660 mV/G ± 5%
Noise characteristics	50 μG/√Hz
Operating temperature (°C)	-40 - +85

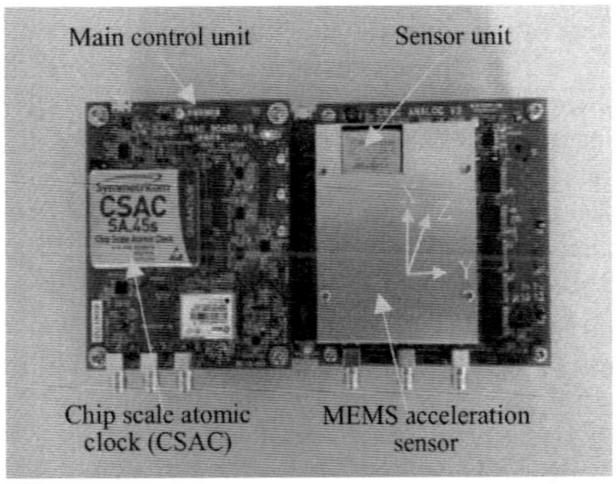

Figure 3. Improved Sensor Module with CSAC.

Table III shows the specifications of the mounted tri-axial MEMS acceleration sensor. The wireless communication unit enables data collection using a wireless system and allows selectable use of either a general wireless LAN (Wi-Fi) or 3G. The basic performance of the prototype of the developed sensor device was examined [10][11].

The prototype of the developed sensor device was improved in the following ways, with the aim of achieving increased functionality and practical usability:

a) Generation of three channels for serving as an external analog sensor input interface
b) Addition of a 24-bit A/D converter
c) Reinforcement of FPGA
d) Separation of the wireless communication unit and adoption of a commercially available motherboard (Raspberry Pi 2 Model B)
e) Loading of the IEEE 1588-based time synchronization function

By including the 24-bit A/D converter and using three channels as the external analog sensor input interface, a sensor that requires a wide dynamic range, such as a servo-type acceleration sensor, can be connected. Furthermore, by joining three units of a strain or displacement sensor, the sensor device can be used as a data logger. In addition, with the wireless communication unit and the use of commercially available Raspberry Pi, the system is capable of responding to a new wireless communication system quickly. Finally, by equipping the interface based on the IEEE 1588 standard for time synchronization of networks, the measurement timing can be initialized among the sensor devices for synchronization. Figure 3 shows the improved sensor device that was produced.

V. FORMULATION OF AN AUTONOMOUS TIME SYNCHRONIZATION SENSING SYSTEM

Herein, the construction of an autonomous time synchronization sensing system with the sensor device described in Section III is discussed. To construct the sensing system composed of multiple sensors using the CSAC equipped sensor devices, it is necessary to prepare one device as the master, define absolute time information on it, and synchronize the other devices as slaves. The main control unit of each sensor device is armed with an I/O connector for 1 Pulse Per Second (PPS) signals of the CSAC. By using this, the master device outputs 1 PPS signals to each slave device to synchronize them, and adjusts the clock phase of the CSAC of the slave devices. Although a CSAC has a high time-keeping accuracy, it is necessary to define the absolute time information separately, because it originally has no such information. At the time of initial setting, the GPS module installed in the main control unit is used. The data is transmitted from the master device to the slave devices based on the IEEE 1588 method. Once all the sensor devices have been initially synchronized, they will autonomously retain the high-precision time information, and they only need to be set at arbitrary places for data collection. As mentioned previously, since accurate time stamps are recorded for the measured data, the data can be collected via any system including Ethernet, Wi-Fi, and 3G. Furthermore, even in places where GPS signals are not available and wireless or wired networks cannot be prepared, the data can be measured and collected. Therefore, this system can be used for mobile measurement or as a portable sensing system.

Figure 4 shows the configuration of the autonomous time synchronization sensing system. The sensor devices, which are individually equipped with the acceleration sensor board containing the MEMS acceleration sensor, can be freely combined with the other sensor devices having displacement sensors or strain sensors via external sensor boards.

VI. BASIC PERFORMANCE TEST OF IMPROVED SENSOR DEVICE

a) *Vibration table test with built-in MEMS acceleration sensor*

To check the basic performance of the improved sensor device proposed in Section III, a vibration table test was conducted. During the vibration table test, measurements were made with the built-in MEMS acceleration sensor in each sensor device.

The purpose was to check the measurement performance of the MEMS acceleration sensor and the time synchronization performance of the sensor device. As shown in Figure 5, four sensor devices were fixed on the vibrating table, the same vibration was applied towards one horizontal direction, and the measured results were compared. In the test, a swept sine wave of 0.1 to 2 Hz and 2 to 10 Hz was applied as the input wave, as shown in Figure 6. The measurement sampling frequency of the sensor device was set as 100 Hz in this case.

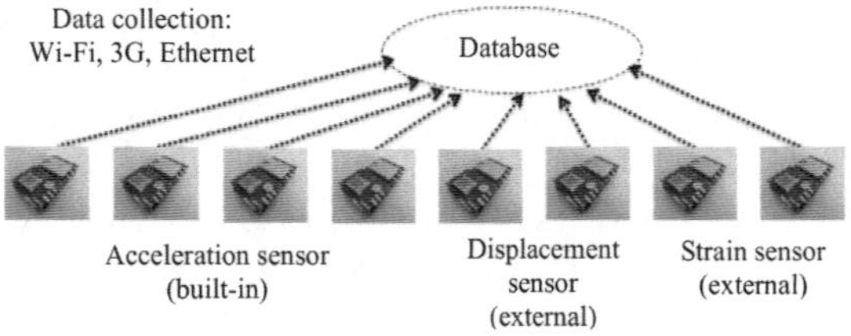

Figure 4. Configuration of Autonomous Time Synchronization Sensing System.

A vibration was applied along the Y direction of the sensor devices and measurements were made with the sensor devices and a comparative servo-type acceleration sensor. Figure 7 shows the calculated results of the Fourier amplitude spectral ratio for the acceleration waveforms measured with the four sensor devices and the servo acceleration sensor (for control). Compared to that of the servo acceleration sensor, the amplitudes of the four sensor devices were flat in the frequency bands of 0.1 to 2 Hz and 2 to 10 Hz, and the MEMS acceleration sensors loaded on the sensor devices showed a good performance for the components in the Y direction. Figure 8 shows the calculated results of the Fourier phase spectrum ratio of the acceleration measurement waveforms of the three (slave) devices with one sensor device on the vibration table as the master. If there is no phase delay among the sensor devices and time synchronization is secured, the Fourier phase spectrum ratio should be close to zero in all the frequency bands. In Figure8, a phase delay within 0.001 s is plotted with a dotted line. This indicates that the time synchronization realized among the sensor devices was within 0.001 s.

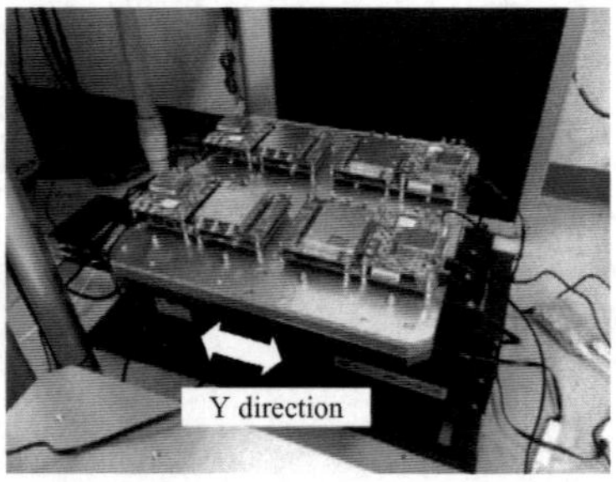

Figure 5. Vibration Table Test in Y Direction.

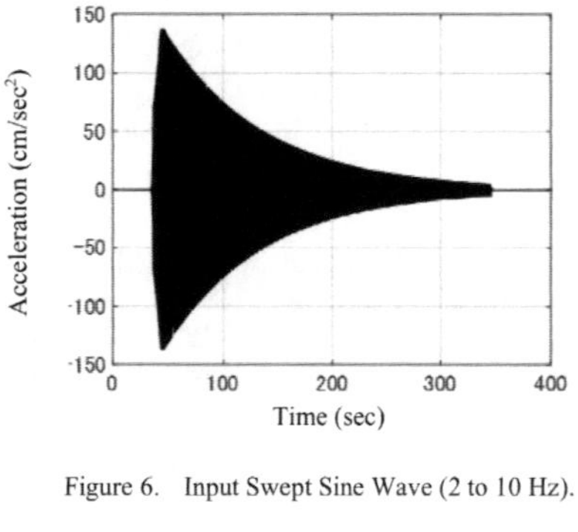

Figure 6. Input Swept Sine Wave (2 to 10 Hz).

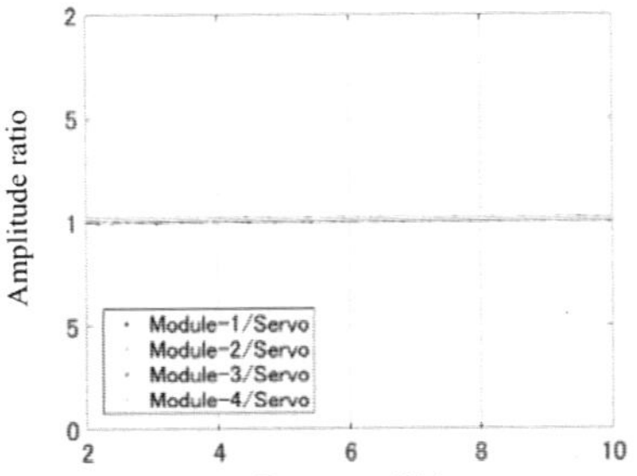

Figure 7. Spectrum Ratios of Fourier Amplitudes of Four Sensor Modules to Servo-Type Acceleration Sensor (Y direction).

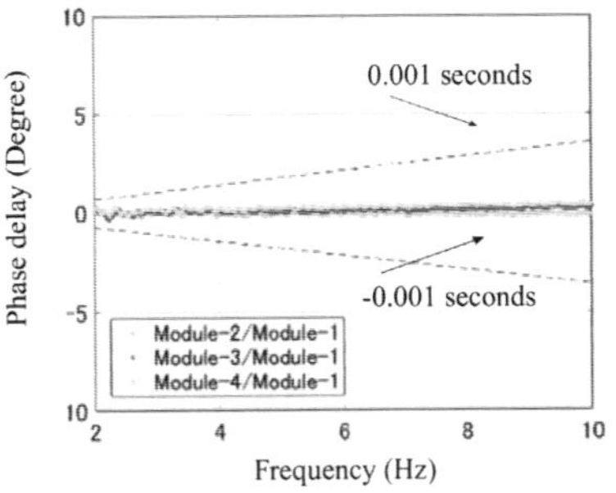

Figure 8. Spectrum Ratios of Fourier phase of Three Slave Modules to Master Module (Y direction)

b) *Displacement measurement test using external analog sensor input interface*

In order to examine the time synchronization performance when using an external analog sensor input interface, a test was performed using a displacement gauge. As shown in Figure 9, the voltage output of one displacement gauge was branched and given as input to the eight sensor devices equipped with an external sensor board. In the test, the displacement was changed by about 1 cm each time and it was measured using the eight sensor devices. Figure 10 shows the measurement results. The measurement results obtained by the eight sensor devices exactly match each other, indicating that they had correctly synchronized time data.

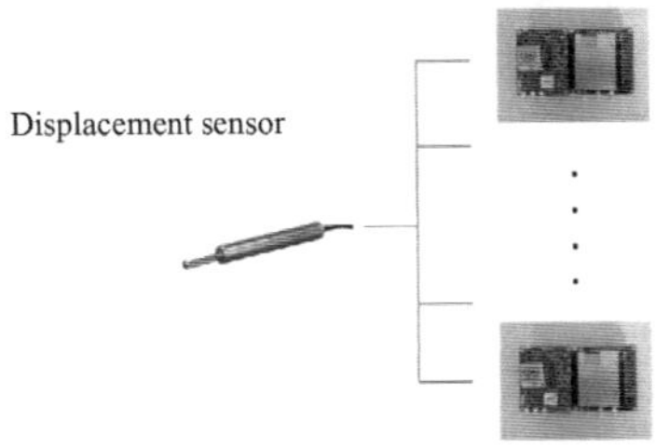

Figure 9. Measurement Test with the Displacement Sensor Connected to the External Analog Sensor Input Interface.

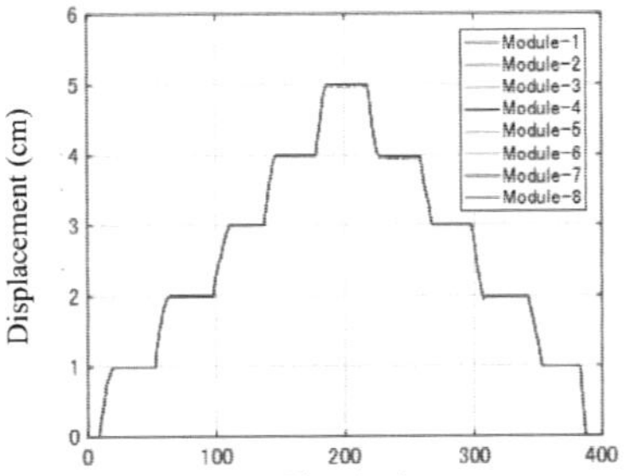

Figure 10. Measurement Test Results with Connected Displacement Sensor

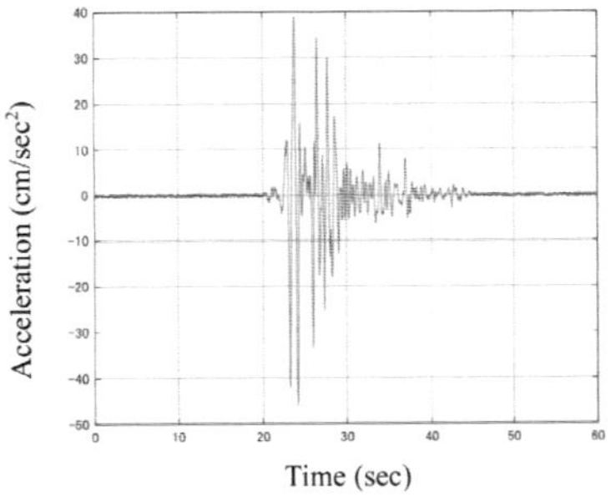

Figure 11. Acceleration of Measurement Results of Earthquake Detection Test

c) *Earthquake detection test*

In order to use the sensor device for earthquake observation, it is necessary to detect the occurrence and end of an earthquake. The developed sensor device realizes earthquake detection by comparing the measured values with the threshold values during sensing. When the occurrence of an earthquake is detected during the sensing operation, it starts saving the measurement data. At this time, immediately after the earthquake occurs, it also saves the data measured for several tens of seconds before the earthquake and the data measured for several tens of seconds immediately after the end of the earthquake, to secure the data of the total event of the earthquake.

In order to check the earthquake detection performance, a test was conducted with a vibration table. An earthquake wave excitation was provided in the Y direction of the sensor devices and the data was measured with a threshold value of 0.5 cm/s^2. The input earthquake wave was the NS direction component of the strong motion record observed at the JMA Kobe during the 1995 Southern Hyogo Prefecture Earthquake. Figure 11 shows the measurement results. It shows that the earthquake detection algorithm was able to first detect the occurrence and end of the earthquake with the set threshold values and then save the measured data.

VII. CONCLUSION

Our research and development efforts for designing an autonomous time synchronization sensor device equipped with a chip scale atomic clock (CSAC), which records and maintains high-precision time information, for earthquake observation and structural health monitoring of buildings and civil engineering structures was reported in this paper. First, the concepts of autonomous time synchronization and CSACs were explained, and the mechanism to assign ultra-precision time information to sensor data using a CSAC was presented. Then, the development of the sensor device as a prototype and the improvements applied to it were described in detail. The improved prototype was used to develop a sensor device for practical application, and a vibration table test was conducted to examine the performance of the improved sensor device.

To apply the device for earthquake observation, the logic to detect the occurrence of an earthquake according to set threshold values and to save the data of only the earthquake event was prepared, and its function was confirmed using the vibration table test. These results demonstrate that the developed autonomous time-synchronization sensor device has good performance and that it can be applied for earthquake observation and structural health monitoring.

One of the future challenges is to consider how to operate the sensing system for measurement purposes, assuming that even CSAC will undergo aging in the long term. In addition, it is not easy to fully utilize the high-precision time-keeping performance of the CSAC device. For example, even with a dedicated built-in FPGA, its clock is just 125 MHz, and it can give time stamps to the measurement data only within a time interval of 8 ns. When the 1 PPS output of CSAC is used to synchronize the sensor devices, a delay occurs due to the length of the cable connecting them. Furthermore, even though it is expected that CSACs will eventually be installed on all computers and smartphones worldwide, at present, only one US company manufactures and sells CSAC products, and therefore, they are very expensive. It can be hoped that more sensor companies will join the market and several products will be actively used in various fields. My future research plan includes detailed verification of the time-keeping performance of a CSAC as an atomic clock and the confirmation of the wireless communication function. In addition, it will be applied for actual earthquake observation, and demonstration tests will be conducted on actual buildings and bridges.

ACKNOWLEDGMENT

This research was partially supported by the New Energy and Industrial Technology Development Organization (NEDO) through the Project of Technology for Maintenance, Replacement and Management of Civil Infrastructure, Cross-ministerial Strategic Innovation Promotion Program (SIP). This research was also partially supported by JSPS KAKENHI Grant Number JP16K01283.

REFERENCES

[1] N. Kurata, B. F. Spencer, and M. Ruiz-Sandoval, "Risk Monitoring of Buildings Using Wireless Sensor Network," Journal of Structural Control and Monitoring, vol. 12, Issue 3-4, pp. 315-327, July-Dec. 2005, doi: 10.1002/stc.73.

[2] N. Kurata, M. Suzuki, S. Saruwatari, and H. Morikawa, "Actual Application of Ubiquitous Structural Monitoring System using Wireless Sensor Networks," Proc. 14th World Conference on Earthquake Engineering (14WCEE), Beijing, China, Oct. 2008, Paper ID:11-0037, pp. 1-8.

[3] N. Kurata, M. Suzuki, S. Saruwatari, and H. Morikawa, "Application of Ubiquitous Structural Monitoring System by Wireless Sensor Networks to Actual High-rise Building," Proc. the 5th World Conference on Structural Control and Monitoring (5WCSCM), Tokyo, Japan, July 2010, Paper No. 013, pp. 1-9.

[4] M. Maroti, B. Kusy, G. Simon, and A. Ledeczi, "The Flooding Time Synchronization Protocol," Proc. the 2nd International Conference on Embedded Networked Sensor Systems (SenSys '04), Baltimore, USA, Nov. 2004, pp. 39-49, ISBN:1-58113-879-2.

[5] D. L. Mills, "Internet time synchronization: the network time protocol," IEEE Transactions on Communications, vol. 39, Issue 10, pp. 1482-1493, Oct. 1991, doi:10.1109/26.103043.

[6] B. W. Parkinson, and J. J. Spilker Jr. eds, "Global Positioning System: Theory and Applications," Vol. I & II, American Institute of Aeronautics and Astronautics (AIAA), 1996, ISBN: 978-1-56347-106-3.

[7] S. Knappe, et al., "A microfabricated atomic clock," Applied Physics Letters, vol. 85, Issue 9, pp. 1460-1462, Aug. 2004, doi:10.1063/1.1787942.

[8] Q. Li, and D. Rus, "Global Clock Synchronization in Sensor Networks," IEEE Transactions on Computers, vol. 55, Issue 2, pp. 214-226, Jan. 2006, ISSN: 0018-9340.

[9] R. Lutwak, et al., "The Chip-Scale Atomic Clock - Prototype Evaluation," Proc. the 39th Annual Precise Time and Time Interval (PTTI) Meeting, Long Beach, USA, Nov. 2007, pp. 269-290.

[10] N. Kurata, "Disaster Big Data Infrastructure using Sensing Technology with a Chip Scale Atomic Clock," World Engineering Conference and Convention (WECC2015), Kyoto, Japan, Dec. 2015, pp. 1-5.

[11] N. Kurata, "Basic Study of Autonomous Time Synchronization Sensing Technology Using Chip Scale Atomic Clock," Proc. the 16th International Conference on Computing in Civil and Building Engineering (ICCCBE2016), Osaka, Japan, July 2016, pp. 67-74.

[12] J. Elson, L. Girod and D. Estrin, "Fine-Grained Network Time Synchronization using Reference Broadcasts," Proc. 5th Symposium on Operating Systems Design and Implementation (OSDI'02), Boston, Massachusetts, Dec. 2002, pp. 147-163.

[13] S. Ganeriwal, R. Kumar and M. B. Srivastava, "Timing-sync Protocol for Sensor Networks," Proc. the 1st international conference on Embedded networked sensor systems (SenSys '03), Los Angeles, California, Nov. 2003, pp. 138-149.

[14] K. Romer, "Time Synchronization in Ad Hoc Networks," Proc. the 2nd ACM International Symp. on Mobile Ad Hoc Networking & Computing (MobiHoc'01), Long Beach, California, Oct. 2001, pp. 173-182.

TomoSense: Towards Low Cost Multi-Device Aware Independent Planar Surface Sensing

Andrzej Romanowski, Przemysław Kucharski,
Krzysztof Grudzień, Laurent Babout
Institute of Applied Computer Science
Lodz University of Technology
Łódź, Poland
Email: {pkuchars,androm,kgrudzi,lbabout}@kis.p.lodz.pl

***Abstract*—We present a plane surface non-invasive sensing system for creating new cross-device interaction in the wild based on electrical capacitance tomography (ECT) measurement setup. The core element of the system is the plane capacitance sensor consisting of 32 electrodes built into an experimental tabletop assembly coupled with the spatial-awareness concept. The interaction is enabled taking the advantage of the principle of physical objects interfering with the electrostatic field in proximity of the surface, which is shown here for a set of mobile devices. The presented system is independent, i.e. does not require any external sensing methods to be coupled with in order to detect devices in the proximity. Additionally, no technical requirement concerning the type of interaction device is posed hence, we enable to embed devices world into the natural environment. Moreover, the system design and operational foundations in terms of both simplicity and measurement protocol make the equipment easily scalable. All these properties open way to elaborate new interaction techniques that are even more allusive. This paper offers a glimpse of technical details of the system as well as discussion on the further exploration of the TomoSense potential.**

Keywords- capacitance sensing; interactive surface; ECT; multi-device sensing, spatial-awareness.

I. INTRODUCTION

Spatial awareness concept is a key to development of multi device systems and especially interactions in these multi device environments, such as presented in [1, 3]. Recent work on sensemaking shows specific scenarios for multi device interactions emerging, while the range of possible areas where users already use multiple devices simultaneously grows [4]. However, the methods for determination of mutual position of devices are not perfect. Most of published research and applications involve techniques that require mounting external sensors/cameras and/or satisfaction of conditions, such as the line-of-sight for camera based systems or direct contact with special surface such as the specialized interactive tabletop displays in order to elaborate spatial-awareness for these systems. Consequently, most of them are either difficult to deploy in-the-wild conditions or spatial-awareness can be explored in the laboratory conditions only. Therefore, we propose TomoSense: an ECT-based prototype sensing system constituted of a plane capacitance sensor easy to be embedded within an ordinary table and a process tomography measurement equipment coupled with a dedicated measurement protocol. TomoSense enables to identify devices in the close proximity of the electrodes that are hidden below the plane (i.e. table) surface thus enabling ad hoc interactions in different locations, as proposed in [2]. This paper covers a short technical overview of the prototype concept as well as first results and discussion on the further studies.

However, while a number of interaction techniques have been proposed, the method of sensing the relative position of the devices still remains a challenge. Past experiments often used stationary and costly sensing, such as interactive tabletops [1] or motion tracking systems [2]. Alternatively, Rädle et al. [3] developed a Kinect-based system for spatial awareness that required placing a sensor above the surface on which the devices were placed. All of the past approaches have certain limitations, such as the need for line-of-sight for camera-based systems, or the need for direct contact with the surface for interactive tables. As a consequence of these constraints, studies of multi-device systems either do not use spatial awareness or focus solely on laboratory experiments [4], [5] . As more and more users carry multiple mobile devices simultaneously [6], a need emerges for a versatile sensing method that would enable in situ studies and create possibilities for a wide deployment.

This paper introduces TomoSense — an electrical capacitance tomography sensor embedded in an ordinary table that enables identifying devices on and above the table and acquiring positional information. TomoSense is a research prototype that enables more ubiquitous positional sensing for devices and approximates the concept of an interactive tablecloth (a concept first proposed by Müller-Tomfelde and Fjeld [7]) — the possibility to create ad-hoc interactive surfaces in any location. Here, we provide a description of TomoSense, details of the sensing method used, preliminary insights from its application to device sensing and plans for future studies as further development of a concept initially postulated here [8].

II. TOMOSENSE

TomoSense is a rectangular planar sensor dedicated to electrical process tomography measurement modality that consists of 32 electrodes arranged in 4 rows and 8 columns all embedded just below the surface of an ordinary table. Fig. 1 is a photo of the table with a sensor intentionally (showing the principle of operation, while to be easily hidden with an opaque layer during normal operation) visible underneath the transparent plastic layer (3mm thickness) of the upper table surface. It is worth to note that, while we use an ordinary utility table for our experiments, the system itself can be a part of virtually any other surface as well. The table presented as an example here has a size of $610mm$ x $450mm$, while each electrode is $95mm$ x $60mm$ with the gaps in between the electrodes of $10mm$. The bottom part of sensor ($10mm$ below the table surface) was electrically screened in order to improve the signal-to-noise ratio (SNR) and thus improving the sensing properties of the system in the space above the sensor. Electrical capacitance tomography is based on the principle of measuring the change of capacitance between all the consecutive pairs of sensing electrodes (irrespective of their position or orientation) quickly switching the excitation to successive electrodes, while grounding the rest. Experiments were conducted with sensor of 32 electrodes located as shown in Figure 1, using 32 channel quality equipment enabling real time on-the-fly monitoring of the measurement space; further details on ECT process tomography can be found here [6]. In order to better illustrate the working concept of the proposed system, we show here 2D reconstructed images (using basic LBP algorithm), while it is reasonable to store and process only the relative position of the devices omitting the imaging and visualization at all in further research work [6].

Electrical capacitance tomography is based on the principle of measuring the change of capacitance between consecutive pairs of sensing electrodes, irrespective of their position or orientation. In order to conduct the measurement, one of the electrodes is excited with a certain electrical potential (in the range of $5 - 15V$) while the rest of electrodes are grounded. This work was conducted using a custom-made 32 channel research-grade ECT device. The device is fully flexible as it allows to adjust the interchannel gains of separate measurement channels. All the electrodes in TomoSense are connected to the device and monitored in real time.

III. SENSING

A typical electrical capacitance tomography system consists of three major components (Figure 2); the ECT sensor with electrodes placed around the monitoring object, the data-acquisition ECT measurement unit, which excites the electrodes and measures the capacitance between each pair of electrodes, and the computer with complementary software installed, for image reconstruction, image analysis and sensitivity matrix of the used ECT sensor. Typically, used sensors consisting of N electrodes (e.g. $N = 8, 12, 16$) lead to M capacitance measurements $M = (N - 1) * N/2$, ($M = 28, 66, 120$) [9]. The number of the amounted electrodes in ECT sensor is related to image acquisition rate and the required resolutions. The use of 12 electrodes allows the acquisition of 100 frames per second. In the presented ECT sensor ($N = 32$) and with the applied ECT measurement unit, the acquisition rate was at 11 frames per second that gives $M = 496$ measurement records for one frame. The

Fig. 1. Photo of TomoSense - top view of the system with a single mobile device (iPhone 6) placed on the table. Note the size of the sensed surface relative to the smartdevice.

measured capacitance records are collected in a matrix where i, j represent the numbers of the electrodes in between the successive pairs of measurement electrodes [10]. The changes of capacitance between each pair of electrodes are dependent mainly on the permittivity value of the space between electrodes and the distance between electrodes. In order to prepare the image of permittivity distribution in space between each pair of electrodes, it is necessary to calculate the sensitivity matrix, which provides information about the influence of the level of permittivity changes in each part of the measurement space (in our case, above the table) on particular capacitance measurements [11]. Before starting the reconstruction process, the sensitivity matrix has to be calculated. The measurement procedure is conducted by connecting each electrode to an ECT system. The measurement of capacitance C was conducted between each pair of electrodes, C_{1-2}, C_{1-3}, ..., C_{1-32}, C_{2-3}, C_{2-4}, ... , C_{2-32}, ... , C_{31-32}. The measurement vector M_{1x496} consist of $N = 496$ measurements. The reference vector for empty measurement space M_{ref} is recorded in order to eliminate the influence of the distance between the distant electrodes on the results. The sensing area is divided into 23x30 pixels. The reference data is used to create the reconstructed image of the objects placed on or above the surface of TomoTable. In order to obtain the image, a sensitivity weight matrix $W_{496x690}$ is calculated. It provides information on how the changes in each pixel influence the measurements of capacitances between each pair of electrodes. The values of weight matrix are calculated based on distance of a pixel from a given electrode. For electrodes located farther away from each other, the influence on pixel changing is much smaller than for adjacent electrodes. The resulting image I is obtained by first subtracting M_{ref} from M to obtain the relative measurement vector M_e and then multiplying M_e by the weight matrix W.

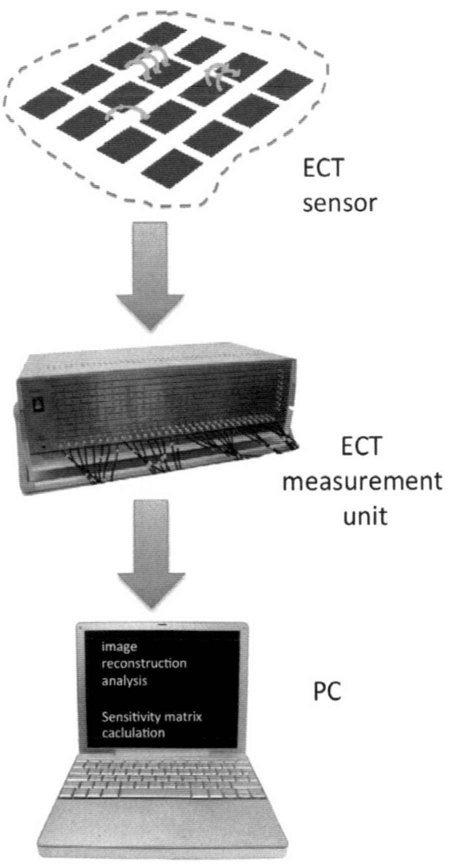

Fig. 2. Components of ECT

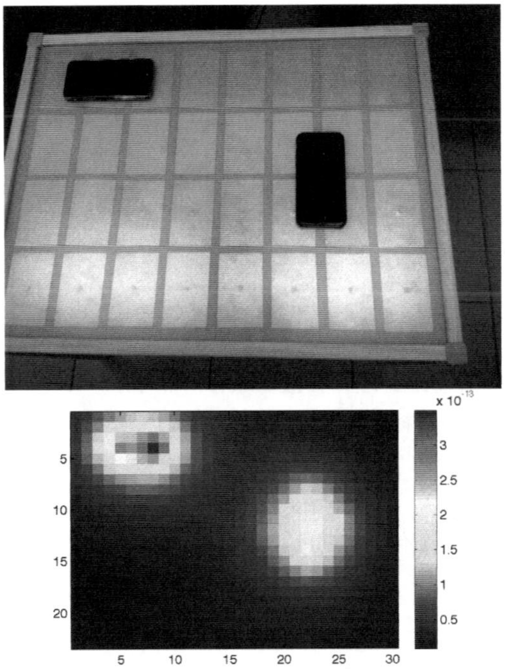

Fig. 3. Two iPhone 6 units placed on TomoTable and the resulting reconstructed image. Top: The phone on the upper left-hand side is located above the center of one electrode and covering two adjacent electrodes partially. The phone on the lower right-hand side is placed in between four adjacent electrodes covering only about one fourth of each of them. Bottom: The reconstructed 2D image of the device configuration view on top. The color scale show measurement intensity that varies empty space (blue) to the solid body of a device (dark red).

IV. Preliminary Results

Figures 3 and 4 show the reconstructed images of the distribution of the objects on the sensed surface. The examples shown here illustrate different possible configurations of devices and varying alignment with respect to the electrode array.

While it is apparent that an object is present on the sensed surface, its exact location is harder to determine. This is caused by the fact that the capacitance between adjacent electrodes (when the sensed surface is empty) increases with the distance between the electrodes. That is why a reference vector needs to be obtained before any object detection is performed.

Our next observation is that the introduction of mobile devices onto the sensed surface produced an easily sensed change in capacitance. The differences of capacitance we observed are in range of a few picofarads (from $6pf$ (empty space) to $14pf$ (space with a mobile device)). The advanced research system we used can detect differences in the range of fF and thus a lower grade device would be sufficient. Consequently, ECT sensing for mobile devices does not require highly accurate capacitance sensors, which creates opportunities for low-cost deployments. The number of elements into which the sensor plane was discretised in order to conduct the image reconstruction is relatively low and the resolution of the image is relatively low (e.g. compared to an interactive table). The image reconstruction procedure applied here was a simplified version of the LBP algorithm — a fairly naïve one that neglects the nonlinear character of the electrical field response to the objects present in the measurement space. Albeit using basic reconstruction method and choosing low resolution of the visualization (23x30 pixels) the size and orientation of the devices can be easily seen on the resulting reconstructed image. As a reference, we we show two cases with different orientation of the devices with respect to each other as well to the sensing electrodes area and the table itself (upper photos on Fig. 3 and Fig. 4) as well as the resulting reconstructed images of the distribution of the objects on the sensed surface (bottom pictures on Fig. 3 and Fig. 4). There are observable differences in the produced images depending on how the devices are positioned in relation to the electrodes and other devices. This showcases the potential of electrical capacitance tomography to provide accurate sensing for multi-device systems.

There are observable differences in the produced images depending on how the devices are positioned in relation to the electrode array and other devices. This showcases the potential of electrical capacitance tomography to provide accurate sensing for multi-device systems, namely we demonstrate

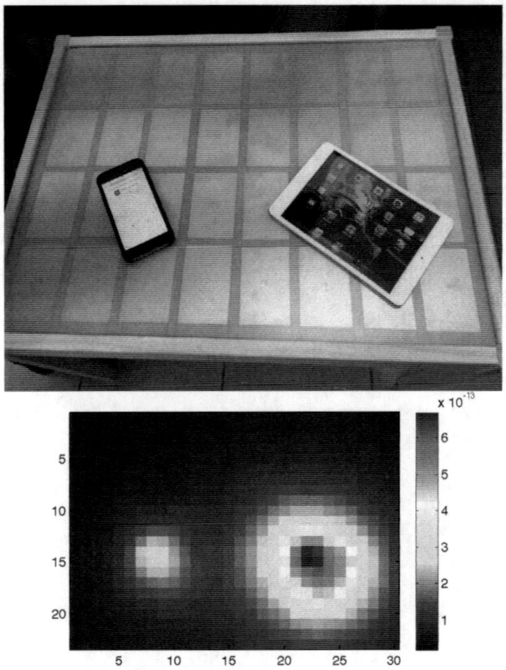

Fig. 4. An iPhone 6 and an iPad mini placed on TomoTable and the resulting reconstructed image. Top: The spatial arrangement of the devices is more chaotic and more likely in an in-the-wild scenario. The rotation of the devices is misaligned with TomoTable's electrode array. Bottom: The reconstructed 2D image of the two devices. The color scale show measurement intensity that varies empty space (blue) to the solid body of a device (dark red).

it is feasible to: (1) localize the position of the device (2) distinguish the size (3) detect the rotation angle and (4) sense several distinct devices.

V. CONCLUSIONS AND FUTURE WORK

In this paper, we demonstrated that TomoSense detects on-top placed devices with ease; measurement records taken during experiments revealed significant changes in sensed capacitance and these varied from a few to over a dozen in the range of picoFarads (from 6pF for empty space to 14pF when sensing a device), while the ECT unit is capable to work in far more narrow range of femtoFarads. With this, we can conclude that it is possible to use a custom made device with lower sensitivity capacitance measurement devices for future wide deployment. One can observe that, even for the same type of devices, the particular position of the device with respect to electrode distribution (coverage over the distinct electrodes area) influences the values of reconstructed pixels (Fig. 2). This property may provide additional knowledge about devices orientation with respect to electrodes positions and hence shall improve the eventual spatial position calculations. ECT normally can produce tens up to hundreds of images per second for the all-inter-electrode measurement vectors. However, using contextual knowledge of the monitored process, such as the specific movements of mobile devices as reported here [5], we can adjust the measurement protocol. The protocol may support more rapid detection of spatial location with the aid of the "traveling measurement window" concept using a mask of 9 or 16 electrodes. While spatial awareness becomes an important feature in a class of applications such as sense making in a multi device environment, a question of a balance between required sensing accuracy vs. complexity and ease of application remains open. The proposed prototype offers limited spatial resolution compared to infrared based positioning. However, further research on refining the design (in terms of different electrode arrangements coupled with dedicated measurement protocols as well as contextual data processing algorithms) shall provide sufficient accuracy for spatial-aware based multi device applications. On the other hand, our design preserves the biggest advantage over the other modality systems, i.e. the possibility to be easily embedded into different surfaces and, therefore, to keep the promise of in-the-wild applicability. It will be interesting to test the device for advanced domain expert analytical meetings for last stage of scientific crowdsourcing applications [12]. Lastly, with the improved prototype, it is worth to conduct in-situ study on possible ways of interaction with various everyday objects.

REFERENCES

[1] P. Wozniak, B. Schmidt, L. Lischke, Z. Franjcic, A. E. Yantaç, and M. Fjeld, "Mochatop: Building ad-hoc data spaces with multiple devices," in *CHI '14 Extended Abstracts on Human Factors in Computing Systems*, ser. CHI EA '14. ACM, 2014, pp. 2329–2334.

[2] K. Hasan, D. Ahlström, and P. Irani, "Ad-binning: leveraging around device space for storing, browsing and retrieving mobile device content," *Proceedings of CHI 2013*, pp. 899–908, 2013.

[3] R. Rädle, H.-C. Jetter, N. Marquardt, H. Reiterer, and Y. Rogers, "Huddlelamp: Spatially-aware mobile displays for ad-hoc around-the-table collaboration," in *Proceedings of the Ninth ACM International Conference on Interactive Tabletops and Surfaces - ITS '14*. ACM Press, 11 2014, pp. 45–54.

[4] P. Hamilton and D. J. Wigdor, "Conductor: enabling and understanding cross-device interaction," in *Proceedings of the 32nd annual ACM conference on Human factors in computing systems - CHI '14*. ACM Press, 4 2014, pp. 2773–2782.

[5] A. Lucero, T. Jokela, A. Palin, V. Aaltonen, and J. Nikara, "Easygroups: binding mobile devices for collaborative interactions," in *Proceedings of the 2012 ACM annual conference extended abstracts on Human Factors in Computing Systems Extended Abstracts - CHI EA '12*. ACM Press, 5 2012, p. 2189.

[6] K. Zickuhr, "Tablet ownership 2013," *Pew Research Center report, pewinternet.com*, p. 11, 2013.

[7] C. Müller-Tomfelde and M. Fjeld, "Tabletops: Interactive horizontal displays for ubiquitous computing," *Computer*, vol. 45, no. 2, pp. 78–81, 2012.

[8] P. Kucharski, A. Romanowski, K. Grudzień, and P. Woźniak, "TomoTable: Towards Multi-Device Spatial Awareness Based on Independent Plane Sensing," in *Cross Surface 2016 at ACM CHI'16*, 2016.

[9] A. Romanowski, K. Grudzien, R. A. Williams, and R. West, "A review of data analysis methods for electrical industrial process tomography applications," in *Proceedings of the 2005 4th World Congress on Industrial Process Tomography – WCIPT4 Japan*, vol. 2. VCIPT, 2005, pp. 916–921.

[10] D. Sankowski and J. Sikora, *Electrical Capacitance Tomography: Theoretical Basis and Applications*, 2010.

[11] Z. Ye, R. Banasiak, and M. Soleimani, "Planar array 3d electrical capacitive tomography," *Insight*, vol. 55, pp. 675–680, 2013.

[12] C. Chen, P. W. Woźniak, A. Romanowski, M. Obaid, T. Jaworski, J. Kucharski, K. Grudzień, S. Zhao, and M. Fjeld, "Using crowdsourcing for scientific analysis of industrial tomographic images," *ACM Trans. Intell. Syst. Technol.*, vol. 7, no. 4, pp. 52:1–52:25, Jul. 2016.

Fine-grained Indoor Localization:

Visible Light Communication

M. Vieira, M. A. Vieira, P. Louro, A. Fantoni
ADETC/ISEL/IPL,
R. Conselheiro Emídio Navarro, 1959-007
Lisboa, Portugal
CTS-UNINOVA
Quinta da Torre, Monte da Caparica, 2829-516,
Caparica, Portugal

e-mail: mv@isel.ipl.pt, mv@isel.pt, plouro@deetc.isel.pt, afantoni@deetc.isel.ipl.pt

P. Vieira
ADETC/ISEL/IPL,
R. Conselheiro Emídio Navarro, 1959-007
Lisboa, Portugal
Instituto das Telecomunicações
Instituto Superior Técnico, 1049-001,
Lisboa, Portugal
e-mail: pvieira@isel.pt

Abstract—**An indoor positioning system where trichromatic white Light Emitting Diodes (LEDs) are used both for illumination proposes and as transmitters and an optical processor, based on a-SiC:H technology, as mobile receiver is presented. On-Off Keying (OOK) modulation scheme is used, and it provides a good trade-off between system performance and implementation complexity. The relationship between the transmitted data and the received digital output levels is decoded. LED bulbs work as transmitters, sending information together with different identifiers, IDs, related to their physical locations. A triangular topology for the unit cell is analysed, and a 2D localization design, demonstrated by a prototype implementation, is presented. Fine-grained indoor localization is tested. The received signal is used in coded multiplexing techniques for supporting communications and navigation concomitantly on the same channel. The location and motion information is found by mapping the position and estimating the location areas.**

Keywords- a-SiC: H technology; optical sensor; transmitter; receiver; demultiplexer; WDM; indoor positioning.

I. INTRODUCTION

Research on indoor localization and navigation has long been a popular topic. Localization is one of the essential modules of many mobile wireless applications. Although Global Positioning System (GPS) works extremely well for an open-air localization, it does not perform effectively in indoor environments, due to the inability of GPS signals to penetrate through in-building materials. Therefore, precise indoor localization is still a critical missing component and has been gaining growing interest from a wide range of applications, e.g., location detection of assets in a warehouse, patient tracking inside the hospital, and emergency personnel positioning in a disaster area. Although many methods are available, such as WiFi-based [1], [2] and visual indoor topological localization [3], [4], they require dense coverage of WiFi access points or expensive sensors like high-performance cameras to guarantee the localization accuracy. In the sequence, we propose to use modulated visible light (carried out by white low cost Red, Green, and Blue, RGB, LEDs) to provide globally consistent signal-patterns to perform indoor localization.

We present a 2D localization design, demonstrated by a prototype implementation. The main issue is to divide the space into spatial beams originating from the different light sources, and identify each beam with a unique time sequence of light signals. The receiver, equipped with a light sensor, determines its spatial beam by detecting the light signals, followed by optimization schemes to refine its location within the beam. Fine-grained indoor localization can enable a multitude of applications. In supermarkets and shopping malls, exact location of products can greatly improve the customer's shopping experience and enable customer analytics [5], [6].

Visible Light Communication (VLC) is a data transmission technology [7], [8], [9], and [10], based on the use of visible light. Due to the combination of illumination and communication, a lot of research has been performed for VLC applications [11], [12], and [13]. With this technology, it is possible to achieve simultaneous illumination and data transfer by means of LEDs. This functionality has given rise to VLC, where LED luminaires are used for high-speed data transfer [14], [15]. Moreover, both interior lighting of a room and data transfer will be achieved without the need of an additional communication system. Aside from integrability with the illumination system, VLC has many advantages compared with other radio based technologies: radio frequency (RF) interference free, RF interference immune, safe for human health, and more secure [16]. Luminaires equipped with multi colored LEDs can provide further possibilities for signal modulation and detection in VLC systems [17].

The use of Red-Green-Blue (RGB) LEDs is a promising solution to high-speed VLC systems as they offer the possibility of the Wavelength Division Multiplexing (WDM), which can greatly increase the transmission data rate. In the recent past, we have developed a WDM device that enhances the transmission capacity of optical communications in the visible range. The device was based on tandem a-SiC:H/a-Si:H pin/pin light controlled filter with two optical gates that select the different channel wavelengths. When different visible signals are encoded in the same optical transmission path [18], [19] the device multiplexes the different optical channels, and performs different filtering processes: amplification, switching, and wavelength conversion. Finally, it decodes the encoded signals recovering the transmitted information.

This paper provides detailed characteristics of various components in a VLC system such as transmitter and receiver, multiplexing techniques, system design and visible light sensing and applications, such as indoor localization and motion recognition. A 2D localization design, demonstrated by a prototype implementation will be analyzed. Fine-grained indoor localization is tested. The proposed system, composed data transmission and indoor positioning, involves wireless communication, smart sensor and optical sources network, which constitutes a transdisciplinary approach framed in cyber-physical systems.

This paper is organized as follows. In Section I, an introduction is presented. In Section II, the system configuration and its characterization is explained. In Section III, indoor positioning is analyzed while, in Section IV, some navigation system examples are shown. Finally, Section V summarizes the conclusions.

II. SYSTEM CONFIGURATION AND CARACTERIZATION

A. Transmitter

The positioning system's topology is a self-positioning system in which the measuring unit is mobile. This unit receives the signals of several transmitters in known locations, and has the capability to compute their location based on the measured signals. LED bulbs work as transmitters, sending information together with different IDs related to their physical locations. Each LED lamp transmits data during the time slot it occupies, i.e., the individual LED lamp transmits its own data depending on the area it locates. An optical receiver inside the mobile terminal extracts the location information to perform positioning and, concomitantly, the transmitted data from each transmitter.

The beam area of light radiation of an LED, in the array, has the form of a circle. The estimate distance from the ceiling is used to generate a circle around each transmitter (see Figure 1) on which the device must be located in order to receive the transmitted information (generated location and coded data). To receive the information from several transmitters, the device must be positioned where the circles from each transmitter overlap, producing at the receiver a MUX signal that, after demultiplexing, acts twofold as a positioning system and also a data transmitter. The receiver detects one or more signals from light beams of different LEDs. If the signal it receives is only from one LED, the coordinates of the LED are assigned the device's reference point. If the device receives multiple signals, i.e., if it is in the overlapping region of two or more LEDs, it finds the centroid of the received coordinates and stores it as the reference point. Thus, the overlap region is used as an advantage to increase the accuracy in position estimation because more overlapping region means more reference points.

The proposed system considers a set of LED bulbs on the ceiling and a mobile terminal. The ceiling plan for the LED array layout of a unit cell is shown in Figure 1a (LED array = RGBV color spots). A triangular topology was considered for the unit cell (Figure 1a). The proposed arrangement employs four modulated LEDs (RGBV), three of them (RGB-LED) are located at the vertices of an equilateral triangle and a fourth one (V) is located at its centroid. The geometric scenario used for calculation uses a calibration grid (triangular), smaller, to improve its practicality. Here, a beam radius of 2 cm was assumed for each LED. The chips of the white LEDs can be switched *on* and *off* individually in a desired bit sequence and are 3 cm away from the receiver. For each RGB-LED, only one chip (R, G, B) is modulated in order to broadcast the specific information (payload data). The extra violet LED sends the network cell's. We name point 1 where all the four locations overlap. Points 2, 3 and 4 refer to the locations with three overlaps, points 5, 6 and 7 with two overlaps, and finally 8, 9 and 10 where no overlap occurs. The grid size was chosen in order to have the triangle inscribed inside the generated circle estimated around the violet transmitter.

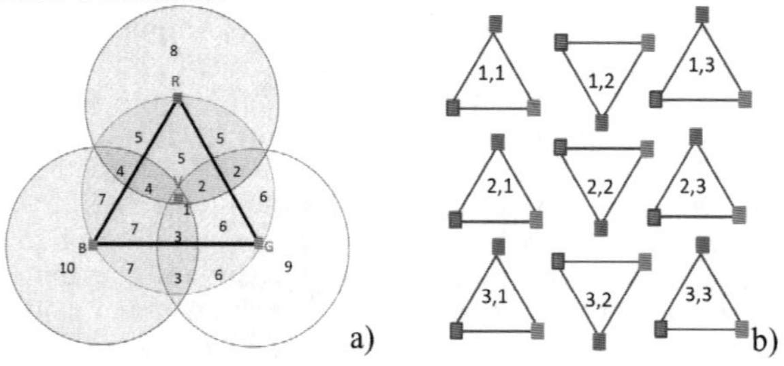

Figure 1. The next closest grid positions in lighting design. a) unit navigation cell. b) network cell's

The triangular topology allows the use of clusters cells and can be applied on large surfaces (Figure 1b). A large-dimension indoor environment, like a supermarket or a library can be considered by dividing the room into unit navigation cells with an appropriate side length. In Figure 1b, the unit cell was repeated in the horizontal and vertical directions in order to have a *mxn* matrix of unit cells that fill all the space and gives the geographical position assigned to each unit cell. The violet signal carries the ID of the unit cell. Cell's IDs are encoded as rows and columns [rrrr; cccc] using a binary representation for decimal number. For instance, number 11 is coded as "1011" (2^3+0+2^1+2^0). In case of the presented cell in Figure 1a being part of the cluster (Figure 1b) the ID from the cell located at row 1: column 1, will be [0001 0001], whereas in case of row 2 column 3, an ID_BIT [0010 0011] will be send by the violet LED. With perfect information, this method will give an exact, unique answer, i.e., the cell location in the cluster and for each unit navigation cell, the single region at the intersection of the circles.

As stated, the employment of trichromatic RGB LEDs as transmitters offers the possibility of WDM, which can greatly increase the transmission data rate.

Light produced by the LEDs is assumed to propagate as a Gaussian Beam. Under this assumption, in agreement with the LED's datasheet used for the laboratory experimental measurement, the electric field intensity propagates in free space in its unique fundamental mode [20]. Applying this model, we calculate the light intensity projected on the target screen based on the LED characteristics: wavelength, intensity and divergence angle (60º). In Figure 2, the simulation of the projected light intensities is shown for the unit triangular cell. The coordinates of the LEDs, in centimeters, were set as: V (0, 0), R (0, 2), B(-1.72, -1), G (1.72, -1).

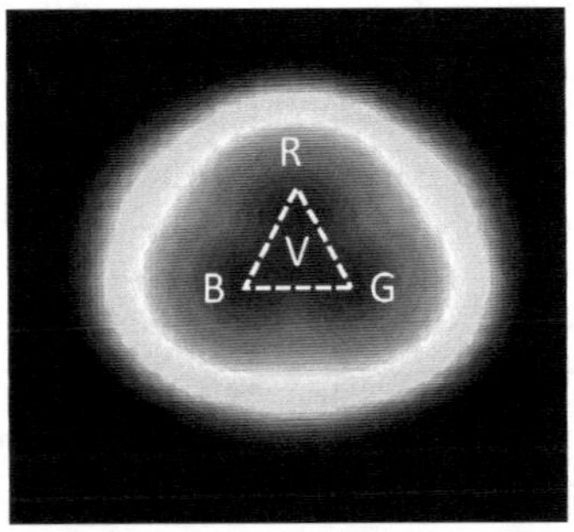

Figure 2. Simulated light intensity in a triangular unit cell.

To transmit the data, an On-Off Keying (OOK) code was used. In Figure 3, an example of the digital signals (RGBV codeword) used to drive the LEDs is displayed. In this example, the ID_BIT [0101 0011] was sent by the violet LED and corresponds to the unit cell (5,3). The red, the green and the blue LED send the payload data.

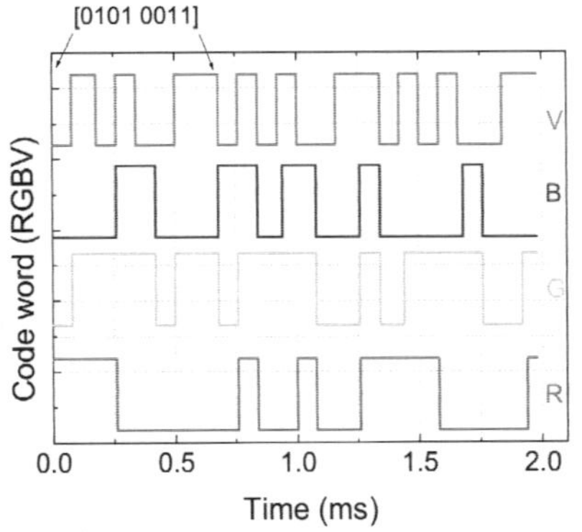

Figure 3. Representation of the original encoded message [R G B V] ascribed to the cell (5,3).

B. Receiver

The optoelectronic sensor is a 1x1 cm double pin heterostructure produced by PECVD (Plasma Enhanced Chemical Vapor Deposition) sandwiched between two transparent conductive contacts (TCO). The device configuration is shown in Figure 4. In the heterostructure, p-i'(a-SiC:H)-n/p-i(a-Si:H)-n [17], the intrinsic layer of the front p-i-n photodiode is built of a-SiC:H while the back intrinsic layer is based on a-Si:H. As a result, both front and back diodes act as optical filters confining, respectively, the optical carriers resultant from the blue and red wavelength photons apart, while the optical carriers generated by the green wavelength photons are absorbed across both.

The device operates within the visible range using for data transmission modulated low power light supplied by a violet (V), and three trichromatic LEDs. The RGB-LED are used together for illumination proposes and individually, one only chip, to transmit the channel location and data information. So, a polychromatic mixture of red, green, blue and violet; $\lambda_{R,G,B,V;}$ pulsed communication channels (input channels, transmitted data) are combined together, each one with a specific bit sequence and absorbed accordingly to their wavelengths (see arrow magnitudes in Figure 4). The combined optical signal (multiplexed signal; received data) is analyzed by reading out the generated photocurrent under negative applied voltage (-8V), with and without 390 nm background lighting, applied either from front or back sides [18].

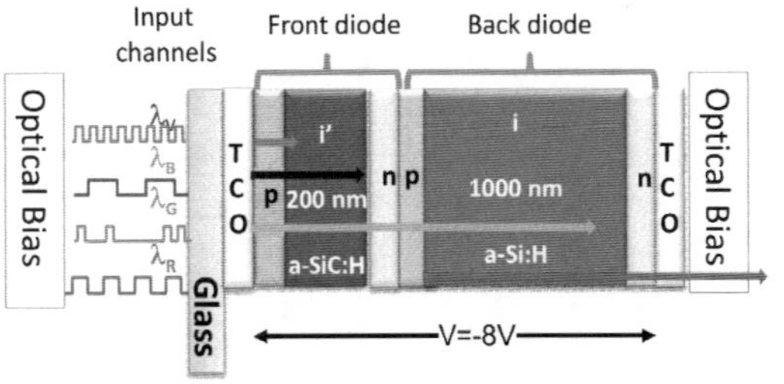

Figure 4. Double pin configuration and device operation.

In Figure 5, the measured signal due to the overlap of the four independent input channels (MUX signal) is displayed without applied optical bias (dark) and under front and back irradiation. On the top the driving signal applied to each R, G, B and V LED is presented, the bit sequence was chosen in order that when one channel is *on* the others are always *off*.

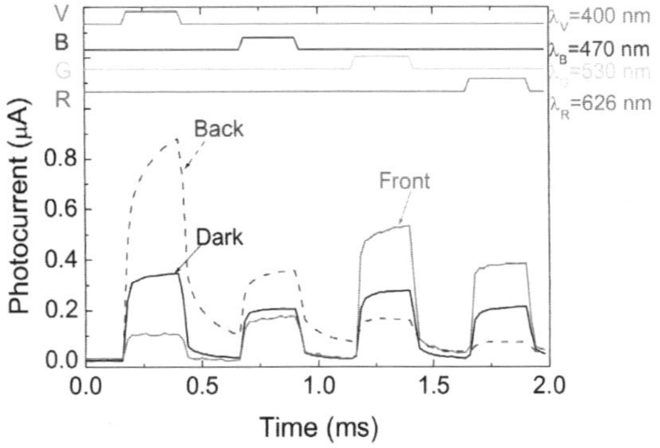

Figure 5. Transient photocurrent without (Dark) and under front (Front) and back (Back) 390 nm irradiation.

Data analysis shows that the photocurrent depends, under irradiation, on the irradiated side and on the incoming wavelength, the irradiation side acting as the optical selector for the input channels. Under front irradiation, the long wavelength channels are enhanced and the short wavelength channels quenched while the opposite occurs under back irradiation. Note that, under back lighting, as the wavelength increases the signal strongly decreases while the opposite occurs under front irradiation. This nonlinearity is the main idea for decoding the MUX signal at the receiver.

C. *MUX/DEMUX device*

For the unit cell, and with the receiver at position generation 1 (see Figure 1), the photocurrent generated by all the input channels was measured under front and back lighting.

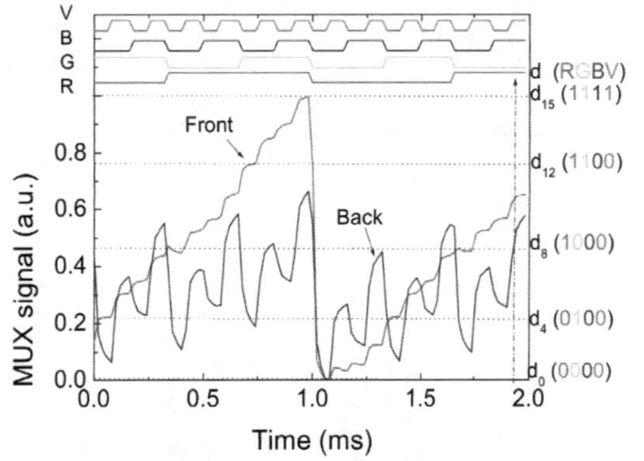

a)

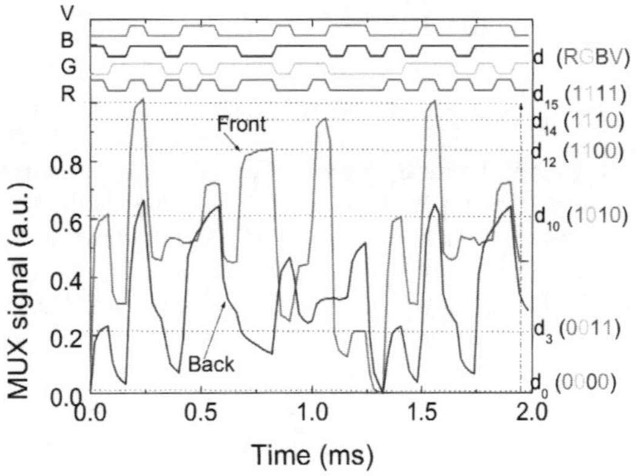

b)

Figure 6. MUX signal under front and back irradiation. On the top the transient optical signal from each RGBV are decoded.

The bit sequence of each channel was adjusted in order to have all the *on/off* possible states in an ordered sequence. The photocurrent was normalized to its maximum value. In Figure 6a this "standard" MUX signal is displayed, under front and back irradiation. In Figure 6b a random sequence is shown under the same conditions. In the top of the figures, the digital decoded information is shown.

The MUX signal under front irradiation is quite different from the one under back lighting. Results from the "standard" sequence (Figure 6a) show that for each possible 2^4 *on/off* states, it corresponds a well-defined level. Under front irradiation, sixteen separate levels are detected (d_0-d_{15}) and correspond to all possible combinations of the *on/off* states, concerning the input channels. Under back irradiation, the MUX signal trend is very close to the one of the violet input channel and allows the readout of the cell´s ID-BIT. In Figure 6b, some *on/off* states are missing, but, as expected, the behavior is the same: front irradiation enhances the red/green channels while under back irradiation the violet channel is readout.The functional principle to decode the transmitted information is based on the adjustable penetration depths of the photons into the front and back diodes (see Figure 4), which is linked to their absorption coefficient in the intrinsic front and back collection areas. Front irradiation is strongly absorbed at the beginning of the front diode and, due to the self-bias effect, increases the electric field at the back diode, where the red incoming photons are absorbed, resulting in an increased collection. Under back irradiation, the electric field decreases, mainly at the i-n back interface, quenching the red signals and enhancing the blue /violet ones (see Figure 5).

The algorithms to decode the coded information are relatively straight-forward since the background acts as selector that chooses one of the 2^n sublevels, being n the number of transmitted channels, and associates to each level an unique n-bit binary code [21]. The combination of the four channels under irradiation, denotes the presence of all the possible sixteen (2^4) *on/off* states, clearly observed in Figure 6a. Here, each level is ordered by the correspondent gains in a 4 bit binary code [X_R, X_G, X_B, X_V], with X=1 if the channel is *on* and X=0 if it is *off.* In Figure 6, in the right side, it is presented the selection index for the 16-element look-up (d_0-d_{15}) table, each one in its 4-bit binary code (RGBV) [18]. Therefore, by assigning each output level to a n digit binary code weighted by the optical gain of each channel, the signal can be decoded. A maximum transmission rate capability of 30 kbps was achieved in a four channel transmission using this device. In the top of the figure, the digital decoded information is shown.

III. INDOOR POSITIONING

In Figure 7, the MUX signals with the receiver at the nearest positions 2 and 6, under front lighting, are presented. In Figure 7a, the "standard" bit sequence (Figure 6a) was analyzed, while in Figure 7b, the random one (Figure 6b) was imposed.

Along n channel WDM message transmission, 2^n *on/off* states are possible during an interval of time T (see Figures 6 and 7). The position of the device during the receiving process will be given by the highest detected level, i. e., the level where all the n received channels are simultaneously *on* [22]. So, the four (RGBV, Figure 6), the three (RGV, Figure 7) or two (GV, Figure 7) received messages will be given by the decoding of the n received channels while the device position will be confirmed by looking at the highest level (dot-dash line).

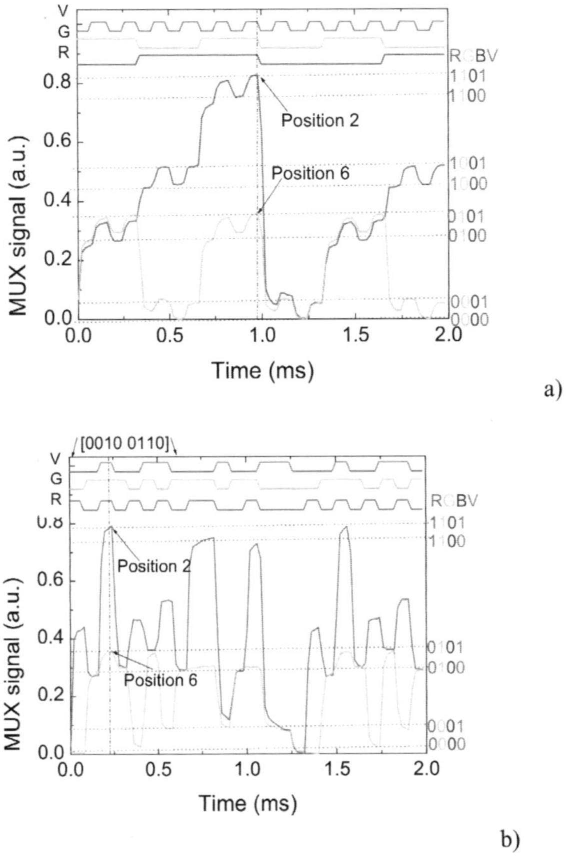

Figure 7. MUX signals under 390 nm front and back irradiation. On the top the transmitted channels were decoded. a) Standard bit sequence. b) Random bit sequence.

The position ID for the analyzed examples will appear as [1111] (point generation 1, ([1111] in Figure 6) or [1101] (point generation 2, in Figure 7), and [0101], (point generation 6, in Figure 7). In Figure 7b, the eight first bits of the violet packet will give the 8-bit address of the unit cell, [0010 0110], that is located at line 2, column 6 from the network.

IV. NAVIGATION DATA BITS

A challenge in LED-based navigation system is the way to improve the data transmission rate while maintaining the capability for accurate navigation. The input of the aided navigation system is the MUX signal, and the output is the system state estimated at each time step. For each transition between an initial location and a final one, two code words are generated, the initial (*i*) and the final (*f*). If the receiver stays under the same region, they should be the same, if it moves away they are different [23], [24].

The suitability of the navigation data bit transition was tested. The navigation solution is to move the sensor unit along a known pattern path. One can performed signal acquisition on the different generated locations, for instance: beginning in point 5 and ending in point 3 (see Figure 1), in four consecutive instants (t_1, t_2, t_3 and t_4).

In a segment where the initial position of the receiver is point generation 5, then it moves to point 4, after that goes to point 7 and finally arrives to point 3, the acquired MUX signal at the instants t_1, t_2, t_3, and t_4 is displayed in Figure 8a. The decoded channels are depicted on top. On the right hand, the highest levels (horizontal dotted lines), in each time interval, and the correspondent code words are pointed out.

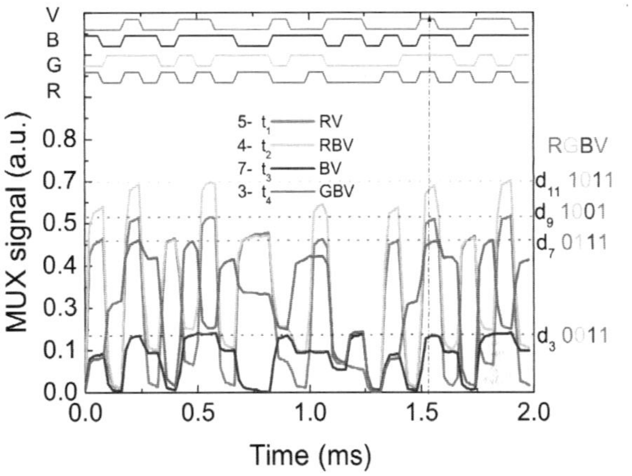

Figure 8. Triangular topology. a) MUX/DEMUX signals under different generation regions (5, 4, 7, 3). b) Compass needle.

As the receiver moves between generated point regions, the received information changes. In turn, red, green or blue channels are added or removed, but the violet is always present giving the location of the cell inside the cluster. In the considered example, the 8-bit positioning ID decoded from the violet channel was [0010 0110], which corresponds to line 2, column 6 of the network. Hence, the retrieved information when the receiver was under point generation 4 (t_2) was: 8-bit positioning ID from the cell in the network [violet channel, 0010 0110], 4-bit positioning ID from the point generation cell: [RGBV, 1011], red channel payload packet: [1010 1010 1100 0100…]. When it moves to generation point 7 (t_3) the cell 4-bit positioning ID changes to [0011] the red information is lost and the blue payload data is maintained as: [1011 0111 0011 1010…]. Nevertheless, the 8-bit violet ID stays the same [0010 0110] since it corresponds to the same unit cell (line 2, column 6) in the network.

V. CONCLUSION

This paper presents a coupled data transmission and indoor positioning by using transmitting trichromatic white LEDs and an a-SiC:H/a-Si:H pin/pin SiC optical MUX/DEMUX mobile receiver. For data transmission, an On-Off Keying code was used. A triangular topology was considered for the unit cell. The proposed arrangement employs four modulated LEDs. Three of them are located at the vertices of an equilateral triangle to transmit the payload data and a fourth one is located at its centroid to send the positioning BIT ID from the unit cell in the network. Fine-grained indoor localization was tested. A 2D localization design, demonstrated by a prototype implementation was developed.

A detailed analysis of the component's characteristics within the VLC system, such as transmitter and receiver, multiplexing techniques, system design, visible light sensing, and indoor localization and navigation recognition were discussed. The results showed that, by using a pinpin double photodiode based on a a-SiC:H heterostucture as mobile receiver and RBG-LED as transmitters, it is possible not only to determine the position of a mobile target inside the unit cell but also in the network and concomitantly to infer the travel direction along the time. For future work, by using multiple emitters and receivers, the transmission data rate through parallelized spatial multiplexing can be improved.

ACKNOWLEDGEMENTS

This work was sponsored by FCT – Fundação para a Ciência e a Tecnologia, within the Research Unit CTS – Center of Technology and systems, reference UID/EEA/00066/2013 and by the IPL project VLC_MIMO, 2016.

REFERENCES

[1] Y. X. Sun, M. Liu, and Q. H. Meng, "Wifi signal strength-based robot indoor localization," in IEEE International Conference on Information and Automation, 2014.

[2] P. Bahl, and V. N. Padmanabhan, "Radar: an in-building rf-based user location and tracking system," in Proc. of IEEE INFOCOM, 2000.

[3] M. Liu, and R. Siegwart, "Dp-fact: Towards topological mapping and scene recognition with color for omnidirectional camera," in Robotics and Automation (ICRA), 2012 IEEE International Conference, may, pp. 3503 –3508, 2012.

[4] M. Liu, K. Qiu, S. Li, F. Che, L. Wu, and C. P. Yue "Towards indoor localization using visible light communication for consumer electronic devices," in Proceedings of the IEEE/RSJ International Conference on Intelligent Robots and Systems (IROS), Chicago, the USA, 2014.

[5] A. Jovicic, J. Li, and T. Richardson, "Visible light communication: opportunities, challenges and the path to market," Communications Magazine, IEEE, vol. 51, no. 12, pp. 26–32, 2013.

[6] S T. Komine and M. Nakagawa, "Fundamental analysis for visible-light communication system using led lights," Consumer Electronics, IEEE Transactions on, vol. 50, no. 1, pp. 100–107, 2004.

[7] E. Ozgur E. Dinc, and O. B. Akan, "Communicate to illuminate: State-of-the-art and research challenges for visible light communications," Physical Communication, no.17, pp. 72–85, 2015.

[8] J. Armstrong, Y. Sekercioglu, A. Neild, "Visible light positioning: a roadmap for international standardization," Communications IEEE, vol. 51, no. 12, pp. 68-73, 2013.

[9] K. Panta, and J. Armstrong, "Indoor localisation using white LEDs " Electron. Lett., vol. 48, no. 4, pp. 228–230, 2012.

[10] T. Komiyama, K. Kobayashi, K. Watanabe, T. Ohkubo, and Y. Kurihara, "Study of visible light communication system using RGB LED lights," in Proceedings of SICE Annual Conference, IEEE, pp. 1926–1928, 2011.

[11] Y. Wang, Y. Wang, N. Chi, J. Yu, and H. Shang. "Demonstration of 575-Mb/s downlink and 225-Mb/s uplink bi-directional SCM-WDM visible light communication using RGB LED and phosphor-based LED," Opt. Express vol. 21, no. 1, pp. 1203–1208, 2013.

[12] D. Tsonev, H. Chun, S. Rajbhandari, J. McKendry, S. Videv, E. Gu, M. Haji, S. Watson, A. Kelly, G. Faulkner, M. Dawson, H. Haas, and D. O'Brien, "A 3-Gb/s single-LED OFDM-based wireless VLC link using a Gallium Nitride μLED," IEEE Photon. Technol. Lett., vol.26 no.7, pp. 637–640, 2014.

[13] D. O'Brien, h. L. Minh, L. Zeng, G. Faulkner, K. Lee, D. Jung, Y. Oh, and E. T. Won, "Indoor visible light communications: challenges and prospects," Proc. SPIE 7091, 709106, 2008.

[14] S. Schmid, G. Corbellini, S. Mangold, and T. R. Gross, "An LED-to-LED Visible Light Communication system with software-based synchronization," in 2012 IEEE Globecom Workshops, pp. 1264–1268, 2012.

[15] Z. Zhou, M. Kavehrad, P. Deng, "Indoor positioning algorithm using light-emitting diode visible light communications " *Opt. Eng*. Vol.51, no. 8, 085009, 2012.

[16] S T. Komine and M. Nakagawa, "Fundamental analysis for visible-light communication system using led lights," Consumer Electronics, IEEE Transactions on, vol. 50, no. 1, 100–107, 2004.

[17] E. Monteiro, and S. Hranilovic, "Constellation design for color-shift keying using interior point methods," in Proc. IEEE Globecom Workshops, Dec., pp. 1224–1228, 2012.

[18] M. Vieira, P. Louro, M. Fernandes, M.A. Vieira, A. Fantoni and J. Costa, "Three Transducers Embedded into One Single SiC Photodetector: LSP Direct Image Sensor, Optical Amplifier and Demux Device," Advances in Photodiodes", InTech, Chap.19, pp. 403-425, 2011.

[19] M. A. Vieira, P. Louro, M. Vieira, A. Fantoni, and A. Steiger -Garção, "Light-activated amplification in Si-C tandem devices: A capacitive active filter model," IEEE sensor jornal, 12, no. 6, pp.1755-1762, 2012.

[20] E. A Saleh Bahaa and M. C. Teich, "Fundamentals of Photonics", John Wiley & Sons. Chapter 3, "Beam Optics," pp. 80–107, 1991.

[21] M. A. Vieira, M. Vieira, V. Silva, P. Louro, and M. Barata, "Optoelectronic logic functions using optical bias controlled SiC multilayer devices,". MRS Proceedings, vol. 1536, pp. 91-96, 2013.

[22] M. A. Vieira, M. Vieira, P. Louro, V. Silva, P. Vieira, "Optical signal processing for indoor positioning using a-SiCH technology," Opt. Eng. Vol. 55, no. 10, 107105, doi: 10.1117/1.OE.55.10, 2016.

[23] M. A. Vieira, M. Vieira, P. Louro, L. Mateus, and P. Vieira, "Indoor positioning system using a WDM device based on a-SiC:H technology," Journal of Luminescence, doi.:10.1016/j.jlumin.2016.10.005, 2016.

[24] P. Louro, J. Costa, M. A. Vieira, M. Vieira, "Optical Communication Applications based on white LEDs," J. Luminescence. doi.:10.1016/j.jlumin.2016.11.036, 2016.

Cu_2O Photosensitive Thin Films for Solar Cell Application

Ørnulf Nordset and Sean Erik Foss
Institute for Energy Technology, IFE
Kjeller, Norway
email: Ornulf.Nordseth@ife.no
email: Sean.Foss@ife.no

Bengt Gunnar Svensson and Raj Kumar
University of Oslo
Oslo, Norway
email: b.g.svensson@fys.uio.no
email: raj.kumar@smn.uio.no

Irinela Chilibon, Cristina Vasiliu,
Raluca Iordanescu, Laurentiu Baschir,
Dan Savastru, Adrian Kiss and Anca Parau
National Institute of Research and Development for Optoelectronics, INOE-2000
Bucharest-Magurele, Romania
emails: qilib@yahoo.com, icvasiliu@inoe.ro, iorda85@yahoo.com, baschirlaurentiu@inoe.ro, dsavas@inoe.ro, adrian.kiss@inoe.ro, anca.parau@inoe.ro

Laurentiu Fara
University Politehnica of Bucharest
Bucharest, Romania
email: lfara@renerg.pub.ro

Roxana Trusca
METAV-CD
Bucharest, Romania

Abstract—**Among copper oxides, Cu_2O is intensively studied due to its high optical absorption coefficient and relatively good electrical properties. Copper oxide thin films properties depend on the deposition method as an effect of detailed arrangement of Cu and O atoms that induce different physical properties. Cu_2O is a p-type semiconductor having a band gap sufficiently close to the optimal band gap under AM1.5 radiation spectrum, which makes it an attractive material for photovoltaic applications and solar cells. The structural and morphological properties of deposited thin films were investigated by Scanning Electron Microscopy (SEM) and Atomic Force Microscopy (AFM). The thin film thickness and optical constants were determined by Spectroscopic Ellipsometry (SE). The purpose of the paper was to study the technological possibilities of preparing high quality Cu_2O thin films, used in photovoltaic applications. The sputter-deposited Cu_2O thin films presented in this work show good potential as absorber layers for photovoltaic applications.**

Keywords-copper oxide; solar cell; magnetron sputtering; SEM; AFM; ellipsometry.

I. INTRODUCTION

In recent years, cuprous oxide (Cu_2O) has been intensively studied due to its high optical absorption coefficient and favorable electrical properties. Cu_2O thin films properties are depending on the deposition method, as a result of the detailed arrangement of Cu and O atoms that induce different physical properties. Several methods can be used to prepare Cu_2O thin films, including thermal oxidation, chemical vapor deposition, plasma evaporation, reactive sputtering, and electrodeposition [1][2]. It has been reported that most of these synthesis methods result in a combined growth of Cu_2O and CuO phases, which is unfavorable in photovoltaic applications. Cu_2O is very promising candidate for solar cell applications as it is a suitable material for photovoltaic energy conversion [2]. In this work, we analyze Cu_2O thin films, deposited on SiO_2 and quartz substrates by magnetron sputtering. The purpose of the paper was to study the technological possibilities of preparing high-quality Cu_2O thin films for photovoltaic applications.

The optical transmittances of the films show a strong dependence on the flow rate during deposition [1].

Ohajianya and Abumere [3] show that the efficiency of Cu_2O/Cu solar cell increases as the thickness of the Cu_2O decreases, up to a limiting thickness of 26.30 μm, after which the efficiency decreases as the thickness decreases.

This paper is organized as follow: Section I. Introduction presents the applications of cuprous oxide (Cu_2O); Section II. describes the method for preparing copper oxide thin film; Section III. describes the structural investigations; Section IV. presents the results of the research, and the paper concludes in Section V.

II. CUPROUS OXIDE THIN FILM PREPARATION METHOD

Cu_2O is a p-type semiconductor having a band gap sufficiently close to the optimal band gap under AM1.5 radiation spectrum, which makes it an attractive material for photovoltaic applications and solar cells.

Cu_2O thin films were deposited on 1 × 1 cm^2 quartz and silicon substrates by a direct current (DC) magnetron sputtering system (Semicore Triaxis). The quartz substrates were cleaned in piranha and rinsed in deionized water. The substrates were dried with nitrogen and loaded into the deposition chamber. Cu_2O was deposited by reactive sputtering of Cu target (99.999%) in O_2/Ar (6/49 sccm) with a substrate temperature of 400 °C. The power density was fixed at 2.2 W/cm^2, and experimentally established. During the magnetron sputtering deposition, the base pressure was kept below 3.0 x 10^{-7} Torr and the sample stage was rotated at a constant speed of 12 rpm. The Cu_2O thin films were deposited in two different thickness ~ 200 nm and ~ 500 nm with a deposition rate ~ 25 nm/min. As-grown Cu_2O films were annealed at 900 °C for 3 minutes in vacuum (pressure ~10^{-1} Torr) in order to enhance the optical and electrical properties [4].

III. STRUCTURAL INVESTIGATIONS

The structural and morphological properties of deposited thin films were investigated by SEM and AFM. The thin film thickness and optical constants were determined by SE. Several variants of Cu_2O thin film preparation have been considered, resulting in films of approximately 200 nm and 500 nm thickness.

TABLE I. SAMPLES AND DEPOSITION CONDITIONS FOR Cu_2O THIN FILMS DEPOSITED BY MAGNETRON SPUTTERING

Sample name	*Film deposition conditions*
Sample 1	Cu_2O (as-grown): deposited at 400 ^{0}C; film thickness ≅ 200 nm, on n-type Si substrate
Sample 2	Cu_2O (as-grown): deposited at 400 ^{0}C; film thickness ≅ 500 nm, on n-type Si substrate
Sample 3	Cu_2O (as-grown): deposited at 400 ^{0}C; film thickness ≅ 200 nm, on quartz substrate
Sample 4	Cu_2O (annealed): deposited at 400 ^{0}C; film thickness ≅ 500 nm, on quartz substrate
Sample 5	Cu_2O (annealed): deposited at 400 ^{0}C; film thickness ≅ 200 nm and annealed at 900 ^{0}C, 3 min in vacuum, on quartz substrate
Sample 6	Cu_2O (annealed): deposited at 400 ^{0}C; film thickness ≈ 500 nm and annealed at 900 ^{0}C, 3 min in vacuum, on quartz substrate

Table I presents the experimental samples and deposition conditions for Cu_2O thin films deposited by magnetron sputtering.

IV. RESULTS

The structural and morphological properties of deposited thin films were investigated by SEM and Atomic Force Microscopy AFM. The thin film thickness and optical constants were determined by SE.

A. *Scanning electron microscopy*

SEM images of 200 nm and 500 nm film deposited on SiO_2 substrate are shown in Figures 1 and 2. For 200 nm films, the grain size is around 30 to 40 nm (Figure 1) and rarely more than 60 nm. For films of thickness 500 nm the grain size increased to 60 - 70 nm (Figure 2).

a) *b)*

Figure 1. SEM images of a) 200 nm as-grown Cu_2O thin film on Si substrate, *Sample 1* and b) SEM image of 500 nm as-grown Cu_2O thin film on Si substrate, *Sample 2*.

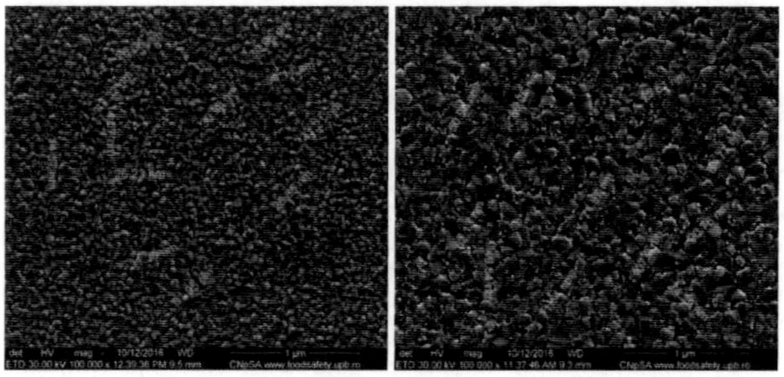

a) *b)*

Figure 2. SEM images of a) SEM image of 200 nm as-grown Cu_2O thin film on quartz substrate, *Sample 3* and b) SEM image of 500 nm as-grown Cu_2O thin film on quartz substrate, *Sample 4*.

a) *b)*

Figure 3. SEM images of a) 200 nm annealed Cu_2O thin film on quartz substrate, *Sample 5* and b) 500 nm annealed Cu_2O thin film on quartz substrate, *Sample 6*.

Figure 3 presents SEM images for *Sample 5* and *Sample 6*, deposited on quartz substrate. It is noticeable that for the Cu_2O thin film on quartz, average grain size increases from ~70 nm for the as-grown film to ~600 nm for the annealed film [4].

The size of the grains depends on the thickness of the films deposited and the type of substrate material. For the SiO_2 substrate it is noticeable that the grains deposited are more uniform and smaller than the films deposited on the quartz.

For the quartz substrate, increasing the thickness of Cu_2O films, from 200 nm to 500 nm, also increases grain size.

B. *Atomic force microscopy*

In order to study the effect of the deposition condition on the morphology of the Cu_2O thin film, the morphologies of all samples have been analyzed using an Atomic Force Microscope (AFM), (INNOVA, Veeco Company). For the data acquisition, we used an AFM probe model RTESPA, doped with Si and for image analysis we used Scanning Probe Microscopy with special SPM Lab Analysis v.7.0 software (from Veeco Company). The scanning was made in tapping mode and the scanning speed was about 2.5 μm/s on a surface area of 10×10 μm^2. The AFM images had a resolution of 512×512 pixels. For all the samples, the AFM images were performed first on 30×30 μm^2 area and then on the 10×10 μm^2 area, representing the cleanest zone of the large area.

AFM data analysis allows quantitative information to be extracted on surface roughness. A systematic description of various analytical methods used for roughness characterization can be found in [5]. The root-mean square roughness (R_{RMS}) is defined as the standard deviation of the surface height profile from the mean height, (1).

$$R_{RMS} = \left[\frac{1}{N} \sum_{n-1}^{n} \left(h_i - \langle h \rangle \right)^2 \right]^{\frac{1}{2}} \quad (1)$$

where N is the number of pixels in the image (or data points), h_i is the height of the ith pixel, and h is the mean height of the image [5].

The AFM has been employed to determine the morphology, the grain size and the root mean square (RMS) surface roughness of all deposited films at 400 °C as-grown for 200 nm and 500 nm thicknesses of films, and annealed at 900 °C for 200 nm and 500 nm thicknesses of films.

The 2D and 3D AFM images of Cu_2O thin films deposited at different conditions show the surface morphologies of the films (*Figures* 4 to 8). Generally, we found that an increase in the thickness of Cu_2O films potential results in an increase of the grain size and RMS surface roughness, as shown in Table II.

TABLE II. RMS FOR Cu_2O THIN FILMS

Sample name	*RMS roughness [nm]*
Sample 2	6.31
Sample 3	1.58
Sample 4	7.95
Sample 5	15.65
Sample 6	20.60

For the same thickness of 500 nm, the roughness on Si substrate is smaller than the roughness on quartz. Sample 6 has the greatest RMS roughness.

Generally, during the Cu_2O film making, we found that an increase in film thickness and the treatment temperature increase the grain size and implicitly the roughness of the films.

Samples 2 and 4 had similar roughness, the coating was not influenced by the two selected substrates (Si and quartz substrates). However, we notice that the coating on Si substrate (*Sample 2*) had more dense and compact columns, compared with *Sample 4*.

After the film deposition at 400 °C, it was observed the fine structure for the coatings on *Samples* 3 and 4, emphasized by the low roughness values (1.58 nm, respectively 7.95 nm).

The annealing at 900 °C, 3 min in vacuum led to an increase of roughness for both samples with different layers thickness deposited on quartz substrate (*Samples* 5 and 6).

Sample 6, with a thickness of 500 nm, after the annealing, presented the largest grains size and therefore the highest value of roughness parameter (20.60 nm).

C. *Spectroscopic ellipsometry*

Spectroscopic ellipsometry and reflectivity measurements are used for determination of Cu_2O film thickness [6].

For determination of the optical properties of the Cu_2O films, a layer-by-layer growth model was used as presented in Figure 9 [7]. In the calculation process, optical constants of each material in the respective layer are cited from the literature. The surface roughness is modeled by mixing the optical constants of surface material (Cu_2O) and 50% air (i.e., n = 1 and k = 0) as shown in Figure 9.

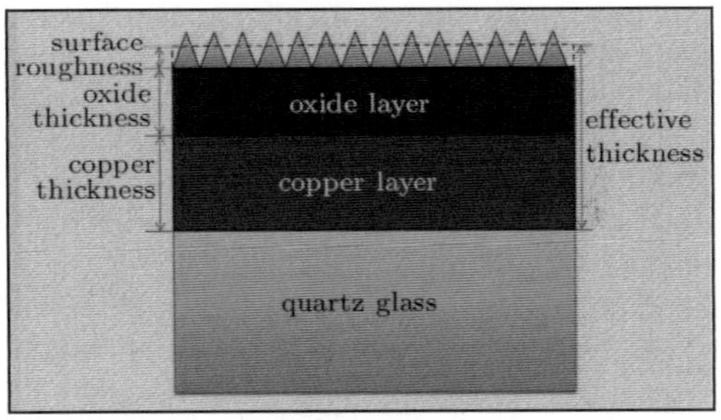

Figure 9. Schematic illustration of 3-layer model for oxidized Cu layer on quartz substrate [7].

We used the UVISEL Spectroscopic Ellipsometer equipment from HORIBA Jobin Yvon in the spectral range 190-2100 nm [8]. All calculations were performed using DeltaPsi vs 2.6 software.

Tan Ψ and cos Δ spectra were modeled until the best fit was obtained. The model consists of a main copper oxide layer with a surface roughness layer and an interlayer layer above the (Qz / Si) quartz / Si substrate. The Tauc - Lorentz dispersion law was used for the Cu_2O layer, while the surface roughness layer was formed by one layer of Cu_2O, CuO and voids. The model used is shown in Figure 10.

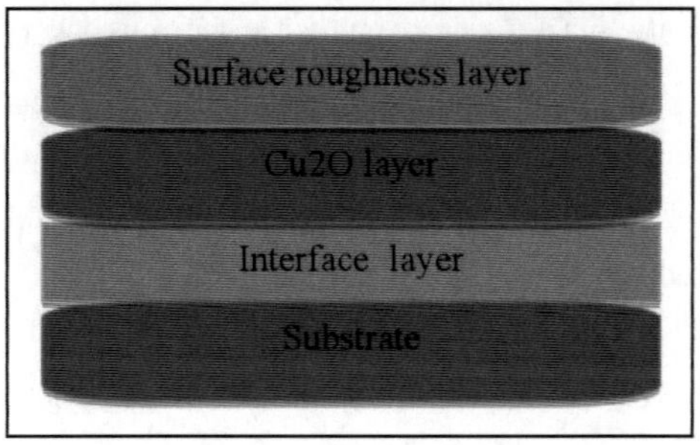

Figure 10. Model of multilayer thin copper oxide

Figure 11 presents the graphs of n, k constants for *Sample 1*, i.e., a ~200 nm thick Cu_2O thin film deposited by magnetron sputtering at 400 °C on Si substrate. The model details of *Sample 1* are: Thickness 314 nm +/- 19,728 nm; oscillator used Tauc-Lorentz; points number 27; fit quality factor 5.120504; roughness layer 115 nm +/- 46.393 nm; band gap E_g = 2.1816.

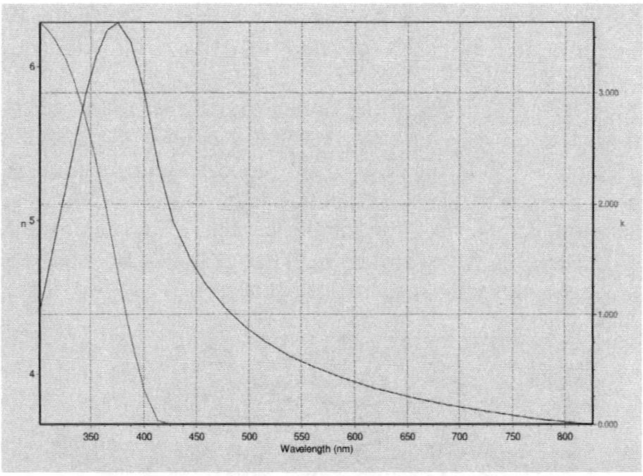

Figure. 11. Graphs of n (blue curve), k (red curve) constants for *Sample 1*.

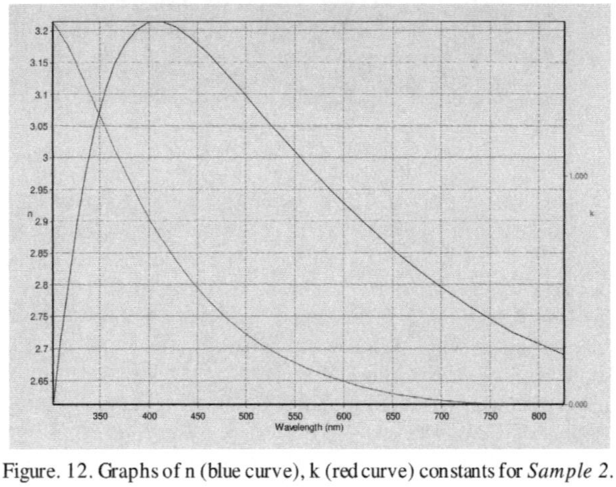

Figure. 12. Graphs of n (blue curve), k (red curve) constants for *Sample 2*.

Figure 12 presents the graphs of n, k constants for *Sample* 2, i.e., a ~500 nm thick Cu_2O thin film deposited by magnetron sputtering at 400 °C on Si substrate. The model details of *Sample 2* are: Thickness 471 nm +/- 9.232 nm; oscillator used Tauc-Lorentz; points number 27; fit quality factor 7.929797; roughness layer 12 nm +/- 3.592 nm; band gap E_g = 1.8945.

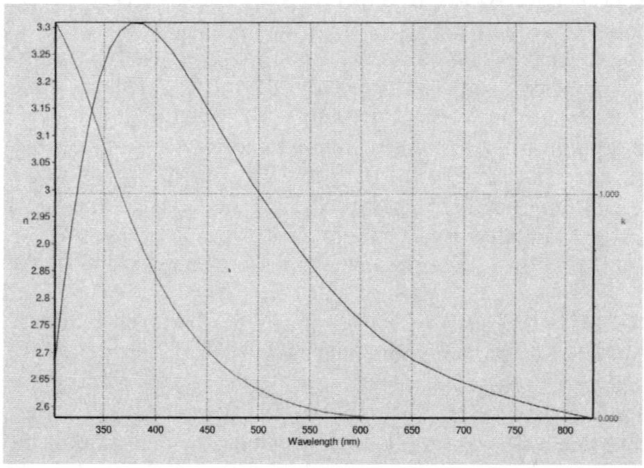

Figure 13. Graphs of n (blue curve), k (red curve) constants for *Sample 4*.

Figure 13 presents the graphs of n, k constants for *Sample 4*, i.e., a ~500 nm thick Cu_2O thin film deposited by magnetron sputtering at 400 °C temperature on quartz substrate. The model details of *Sample 4* are: Thickness 561 nm +/- 16.858 nm; oscillator used Tauc-Lorentz; points number 27; fit quality factor 14,251030; roughness layer 15 nm +/- 1.663 nm; band gap E_g = 1.8590.

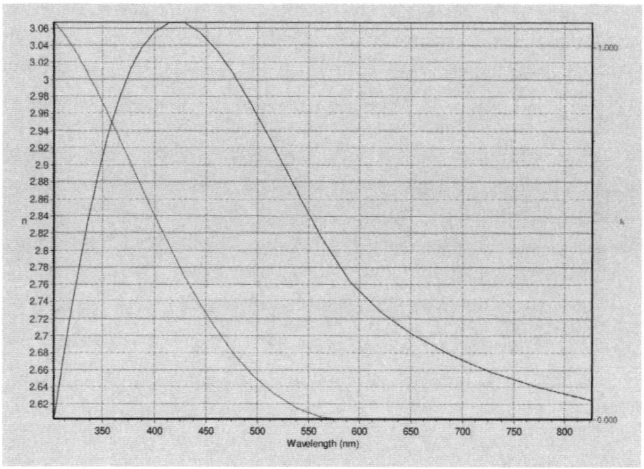

Figure 14. Graphs of n (blue curve), k (red curve) constants for *Sample 6*.

Figure 14 presents the graphs of n, k constants for *Sample 6*, i.e., a ~500 nm thick Cu_2O thin film deposited by magnetron sputtering at 400 °C and treated at 900 °C on quartz substrate. The model details of *Sample 6* are: Thickness 590 nm +/- 9.964 nm; oscillator used Tauc-Lorentz; points number 27; fit quality factor 10.042980; roughness layer 21 nm +/- 1.509 nm; band gap E_g = 1.6900.

V. CONCLUSIONS

Characterization of sputter-deposited Cu_2O thin films by scanning electron microscopy and atomic force microscopy showed that the average grain size and the RMS surface roughness increases with film thickness. Spectroscopic ellipsometry measurements showed that annealing of the Cu_2O film at 900°C reduces optical absorption, i.e., the extinction coefficient is reduced, presumably as a result of increased grain size [4]. In conclusion, the sputter-deposited Cu_2O thin films presented in this work show good potential as an absorber layer for photovoltaic applications.

ACKNOWLEDGMENT

This work was conducted under the research project "High-performance tandem heterojunction solar cells for specific applications" (SOLHET), financially supported by the Research Council of Norway (RCN) and the Romanian Executive Agency for Higher Education, Research, Development and Innovation Funding (UEFISCDI) through the M-ERA.NET Program and 2017 Core Program, PN16-400102.

REFERENCES

[1] F. K. Mugwang'a, P. K. Karimi, W. K. Njoroge, O. Omayio, and S. Waita, "Optical characterization of Copper Oxide thin films prepared by reactive dc magnetron sputtering for solar cell applications", Int. J. Thin Film Sci. Tec., vol. 2, no. 1, pp. 15-24, 2013.

[2] M. R. Johan, M. Shahadan, M. Suan, N. L. Hawari, H. A. Ching, "Annealing Effects on the Properties of Copper Oxide Thin Films Prepared by Chemical Deposition", Int. J. Electrochem. Sci., vol. 6, pp. 6094–6104, 2011.

[3] C. A. Ohajianya and O. E. Abumere, "Effect Of Cuprous Oxide (Cu_2O) Film Thickness On The Efficiency Of The Copper-Cuprous Oxide (Cu_2O/Cu) Solar Cell", The International Journal of Engineering and Science (IJES), vol. 2, no. 5, pp. 42-47, 2013.

[4] Ø. Nordseth, R. Kumar, K Bergum, L. Fara, S. E. Foss, H. Haug, F. Dragan, D. Crăciunescu, P. Sterian, I. Chilibon, C. Vasiliu, L. Baschir, D. Savastru, E. Momakhov, and B. G. Svensson, "Optical analysis of a ZnO/Cu_2O subcell in a silicon-based tandem heterojunction solar cell", Green and sustainable chemistry, vol. 7, no. 1, pp. 57-69, 2017.

[5] J. M. Bennett and L. Mattson, "Introduction to Surface Roughness and Scattering", Optical Society of America, Washington, DC, 1989.

[6] O. Messaoudi, et al., "Correlation between optical and structural properties of copper oxide electrodeposited on ITO glass", J. of Alloys and Compounds, vol. 611, pp. 142–148, 2014.

[7] J.-B. Gong, et al. "Thickness dependence of the optical constants of oxidized copper thin films based on ellipsometry and transmittance", Chin. Phys. B, vol. 23, no. 8, pp. 087802-1–087802-5, 2014.

[8] HORIBA International Corporation [accessed August 2017] (http://www.horiba.com/us/en/scientific/products/ellipsometers/)

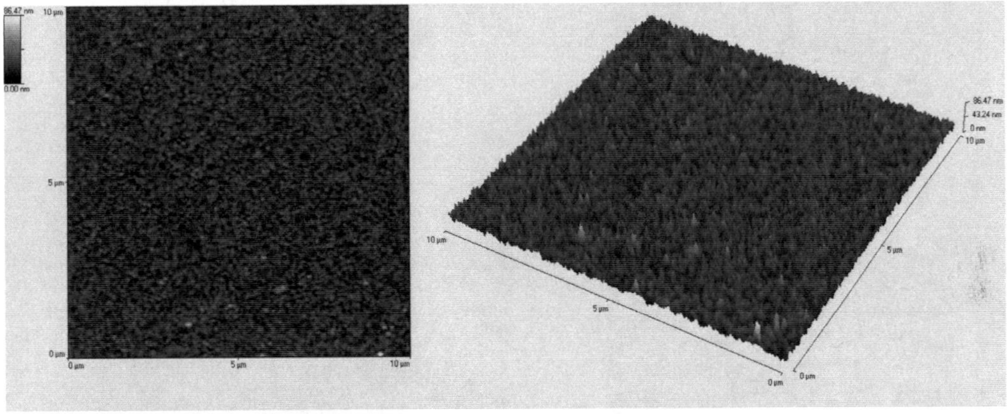

Figure 4. 2D and 3D AFM images of *Sample 2*.

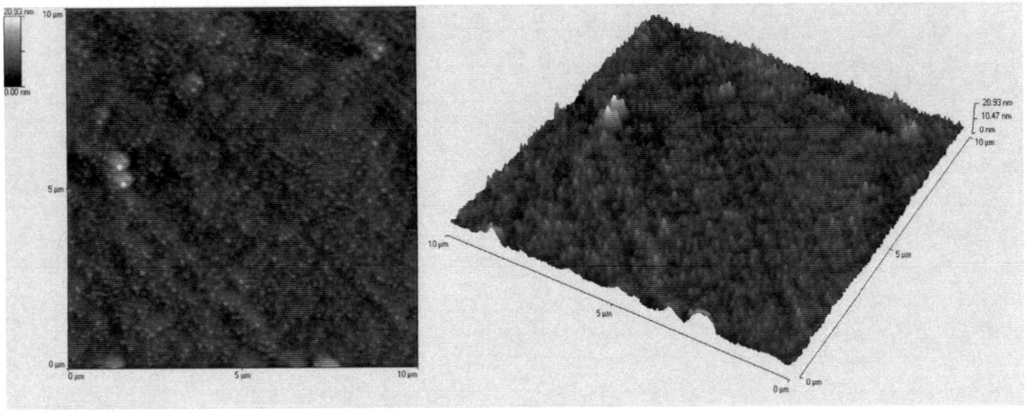

Figure 5. 2D and 3D AFM images of *Sample 3*.

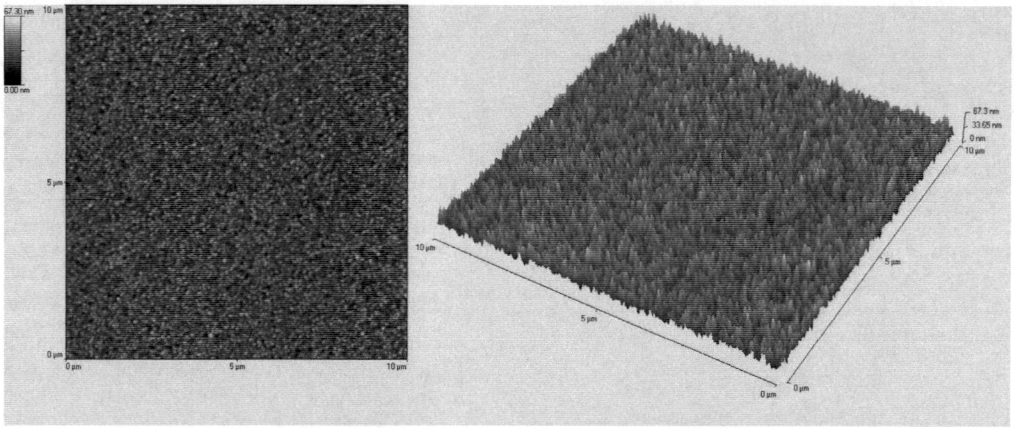

Figure 6. 2D and 3D AFM images of *Sample 4*.

Figure 7. 2D and 3D AFM images of *Sample 5*.

Figure 8. 2D and 3D AFM images of *Sample 6*.

Design of SiN_x Optical Sensor Using Polygonal Resonator Structure

Jun-Hee Park, Su-Jin Jeon, Ji-Hoon Kim, Eudum Kim, Sun-Ho Kim and Young-Wan Choi*
School of Electrical and Electronics Engineering, Chung-Ang University
221 Heuksuk-Dong, Dongjak-ku, Seoul, 156-756, Korea
Email: kp9934@hanmail.net, jeonsujin0601@gmail.com, kjh41067206@gmail.com, eudum.kim@gmail.com, locsksh@gmail.com and ychoi@cau.ac.kr

Kwang Ryong Oh
Electronics and Telecommunications Research Institute
138 Gajeongno, Yuseong-Gu, Daejeon, Korea
Email: kroh@etri.re.kr

Chil-Min Kim
Department of Emerging Materials Science
DGIST
711-873, Daegu, Korea
Email: chmkim@dgist.ac.kr

Kyung-Jin Choi
Meterials Science and Engineering
UNIST
UNIST-gil 50, 689-798, Ulsan, Korea
Email: choi@unist.ac.kr

***Abstract*—In this paper, SiN_x polygonal resonator is carefully simulated for an optical sensor. The polygonal resonator has recently attracted much attention for application in bio and chemical sensors because it does not have a bending loss, which can be fabricated with high integration rate, and it has an advantage of using Multi Mode Interference (MMI) coupler. In polygonal resonator sensor design, high Q-factor and low loss Total Internal Reflection (TIR) mirror are important factors. Therefore, a 125 degrees TIR mirror that has a 97% reflectance considering the Goos-Hânchen shift and critical angle is designed. For rib type waveguide, we designed it to have 3 µm width, 0.5 µm height, and 0.25 µm etching depth. Regarding the simulation results of Finite Domain Time difference (FDTD) method, the Q-factor of SiN_x polygonal resonator was 5736 and Free Spectral Range (FSR) was 16.3 nm. When we changed the refractive index, the shift of the peak was 26.5 nm/Refractive Index Unit (RIU).**

Keywords- photonics; optical resonator; optical sensors.

I. INTRODUCTION

In recent years, optical resonators have been researched for their use as sensors and filter devices. When using these optical resonators as a biosensors, attaching antibodies on the surface are used for monitoring the change of refractive index after an antibody-antigen reaction. These sensors are called refractometric sensors [1]–[2]. They detect the variation of refractive index by measuring the output power at a fixed wavelength or shift of resonance wavelength. In order to obtain high sensitivity, a resonator should have a high Q-factor. The most common type of resonator is a ring resonator [3]. However, during the fabrication progress, it has the disadvantage of mass-production because a single mode condition should be applied. In the ring resonator structure, the waveguide width is too narrow to fabricate the resonator using photolithography because the common waveguide core material is Si, which has about 400 nm width for a single mode waveguide. When the waveguide of the ring resonator is at multimode, the output of the resonator has a lot of peaks and thereby, it is not suitable to be used as an optical sensor. For establish the single mode condition, a common method is to design the rib type waveguide or to use a low refractive index core material. However, bending loss is another disadvantage of the ring resonator. It has a high bending loss which limits the minimization of the resonator. This disadvantage reduces the integration rate. To overcome these drawbacks, we designed a polygonal resonator that does not have bending loss. Also, a polygonal resonator can use MMI coupler. Therefore, a polygonal resonator can be an alternative solution. In this paper, we simulated the polygonal resonators based on SiN_x material which has a refractive index of 1.9827 at 1.55 µm wavelength.

II. THEORETICAL ANALYSIS OF RESONATOR

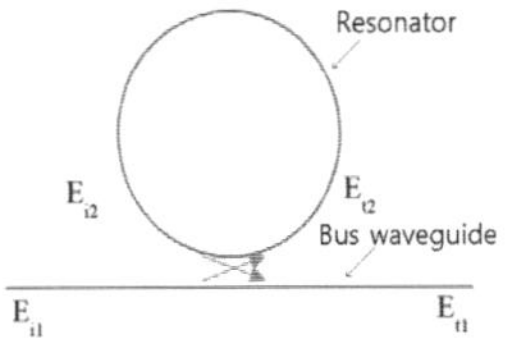

Figure 1. A Resonator structure

As shown in Fig.1, a resonator structure is composed of a bus waveguide and a resonator [4]. It has been used as sensor and filter device. E_{i1} is the input electric field, E_{t2} is the coupling electric field from waveguide to resonator, E_{i2} is the coupling electric field from resonator to waveguide and E_{t1} is the output electric field. The equation in this resonator can be expressed as:

$$\begin{pmatrix} E_{t1} \\ E_{t2} \end{pmatrix} = \begin{pmatrix} t & \kappa \\ -\kappa^* & t^* \end{pmatrix} \begin{pmatrix} E_{i1} \\ E_{i2} \end{pmatrix} \quad (1)$$

$$E_{i2} = \alpha \cdot e^{j\theta} E_{t2} \quad (2)$$

Here, t is the transmission coefficient, κ is the coupling coefficient and α is the attenuation coefficient. Using (1) and (2), the output of the resonator can be expressed as:

$$P_{t1} = |E_{t1}|^2 = \frac{\alpha^2 + |t|^2 - 2\alpha|t|\cos(\theta + \varphi_t)}{1 + \alpha^2|t|^2 - 2\alpha|t|\cos(\theta + \varphi_t)} \quad (3)$$

III. WAVEGUIDE DESIGN AND TIR MIRROR

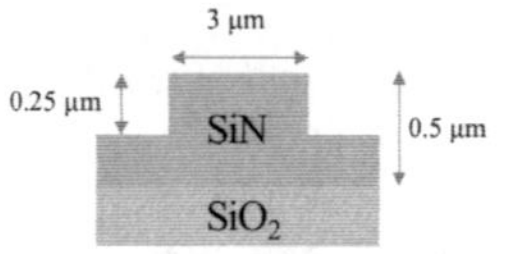

Figure 2. Waveguide structure

The design of a waveguide is important because it determines the propagation loss. Firstly, we designed the waveguide to have a SiN_x core and SiO_2 cladding material. SiN_x material has a refractive index of 1.9827 at 1.55 μm wavelength [5] and SiO_2 material has a refractive index of 1.44 at 1.55 μm wavelength [6]. As shown in Fig.2, the waveguide width, height and etching depth are 3 μm, 0.5 μm and 0.25 μm, respectively. This structure makes it possible to fabricate the resonator using a contact aligner that costs lower and has a higher productivity than using e-beam lithography. We also designed a TIR mirror which is a significant factor for the polygonal resonator. The critical angle and Goos-Hanchen shift should be considered carefully in designing a TIR mirror [7]. The critical angle of the SiN_x waveguide structure is 46.57 degrees and the estimated value of the Goos-Hånchen shift is calculated about 200 nm. The designed TIR mirror has an angle of 125 degrees and the reflectance is 97% as shown in Fig.3. According to the simulation, there are 5 Transverse Electric (TE) and Transverse Magnetic (TM) modes in the waveguide structure because of its wide width. However, the surface roughness of the SiN_x waveguide and the long path length of the resonator make higher order modes disappear. Therefore, the output of the polygonal resonator has a single mode electric field.

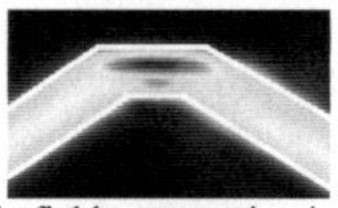
Figure 3. Electric field propagation in TIR mirror

IV. POLYGONAL RESONATOR

The polygonal resonator is an attractive structure because it has no bending loss and MMI coupler can be applied for use. These advantages make fabrication easier than the ring type resonator. However, sophisticated TIR mirror design should be required for low bending loss of the polygonal resonator. In the designed TIR mirror, each TIR mirror has 3% loss, so the total resonator loss is about 22%. Using equation (3), a 50:50 coupler is needed for high on-off ratio. Therefore, we designed 50:50 MMI coupler, which has 193 μm length. The total length of the polygonal resonator is 800 μm. The simulation results of the octagonal resonator is shown in Fig. 4. The results showed that the Q-factor of the polygonal resonator was 5736 and the FSR was 16.3 nm. When the refractive index was changed, the shift of the peak was 26.5 nm/RIU.

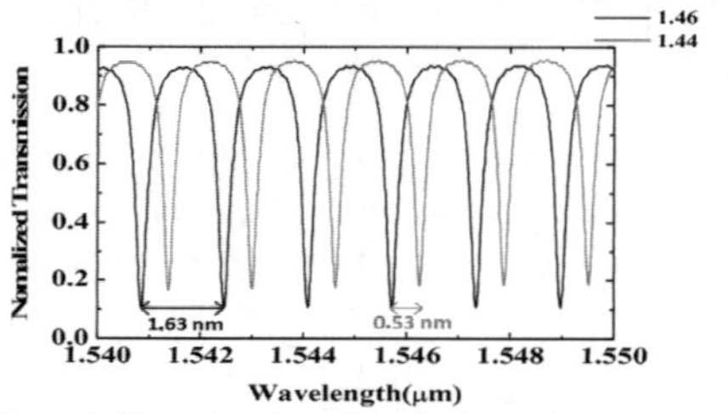

Figure 4. The output intensity of polygonal resonator

V. CONCLUSIONS

In this paper, we designed a polygonal resonator as an optical sensor. In contrast to ring resonators, having no bending loss and using MMI are the advantages of polygonal resonator. These advantages increase the integration rate and make fabrication easier. Also, wide width waveguide can be fabricated through photolithography just as a contact aligner. The polygonal resonator will be a good solution to overcome the disadvantages of a ring type resonator.

ACKNOWLEDGMENT

This work was supported by the Pioneer Research Center Program through the National Research Foundation of Korea (NRF) funded by the Ministry of Science, ICT & Future Planning (No. NRF-2014M3C1A3051969) and was supported by Basic Science Research Program through the National Research Foundation of Korea (NRF) funded by the Ministry of Education (2009-0093817).

REFERENCES

[1] N. A. Yebo, D. Taillaert, J. Roels, D. Lahem, M. Debliquy, D. Van Thorhout and R. Baets, "Silicon-on-insulator(SOI) ring resonator-based integrated optical hydrogen sensor," IEEE photonics technology letters, 21(14), 2009

[2] Z. Vanessa, L. Peter, W. Martin and P. Daniel, "A highly sensitive refractometric sensor based on cascaded SiN microring resonators," Sensors, 13, 14601-14610, 2013

[3] Vittorio M. N. Passoro, "Ammonia optical sensing by microring resonators," Sensors, 7, 2741-2749, 2007

[4] John E. Heebner, Vincent Wong, A. Schweinsberg, R. W. Boyd and D. J. Jackson, "Optical transmission characteristics of fiber ring resonators," IEEE journal of quantum electronics, 40(6), 2014

[5] Tryggve Bååk, "Silicon oxynitride; a material for GRIN optics," Applied optics, 21(6), 1069-1072, 1982

[6] S. O. Kasap, Optoelectronics and photonics, Pearson, Canada, 33, 2013

[7] Tae-Kyeong Lee, *et al.*, "A high-Q biochemical sensor using a total internal reflection mirror-based triangular resonator with an asymmetric Mach-Zehnder interferometer," Optics communications, 285(7), 1807-1813, 2012

An Electrochemical Sensor for Environmental Detection Based on Reduced Graphene Oxide Modified Electrodes

Chiaying Chen, Yen-Chun Chen, and Yu-Ting Hong
Department of Environmental Engineering,
National Chung Hsing University,
Taichung City 402, Taiwan
e-mail: chiayingchen@nchu.edu.tw
{g104063204, g105063217}@mail.nchu.edu.tw

Abstract—**The increasing use and associated environmental release of consumed human and veterinary antibiotics have drawn great attention recently. A high percentage of the excreted antibiotics remains in an intact form and enters the natural aquatic systems via the effluent and sludge from wastewater treatment plants, hospitals, and livestock farms. These released antibiotics may lead to bacterial resistance proliferation, contamination or adverse impacts on non-target organisms and microbial ecosystems. Therefore, this situation has created a compelling need to develop sensitive on-site detection techniques for monitoring these antibiotics in the environment. However, delicate instrumentation and complex sample pretreatment requirement of conventional analytical techniques such as spectrophotometry, electrophoresis, and chromatography have hindered their practical applications in real time and in situ sensing task. On the other hand, electrochemical techniques have served as sensitive methods for on-site monitoring with low cost, high efficiency, and minimum sample pretreatment necessity. In the present work, an electrochemical sensor for rapid determination of sulfamethoxazole, one of the most widely used antibiotics, has been developed. Functionalized reduced graphene oxide was used to modify the electrodes owing to its high charge mobility, low background noise, and high surface area. The response was optimized in terms of pH, scan mode, and applied potential. Moreover, the modified electrodes showed great selectivity and stability, and thus collectively, renders it a promising sensor toward detecting sulfamethoxazole in the aquatic system.**

Keywords-electrochemical sensor; emerging contaminants; graphene oxide; environmental detection.

I. Introduction

Up to 95% of antibiotics could be excreted in an unchanged state from animals and humans [1]. Throughout the conventional biological wastewater treatment processes, many antibiotics such as β-lactams, sulfonamides, trimethoprim, macrolides, fluoroquinolones, and tetracyclines have been reported to remain in the final effluents and be released to the environment [2-4]. Also, treated-wastewater irrigation in arid regions has caused elevated levels of bacterial antibiotic resistance in both aquatic system and treated-wastewater-irrigated soils [1]. These released antibiotic compounds in discharge or reused wastewater have raised increasing concern, owing to their adverse impact to the aquatic environment or proliferation of resistant strains of bacteria [2]. Sulfonamides, one of the most commonly used antibiotic groups, are used for the treatment of urinary-tract infections, pneumocystis pneumonia, chronic bronchitis, meningococcal meningitis, acute otitis, toxoplasmosis, skin and soft tissue infections [5]. Sulfamethoxazole is a representative sulfonamide antibiotic and frequently found in surface water and groundwater worldwide [6, 7]. Given the wide usage of sulfamethoxazole, its real-time and in-situ detection is of great importance. A variety of analytical techniques, including chromatography, spectrophotometry, and electrophoresis, are time-consuming, expensive and pretreatment-needed. On the other hand, electrochemical techniques, which have fast response, low cost, simplicity for operation, are promising for sulfamethoxazole detection. A few studies have used electrochemical approach for determination sulfamethoxazole [5, 8-10]. Herein, we propose an electrochemical sensor for selective detection of sulfamethoxazole based on modified electrodes with functionalized reduced graphene oxide (RGO), owing to its high charge mobility, low background noise, and high surface area. Methods of sample preparation and characterization of the present work are introduced in Section II. Then we demostrate electrochemical responses of the developed sensors for sulfamethoxazole determination in Section III, and finally, we conclude in Section IV.

II. Materials and Methods

Chemicals of the highest purity available from Sigma Aldrich (Missouri, USA) [11] and Acros Organics (New Jersey, USA) [12], unless stated otherwise, were used without further purification. Aqueous solutions were prepared in water that purified to $\geq$ 18.2 MΩ·cm. The pH adjustment was achieved by adding $HClO_4$ and NaOH solutions. Synthesized graphene oxide and reduced graphene oxide were characterized by UV-Vis measurements (HITACHI U-3900 spectrophotometer). The cyclic voltammetry (CV) measurements were performed on an electrochemical system (CH Instruments). Graphene oxide (GO) was prepared from purified natural graphite by a modified Hummers' method. Functionalized RGO, N-RGO, was prepared by reducing GO via a solvothermal reaction with ammonia solution.

III. Results and Discussion

In the UV-Vis absorption spectra (Figure 1 (a)), the absorption peaks at 230 and 300 nm are assigned to the π-π transition of aromatic C=C bonds and C=O bonds, respectively. After the reduction, the absorption peak was red-shifted to 271 nm, indicating a successful GO reduction, in which the conjugated C=C bonds were restored. The electrochemical oxidation of sulfamethoxazole on the bare and modified electrode surfaces was examined, as shown in Figure 1 (b). The relative ordering of CV current has been determined to be N-RGO > bare electrode > GO. In the presence of sulfamethoxazole (50 μM), a relevant increase in the current was observed for N-RGO, as compared to bare electrode and GO modified electrode (Figure 2), implying an enhanced electrochemical response of the N-RGO modified electrode. This indicates a promising sensing feature of N-RGO toward sulfamethoxazole detection.

IV. Conclusions

In the present work, the characterization and evaluation of functionalized RGO modified electrodes for determination of sulfamethoxazole were performed. The fabricated electrode is promising as an on-site detection tool for point-of-care monitoring of sulfamethoxazole with fast-response, sensitive, and cost-effective characters.

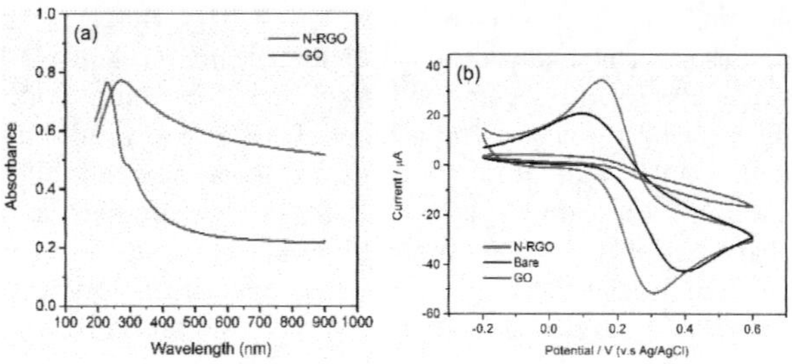

Figure 1. (a) UV-Vis spectra of GO and N-RGO, (b) Cyclic voltammograms of bare electrode, GO, and N-RGO in 0.1 M KCl solution containing 5 mM $[Fe(CN)_6]^{3-}$/ $[Fe(CN)_6]^{4-}$.

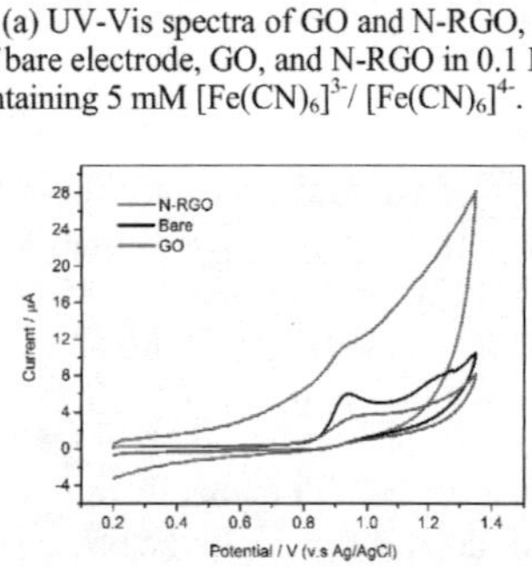

Figure 2. Cyclic voltammograms of bare electrode, GO, and N-RGO in the presence of sulfamethoxazole (50 μM).

References

[1] Y. Negreanu, Z. Pasternak, E. Jurkevitch, and E. Cytryn, "Impact of treated wastewater irrigation on antibiotic resistance in agricultural soils," Environ. Sci. Technol., vol. 46, May. 2012, pp. 4800-4808, doi: 10.1021/es204665b.

[2] N. Le-Minh, S. J. Khan, J. E. Drewes, and R. M. Stuetz, "Fate of antibiotics during municipal water recycling treatment processes," Water Res., vol. 44, Aug. 2010, pp. 4295-4323, doi: 10.1016/j.watres.2010.06.020.

[3] Y. L. Zhang, C. F. Marrs, C. Simon, and C. W. Xi, "Wastewater treatment contributes to selective increase of antibiotic resistance among acinetobacter spp," Sci. Total Environ., vol. 407, Jun. 2009, pp. 3702-3706, doi: 10.1016/j.scitotenv.2009.02.013.

[4] I. Michael, L. Rizzo, C. S. McArdell, C. M. Manaia, C. Merlin, T. Schwartz, C. Dagot, and D. Fatta-Kassinos, "Urban wastewater treatment plants as hotspots for the release of antibiotics in the environment: A review," Water Res., vol. 47, Mar. 2013, pp. 957-995, doi: 10.1016/j.watres.2012.11.027.

[5] M. Meshki, M. Behpour, and S. Masoum, "Application of fe doped ZnO nanorods-based modified sensor for determination of sulfamethoxazole and sulfamethizole using chemometric methods in voltammetric studies," J. Electroanal. Chem., vol. 740, Mar. 2015, pp. 1-7, doi: 10.1016/j.jelechem.2014.12.008.

[6] Q. Q. Zhang, G. G. Ying, C. G. Pan, Y. S. Liu, and J. L. Zhao, "Comprehensive evaluation of antibiotics emission and fate in the river basins of china: Source analysis, multimedia modeling, and linkage to bacterial resistance," Environ. Sci. Technol., vol. 49, Jun. 2015, pp. 6772-6782, doi: 10.1021/acs.est.5b00729.

[7] Y.-C. Lin, W. W.-P. Lai, H.-h. Tung, and A. Y.-C. Lin, "Occurrence of pharmaceuticals, hormones, and perfluorinated compounds in groundwater in taiwan," Environmental Monitoring and Assessment, vol. 187, 2015, pp. 256, doi: 10.1007/s10661-015-4497-3.

[8] L. F. Sgobbi, C. A. Razzino, and S. A. S. Machado, "A disposable electrochemical sensor for simultaneous detection of sulfamethoxazole and trimethoprim antibiotics in urine based on multiwalled nanotubes decorated with prussian blue nanocubes modified screen-printed electrode," Electrochim. Acta, vol. 191, Feb. 2016, pp. 1010-1017, doi: 10.1016/j.electacta.2015.11.151.

[9] H. Chasta, and R. N. Goyal, "A simple and sensitive poly-1,5-diaminonaphthalene modified sensor for the determination of sulfamethoxazole in biological samples," Electroanalysis, vol. 27, May. 2015, pp. 1229-1237, doi: 10.1002/elan.201400688.

[10] I. Cesarino, V. Cesarino, and M. R. V. Lanza, "Carbon nanotubes modified with antimony nanoparticles in a paraffin composite electrode: Simultaneous determination of sulfamethoxazole and trimethoprim," Sens. Actuator B-Chem., vol. 188, Nov. 2013, pp. 1293-1299, doi: 10.1016/j.snb.2013.08.047.

[11] Sigma-Aldrich Co. LLC., https://www.sigmaaldrich.com/united-states.html (accessed July, 2017).

[12] Acros Organics, https://www.fishersci.com/us/en/brands/I9C8LQ1I/acros-organics.html (accessed July 2017).

Smart Vehicle Lighting System in the Visible Range: Vehicle-to-Vehicle Communication

M. A. Vieira, M. Vieira, P. Louro
ADEETC/ISEL/IPL,
R. Conselheiro Emídio Navarro, 1959-007
Lisboa, Portugal,
CTS-UNINOVA
Quinta da Torre, Monte da Caparica, 2829-516,
Caparica, Portugal
email: mv@isel.ipl.pt, mv@isel.pt, plouro@deetc.isel.ipl.pt

P. Vieira
ADEETC/ISEL/IPL,
R. Conselheiro Emídio Navarro, 1959-007
Lisboa, Portugal
Instituto das Telecomunicações
Instituto Superior Técnico, 1049-001,
Lisboa, Portugal,
email: pvieira@deetc.isel.pt

***Abstract*— This paper proposes the use of Visible Light Communication (VLC) for vehicle safety applications, creating a smart vehicle lighting system that combines the functions of illumination and signaling, communications, and positioning. The feasibility of VLC is demonstrated by employing trichromatic Red-Green-Blue (RGB) LEDs as transmitters, since they offer the possibility of Wavelength Division Multiplexing (WDM), which can greatly increase the transmission data rate, when using SiC double p-i-n receivers to encode/decode the information. Each chip, individually, is used to transmit the driving range distance and data information. An on-off code is used to transmit the data. Free space is the transmission medium. The receivers consist of two stacked amorphous a-H:SiC cells. Multiple Input Multiple Output (MIMO) architecture is used. For data transmission, two headlights based on commercially available modulated white RGB-LEDs are used. For data receiving and decoding, three a-SiC:H double pin/pin optical processors symmetrically distributed at the vehicle tail are utilized. The process of accurately encoding and decoding positioning and the design of SiC navigation system are discussed and tested. A visible multilateration method estimates the drive distance range.**

Keywords*- *a-SiC:H technology; LED; Visible Light Communication; Intelligent Transportation System; optical sensor; WDM.

I. INTRODUCTION

Recently, the demand for the solution of road traffic problems such as accidents, congestion and the associated environmental pollution, has significantly increased. By enabling wireless communication among vehicles and between vehicles and infrastructure, the safety and the efficiency of road traffic can be substantially improved. Current solutions, such as intelligent traffic control systems, provide communication infrastructures along the road; vehicular communication and likewise, are research trends under the area of Intelligent Transportation Systems (ITS) [1], [2] and [3].

Several modes of vehicular communications, such as infrastructure-to-vehicle (I2V), vehicle-to-vehicle (V2V) and vehicle-to-infrastructure (V2I) are becoming increasingly popular, boosted by navigation safety requirements [4].

Recently, LED-based optical wireless communication has been also proposed for car to car message delivery. This option turned out to be particularly effective in short range direct communications to explore Line-of-Sight (LoS) and overcome the issues related to the isotropic nature of radio waves. One additional benefit of LEDs is that they can switch to different light intensities at a very fast rate. This functionality has given rise to a novel communication technology (Visible Light Communication - VLC) where LED luminaires can be used for high speed data transfer [5], [6]. In the recent past, we have developed a WDM device that enhances the transmission capacity of optical communications in the visible range. When different visible signals are encoded in the same optical transmission path [7], [8] the device multiplexes the different optical channels, performs different filtering processes (amplification, switching, and wavelength conversion) and finally decodes the encoded signals recovering the transmitted information. This device is used as a receiver. Therefore, by utilizing VLC between vehicles, drivers are given a clearer knowledge of the preceding and nearby vehicles status.

In this paper, a traffic scenario is established. The transmitters and the receivers are characterized. To achieve vehicular communication (V2V) 4 bit string color messages in the visible range and their three parity bits for error control are used to transmit a codeword that is received and decoded by the SiC pinpin devices. Code and parity multiplex/demultiplex (MUX/DEMUX) signals are designed, transmitted and analyzed. The dependence of distance between the transmitter and receiver on the shape and magnitude of the encoded signal is presented. Driving range distance is discussed and tested using the VLC system. The proposed smart vehicle lighting system considers wireless communication, computer based algorithms and smart sensor and optical sources network, which builds a transdisciplinary approach framed in cyber-physical systems.

This paper is organized as follows. In Section I, the introduction is present and in Section II, the system design is explained. Section III reports the encoder/decoder method and in Section IV, the driving distance is analyzed. Finally, in Section V, conclusions are drawn.

II. SYSTEM DESIGN

A. The traffic scenario

White RGB-LEDs using WDM can achieve higher data transfer rates and can also be used for lighting purposes [9]. For data transmission, we propose the use of two headlights based on commercially available modulated white RGB-LEDs. For data receiving and decoding, three a-SiC:H double pin/pin optical processors symmetrically distributed at the vehicle tail are used (see Figure 1).

This VLC system enables the data transmission between vehicles, which is crucial to stack the information concerning the status of the vehicle (e.g., brake, speed, acceleration, engine failure, traffic congestion). To build a one-way VLC system that allows a feedback channel between the leader vehicle and the follower vehicle. The follower vehicle is assumed to be equipped with two headlamps transmitters. They send a codeword message [RGBV: P_R, P_G, P_B] composed of red, green, blue and violet 4-binary bits (four input data bits [R G B V]) and generate three additional parity bits [P_R, P_G, P_B] for easy decoding and error control [10]. The parity bits are SUM bits of the three-bit additions of violet pulsed signal, with two additional bits of RGB. The leader vehicle is assumed to be equipped with three a-SiC pinpin receivers to detect optical messages, as in Figure 1. The spacing of the two transmitters is fixed while their distance to the receivers varies and depends on the speed (v_1, v_2). Both transmitters are oriented towards the receivers.

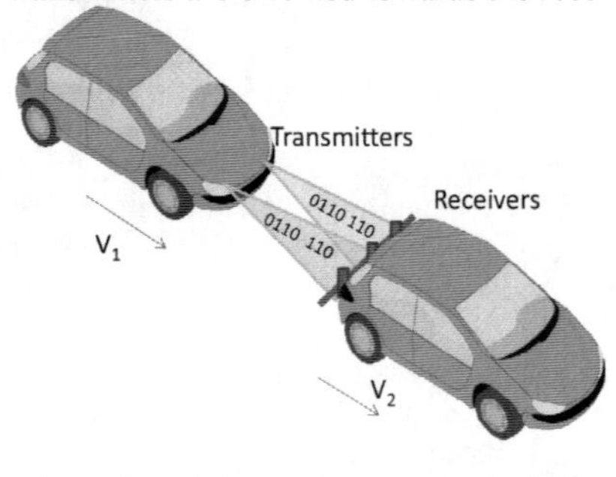

Figure 1. Illustration of the V2V. Use Case: the follower vehicle sends the message that is received by the leader and can be retransmitted for the next car.

In Figure 2, the geometrical relation between the two vehicles (leader vehicle and follower vehicle) and the separating distances (A, B and C) are displayed. Here, the follower vehicle sends the information using the modulated light from the headlamps forming a lighting coverage. The leader vehicle receives and decodes the message in three separated receivers at the tail and compares them. It was assumed that each LED chip sends light only perpendicular to the semiconductor's surface, and a few degrees to the side, which results in a light cone pattern (Figure 2). Three situations are possible: A, the vehicles are at a safety distance and the three sensors receive the same message with the same intensity; B, the vehicles are in a warning distance, they are approaching and the left and the right sensor receive the same message but at the middle sensor the message arrives with double intensity; C the vehicles are too close, in the automatic braking distance, and the same message arrives to the left and to the right sensor and no message is read out by the middle one. Based on that, the driving range distance is calculated and a warning is sent to the driver or eventually activates the automatic braking system.

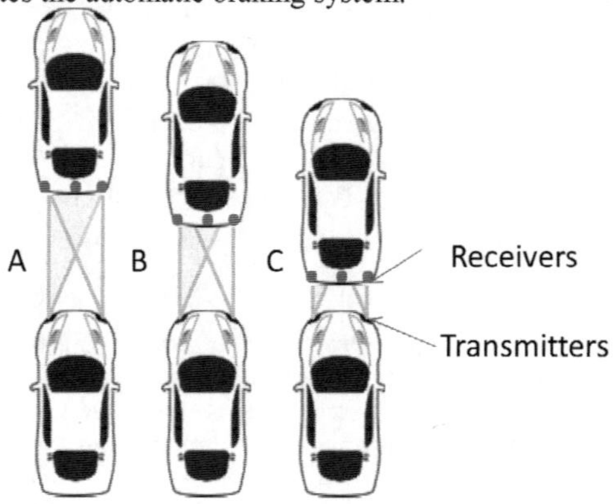

Figure 2. Driving range distance showing the inter-vehicle distance decreasing as total photocurrent on the three receivers changes.

B. Transmitters

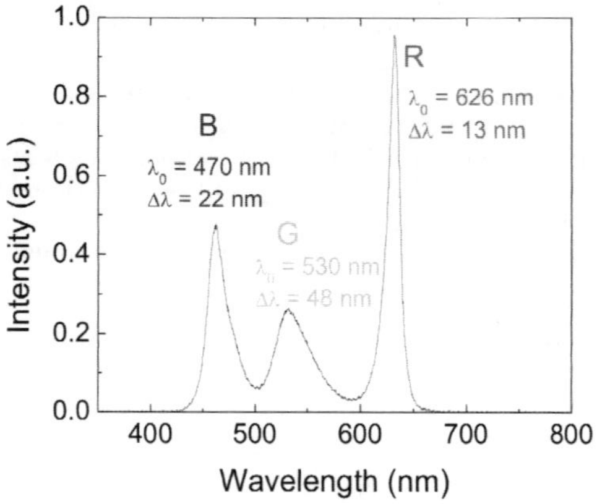

Figure 3. Normalized emission spectra for the white RGB-LED.

The usage of trichromatic RGB-LEDs as transmitters offers the possibility of WDM which can greatly increase the transmission data rate. For data transmission, we use commercially available violet and white RGB-LEDs whose spectra is displayed in Figure 3.

The output spectra of the white LED contains three peaks assigned to the colors red, green and blue that mixed together provide the white perception to the eye. They are used for lighting purposes and when modulated, to transmit data. Each chip, in the trichromatic LED, can be switched *on* and *off* individually for a desired bit sequence [R G B]. An extra violet modulated LED [V] was added to increase data transmission and to generate parity bits [11] that allow error control [12].

For data transmission an on-off keying (OOK) code was used. In Figure 4, an example of the digital signals (codeword) used to drive the LEDs is displayed. All the sixteen (2^4) *on/off* possible combinations of the 4 input channels (RGBV) are reported as well the corresponding parity bits. The arrow sets the seven bit [1111:111] codeword.

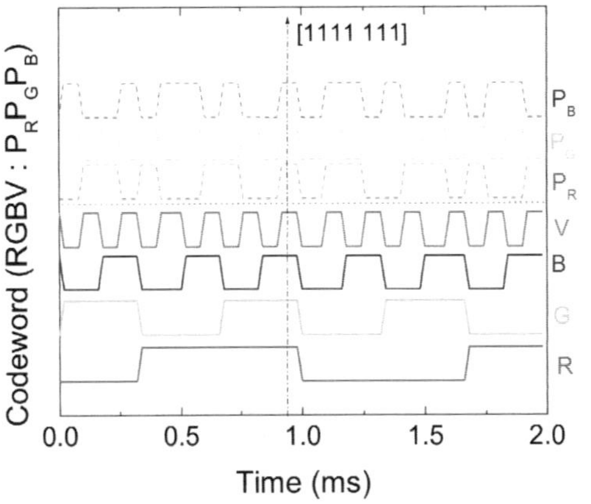

Figure 4. Representation of the original encoded message [R G B V; P_R P_G P_B].

Here, the Hamming (7,4) code [11] encodes the 4 bits (four input channels, RGBV) of data into 7 bits by adding 3 parity bits. The encoder takes four input data bits [R G B V] to which corresponds one of the possible 16 combinations and generates three additional parity bits, i.e., the parity bits are SUM bits of the three-bit additions of violet pulsed signal with two additional bits of RGB [12] and are given by:

$$P_R\text{-(VRB)} = V \oplus R \oplus B \quad (1)$$
$$P_G\text{-(VRG)} = V \oplus R \oplus G \quad (2)$$
$$P_B\text{-(VGB)} = V \oplus G \oplus B \quad (3)$$

Moreover, the seven-bit codeword at the output of the encoder will be in a format, with the data and the parity bits [R G B V ; P_R P_G P_B] separated.

C. Receiver

The optoelectronic sensor is a double pin heterostructure produced by Plasma Enhanced Chemical Vapour Deposition (PECVD) sandwiched between two transparent conductive contacts (TCO). The device configuration is shown in Figure 5. In the stacked structure, p-i'(a-SiC:H)-n/p-i(a-Si:H)-n, the intrinsic layer of the front p-i-n photodiode in made of a-SiC:H while the back intrinsic layer is based on a-Si:H. The deposition conditions and optoelectronic characterization of the single layers and device as well as their optimization were described in [8] and [13]. Both front and back diodes act as optical filters confining, respectively, the optical carriers produced by the blue and red photons, while the optical carriers generated by the green photons are absorbed across both.

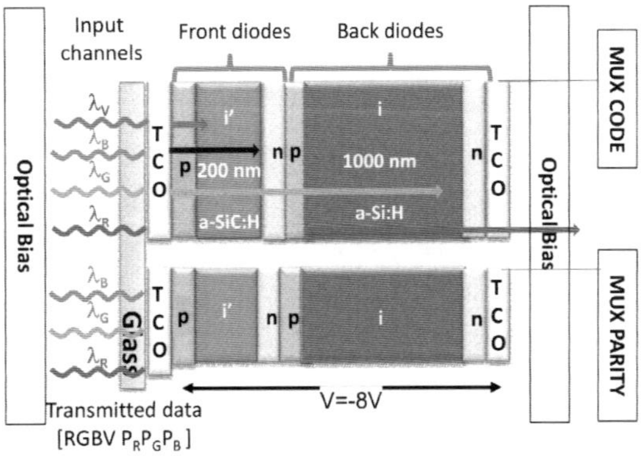

Figure 5. Receiver configuration and operation.

A polychromatic mixture of red, green, blue and violet; $\lambda_{R,G,B,V}$; pulsed communication channels (input channels; transmitted data) are combined together, each one with a specific bit sequence and absorbed according to their wavelengths (see arrow magnitudes in Figure 5). The combined optical signal (multiplexed signal; received data) is analyzed by reading out the generated photocurrent under negative applied voltage (-8V), with and without 390 nm background lighting, applied either from front or back sides [14]. The RGB-LEDs are used together for illumination purposes and individually to transmit the channel location and data information.

D. Optical filter

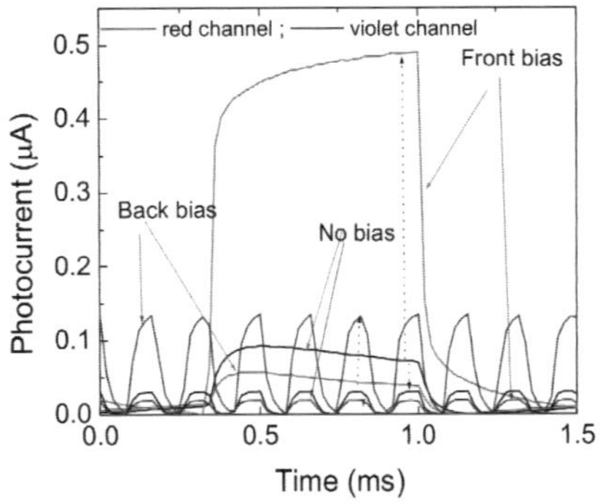

Figure 6. Red and violet signals without (No bias) and under front (Front bias) and back (Back bias) irradiation

Four monochromatic input channels illuminated the device separately (transmitted data) or combined (MUX signal) with 12 kbps transmission rate. The generated photocurrent was measured. For the red and violet channels, the photocurrents without optical bias (no bias) and under front and back lighting are displayed in Figure 6. Results show that front irradiation enhances the red signal and decreases the violet, while back irradiation has the opposite effect (see arrows in the figure).

The gathered data confirms that the optical gain, under irradiation, depends on the irradiated side and on the incoming wavelength acting as an active filter for the input channels [14]. Under front irradiation, the long wavelength channels are enhanced and the short wavelength channels quenched while the opposite occurs under back irradiation.

III. ENCODER /DECODER

The algorithm to decode the information is relatively straightforward and the knowledge of the background acting as selector that chooses one or more of the 2^n sublevels (with n being the number of transmitted channels) and their n-bit binary code makes the communication reliable [15].

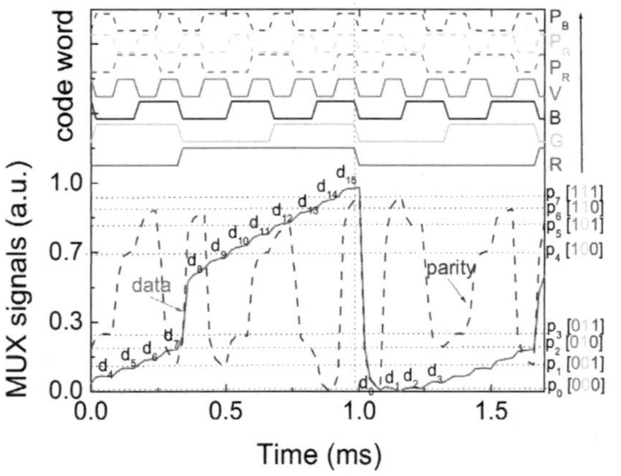

Figure 7. Code and parity MUX/DEMUX signals under 390 nm front irradiation. On the top the transmitted channels [R G B V : P_R P_G P_B] are decoded.

In Figure 7, the received data, i.e., the MUX code signal, due to the combination of four (400 nm, 470 nm, 530 nm, 626 nm) input channels and the correspondent parity bits are displayed under front irradiation. The solid lines show the MUX signal that arises from the transmission of the four (R, G, B, V) wavelength channels. The dashed line marks the synchronized parity MUX signal transmitted with the data code. Due to the different optical gains, the colors red, green and blue were assigned respectively to the transmission of P_R, P_G and P_B. The sixteen ordered levels (d_0-d_{15}) of the data MUX signal are pointed out at the correspondent levels, and the ordered eight levels (p_0-p_7) ascribed to the parity bits are displayed as horizontal dotted lines. On the right hand side of Figure 7, the correspondence between the parity levels and the parity bits is shown. In the top, the decoded seven bit word [R,G,B,V, P_R, P_G, P_B] of the transmitted inputs is displayed. Results show that each of the 2^n possible *on/off* states corresponds to a well-defined level. In Figure 7, all the *on/off* states are possible hence, 2^4 ordered levels are detected (d_0-d_{15}) and correspond to all the possible combinations of the *on/off* states. Under front irradiation, each of those n channels is enhanced or quenched differently, resulting in an increase of red/green magnitude and a decrease on the blue/violet magnitude. In the sequence, by assigning each output level to a n digit binary code (weighted by the optical gain of the each channel), the signal can be decoded. A maximum transmission rate capability of 30 kbps was achieved in a four channel transmission.

The proximity of the magnitude of consecutive levels (Figure 7) causes occasional errors in the decoded information that is corrected using the parity bits. For instance, levels d_1, d_2, and d_3 have similar magnitude and can be confused when reading a word message, however their parity levels, respectively, p_7, p_5 and p_2, are quite different. The parity of the word is checked after reading the word. The word is accepted if the parity of the bits read out is correct. If the parity of the bits is incorrect, an error is detected and should be corrected [12].

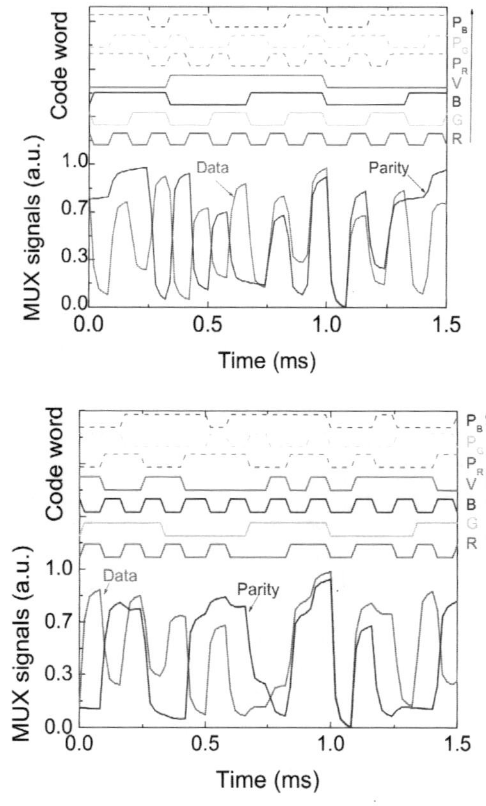

Figure 8. Two different code and parity MUX/DEMUX signals under 390 nm front irradiation. On the top the transmitted channels are decoded.

To automate the process of recovering the original transmitted data, an enhanced algorithm was developed. The transmitted information is decoded by comparing both the signal from the code and parity MUX levels under front irradiation, as shown in Figure 7. The decoding algorithm is based on a proximity search [16]. The vector components are determined by the signal currents I_1 and I_2, where I_1 (d levels) and I_2 (p levels) are the currents measured simultaneously, under front optical bias, for the 4-bit codeword (RGBV) and for the 3-bit parity [P_R, P_G P_B]. The result is then compared with all vectors obtained from a calibration sequence (see Figure 7) where each code level, d(0-31), is assigned the correspondent parity level, p(0-15). The color bits of the nearest calibration point are assigned to the time slot. An Euclidean metric is applied to measure the distances. We have tested the algorithm with different random sequences of the channels and we have recovered the original color bits, as shown in the top of Figure 8.

IV. DRIVING DISTANCE

Lumens of light emitted by an LED depend on the current passing through the LED. For the luminous path loss (L_L), the conversion of the current flowing through the LED to lumens is given by [17].

$$L_L = \frac{1}{D^2} \times (\text{emitted power of the LED}) \quad (4)$$

where D is the distance between the LED and the receiver. The light generated by an LED is directly proportional to the forward current flowing through the device. In order to analyze the influence of white LED brightness (headlight-like) on the sensor response, the drive current applied to each chip was changed, keeping all the same level for equal white perception. The intensity of the violet LED was kept constant at 30 mA. Each chip was modulated as shown on the top of Figure 7. In Figure 9a, the MUX signal is displayed for different applied drive currents. In Figure 9b, the [1111] code level magnitudes, d_{15}, (arrow in Figure 9a) as a function of the drive current is displayed. The dotted curve shows the trend of the photocurrent with the relative distance from the receiver to the transmitter. Experimental results show that as the drive current increases, the intensity of the MUX signal also increases, but its shape remains the same. The sixteen levels, each one ascribed to an *on/off* possible state, are all detected allowing at the receiver the demultiplexing operation and the recovery of the transmitted information. Figure 9b, also shows that the code levels magnitude increases in a fast rate up to driving currents around 10 mA and then the photocurrent keeps increasing with the driving current but at a slow rate. Here, if we plot the photocurrent as a function of the one over the square of the driving current (dot plot) we can map the relative distances between the receiver and the transmitter. If the irradiance is calibrated for a known separation between the transmitter and the receiver, the irradiance at a given distance can be calculated using the inverse square law, hence, as the photocurrent increases the relative distance decreases exponentially. Three regions are detected: region A where the photocurrent decreases slowly with the distance; region B where its decrease is gradual; and region C, where a fast decrease occurs. These three regions can be directly correlated with the inter-vehicle driving distance from Figure 2, after a calibration. So, by measuring the photocurrent at fixed code level it enables the prediction of the distance between vehicles and provides information to warn the driver about the safety distance (Figure 2). This warning can be transmitted through one of the four available channels.

The VLC system compares the three received messages and infers the driving distance between the leader and the follower vehicles by reading the magnitude of the higher level (dash dot arrow in the figure) in the middle sensor. A warning message should be sent if the distance is lower than the safety distance.

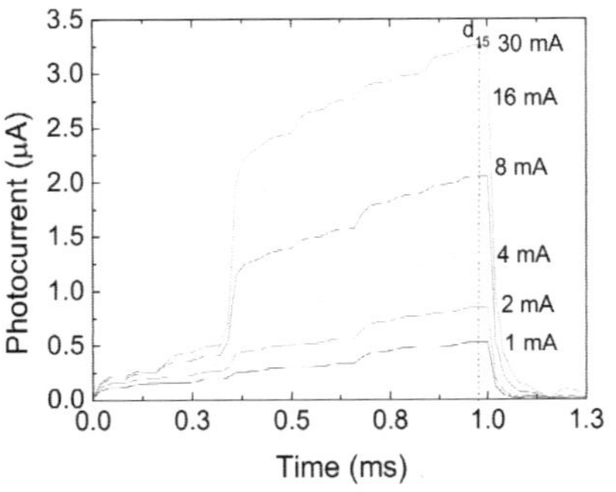

a)

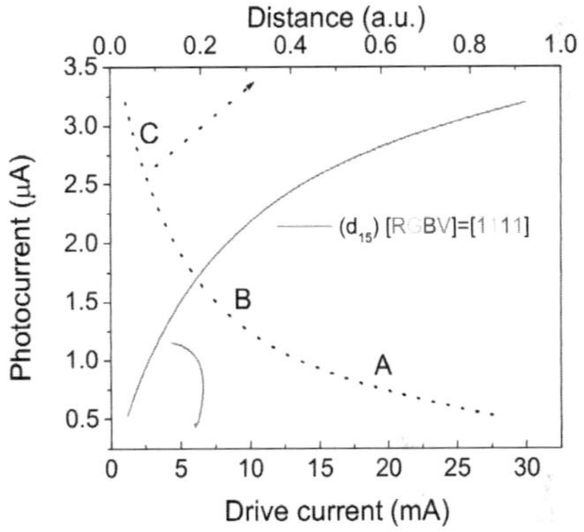

b)

Figure 9. a) MUX signal under different drive currents applied to the chips of the trichromatic LED. b) [1111] code level magnitude as a function of the drive current applied to the RGB chips.

We have simulated the scenario B (Figure 2). The drive current applied to the two LEDs (headlamps-like) was the same and adjusted in order to have the same lighting conditions of this region. Here, the right and the left sensor receive the same message and the one in the middle receives the overlap of both. We have applied to the RGB LED a current of the order of 4 mA and 30 mA to the violet one. In Figure 10, the received MUX signals on the right and left sensors or in the middle one are displayed. The solid lines are ascribed to the MUX data word and the dotted lines to the correspondent parity MUX. The same 4:3 binary information (on the top of the figure) was sent simultaneously by both LEDs.

As expected, the shape of both code and parity MUX signals are the same but the intensity in the middle sensor (≅1 µA) is almost twice of the one received in the two others (≅0.5 µA).

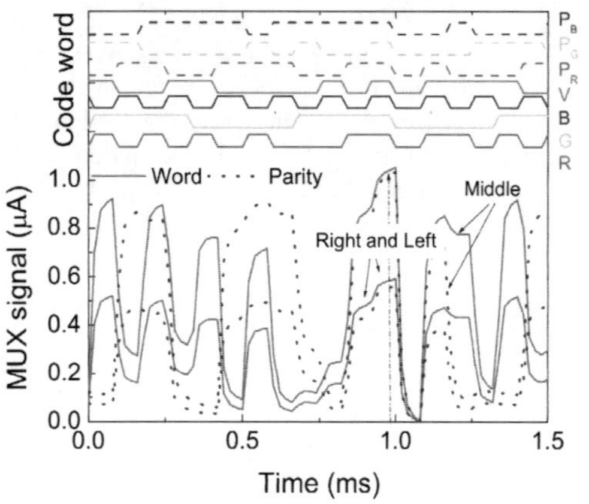

Figure 10. MUX (solid line) and parity (dotted line) signals acquired by the right, the left and the middle receivers.

Note that, when applying to each chip a forward current of the order of 4 mA, the magnitude of the data MUX signal is ≅1 μA (Figure 9b) to which corresponds a relative distance around 0.4 that leads to region B.

V. CONCLUSION

In this paper, a VLC system, for vehicle safety applications, was presented. The system is composed of a VLC transmitter that modulates the light produced by white RGB-LEDs, and by VLC receivers based on photosensitive elements (a-SiC:H pinpin photodiodes) that code and decode the modulated signals. A scenario for the VLC system was tested and analyzed and a traffic scenario was simulated. By reading out in the receivers the magnitude of the multiplexed signal, it was possible, concurrently, to decode a transmitted message and to infer the driving distance between the transmitter and the receiver.

ACKNOWLEDGEMENTS

This work was sponsored by FCT – Fundação para a Ciência e a Tecnologia, within the Research Unit CTS – Center of Technology and systems, reference UID/EEA/00066/2013 and by the IPL project VLC_MIMO, 2016.

REFERENCES

[1] N. Kumar, N. Lourenço, D. Terra, L. N. Alves, and R. L. Aguiar, "Visible Light Communications in intelligent transportation systems", IEEE Intelligent Vehicles Symposium, pp.748-753, 2012.

[2] C. Liu, B. Sadeghi, and E. W. Knightly, "Enabling vehicular visible light communication (V2LC) networks," Proceedings of the Eighth ACM international workshop on Vehicular inter-networking (VANET '11), ACM, New York, NY, USA, pp. 41-50, 2011.

[3] P. Papadimitratos, A. La Fortelle, K. Evenssen, R. Brignolo, and S. Cosenza, "Vehicular communication systems: Enabling technologies, applications, and future outlook on intelligent transportation" Communications Magazine, IEEE , vol.47, no.11, pp. 84-95, November 2009.

[4] S. Yousefi, E. Altman, R. El-Azouzi, and Fathy, M., "Analytical model for connectivity in vehicular Ad Hoc networks", IEEE Transactions on Vehicular Technology, vol. 57, pp. 3341-3356, 2008.

[5] S. Schmid, G. Corbellini, S. Mangold , and T. R. Gross, "An LED-to-LED Visible Light Communication system with software-based synchronization," in 2012 IEEE Globecom Workshops, pp. 1264–1268, 2012.

[6] D. O'Brien, H. L. Minh, L. Zeng, G. Faulkner, K. Lee, D. Jung, Y. Oh, and E. T. Won, "Indoor visible light communications: challenges and prospects," Proc. SPIE 7091, 709106, 2008.

[7] M. Vieira, P. Louro, M. Fernandes, M. A. Vieira, A. Fantoni and J. Costa, "Three transducers embedded into one single SiC photodetector: LSP direct image sensor, optical amplifier and Demux device" Advances in Photodiodes InTech, Chap.19, pp.403-425, 2011.

[8] M. A. Vieira, P. Louro, M. Vieira, A. Fantoni, and A. Steiger-Garção, "Light-activated amplification in Si-C tandem devices: A capacitive active filter model" IEEE Sensor Jornal, 12, no. 6, pp. 1755-1762, 2012.

[9] I. L. Azevedo, M. G. Morgan, and F. Morgan, "The transition to solid-state lighting," Proceedings of the IEEE , vol.97, no.3, pp. 481-510, March 2009.

[10] M. A. Vieira, M. Vieira, P. Louro, V. Silva, "Error detection on a spectral data using an optical processor based on a-SiC technology" Sensors & Transducers, Vol. 184, Issue 1, January 2015, pp. 116-122. © 2015 by IFSA Publishing, S. L., 2015.

[11] R. W. Hamming, ''Error detecting and error correcting codes'', Bell Syst. Tech. J. 29, pp.147–160 , 1960.

[12] M. A. Vieira, M. Vieira, V. Silva, P. Louro, and J. Costa, "Optical signal processing for data error detection and correction using a-SiCH technology" Phys. Status Solidi C 12, No. 12, pp. 1393–1400, 2015.

[13] Vieira, M., Louro, P., Fernandes, M., Vieira, M. A., Fantoni, A., and Costa J., "Three transducers embedded into one single SiC photodetector: LSP direct image sensor, optical amplifier and Demux device", Advances in Photodiodes, InTech, Chap.19, 403-425 (2011).

[14] Vieira, M., Vieira, M.A., Louro, P., Costa, J., Fernandes, M., Fantoni, A., and Barata, M., "Multilayer architectures based on a-SiC:H material; Tunable wavelength filters in optical processing devices" J. Nanosci. Nanotechnol., Vol 11, no.6, 5299-5304 (2011).

[15] M. A. Vieira, M. Vieira, V. Silva, P. Louro, and M. Barata, "Optoelectronic logic functions using optical bias controlled SiC multilayer devices". MRS Proceedings, 1536, pp. 91-96, 2013.

[16]M. A. Vieira, M. Vieira, P. Louro, V.Silva, J. Costa, and A. Fantoni, "SiC multilayer structures as light controlled photonic active filters" Plasmonics 8 (1), pp. 63-70, 2013.

[17] I. Raza, S. Jabeen, S. R. Chaudhry, S. A. Hussain, M. S. Bhatti, M. H. Raza, "Optical wireless channel characterization for indoor Visible Light Communication", Indian Journal of Science and Technology, Vol 8 (22), 2015.

Aircraft Detection at Short Distances by GPS FSR System

Christo Kabakchiev
Sofia University
Sofia, Bulgaria
e-mail: ckabakchievr@fmi.uni-sofia.bg

Ivan Garvanov
ULSIT
Sofia, Bulgaria
e-mail: i.garvanov@unibit.bg

Vera Behar
IICT-BAS
Sofia, Bulgaria
e-mail: vera.behar@yahoo.com

Dorina Kabakchieva
UNWE
Sofia, Bulgaria
e-mail: dkabakchieva@unwe.bg

Abstract—**The paper considers the concept of a Global Position System (GPS) shadow Forward-Scatter Radar (FSR) for detection of air targets at short distances. This paper discusses the experimental results obtained after processing the GPS signals received near the airport in Sofia, Bulgaria. This research aims to demonstrate the ability to automatically detect low-flying aircrafts by a Forward Scattering GPS system. The other goal of this article is to study and estimate different types of GPS shadows created by aircrafts of different sizes and shapes.**

Keywords- Forward scattering radar (FSR); radio shadow.

I. Introduction

In recent years, passive radar systems where GPS satellites are used as transmitters have become increasingly popular as an alternative to traditional radar systems. The GPS Forward Scatter Radar (GPS FSR) is a specific case of FSR, where GPS satellites are exploited as 'transmitters of opportunity'. In [1], [2], [3], [4] and [5], the authors consider the possibility of detecting air targets in bistatic and forward scatter radar, which exploit GPS satellites as transmitters. A possible algorithm for air target detection using GPS L5-based FSR system is described in [6], and the detection probability characteristics are analytically calculated in [7] for low-flying and poorly maneuverable air targets in the urban interference environment. In [6] and [7], the authors have discussed the potential to increase the Signal-to-Noise Ratio (SNR) to detect aircrafts with GPS L5-based FSR system.

Papers [5], [6], [7] and [8] are devoted to experimental measurements made by using the GPS L1-based FSR system and the Software-Defined GPS receiver, developed by the Aerospace Department at the University of Colorado [9], allowing to observe the geometric shadows (signal blocking) of ground objects of different sizes, mobile and stationary.

Our hypothesis was that, since there is a very weak signal on the surface of the Earth from a GPS L1-based FSR system, in order to register the radio shadow of some object, the object size must be large, and the distance from the receiver to the object must be small.

The purpose of our experiments was to clarify the real possibilities of the proposed system for recording radio shadows created by different objects - depending on the object's size, distance from the receiver to objects, speed of objects, and satellite constellation at the time of recording. Our GPS L1-based FSR system contained a Universal Serial Bus USB-based recording system with a small commercial GPS antenna, which recorded the GPS data flow and stored it as binary files in our computer, and a Software-Defined GPS receiver to process the recorded data in MATLAB [9]. The Software-Defined GPS receiver contains the Acquisition block to identify satellites, and the Code & Carrier Tracking block to form the navigation message. Next, the obtained navigation message was integrated within hundreds milliseconds in order to form the radio shadow of the object and the integrated message was used for further detection of the object based on its radio shadow. During the experiments, the choice of satellites to observe the deepest shadow from the object, the estimation of the type and parameters of radio shadows, were all carried out manually by the operator; they were not automated.

The purpose of this article is to explore different types of GPS shadows created by aircrafts of different sizes and shapes. This knowledge is necessary to extract the characteristic parameters of the radio shadows, which can be used for the further classification of different types of aircrafts.

The originality of the research is that we propose to use additional information derived from radio shadows of different aircrafts in order to improve the detection of low-flying aircrafts. The innovation is to develop new secondary applications of GPS technology.

The rest of the paper is structured as follows. Section 2 describes the principle of the diffraction in forward scattering radar system. The algorithm for signal processing is presented in Section 3. Section 4 discusses the experimental scenario and the experimental results. Finally, Section 5 draws conclusions based on the obtained results.

II. Diffraction in Forward Scattering Radar

The forward scattering radar technology exploits the phenomenon of diffraction of electromagnetic waves in order to detect targets. The diffraction is observed when the wavelength of electromagnetic waves, incident on the target, is much less than the size of the target.

If the distance from the receiver to the target (R_t) is comparable to the size of the object (D), then the target creates the "geometric shadow" of electromagnetic waves incident on the target. In the zone of "geometric shadow", act the laws of geometrical optics, i.e., electromagnetic waves spread straightforward. In that zone, the distance from the transmitter to the target meets the inequality R << D2/λ where λ is the wavelength. In the near diffraction zone, i.e., Fresnel zone, the diffracted electromagnetic waves mutually interfere, and the approximate inequality R ≤ D2/λ holds for the distance between the receiver and the target. In the far zone of diffraction, i.e. Fraunhofer zone, the distances from the transmitter to the target and from the target to the receiver are much larger than the size of the target. In this area, the inequality R >> D2/λ holds. The diffraction of light passed through the circular aperture is shown in Figure 1.

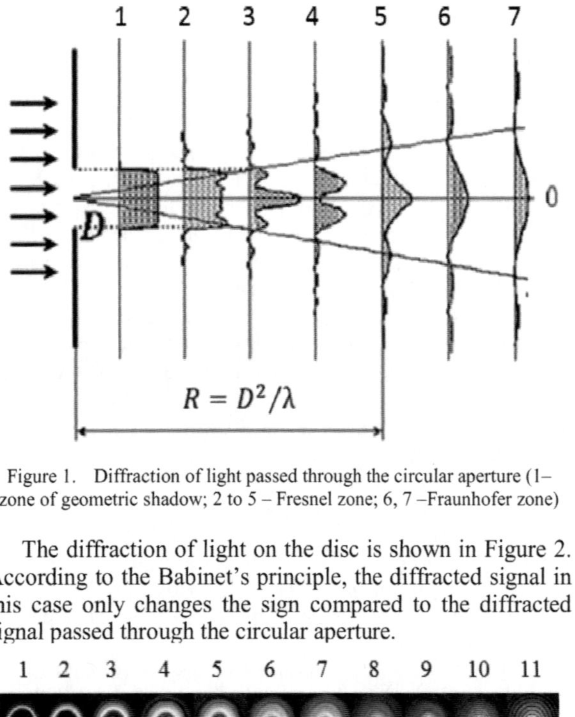

Figure 1. Diffraction of light passed through the circular aperture (1– zone of geometric shadow; 2 to 5 – Fresnel zone; 6, 7 –Fraunhofer zone)

The diffraction of light on the disc is shown in Figure 2. According to the Babinet's principle, the diffracted signal in this case only changes the sign compared to the diffracted signal passed through the circular aperture.

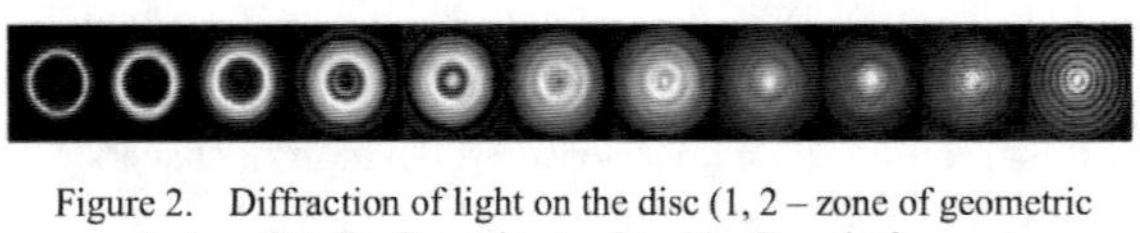

Figure 2. Diffraction of light on the disc (1, 2 – zone of geometric shadow; 3 to 7 – Fresnel zone; 8 to 11 – Fraunhofer zone)

The FSR technology actively exploits the diffraction of the transmitted electromagnetic waves in the far zone of Fraunhofer when the target moves near the baseline "receiver – transmitter" and far from the receiver. In that case, the Forward Scatter (FS) effect is observed, the most attractive feature of which is the drastic increase in the forward scattering radar cross-section, and, therefore, the strong increase of Signal-to-Noise Ratio (SNR) of the received signal.

This paper considers the case when a target fully blocks the signal from the GPS satellite (geometric shadow), Figure 3. This way, the formed GPS radio shadow can be used for target detection, estimation and classification.

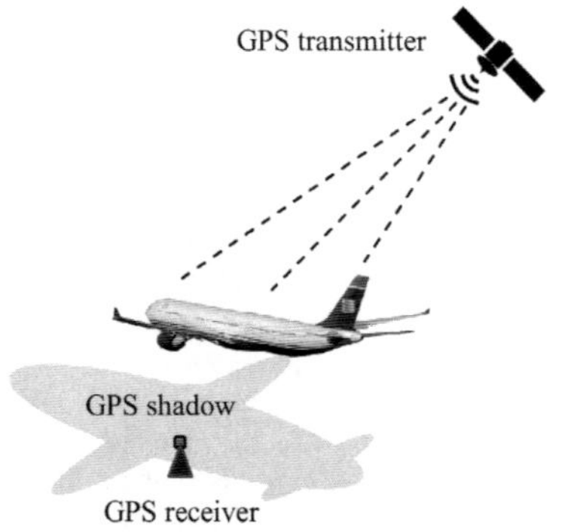

Figure 3. FS GPS Shadow

III. Signal Processing

The use of GPS signals as a passive radar system is becoming increasingly popular as an alternative to radar systems. The general block-scheme for target radio shadow detection using a Software-Defined GPS receiver [3] is shown in Figure 4.

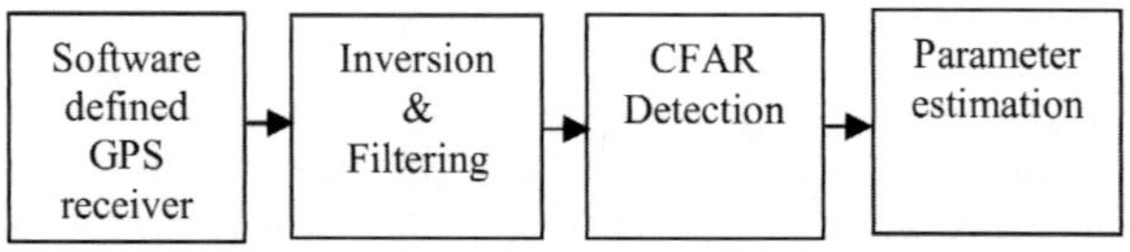

Figure 4. Block-scheme of signal processing

According to Figure 4, in the software-defined GPS receiver, the message is obtained in result of execution of a set of program files for acquisition and tracking, presented in [5]. The message is further inverted as follows:

$$y = [(x - \max(x)]^2 \text{, where } x = abs(I_P) \quad (1)$$

where I_p is the component at the output of the Code & Carrier tracking block, x is the absolute value of I_p, y is the inverted signal x.

The SNR of the signal y is further improved by filtering using the Jumping Average Filter. The Neyman–Pearson algorithm for signal detection can be used for testing a simple hypothesis H_1 (target is present) against a simple alternative H_0 (target is absent):

$$\begin{aligned} H_1 &: if \max\{y_f(n)\} \geq T_{fa} \cdot \sum_{l=1}^{L} y_f'(l) \\ H_0 &: \qquad otherwise \end{aligned} \quad (2)$$

where $y_f'(l)$ is the filtered signal within the reference window of size L needed for power noise estimation. The scale factor T_{fa} is determined in accordance with the probability of false alarm P_{fa}, which should be maintained by the detection algorithm.

The registered GPS radio shadows are characterized by the following parameters:

1) The length of a target shadow, obtained by the FS GPS system can be approximately related to the physical size of the object. The length of the target shadow (*dT*) in seconds is estimated as:

$$dT = T_2 - T_1 \tag{3}$$

where T_1 and T_2 are the beginning and the end of the target shadow in the time domain, which are estimated manually by the operator when processing the experimental records of the target shadow in MATLAB.

2) The peak signal-to-noise ratio (SNR_{peak}) is estimated as the difference between the average noise power in dB and minimal value of the radio shadow in dB, found in the interval $[T_1, T_2]$.

$$SNR_{peak}[dB] = mean(P_n) - \min(P_s) \tag{4}$$

In (4), P_n is the noise power in dB and P_s is the power of the target shadow in dB.

IV. EXPERIMENTAL RESULTS

In this experimental study, the GPS L1-based recording system (1575.42 GHz) consists of two types of GPS receivers and a GNS 5490 ADS-B receiver for verification of measurements (Figure 5). The first GPS receiver (Antaris AEK-4R) is used to determine the location of the satellites over the horizon, while the other software GPS recording system (GNSS_SDR) is used to record and store GPS signals from different targets.

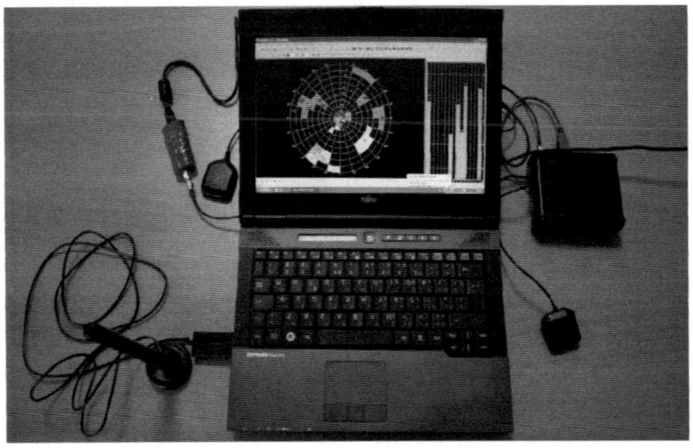

Figure 5. Experimental equipment

The GPS receiver GNSS_SDR was proposed and developed in the Aerospace Department of the Colorado University, USA [9]. This recording system receives and records the GPS data flow using a small commercial GPS antenna and an USB-based device. The recorded GPS signals are saved as binary files in the computer memory. The position of the satellites at the time of the experiment obtained from the GPS receiver "Antaris AEK-4R" is shown in Figure 6.

In our experiment, only signals from visible satellites that are located close to the line "target-receiver" at high elevation angles, are recorded for further processing. The air target crosses the baseline "satellite-receiver" and forms GPS geometric shadow, (falling of the received signal) which is observed as a deep "hole" in the received signal.

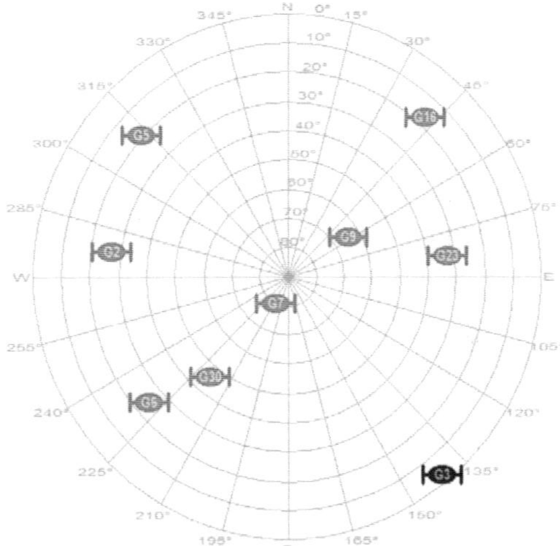

Figure 6. Satellite constellation during the experiment

The two recording systems use the same GPS antennas mounted on the roof of a car, which was stopped 900 meters from the start of the runway of the Sofia airport (Figure 7). During the experiment, the length of the airplanes is about 30-40 m and the distance from the airplane to the receiver is about 80 m.

Figure 7. Receiver scenarios

During the experiment, airplanes that take off from the west fly over the GPS receiver. The visible satellites shown in Figure 6 are: 2, 5, 6, 7, 9, 16, 23, and 30. The filtered signals from all visible satellites are shown in Figure 8. It can be seen that the signal from satellite 7 was blocked by the airplane.

As shown on Figure 8, the deepest "hole" in the signal strength is created by the airplane in case of the satellite 7.

The detection sensitivity depends on the satellite position. The detection probability is a function of the signal-to-noise ratio. In our case, the highest signal to noise ratio is achieved when the air target is located near the baseline "satellite-receiver", which means that the bistatic angle is close to 180 degrees.

Assessing the shadow parameters of two types of aircraft, it was found that the parameters were very sensitive to the geometry of the experiment. The position of the satellite is very important. The biggest shadow comes from the satellites located 90 degrees above the horizon. When using the same GPS satellites for detecting an aircraft, it was found that the distance from the airplane to the receiver strong influenced over the GPS shadow.

After the preliminary analysis of data, the filtered data has been statistically processed in order to calculate the statistical parameters of all shadow parameters. The mathematical expectation and the standard deviation of all measured parameters have been calculated for each aircraft (Table 1). The goal of this statistical processing is to check the possibility of using the resulting parameters for classification of targets by means of a statistical approach.

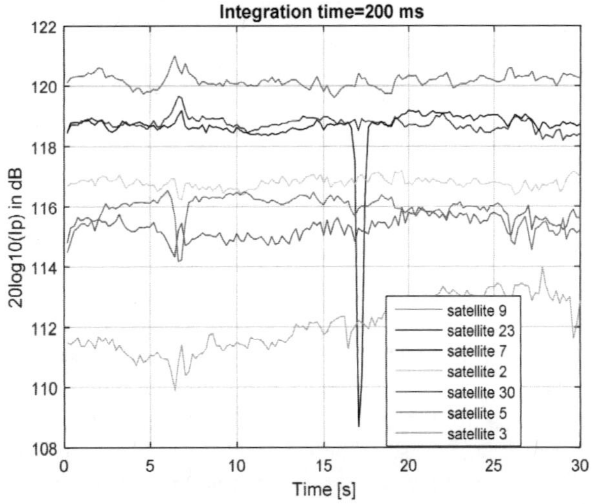

Figure 8. Filtered signals from all visible satellites

The duration of the target shadow (dT) in seconds is estimated as the difference between the beginning and the end of the target shadow in the time domain. The peak signal-to-noise ratio (SNRpeak) is estimated as the difference between the average noise power in dB and the minimal value of the GPS shadow in dB.

TABLE I. MATHEMATICAL EXPECTATION AND STANDARD DEVIATION OF SHADOW PARAMETERS FOR A320 AND ERJ-175

Targets	**Length/ Height (m)**	**Estimation**	***dT* [s]**	***SNR peak* [dB]**
Airbus A320	37.57/ 34.1	**Mean**	2.75	11.33
		STD	0.32	3.91
Embraer ERJ-175	31.68/ 26	**Mean**	2.29	10.12
		STD	0.52	5.34

In Table 1, the results are obtained by statistical processing of 7 records for Airbus A320 and 5 records for Embraer ERJ-175. The geometry of the scenarios was constant in all experiments for correct comparison of the obtained results. All experiments were conducted when the airplanes were taking off, the flying speed was about 300 km/h and the distance from the airplane to the receiver was about 80 m.

V. CONCLUSION

The purpose of the article was to demonstrate the ability to automatically detect of low-flying aircrafts by Forward Scattering GPS system. The other goal of this article was to study and estimate different types of GPS shadows created by aircrafts of different sizes and shapes. The recordings were made both with commercial and with non-professional equipment. The topology of the experiments was the same as that used in the FSR systems. The statistical processing of the resulting estimates of GPS shadow parameters shows that the selected aircrafts create GPS radio shadows with different parameters. From the results, it is evident that we can apply a statistical approach for the classification of aircrafts from their radio shadows. The quality of the classification depends on the size and shape of targets.

The proposed approach and results can be used in various systems for security and surveillance facilities. In addition, the proposed technology can be used to create a passive GPS radar network for detection of air targets based on their GPS radio shadows. The advantage of the proposed GPS FSR system is that it is cheap and costs less than $ 1,000. It is also a passive system using signals from available GPS satellites that cover the entire globe with a signal. Thus, the proposed FSR system can be used around the world.

ACKNOWLEDGMENT

This work was supported by Bulgarian Science Foundation, the project DFNI-T 02/3/2014.

REFERENCES

[1] E. Glennon, A. Dempster and C.Rizos, "Feasibility of air target detection using GPS as a bistatic radar", *Journal of Global Positioning Systems*, vol.5, №1-2, pp. 119-126, 2006.

[2] M. Clarizia, P. Braca, C. Ruf and P. Willett, "Target Detection Using GPS signals of opportunity", *18th International Conference on Information Fusion*, pp. 1429-1436, 2015.

[3] V. Koch and R. Westphal, "New approach to a multistatic passive radar sensor for air/space defense", *IEEE AES Systems Magazine*, pp. 24-32, 1995.

[4] I. Suberviola, I. Mayordome and J. Mendizabal, "Experimental results of air target detection with GPS forward scattering radar", *IEEE Geoscience and Remote Sensing Letters*, vol. 9, № 1, pp. 47-51, 2012.

[5] I. Garvanov, C. Kabakchiev, V. Behar and P. Daskalov, "Air target detection with a GPS forward-scattering radar", *19th International Symposium on Electrical Apparatus and Technologies (SIELA)*, Burgas, Bulgaria, pp.1-4, 2016.

[6] V. Behar and C. Kabakchiev, "Detectability of Air Target Detection using Bistatic Radar Based on GPS L5 Signals", *12th International Radar Symposium*, Leipzig, Germany, pp. 212-217, 2011.

[7] V. Behar, C. Kabakchiev and H. Rohling, "Air Target Detection Using Navigation Receivers Based on GPS L5 Signals", *ION GNSS*, Portland OR, pp. 333-337, 2011.

[8] L. Changjiang, H. Cheng, Z. Tao, W. Li and L. Teng, "Signal modeling and experimental verification in GNSS forward scatter radar", *17th International Radar Symposium*, Krakow, Poland, pp.1-6, 2016.

[9] K. Borre, D. Akos, N. Bertelsen, P. Rinder and S. Jensen, "A Software-Defined GPS and Galileo Receiver: Single-Frequency Approach", Birkhäuser, Boston, MA, 2006.

[10] I. Garvanov, C. Kabakchiev, V. Behar and M. Garvanova, "Target detection using a GPS Forward-Scattering Radar", *IEEE Second International Conference "Engineering & Telecommunications – En&T 2015"*, Moscow-Dolgoprudny, Russia, pp. 29-33, 2015.

[11] I. Garvanov, Chr. Kabakchiev, V. Behar and M. Garvanova, "The Experimental Study of Possibility for Pulsar Signal Detection", *The Second International Conference "Engineering & Telecommunications – En&T 2016"*, Moscow-Dolgoprudny, Russia, pp. 68-72, 2016.

MyEyes - Automatic Combination System of Clothing Parts for Blind People: Prototype Validation

[1]Daniel Rocha, [1,2]Vítor Carvalho, [1]Joaquim Gonçalves, [1]Eva Oliveira
[1]IPCA, School of Technology, DIGARC, Braga, Portugal
[2]Algoritmi R&D, Minho University, Guimarães, Portugal
email: a7517@alunos.ipca.pt, vcarvalho@ipca.pt, jgoncalves@ipca.pt, eoliveira@ipca.pt,

[3]Filipe Azevedo
[3]Association of the Blind and Amblyopic of Portugal
ACAPO, Braga, Portugal
email: filipeazevedo@acapo.pt

Abstract— **Blind people have been, over time, a reason for motivation in the development of solutions to improve their quality of life. The aim of this work is to propose a solution for one of such problems, namely, the selection and combination of clothing for the blind. Thus, this article describes the whole project developed, in agreement with the Portuguese Association of the Blind and Amblyopic of Portugal (ACAPO), for the creation of a Web platform to aid the blind in selecting combinations of clothing. Near Field Communication (NFC) technology is the basis of this project in the identification of garments. The features of the garments are inserted manually, and a combination of features is possible. There is also the possibility to automatically identify the color of the garment. The system has been tested by the ACAPO organization and preliminary feedback is positive, which are a good starting point for the future. This solution helps promote an increased autonomy for blind people.**

Keywords-Inclusion; Blind People; Image Processing; Clothes Combination; NFC.

I. INTRODUCTION

The definition of being human leads us to certain questions: to what extent are we different? Will our society be able to define our species without aesthetic questions? Is our society with its capabilities, whether social, psychological, technological, to help citizens with disabilities? Is there enough technology to minimize the obstacles faced by these people in their daily lives? Certainly, the technology in this field has evolved a lot, but there are still some gaps to be filled.

People with visual impairment face difficulties at various levels, since they are limited in their functional capacity to carry out daily activities, such as different domestic tasks, the choice of clothing, and in all the tasks that are easy for people with visual capacity.

Vision is a sense that dominates human life. It allows us to know and have a perception of the world around us, while giving us meaning for objects, concepts and ideas. Vision is the primary human because it is the dominant sensory channel in the acquisition of information from the outside. Vision accounts for about 80% of our sensory inputs [1][2].

With the advancement of technology, it is important to evolve to minimize all the limitations of a blind person. One issue that remains to be explored is the case of blind people is the selection and combination of garments. Sometimes, even if we do not have any type of disability, we have difficulty choosing what to wear; we can imagine the difficulty of a visually impaired person in this aspect. Not knowing the colors, the type of pattern, or even the place where the garments are found makes this a daily battle in which resources are not the best. Therefore, we proposed this project to address the issue of combining clothing for the blind.

This paper is organized in 5 sections. Section 2 presents some available solutions to help in the autonomy of blind people. Section 3 describes the various components of the solution presented, including system architecture, hardware, software, database as well as Web and windows applications. Section 4 describes the tests performed with blind people to validate the solution presented and finally, Section 5 draws the conclusions and suggests further developments.

II. RELATED WORK

Currently, there is no solution on the market to help blind people with their clothes combination. Indirectly, but not focused on this purpose, we can find applications for mobile devices that can provide, even if far from what is wanted, some help. Some applications already developed in that sense include: Be my eyes, Color Detector, Ibeacons and Colorino.

'By my eyes' [3] is a mobile application considering a video call via the internet to get help from a visually capable person. The color detector is an application of the app store for *iOs* that uses a screenshot to calculate the average color of a chosen area. The Beacons are small devices that use Bluetooth Low Energy (BLE) technology. This technology has an incalculable practical effect. With the beacons, it is possible to identify, for example, landmarks, bathrooms, stairs, shops and many other things. The Colorino is particularly suitable for people who have a reduced vision and even for the blind, as it assists in the choice of clothes, the washing procedure and the color combination.

The research project Context Extraction for the Blind Using Computer Vision (CE4BLIND) is a mobile digital platform that results in a computer application that can be used on a computer, mobile phone or tablet. This project aims to increase the perception of reality to those who cannot use their vision as stated by those responsible for the project, that is, to facilitate and give these people greater autonomy in tasks such as reading a newspaper, a restaurant menu or identifying a route [4].

Another project described in literature is "Assistive Clothing Pattern Recognition for Visually Impaired People" which consists of recognizing patterns of clothing being able to identify 11 clothing colors and recognize 4 categories of clothing patterns [5]-[7]. The paper "Rotation and Illumination Invariant Texture Analysis" suggests a form of clothing combinations of complex patterns for visually impaired people [8][9]. Also, the project described in the paper "Recognizing clothes patterns and colors for blind people using neural network" allows to classify the type of pattern of garments through extracting their characteristics by a camera [10]-[12].

As described, although there are some projects that can be used to help the blind, none of them contains the idea presented in this project. Thus, the development of an application for combinations of clothing pieces was elaborated.

III. DEVELOPED APPLICATION

In this section, the entire system developed is presented, including all the hardware and software.

A. System Architecture

First, to develop this project, it was proposed to develop a Representational State Transfer (REST) system architecture (Figure 1).

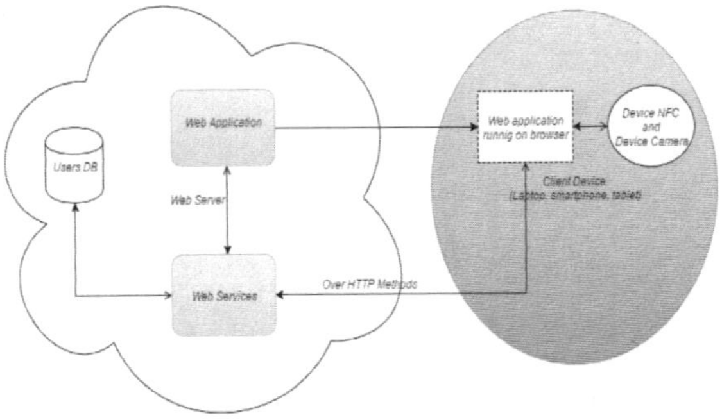

Figure 1. Rest Architecture.

For this, the system is composed of an Application Programming Interface (API) and a front-end application that is all that the user "can see". The API is responsible to process all requests of the user, coming from the front-end interface, such as image acquisition and processing, automatic combinations, among other features.

B. Hardware

The hardware platform focuses on the Arduino Uno, equipped with an Atmel AVR microcontroller and a C++ programming environment (Figure 2).

Since, the technology used for this project is the NFC (Near Field Communication), it requires an NFC shield to Arduino. The reading module is the ITEAD PN532. It has SPI (Serial Peripheral Interface), I2C (Inter-Integrated Circuit) and UART (Universal Asynchronous Receiver/Transmitter) communication interfaces. However, the mode of communication used is the SPI. In this way, the Arduino is connected to a PC and allows the interface with the Web platform.

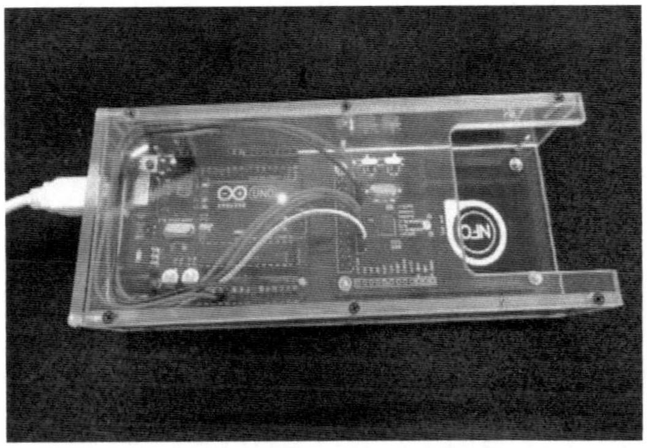

Figure 2. Hardware Developed.

The TAG chosen to place in the clothes is the NTAG216 tag minimally invasive (Figure 3).

Figure 3. Clothes with TAG.

The tag used has the following characteristics:

- Chip - NTAG216;
- Frequency - 13.56MHz;
- Memory - 888 bytes;
- Data transfer: 106 kbit/s;
- Maximum number of characters (URL) – 854.

The NXP NTAG®216 chip offers excellent memory capacity, ideal for storing more information, however, in this project we will not make use of it once it is identified by its UID (Unique Identifier) [13][14].

C. *Software*

The application development uses Laravel, which is a PHP (Hypertext Preprocessor) Framework that uses the MVC (model-view-controller) architecture [15].

This architecture allows simplifying the application in 3 layers, namely user interaction (view), data manipulation layer (model), responsible for reading and writing, and the controller layer, responsible for all user requests that controls the model to be used and the display to be shown to the user.

The database used by default in Laravel is MySQL.

D. *Database*

The database was developed to respond to a set of challenges posed by the system that results in the following key requirements:

1. A user can perform more than one function;
2. Each role is associated with a set of permissions, regardless of which user executes it;
3. Each clothing item (with a unique identifier) is associated with a set of parameterized characteristics:

- Size;
- Washing;
- Printed;
- Season;
- Type;
- Color;
- Style.

The database created was based on the Entity-Relationship (ER) Model. In the database management system, a set of tables will also be considered, which will assist in the decision making. The application also has an administrator level that is composed of the following tables:

- Users;
- Profiles;
- Permissions.

This way, we guarantee privileged access to certain areas of the application and a level of administration.

E. *Web Application*

To understand the structure of the Web application, Figure 4 shows the block diagram of the organization considered.

Considering Figure 4, it is possible to verify that there are four main elements, the "Menu", "About", "Contact" and "Administrator", and, to be able to access them, a user authentication is necessary.

For this purpose, it is necessary to access the "Register" to create the user.

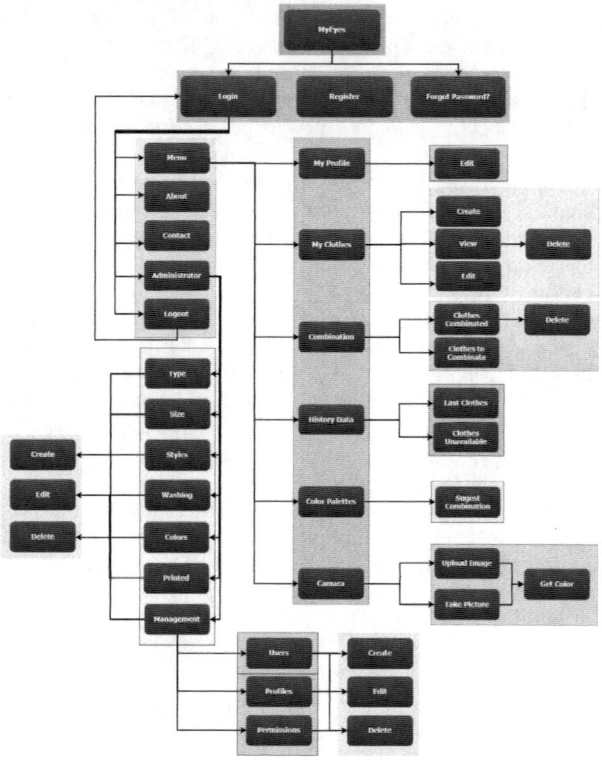

Figure 4. Block Diagram of MyEyes.

With the login done, it is possible to access the "Menu", where there are 6 topics, “My profile”, “My Clothes”, “Combination”, “History Data”, “Color Palettes and Camera” (Figure 5):

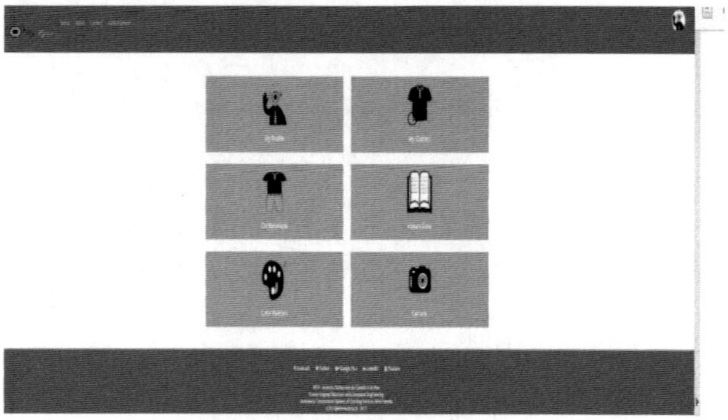

Figure 5. Menu MyEyes.

- **My Profile:** is where all user's personal management is done, where all the user's authenticated fields can be seen, such as name, email and password. This data can be edited at any time.

- **My Clothes:** serves to manage the clothes that the user owns. The clothes can be listed by their attributes, such as: style, type, pattern, size, colors and season. During the listing, the user can edit and delete the part, thus allowing stock management (Figure 6).

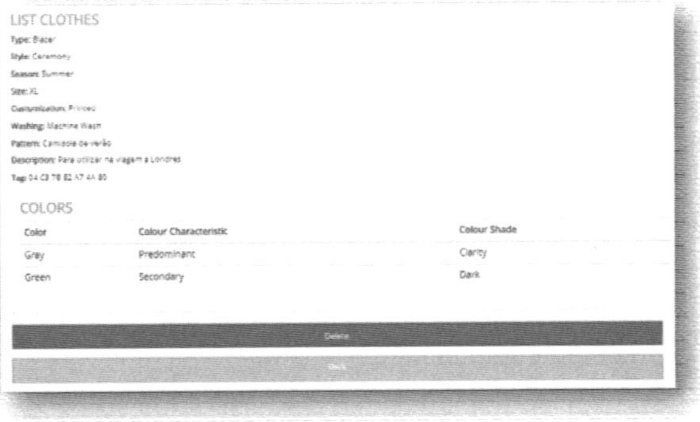

Figure 6. My Clothes Details.

- **Combination:** The whole combination of clothes is implemented here. The user can see their combinations, edit and delete them in "view details" (blue boxes), referring to each piece of clothing (Figure 7).

Figure 7. Part of Combination Layout.

- **History Data:** It allows the user to consult the registry of the last pieces of clothing added, as well as the clothes unavailable. That is, if it is necessary to put a garment in this state, and in case it may be for washing, a quick perception about the state of it is presented.

- **Color Palettes:** This mode is like the combination, but has an automatic mode in which the application makes a filter through the seasons (Autumn, Winter, Spring, Summer), suggesting only parts from the same station or that can be used in both. In this way, we guarantee that all the possible combinations agree with the season of the time, eliminating numerous pieces that would generate confusion to the user.

- **Camera:** Here, it is possible to obtain the predominant color of a garment. There are two ways to do this, one is to upload an image of a garment, and another is to take a photo of the garment with the webcam. After choosing one of the two modes, the predominant color of the garment is shown.

F. *Windows Apllication*

To allow the interface with the NFC reader, a computer application was developed a computer application (Windows operating system) in C # language, capable of performing the readings of NFC tags (Figure 8).

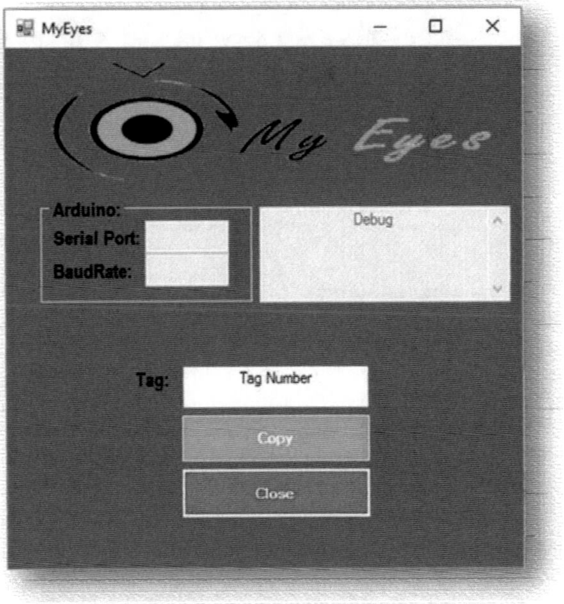

Figure 8. Desktop Application.

In this case, the algorithm has been thought in a way in which the application detects the device automatically, at the time of its connection, autonomously establishing a communication.

IV. VALIDATION

This project was submitted for validation at the Association of the Blind and Amblyopic of Portugal (ACAPO) in Braga, Portugal. Application testing focuses on accessibility and usability (Figure 9).

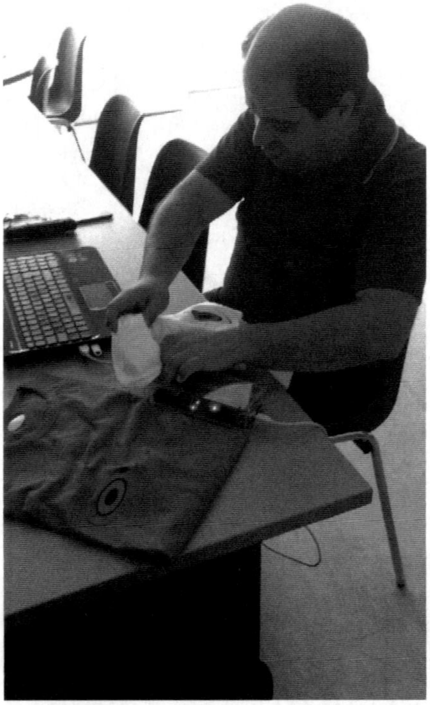

Figure 9. Blind people reading clothes.

During the validation, there were added pieces of clothing and for each one was attached its NFC tag. After, recognize of each clothing was performed with NFC reader.

The feedback was very positive. However, some remarks were discussed to improve the application, like:

- Include more info in social networks (Facebook, YouTube and so on);
- In the windows application, implement a beep sound when detecting a new TAG;
- Create a "back button" at the end of each page to improve usability;
- Invert the order the clothes are shown in when an additional clothing item is added. This means that the last record needs to appear in the first row;
- Exchange the TAG number by Description field when the Clothe is displayed, since that TAG number is insignificant to remember the clothe;
- Remove the confirmation button when attempting to see more details or edit, and keep the confirmation only in case of deleting.

Afterwards, all topics above were considered and a new version of the application was validated again; it means that the second validation was tested without any other additional changes.

Considering the preliminary usability tests performed by the ACAPO member, the blind people community considered that this project will be very useful for the blind population because it could fill a major gap that affects this population, which is related to the identification and characterization of clothing. This solves an obvious difficulty in the task of making combinations at the time of choosing the pieces of clothing that they are going to wear.

These obstacles go so far as to prevent a blind person from being able to choose their daily clothes in a completely autonomous way, forcing them to ask for help from others to describe the pieces that they have, and to organize their wardrobe in order to not be confused by the colors, shades, fabric types and other characteristics of the garment. Moreover, they consider that as there are many blind citizens who live alone and several couples consisting only of blind people, the usefulness of such a tool will increase their autonomy and promote a better inclusion in society. It would be extraordinary if, with this platform, people no longer had the need to ask for help from others regarding clothing combinations. It is true that video calls today make this kind of task much easier, but we must clearly aim for autonomy and independence, and My eyes can offer blind people this legitimate desire to be able to choose in an informed and conscious way the clothes they wear every day.

V. CONCLUSION AND FUTURE WORK

This paper presented a system able to allow visually impaired people to combine cloths based on their taste and options.

The introduction of NFC technology in clothing allows the creation of an autonomous clothing management for a blind person. Being a Web application, it is accessible to all. This application will make possible to contribute to the lack in the existing technology in relation to the aesthetics and visual image of a blind person. The user interface is intuitive and of great usability.

The tests performed with the Portuguese Association of the Blind and Amblyopic of Portugal (ACAPO) validated the proposed solution.

As future work, we intend to implement machine learning in combinations of garments, as well as the insertion of garments automatically using a camera and image processing algorithms in the extraction of characteristics. The multi-language capability needs to be implemented also to increase the number of potential users. Moreover, we intend to use NFC from mobile devices to incorporate this project.

ACKNOWLEDGMENT

We would like to thank ACAPO (Association of the Blind and Amblyopic of Portugal), for their collaboration with the research team, specially the ACAPO from Braga, Portugal.

REFERENCES

[1] "The most important sense that we own is: Vision" [Online]. Available: https://olharomundo.wordpress.com/2010/01/20/e-o-sentido-mais-importante-que-possuimos-e-a-visao/ [Accessed: 28-Jul-2017] (in Portuguese)

[2] A. Zeb, S. Ullah, and I. Rabbi, "Indoor Vision-Based Auditory Assistance for Blind People in Semi Controlled Environments," IPTA 2014, 14-17 October 2014, Paris, France.

[3] "Be My Eyes" [Online]. Available: http://bemyeyes.com/ [Accessed: 28-Jul-2017].

[4] "CE4BLIND" [Online]. Available: http://24.sapo.pt/tag/ce4blind [Accessed: 28-Jul-2017] (in Portuguese)

[5] X. Yang, S. Yuan, and Y. Tian, "Assistive clothing pattern recognition for visually impaired people," IEEE Trans. Human-Machine Syst., vol. 44, no. 2, pp. 234–243, 2014.

[6] K. Jafari-Khouzani and H. Soltanian-Zadeh, "Radon transform orientation estimation for rotation invariant texture analysis," IEEE Trans. Pattern Anal. Mach. Intell., vol. 27, no. 6, pp. 1004–1008, 2005.

[7] Z.-Z. Wang and J.-H. Yong, "Texture analysis and classification with linear regression model based on wavelet transform.," IEEE Trans. Image Process., vol. 17, no. 8, pp. 1421–1430, 2008.

[8] S. Yuan and Y. Tian, "Rotation and Illumination Invariant Texture Analysis," CISP 2010, 16-18 October 2010, Yantai, China.

[9] M. a Akhloufi, X. Maldague and W. Ben Larbi,"A New Color-Texture Approach for Industrial Products Inspection," Journal of Multimedia (JMM), 3 (3), 44-50 (2008).

[10] J. J. R. J, "Recognizing clothes patterns and colours for blind people using neural network,", ICIIESC 2015, 19-20 March 2015, Tamil Nadu, India.

[11] Y. Qian, M. Ye, and J. Zhou, "Hyperspectral image classification based on structured sparse logistic regression and three-dimensional wavelet texture features," IEEE Trans. Geosci. Remote Sens., vol. 51, no. 4, pp. 2276–2291, 2013.

[12] X. Zheng and N. Liu, "Color recognition of clothes based on k-means and mean shift," Proc. - 2012 IEEE Int. Conf. Intell. Control. Autom. Detect. High-End Equipment, ICADE 2012, pp. 49–53, 2012.

[13] N. Semiconductors, "NTAG213F/216F NFC Forum Type 2 Tag compliant IC with 144/888 bytes user memory and field detection."

[14] "TAG NTAG®216 29mm." [Online]. Available: https://www.nfc.pt/home/65-etiqueta-ntag216-29mm.html [Accessed: 01-Aug-2017].

[15] "Laravel" [Online]. Available: https://laravel.com [Accessed: 01-Aug-2017].

Development of a Blood Type Analyzer using Computer Vision and Machine Learning Techniques: A Review

[1,3]Ana Ferraz, [1,2]Vítor Carvalho
[1]Algoritmi Research Centre, University of Minho
[2]IPCA-EST
[1]Guimarães, [2]Barcelos, Portugal
aps_ferraz@hotmail.com; vcarvalho@ipca.pt

[3]José Machado
[3]MetRICs Research Centre
University of Minho
Guimarães, Portugal
jmachado@dem.uminho.pt

***Abstract*—In emergency cases, when the available time for blood transfusions is limited, blood type O (universal donor) is administered. However, sometimes, this can cause a transfusion reaction that can lead to the death of the patient receiving the transfusion. The equipment available on the market is not adequate for emergency scenarios (not portable and slow results). This paper presents the steps taken into consideration in the development of a blood type analyzer using computer vision and machine learning algorithms suitable for emergency situations (small size, lightweight, easy transportation, ease of use, fast results, high reliability and low cost). Several prototypes have been developed with the final version performing real world scenario experiments in hospitals for validation. With this system, it will be possible to contribute to the reduction of casualties in blood transfusions associated to human error or blood incompatibilities.**

Keywords-blood types; computer vision; machine learning; prototype.

I. INTRODUCTION

Blood transfusions are a daily necessity in hospitals and their success depends on various procedures and their execution without errors. A key procedure is the correct identification of the blood type of the patient requiring the blood transfusion, since an error in this procedure leads to incorrect administration of the required blood unit. This procedure becomes more complicated when it comes to emergency situations due to the lack of time and the need to perform the tests in the laboratory. This scenario occurs because automated systems available on the market are bulky and cannot be transported. Additional time is needed for laboratory trips and manual solutions have the possibility of human error in the procedure, while reading and interpreting the results. In urgent situations, the procedure calls for the use of a blood type considered the universal donor (O negative) for the transfusion to be performed. However, because the universal donor is scarce and can induce transfusion reactions, blood transfusions based on the universal blood donor principle should be reserved for emergency situations only. In this sense, the ideal scenario would be to administer the compatible and corresponding blood even in emergency situations and it is necessary to develop a new solution that enables it [1]-[5].

To make it possible even in emergency situations to perform the tests and identify the patient's blood type, avoiding the use of the universal donor, some prototypes were developed that aim to automate the tests and obtain fast results in a portable way. The different prototypes developed are based on the automation of the procedures of an already validated manual test, the slide test, and the use of a camera that captures the images after performing the procedures to obtain test results. The plate test consists of mixing one drop of four different reagents with the blood, separately. Each of the reagents, Anti-A, Anti-B, Anti-AB and Anti-D will identify the presence or absence of a specific antigen found in red blood cells. The identification of the antigens is done through the occurrence of an agglutination reaction that causes the development of agglomerates in the blood [6][7]. These agglomerates are visible to the naked eye, but in this case, they will be detected automatically using the test image and the use of Computer Vision and Machine Learning algorithms. This will allow to reduce or even eliminate the human errors occurrence in blood type identification, enabling to administrate a compatible blood type since the first blood unit, avoiding causalities.

This paper is organized in 5 sections. Section II, describes the functions used to classify the human blood type. Section III shows some results obtained for 40 tests. Section IV presents several prototypes developed in this project and finally, Section V, presents some remarks obtained in this project and indicates some future work considerations.

II. BLOOD TYPE DETECTION ALGORITHMS

As described in [8] several algorithms of Computer Vision were used (below sequence of actions 1-5), to identify the occurrence of the agglutination reaction from the analyzed images. An example of an analyzed image is presented in Figure 1.

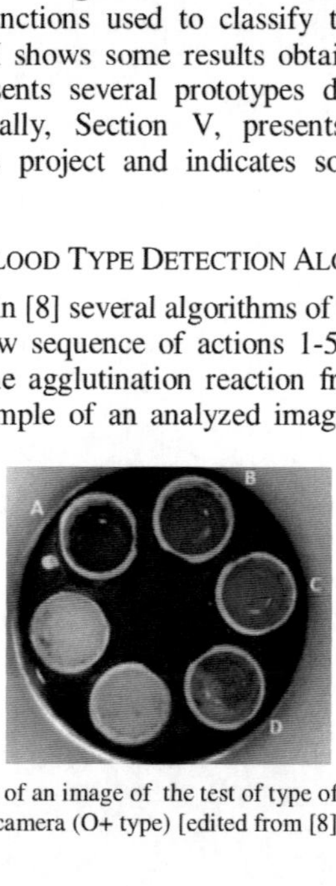

Figure 1. Example of an image of the test of type of blood with an HDD camera (O+ type) [edited from [8])

However, to make the identification of the reaction even more robust, Support Vector Machines (SVMs) (sequence of action number 6 above), were introduced so that, based on experience and consequent learning, blood type identification could be obtained even in the weakest reactions [8]. The following sequence of actions was considered: 1 - Image Acquisition; 2 - Color Plane Extraction; 3 - Pattern Matching; 4 - Geometric Matching; 5 - Features Extraction; and 6 - Support Vector Machines. The 5th action (features extraction) considers obtaining from the analyzed images the Standard Deviation, the Histogram, Histogram of Gradients (HoG) and Fast Fourier Transform (FFT) results, which are presented in the next section (Table I).

III. Results

The different characteristics extracted allowed to obtain better or worse effectiveness. The effectiveness of each of them is represented in Table I for 40 tests carried out, corresponding to 124 samples (4 samples per test) [8].

TABLE I. Results of SVMs with the Different Features Extracted From the Image [8]

Features	Support Vector Machines Results
Standard Deviation	1
Histogram	1
HoG	0.7917
FFT	0.8718

IV. Developed Prototypes

The development of the different prototypes and plates test (where the reagents were placed with the blood) allowed to improve their capabilities, including speed of test, visualization of the reactions, efficacy of detection and the diminution of its dimensions facilitating the portability of the future product [9] [10], Figure 2.

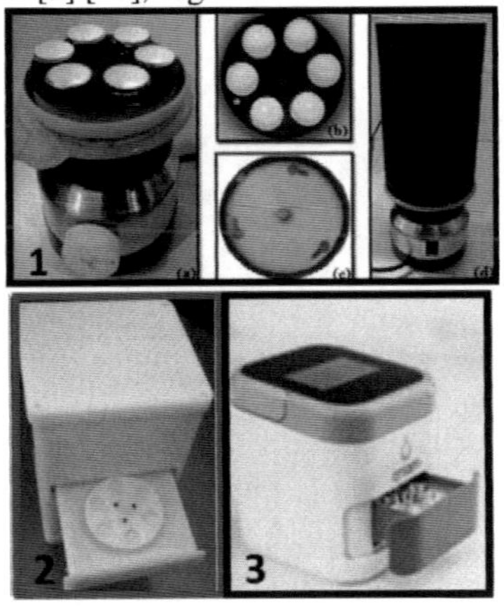

Figure 2. Prototypes and plate tests. (1): with recycled material [9]. (2) with electronics included [10]. (3) with a screen and small dimensions.

As can be seen in Figure 2, throughout the development of the different prototypes, changes were made, which resulted in a final prototype much closer to the intended final device in which the test plate is sealed and there is only a single blood insertion site. This last prototype carries out tests between 3 to 5 minutes, in an efficient and portable way, and ready to be tested in a hospital setting.

V. Final Comments

This project describes a solution developed for detecting human blood types using computer vision and machine learning algorithms. The success of this solution will allow to reduce human errors, minimize the necessity of using the universal donor in blood transfusions being able to be used in emergency scenarios. Several prototypes have been developed, with the last one currently being subject to real world tests in hospitals for validation.

Acknowledgment

Thanks to the Portuguese Foundation for Science and Technology (FCT) for funding this work through the PhD scholarship SFHR/BD/81094/2011.

References

[1] S. R. Rod, P. Tate, and D. S. Trent, Anatomia & Fisiologia, 6th ed., Loures: Lusociência, 2005. (in portuguese)

[2] V. A. Hoffbrand, E. J. Petit, and H. A. P. Moss, Fundamentos em Hematologia, 4ª Edição, Artmed, Porto Alegre, 2004. (in portuguese)

[3] R. Caquet, Guia Prático Climepsi de Análises Clínicas, 1st ed. Climepsi Editores, 2004. (in portuguese)

[4] J. Merck, S. Dohme, Manual de Merck de Saúde para a Família, 2nd ed., Merck Sharp & Dohme, Lisboa, 2004. (in portuguese)

[5] Manual Merck: Biblioteca Médica Online, Merck & Co., Inc. (2009) [online]. Available: http://www.manualmerck.net/?id=179&cn=2100/> (in portuguese)

[6] J. D. Roback, M. R. Combs, B. J. Grossman, and C. D. Hillyer, Technical Manual, AABB, American Association of Blood Banks, Maryland, 2008.

[7] D. M. Hammering, Modern Blood banking & Transfusion Practices, DavidPlus, 6th ed., 2012.

[8] A. Ferraz, J. Brito, V. Carvalho, and J. Machado, "Blood type classification using computer vision and machine learning", Neural Comput & Applic, Vol. 28, Nº 8, pp.2029-2040, 2017.

[9] A. Ferraz, V. Carvalho, and José Machado, "Determination of Human Blood Type Using Image Processing Techniques", Measurement, Vol. 97, pp.165-173, 2017.

[10] A. Ferraz, V. Carvalho, J. Machado, and J. Brito, "Mechatronic system for performing blood pre-transfusion tests", Sensor and Actuators A: Physical, Vol. 246, pp.81-90, 2016.

Design and Implementation of a Low Cost System to Determine the Composition of Biogas

Antonio José Calderón Godoy, Isaías González Pérez
Dept. of Electrical, Electronic and Automatic Engineering
University of Extremadura
Badajoz, Spain
e-mail: {ajcalde, igonzp}@unex.es

***Abstract*—The main objective of this work is the design and development of a device similar to a continuous gas sensor, which can analyze the composition of combustible gases, depending on the types of sensors installed in the capsule designed for this purpose. Some manufacturers of continuous gas analyzers develop equipment with high price. The purpose of this work is the design and implementation of a low cost system, affordable to any type of company, based on the platform Open Hardware Arduino, for measuring and analyzing biogas. This system can be used for many applications and because biogas is a renewable gas fuel, it will be increasingly important in countries committed to the reduction of greenhouse gases. All circuits will be designed and later simulated with the Multisim 12.0 software. The printed circuit boards will be created with the help of the Ultiboard 12.0 software and, finally, the necessary files will be created for the printing of these circuits in the plates with the software LPKF CircuitPro 1.5.**

Keywords-continuous analyzer; combustible gases; biogas.

I. INTRODUCTION

Continuous gas analyzers are equipment that analyzes the composition of gases continuously. That is, as the gas is flowing through the analyzer, the reading of the gas composition can be instantly obtained.

Focusing on combustible gases, these are used for the production of thermal energy from a combustion process. Some gases of this type are natural hydrocarbons and those manufactured solely for use as fuel. Among all possible cases, it has been decided to develop a prototype to determine the composition of biogas. The composition of this combustible gas varies according to the origin of the same [1]. Biogas can be generated in natural media or in a sealed, oxygen-free tank called anaerobic digester, from the reactions of biodegradation that are produced of the organic matter, by the action of microorganisms in the absence of oxygen [2].

This combustible gas consists of a mixture composed of 50-70% of methane (CH_4) and 30-50% of carbon dioxide (CO_2). It also contains minimal amounts of other gases, such as nitrogen (N_2), hydrogen sulphide (H_2S), and some traces of water vapor. The calorific value of the biogas will vary its value depending on the proportion of methane in the mixture [3].

The measurement system designed in this work is based on four sensors that have been chosen according to the composition of this renewable fuel gas. However, it can be extrapolated to any other type of gas simply modifying the set of selected sensors.

The rest of this paper is organized as follows. Section II describes the sensors used. Section III describes the developed prototype. The conclusions and acknowledgement close the article.

II. SENSORS FOR COMBUSTIBLE GASES

Regarding the monitoring of combustible gases, sensors are required that can detect high concentrations of gases, compared to those required for toxic gases that must be more sensitive to lower levels of concentrations.

For both cases, there are five types of sensors, each based on a different foundation for the detection of different gases, namely electrolytic sensors, catalytic sensors, solid state sensors, infrared sensors and photoionization detectors.

Among all types of gas sensors, semiconductor type sensors have been chosen. These sensors have a thin film of metal oxide, on which a piece of silicone is deposited. The absorption of gas at the surface with this oxide results in a change in the electrical resistance, which is related to the measured gas concentration of the sample.

The following sensors have been selected for the implementation of the biogas measurement and analysis system: ammonia (TGS2444), hydrogen (TGS821), methane (TGS3870) and carbon monoxide (TGS5042) sensors [4]. Fig. 1 depicted the sensors selected along with their interface circuitry. The sensors have been bought as ready product but the interface circuitry have been fully designed and built.

III. DEVELOPMENT OF THE PROTOTYPE

This section deals with the design and theoretical development of all the circuits involved in the biogas measurement and analysis system. All circuits will be defined theoretically and, later, simulated by the software Multisim 12.0. Printed circuit boards will be created with the help of Ultiboard 12.0 software. Finally, the necessary files will be created for the machine responsible for printing these circuits on the plates with the LPKF CircuitPro 1.5 software [5].

Figure 1. Sensor used: (a) ammonia, (b) hydrogen, (c) methane and (d) carbon monoxide

In this research, an Arduino board, model MEGA2560 has been used as Data Acquisition system (DAQ) for the set of sensors. It is based on a microcontroller ATmega2560. Analogue input channels are used to measure the voltage of the output circuits of the sensors. The cost of Arduino MEGA is noticeably lower than the cost of a traditional DAQ. The carbon monoxide sensor is the cheapest, 28€, whereas the ammonia sensor costs 90€. The system total cost is about 300€. The cost of the Arduino board is 40 €. A DAQ with analog inputs costs over 450€ in the market, so the low cost character of the proposal is clearly stated.

A methacrylate capsule has been designed with Autodesk AutoCad 2013 and Autodesk Inventor 2014 software, which will circulate the biogas to analyze and house the sensors used (Fig. 2a). Fig. 2b shows a snapshot of the hydrogen sensor as sample of the developed prototype.

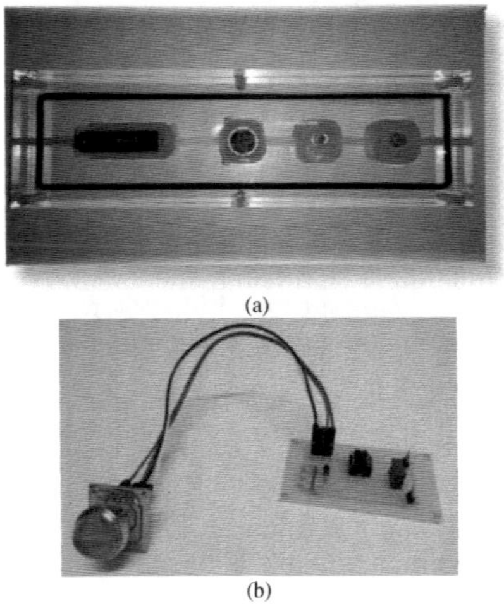

Figure 2. Appearance of: (a) Methacrylate capsule containing the sensors and (b) hydrogen sensor.

Figure 3. Preliminary experimental results.

Early results are shown in Fig. 3 where a snapshot of the system working under laboratory conditions can be observed.

IV. CONCLUSIONS

In this work, the design and development of a cost-effective continuous gas analyzer has been reported. Each of the four sensors chosen for the detection of the biogas composition has been studied and analyzed. Besides, all the circuits necessary for this purpose have being realized. All the circuits that compose the system of measurement and analysis of biogas have been simulated with the software Multisim 12.0, obtaining at all times the corresponding values exposed in the sheets of characteristics of each of them. All the printed circuit boards of the circuits necessary for this project have been implemented with the software Ultiboard 12.0. Currently, the developed meter is in the test phase in order to validate the proposed system.

ACKNOWLEDGMENT

This work has been supported by the FEDER Funds (Programa Operativo FEDER de Extremadura 2014-2020) through the grant "Ayuda a Grupos de Investigación" (ref. GR15178) of Junta de Extremadura.

REFERENCES

[1] K. Cacua, A. Amell, and L. Olmos, "A comparative study of the combustion properties of normal biogas-air mixture and oxygen-enriched biogas-air", Ingeniería e investigación, vol. 31, pp. 233-241, 2011.

[2] D. Deublein and A. Steinhauser, Biogas from Waste and Renewable Resources, Wiley-VCH, 2011.

[3] T. Abbasi, S. A. Abbasi, and S. M. Tauseef, Biogas Energy, Springer, 2012.

[4] Product Information, FIGARO Engineering inc. Available from: http://www.figaro.co.jp/en/product/ (last accessed March 2016)

[5] http://www.lpkfusa.com/support/files/manuals/CircuitPro%202.1.x%20How%20To%20Guide-e-2-1.pdf (last accessed September 2016)

Ultraviolet Photodetectors Fabricated on 4H-SiC

Andrzej Kociubiński, Mariusz Duk, Krzysztof Muzyka
Institute of Electronics and Information Technology
Lublin University of Technology
Lublin, Poland
e-mail: akociub@semiconductor.pl, m.duk@pollub.pl, krzysztof.muzyka.1990@gmail.com

Michał Borecki
Institute of Microelectronics and Optoelectronics
Warsaw University of Technology
Warsaw, Poland
e-mail: borecki@imio.pw.edu.pl

***Abstract*—The aim of the present work is an application of the fabrication technologies of p-n junctions working as photodetectors into the ultraviolet region. Usually, the ultraviolet (UV) photodetectors are fabricated as a standard p-n diode structure with the anode on the top and the cathode on the bottom on silicon carbide (4H-SiC) substrates. The critical part for detectors is the formation of the p-n junction. It can be done by different technological processes, such as ion implantation, epitaxy, etc. This paper presents three different technological approaches to fabricate UV photodetectors as p-n photodiode.**

Keywords- ultraviolet photodetector; semiconductor; thin film; ultraviolet light.

I. INTRODUCTION

Ultraviolet (UV) photodetectors have drawn extensive attention owing to their applications in industrial, environmental and even biological fields. All these applications require very sensitive devices with high signal-to-noise ratio and sometimes high response speed. Compared to UV-enhanced Si photodetectors, a new generation of wide bandgap semiconductors, such as III–V nitrides, gallium nitride (GaN) and SiC, allow to position the p-n junction deeper in the semiconductor structure, which results in lack of sensitivity to unwanted planar defects. Moreover, the SiC material is present in different morphology monolithic and amorphous, which enables realization of advanced stacked photodetecting structures [1]. The monolithic SiC photodiodes are commonly characterized by high responsivity, high thermal stability, robust radiation hardness and high response speed. But, their parameters depend on the material polytype. The 4H-SiC polytype device, due to its large bandgap (Eg=3.26 eV), offers lower leakage current and excess noise factors compared to other SiC polytypes such as the 6H-SiC and 3C-SiC. The aim of this work is the presentation of the fabrication techniques of p-n SiC junctions, aimed to work as photodetectors in UV region, and comparison of obtained results in the form of collected electrical characteristics.

The paper consists of 4 sections. The first section is the introduction, where the new generation of wide bandgap materials for the ultraviolet photodetectors are presented. The second section describes 3 fabrication approaches of SiC p-n junctions. The results of the electrical characterization of the photodiodes are presented in section three. The conclusion is gathered in section four.

II. TECHNOLOGIES AND ELECTRICAL CHARACTERIZATION OF SIC P-N JUNCTIONS

A p-n junction photodiode is just a p-n junction diode that has been specifically fabricated and encapsulated to permit light penetration into the vicinity of the metallurgical junction. The formation of the p-n junction is critical for detectors. It can be done by different technological processes, such as ion implantation, epitaxy etc.

Three different technological approaches to fabricate UV photodetectors as p-n photodiode where the p-n junction is made by [2]–[4]:

- p-type epitaxial layer grown in the chemical vapor deposition process (CVD) (#1),
- 4H-SiC wafers purchased (Cree Inc.) with formed p-n epitaxial layer (#2),
- multiple optimized plasma Al ion implantation (#3),

are under examination. All photodiodes are based on the SiC(n^{++}) substrate with a back metal electrode on the bottom, which use 3-inch diameter 4H-SiC wafers purchased from Cree Inc. The junction is formed from the top by the above mentioned technologies. The whole structure has a metal electrode formed on the top. For experiments, the wafer was diced into segments (10 mm × 10 mm) with a diamond cutting saw.

A. *Approach #1: p-type epitaxial layer grown in the CVD process*

The p-n junctions were fabricated on the substrate having an n-type resistivity of 0.015-0.028 Ωcm (~10^{18} cm^{-3}). A p-type epitaxial layer was grown on the (0001) Si face via CVD to a thickness of 0.5 μm and a carrier concentration of 10^{15} cm^{-3}, as presented in Figure 1.

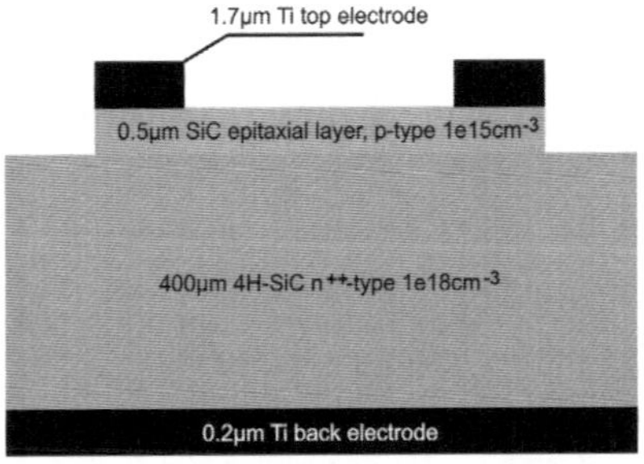

Figure 1. Cross-section of UV photodetector structure with p-type epitaxial layer grown in the CVD process.

The devices are fabricated using mesa geometry to delineate the p-n junction by standard photolithography. The junction was passivated by a thin layer of thermal oxide, which was followed by plasma-enhanced-chemical-vapor deposited silicon oxide (SiO_2). Silicon oxide provides an edge termination of the diode metal contact. The electrodes on n-type and p-type regions were formed by titanium (Ti) and Ti/Al (aluminium) evaporation (lift-off technique), respectively. The contacts were annealed for 5 minutes at 1050°C in argon (Ar) ambient using a rapid thermal annealing (RTP).

B. Approach #2: 4H-SiC wafers purchased (Cree Inc.) with formed p-n epitaxial layer

In the approach #2, contrary to approach #1, the p-type layer was formed by implantation using plasma source of aluminum ions through windows made in a 1um thick deposited oxide. Aluminum is the preferred dopant to produce p-type regions in SiC because of its stability during post-implantation annealing. In fact, the severe ion-induced lattice damage caused by the implantation process requires an appropriate post-implantation annealing for the electrical activation of the dopant and for recovering the crystalline structure, even when an ion implantation at high temperature is performed.

The dopant activation was made by subsequent annealing at 1600°C for 20 min. The electrodes on n-type and p-type regions were formed by Ti/Al/Ti and Ti evaporation (lift-off technique). Both contacts were annealed simultaneously at 1050°C for 5 min. in Ar ambient. The scheme of the obtained structure is presented in Figure 2.

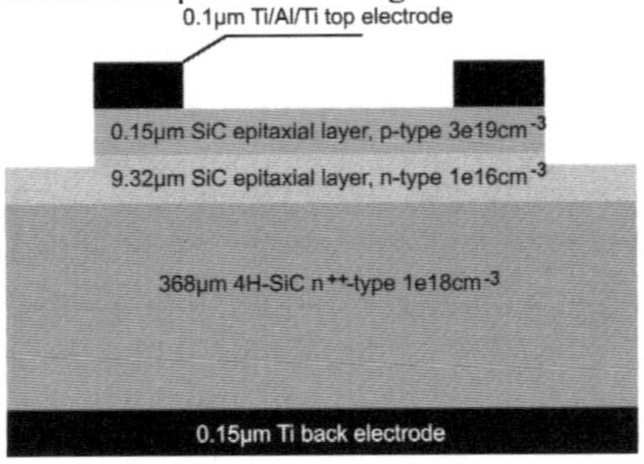

Figure 2. Cross-section of UV photodetector structure with formed p-n epitaxial layer in producer (Cree Inc.).

C. Approach #3 multiple optimized plasma Al ion implantation

The diodes were fabricated on wafers consisting of n-type 4H-SiC substrate with resistivity of 0.021 Ωcm, 0.5 μm thick n-type buffer epitaxial layer with a doping concentration of 1×10^{18} cm^{-3} and 4.5 μm n-type top epitaxial layer with a doping concentration of 1.52×10^{16} cm^{-3}. The cross-section of the fabricated diodes is presented in Figure 3.

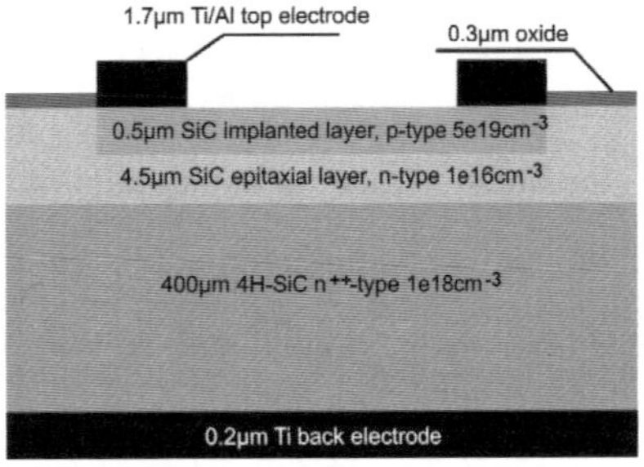

Figure 3. Cross-section of UV photodetector structure with multiple optimized plasma Al ion implantation.

The p-type dopant was again Al and the technology was the implantation. But, the main boundary conditions of implantation as maximally flat (quasi flat, box-shape) profile were taken into implementation. According to the experimental results, it was assumed that minimum implantation energy should be around 55 keV and should not exceed 250 keV. Such process of the flat distribution of p-type Al dopant and a box-shaped profile was realized with multiple energy ion implantations. The total fluence was 7×10^{14} cm^{-2}.

III. RESULTS

The electrical characterization of the p-n photodiodes is mainly covered by measurements of reverse characteristics at room temperature in the dark conditions. These characteristics are most suitable to the leakage current representation, which determines the photodetector quality and sensitivity. The results of the electrical characterization of the prepared photodiodes structures with the use of KEITHLEY SMU 237 [5] are presented in Figure 4.

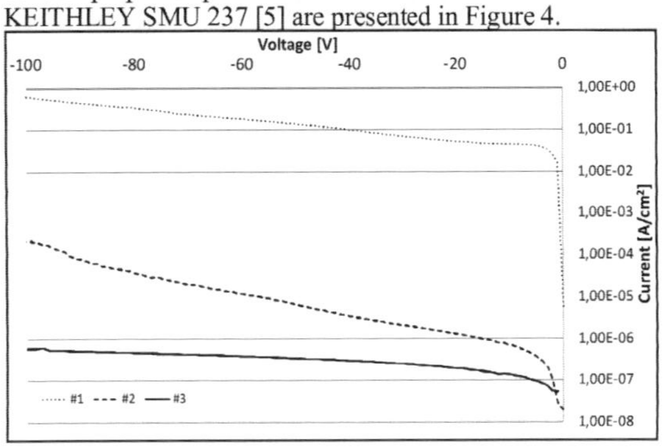

Figure 4. Comparison of reverse I-V characteristics of the circular SiC p-n photodiodes for all three technological approaches.

A comparison of the obtained results shows that the optimization of the quality of p-n junctions leads to expected improvement of photodiode quality by reducing the leakage current by about one order of magnitude. The best characteristics of the device fabricated by approach #3 can also be explained by the fact that the p-type region was formed not by a simple singe implantation, but by an optimized multiple ion implantations.

IV. CONCLUSION

In this paper, the general ideas of various technological approaches of the p-n junctions' formation and characterization were presented. For the UV photodetector purpose, the most suitable technological approach is optimized multiple Al plasma ion implantations. Purchased 4H-SiC substrates with the epitaxial p-n layer are also good for photodiodes preparation. The epitaxial layer grown in the CVD process looks as the least promising technology for use in SiC photodiodes. In future work, we are planning to test structures developed with the use of different UV radiation sources.

ACKNOWLEDGMENT

This work was partially supported by the NCN grant 2012/06/A/ST700398 "Oxide nanostructures for electronic, optoelectronic and photovoltaic applications".

REFERENCES

[1] M. Vieira, M. Vieira, P. Louro, A. Fantoni, and V. Silva, "SiC multilayer photonic structures: A new active filter design," The Third International Conference on Sensor Device Technologies and Applications (SENSORDEVICES 2012) IARIA, Aug. 2012, pp. 25-30, ISBN: 978-1-61208-208-0.

[2] A. Kociubinski et al., "Fabrication and characterization of epitaxial 4H-SiC pn junctions," Proc. SPIE 9228, Optical Fibers and Their Applications 2014, pp. 922804-1 - 922804-6.

[3] A. Kociubiński et al., "Technology and characterization of 4H-SiC p-i-n junctions," Proc. SPIE 8903, Photonics Applications in Astronomy, Communications, Industry, and High-Energy Physics Experiments 2013, pp. 89030V1-89030V6.

[4] M. Borecki et al., "Large-area transparent in visible range silicon carbide photodiode," Proc. SPIE 8903, Photonics Applications in Astronomy, Communications, Industry, and High-Energy Physics Experiments 2013, pp. 89030H1-89030H9.

[5] Keithley Products | Tektronix, https://www.tek.com/keithley.

A Concept for Working Point Determination of Axial Compressors Based on Blade Deflection Measurements with Optical Sensors

Rocco Reinhardt*, Daniel M. Lancelle*, Olaf Magnor*, Olaf Hagendorf† and Peter Dünow†
*IAV GmbH, Powertrain Mechatronics, Gifhorn, Germany
Email: rocco.reinhardt@iav.de, daniel.maurice.lancelle@iav.de, olaf.magnor@iav.de,
olaf.hagendorf@hs-wismar.de, peter.duenow@hs-wismar.de
†University of Wismar, Faculty of Engineering, Dept. of Electrical Engineering and Computer Science, Wismar, Germany

Abstract—**Today, the working point identification of axial compressors is not sufficient, especially of aircraft engine compressors. For this reason, considerable efficiency losses occur in certain working points. The sensors of commonly used measurement methods have to be placed directly in the compressor airflow. This location is not desirable because the sensors are creating vortexes. This paper shows a new method of working point determination of axial compressors. The new developed measurement system with optical sensors provides a contactless blade deflection measurement without influencing the air flow. The assumption is that blade deflections contain information about the actual compressor working point. The advantage of this technique is the minimal invasive nature. Experiments on an axial compressor have approved the assumption and potential of this technique.**

Keywords*—*axial compressor; optical; working point.

I. INTRODUCTION

For many years, strain gauges were usually applied to research blade vibration effects. New methods based on optical sensors have been researched since the 70's [1], [2]. These methods are known as Blade Tip Timing (BTT) or Blade Vibration Monitoring (BVM). In the last fifteen years, the cost for optical equipment, like laser, fast receiver and optical fibers took off rapidly. One of the main reasons for that is the extreme expansion of optical fiber communication. So, optical based blade tip timing is becoming more and more important in compressor research. Other physical sensor principles, like inductive and magneto resistive, microwave or capacitive [3]–[5] are conceivable but they have to show an adequate precision and resolution. The main advantage of BTT is the monitoring of each individual compressor blade with the same sensor set. In addition, BTT do not influence the blades in contrast to strain gauges. With strain gauges, it would be necessary to add them to each blade and implement a telemetry system to monitor them. The time and money invested are extreme in comparison. The tasks in which BTT is most promising currently and in medium term are to extend maintenance intervals on stationary compressors, compressor research in particular stall, flutter and vibration analysis [6]–[8]. A very new approach and still in the beginning of research is the working point determination and optimization [9].

There is a steady development on axial compressors to increase the pressure ratio per stage. This results in a working region which is closer to the non stable state of the axial compressor, the surge line. Currently, accurate working point determination is not possible. To regard the working point uncertainty, the working lines are placed with a greater margin to the surge line. Furthermore, it has to be considered that a compressor aging causes a surge line movement to the working lines. Considerable efficiency losses are the result of these three facts. The sensors of commonly used principles to measure pressure or mass flow have to be placed directly into the air flow. There, they generate vortexes which induce blade vibrations. These vibrations may cause compressor instabilities and so it is not allowed to use intrusive measurement methods. These restrictions lead to uncertainties with working point identifications.

The contribution of this paper is the introduction of a new BTT based working point determination. This method provides a contactless and non-intrusive possibility to detect blade deflections. Aerodynamic effects on compressor blades were analyzed. This analysis leads to the assumption that blade deflections are usable to identify working points. Techniques to prevent or reduce negative influences of engine order (EO) vibrations of blade deflection measurements are presented. To approve the new method, experiments with an axial compressor were done. Therefore, a compressor map was generated to correlate blade deflections with actual working points. These experiments have shown the potential and usability of a working point identification based on blade deflection measurements.

Section 2 describes the aerodynamic effects on the compressor blades to understand the idea of working point identification with blade deflection measurements. Section 3 shows the used measurement principle of BTT to measure blade deflections and also the technical details of the used axial compressor. Section 4 describes preliminary investigations of the compressor blades which allow optimal sensor positioning around the compressor casing. This can prevent or reduce a negative measurement effect because of EO vibration. Section 5 explains the theory of compressor map generation and presents the generated compressor map. Section 6 discusses the reached measurement precision of blade deflection measurements. Furthermore, first measurement results of blade deflections in dependence of the actual compressor working point are presented.

II. AERODYNAMIC EFFECTS ON THE COMPRESSOR BLADE

This section provides a very short insight in the aerodynamic effects on the compressor blades and will help to understand the fundamental idea about working point identification.

Two forces influence the compressor blades during operation, the lift F_L and the drag F_D (Figure 1). The drag force is the sum of the pressure and the friction force. The lift force is the integral in the direction of the free stream velocity of the pressure differences between profile top side p_t and profile bottom side p_b for each surface area element dA:

$$F_L = \int_{A_{\text{blade}}} (p_t - p_b) \cdot dA \quad (1)$$

It is usual to introduce dimensionless coefficents [10]. The dimensionless coefficient for F_D is:

$$c_D = \frac{F_D}{Aq_\infty} \quad (2)$$

q_∞ is the fluid dynamic pressure and A a defined reference area. For a profile, it is the perpendicular to the ground projected cross sectional area. The dimensionless coefficient for F_L is:

$$c_L = \frac{F_L}{Aq_\infty} \quad (3)$$

These forces are generally generated by the airflow. They are dependent on the airflow velocity C_∞, the profile shape, the Reynolds number, the surface friction, boundary layers, laminar and turbulent flow, et cetera. Further information about these effects are illustrated in technical literature [10], [11].

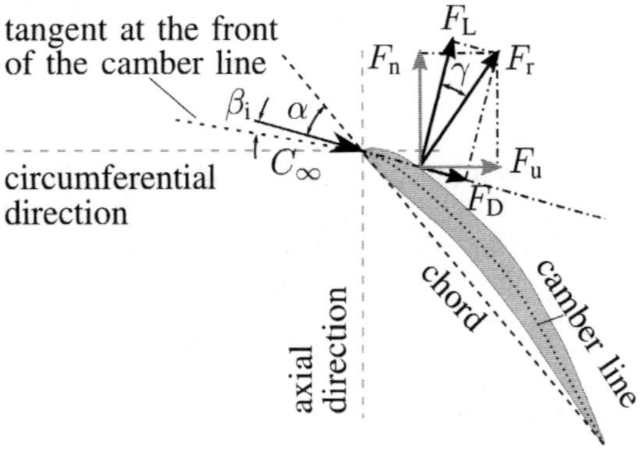

Figure 1. Aerodynamical forces on the compressor blade.

According to the Kutta-Joukowski theorem, the lift force is orthogonal and the drag force is parallel to the direction of flow. F_r is the resulting force. It can be divided into an axial F_n and a circumference force F_u. The angle between the lift and the resulting force is called glide angle γ. The flow direction is described with the angle of attack α. The incidence angle β_i has a major effect on the resulting force. When the compressor is throttled (working point moves left in the compressor map) the pressure ratio increases, the mass flow decreases and the incidence angle increases. Each blade profile shape has a special c_L and c_D behavior depending on the incidence angle [10], [12]. This information can be used to research a working point determination with blade deflections.

III. Measurement Principle and Technical Details of the Axial Compressor

For the BTT measurement principle, one or several blade sensors are arranged around the circumference of the casing. Figure 2 shows this principle. Alternative sensor positions exist in order to prevent the influence of engine order (EO) vibration amplitudes [6], [7]. When a blade crosses the region of one blade sensor, an event will be created. In the absence of blade bending, it is possible to determine the actual undisturbed position s_0 of each blade in relation to the event of the commonly used OPR sensor or, even better, a high resolution reference system and the actual revolution speed or, rather, period of time. If the blade vibrates in none EO modes, the position varies (s_Δ) with time. Additionally, there will be an offset depending on the working point because s_Δ correlates with the resulting force F_r. The actual blade position of blade w in relation to one reference mark can be calculated with (4).

$$s^w = s_0^w + s_\Delta^w \quad (4)$$

$$w : [1, \text{h=Number blades}] \text{ with } w \in \mathbb{Z}$$

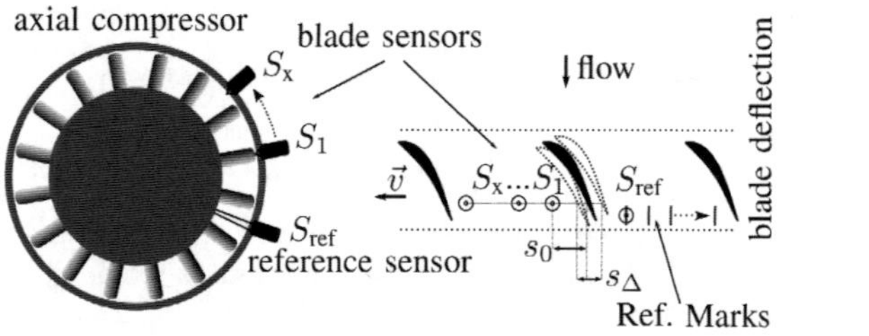

Figure 2. BTT measurement principle on an axial compressor.

In this paper, the individual components of F_r will not be regarded, only the effect in circumferential direction. This will be part of further investigations. For this research, a high resolution reference system was used. Several reference marks are mounted on a suitable load independent position, like the shaft or the disk. They are triggering events at constant angles of the compressor turn. The essential velocity or period of time is calculated with the time difference between two reference events. More details and strategies for a high resolution reference and blade position determination are illustrated in [13].

For the investigation of compressor effects and achievable precisions, a set of three optical blade sensors and one reference sensor is used. Figure 3 shows the principle of the blade sensors. There is one coupling fiber with a core diameter of 4 μm and one outcoupling fiber with a core diameter of 102 μm. Both fibers are guided over a combiner module to one integrated transmitting and receiving end. The combined end has a long ferrule to overcome the width of the compressor casing. The reference sensor is built similarly, except for the ferrule. A ferrule connector for physical contact (FC/PC connector) is used instead. The beam from a laser source with a wavelength of $\lambda = 780\ nm$ and a power of 20 mW is coupled into the sensor module. When the radiated light from the transmitting fiber is reflected by an object, like a blade or a reference mark, the reflected light is collected by the receiving fiber and then guided to an optical receiver. The receiver converts the optical to an electrical signal. A digital storage oscilloscope is used to acquire the data for the following data analysis. Considering that the differences of blade deflections in several working points are often in the range of micrometers, that makes it necessary to regard negative effects, like time walk and time jitter. [14] describes these effects and methods to reduce them. The complete measurement system runs with a sampling rate of $f_s = 250\ MHz$ with a 3 dB bandwidth of approximately $f_{BW} = 200\ MHz$.

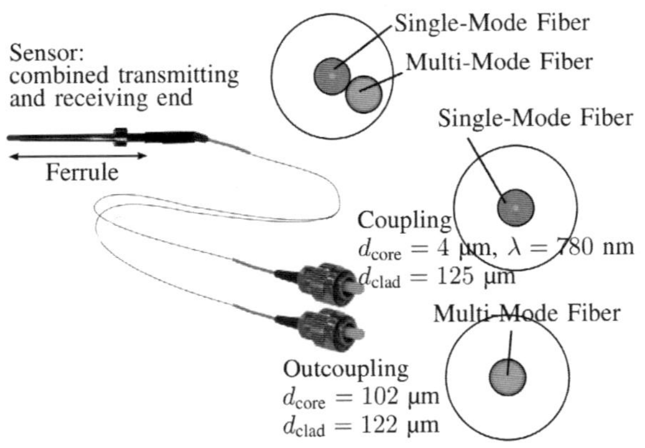

Figure 3. Optical blade sensor setup with special ferrule.

The axial one stage intermediate-pressure-compressor with the internal name EB52 has $h = 58$ blades. It is a research compressor at the Whittle Laboratory of the University of Cambridge and is driven by a synchronous motor to a maximum revolution speed of $n = 3000\ 1/min$. The inner diameter from blade tip to blade tip is $d_c = 0.487\ m$. The compressor can reach an aerodynamic power of about 6 kW and a pressure ratio of $\Pi = 1.02$. The pressure ratio of this research compressor is in comparison to civil engines very small. The engine PW6124 (Airbus A318) from Pratt & Whitney reaches $\Pi = 1.83$ per stage [10]. The one stage compressor HP9 (report AGARD-AR-275) reaches $\Pi = 1.24$. Additionally, the blades of EB52 are very stiff in relation to the maximum aerodynamic power and pressure ratio, so that the blade deflections will be relatively small.

IV. Preliminary Investigation of Axial Sensor Positioning

Usually, blade vibrations f_{blade} have a random character with small amplitudes, thereby averaging is permissible. But, sometimes, varying tip clearances or stator parts lead to excitation of the blades natural frequencies and the vibration amplitudes are rising. For the quality of BTT measurement, this is adverse in the case of EO vibrations. An EO vibration is an integer multiple of the revolution frequency f_{rev} (5).

$$EO = \frac{f_{\text{blade}}}{f_{\text{rev}}} \text{ with } EO \in \mathbb{Z} \tag{5}$$

If the compressor blades vibrate with this kind of frequency, the vibration is synchronized with the compressor revolution. Figure 4 shows a blade vibration with an EO of 6 (blue line). It is defined when the vibration magnitude is negative, the blade comes later to a sensor position because the vibration direction is opposite to the rotational direction. When the magnitude is positive, the blade comes earlier to a sensor position. The sensor positions are called disturbed positions for both states. Only vibration nodes represent undisturbed sensor positions and are usable for direct blade deflection measurements. Furthermore, the blue line can be interpreted as the delta arrival time caused by an EO blade vibration for imaginary sensor positions. If the sensors are located on disturbed positions around the compressor circumference, the measurement result shows a false static blade deflection. If EO vibrations are not considered, blade deflection measurements for working point determination or vibration analysis for flutter or stall may be difficult or impossible. Therefore, one of the main tasks for BTT is an optimal sensor positioning.

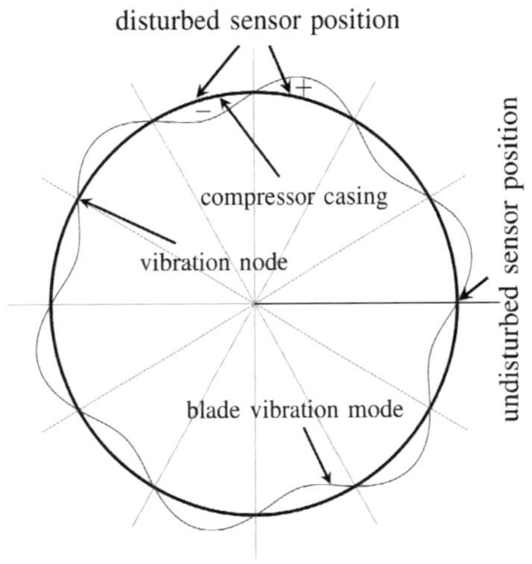

Figure 4. Engine order blade vibration.

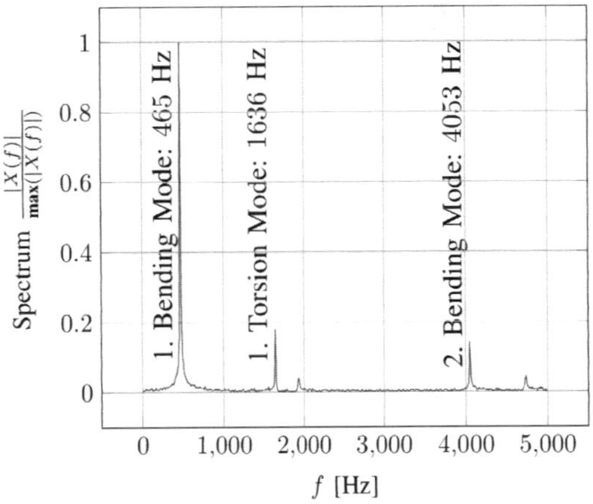

Figure 5. Blade vibration eigenfrequency and eigenform analysis.

The compressor blades were surveyed and the eigenfrequencies (natural frequencies) and eigenforms were identified. Figure 5 shows the resulting frequency spectrum and most significant frequencies. The mode shapes with the most influence on BTT measurement were analyzed in detail.

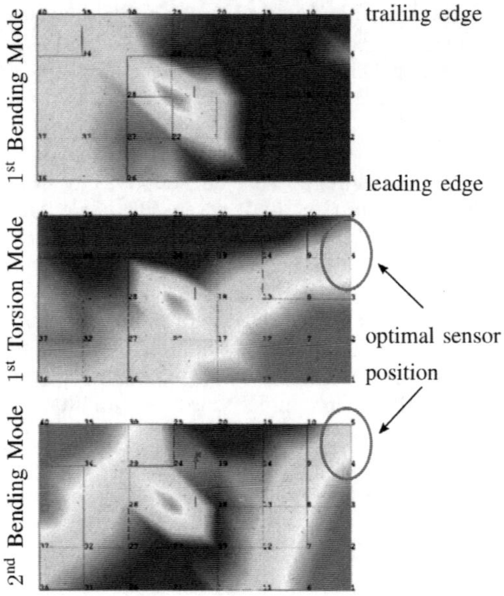

Figure 6. Axial sensor positioning with blade vibration analysis, green region stands for vibration node.

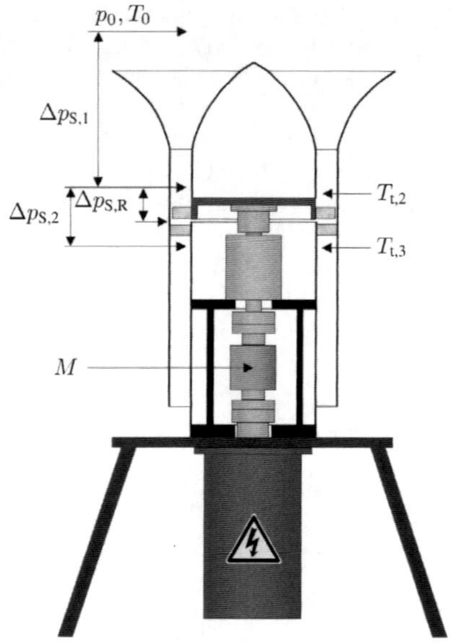

Figure 7. Overview of the probe positions of the test rig.

Figure 6 reveals that the 1st torsion and 2nd bending mode show nodes of vibration close to the trailing edge. This effect is used to minimize their influence to blade deflection measurements for working point determination. The sensors are positioned close to the trailing edge. In the case of EO blade vibration with 1st torsion or 2nd bending mode, they should not affect the measurement. The 1st bending mode shape makes it impossible to use an ideal sensor position. Unfortunately, this mode has the biggest amplitude.

V. Compressor Map Generation

To correlate the acquired blade deformation data to the corresponding working points, all important measurement values need to be recorded. One sample of specific values describes a specific working point. All working points span the compressor map which describes the physical behavior of the compressor. The test rig is equipped with a data acquisition system which measures the revolution speed n, the torque at the shaft M, the static inlet temperature T_0, the total temperature upstream of the rotor $T_{t,2}$, the total inlet pressure $p_{t,0}$, the pressure difference between inlet and the rotor $\Delta p_{S,1}$ and the differential pressure over the compressor stage $\Delta p_{S,2}$. With these values, the compressor map can be determined. Detailed information about compressor map generation are illustrated in [10]. Additionally, the pressure difference over the rotor $\Delta p_{S,R}$ as well as the total temperature downstream of the stage $T_{t,3}$ are measured. Figure 7 shows the probe positions of the test rig.

Figure 8 shows the generated compressor map for the axial compressor presented in this paper.

From the inlet conditions and the pressure drop between inlet and rotor $\Delta p_{S,1}$ the mass flow $\dot{m}$ can be derived. The pressure difference over the stages $\Delta p_{S,2}$ enables to determine

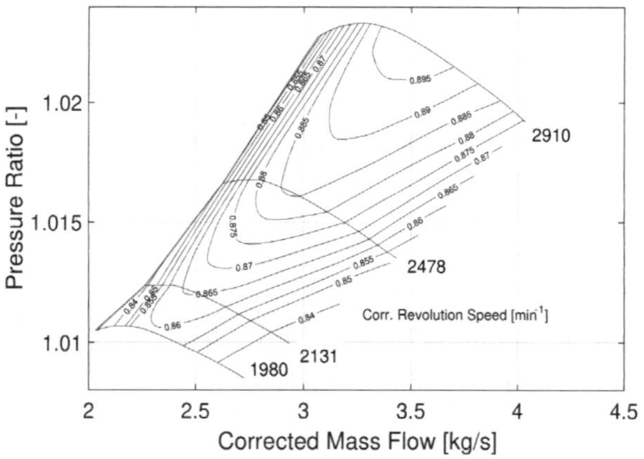

Figure 8. Compressor map for the EB52.

the pressure ratio Π of the compressor. The power at the shaft P_{in} is computed from the torque M and the revolution speed n. The mass flow and the pressure ratio allow the calculation of the required power for the pressure rise under isentropic conditions P_{id}. The ratio of the isentropic and the measured power yields to the compressor efficiency η. To create the compressor map, the compressor is throttled until it stalls. The pressure ratio is plotted versus the mass flow for different rotational speeds. Based on the measured efficiency, a contour plot is created to show lines of constant efficiency. As the compressor's behavior is dependent on the inlet conditions, it is not convenient to use the real mass flow and rotational speed, as the compressor map would not be the same on two different days or two different altitudes. Hereinafter, the different conditions are described with I and II. Therefore, the compressor map is transformed in a way that every point in the map has its specific streamline pattern. This can be achieved if the Mach number in axial (Ma_{ax}) and circumferential direction (Ma_{rad}) are constant for each point in the compressor map. The Mach number in axial direction is:

$$Ma_{ax} = \frac{c_{ax}}{a} = \frac{\dot{m}}{\rho A\sqrt{\kappa RT}} \tag{6}$$

with the flow velocity in axial direction c_{ax}, the sonic velocity a, the isotropic exponent κ, the specific gas constant R, the temperature T of the fluid and the corresponding area A [10].

By replacing the density ρ with the law of an ideal gas and subsequently describing the static pressure and static temperature by their total quantities, a constant axial Mach number is achieved when the following equation is satisfied:

$$\dot{m}_{\mathrm{I}}\frac{\sqrt{T_{\mathrm{t,I}}}}{p_{\mathrm{t,I}}} = \dot{m}_{\mathrm{II}}\frac{\sqrt{T_{\mathrm{t,II}}}}{p_{\mathrm{t,II}}} \tag{7}$$

By defining the corrected mass flow as:

$$\dot{m}_{\mathrm{cor}} = \dot{m}\frac{p_{\mathrm{ref}}}{p_{\mathrm{t}}}\sqrt{\frac{T_{\mathrm{t}}}{T_{\mathrm{ref}}}} \tag{8}$$

with the reference values for pressure p_{ref} and temperature T_{ref}. Often, the values of standard atmosphere are used. The total values p_t and T_t are the values at the compressor inlet.

It is obvious, that a constant axial Mach number is present, when the corrected mass flow is constant. The Mach number in circumferential direction is:

$$Ma_{\mathrm{u}} = \frac{r\omega}{\sqrt{\kappa RT}} \tag{9}$$

Replacing the static temperature with the total temperature and the angular velocity ω with the revolution speed, a constant circumferential Mach number is given when:

$$\frac{n_{\mathrm{I}}}{\sqrt{T_{\mathrm{t,I}}}} = \frac{n_{\mathrm{II}}}{\sqrt{T_{\mathrm{t,II}}}} \tag{10}$$

Introducing the corrected revolution speed:

$$n_{\mathrm{cor}} = n\sqrt{\frac{T_{\mathrm{ref}}}{T_{\mathrm{t}}}} \tag{11}$$

one can see that a constant circumferential Mach number is achieved when the corrected revolution speed is constant. To get a compressor map that is independent of the inlet conditions, the pressure ratio has to be plotted vs. the corrected mass flow. The throttle lines have to be parameterized for constant corrected revolution speeds.

VI. Blade Deflection Results

This section shows the reached measurement precision and discusses the blade deflection results in comparison to the compressor map. Figure 9 shows the single shot resolution θ. The resolution can be calculated with (12). There is v_t the tangential velocity, d_c the compressor diameter (blade tip to blade tip), f_{rev} the revolution frequency and t_s the sampling rate. The single shot resolution is varying from $0.05\ \mu m$ to $0.26\ \mu m$ with the actual revolution speed. All other parameters are constant in the equation.

$$\theta = v_{\mathrm{t}} \cdot t_{\mathrm{s}} = \pi d_{\mathrm{c}} f_{\mathrm{rev}} \cdot t_{\mathrm{s}} \tag{12}$$

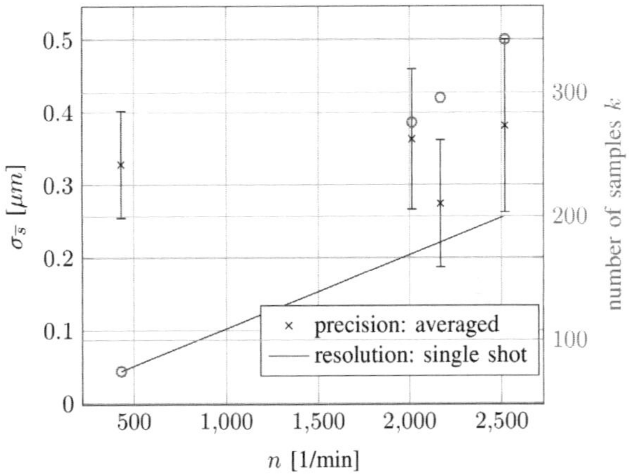

Figure 9. Achieved precision $\sigma_{\bar{s}}$ for all compressor blades, variation $\sigma_{\sigma_{\bar{s}}}$ of precision over all blades and resolution θ of the measurement system.

The resolution is only the first part which describes the quality of a measurement system. The reached precision depending on this resolution is more important. Figure 9 shows also the precision for the distance s^w (4) between a blade w and one reference mark. Each precision value stands for over all compressor blades averaged standard deviation of the arithmetic mean value of each compressor blade. This precision $\sigma_{\bar{s}}$ is calculated with (13):

$$\sigma_{\bar{s}} = \frac{1}{h}\sum_{w=1}^{h}\sigma_{\bar{s}}^{w} \tag{13}$$

with h the number of blades and $\sigma_{\bar{s}}^{w}$ the standard deviation of the arithmetic mean value for blade w.

The arithmetic mean value $\sigma_{\bar{s}}^{w}$ is calculated with (14). σ_{s}^{w} stands for the standard deviation of each individual blade and k for the number of sampled distances s^w.

$$\sigma_{\bar{s}}^{w} = \frac{\sigma_{s}^{w}}{\sqrt{k}} \tag{14}$$

The standard deviation is expressed with (15). For this calculation, the i-th sampled distance s_i^w of blade w to one reference mark and the empirical expected value $\bar{s}^w$ of the sampled distance was used.

$$\sigma_s^w = \sqrt{\frac{1}{k-1}\sum_{i=1}^{k}(s_i^w - \overline{s}^w)^2} = \sqrt{VAR(s^w)} \quad (15)$$

Additionally, in Figure 9 the variation of the standard deviation of the arithmetic mean value over all blades (16) is shown.

$$\sigma_{\sigma_{\overline{s}}} = \sqrt{VAR(\sigma_{\overline{s}}^w)} \quad (16)$$

The precision decreases slightly over the compressor revolution speed and is varying between $0.25\ \mu m$ and $0.4\ \mu m$. The reason for this are the increasing amplitudes of flow induced stochastic blade vibrations. The blades rotate through a steady flow field that is non-uniform in circumferential direction. A forced vibration is induced due to pressure fluctuations.

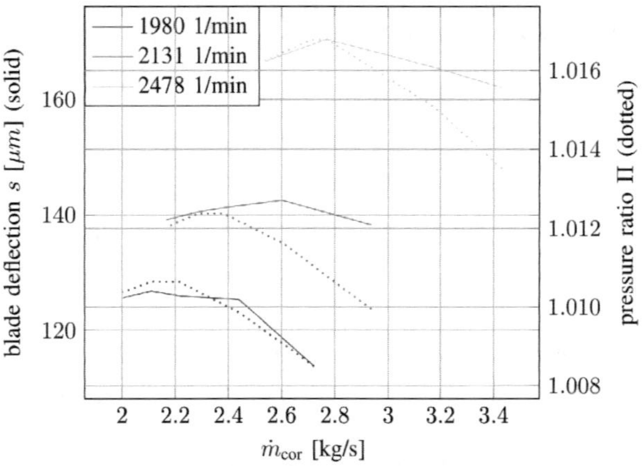

Figure 10. Blade deflection results for several revolution speeds in comparison to pressure ratio Π.

The precision variation of the blades are smaller than $0.125\ \mu m$ and shows the same behavior as the precision. They are increasing with the compressor revolution speed.

Figure 10 shows the first results of averaged blade deflections over the mass flow in comparison with the pressure ratio Π. Each color stands for one corrected revolution speed n_{cor} in the range of 1980..2478 $\frac{1}{min}$. The procedure was to set the revolution speed and change the working point with increasing throttling of the compressor step by step. The increased throttling leads to a reduced mass flow and in the first part to an increased pressure ratio and blade deflection. The working point moves left. Between each step several measurements for the compressor map and the blade deflection were done. The revolution speed lines 1980 and 2478$\frac{1}{min}$ show a good correlation to the pressure ratio. The maximum pressure ratio is very closely to the maximum blade deflection. The speed line at 2131$\frac{1}{min}$ has another behavior. It could be influenced by undetected EO's, not sufficient measurement quality (poor blade edge quality at this working point), not regarding the individual components of the resulting force F_r or another unknown effects.

VII. Conclusion

This paper has introduced a new method of working point identification with blade deflection determination. The theoretical background was explained, the used measurement equipment and several preliminary investigations were presented, and the used statistical values for the analysis were described. The first results were discussed and have proven the possibility of working point identification based on blade deflection measurements. This method allows to increase the efficiency of axial compressors. Further research is recommended to develop more robust sensor principles. It would be desirable to verify this new method on axial compressors with a higher pressure ratio. It is assumed that the measurement effect is much higher there.

Acknowledgment

The authors would like to thank Ivor Day from the University of Cambridge for the interesting professional discussions, the great support and the providing of technical equipment. This research program has been funded by IAV GmbH.

References

[1] I. Zablotskii, Y. A. Korostelev, and L. Sviblov, "Contactless measuring of vibrations in the rotor blades of turbines," DTIC Document, Tech. Rep., 1974.

[2] W. Nieberding and J. Pollack, "Optical detection of blade flutter," in *ASME 1977 International Gas Turbine Conference and Products Show*, American Society of Mechanical Engineers, 1977, V001T01A064–V001T01A064.

[3] M Zielinski and G Ziller, "Noncontact vibration measurements on compressor rotor blades," *Measurement Science and Technology*, vol. 11, no. 7, p. 847, 2000.

[4] P. Procházka and F. Vaněk, "New methods of noncontact sensing of blade vibrations and deflections in turbomachinery," *IEEE Transactions on Instrumentation and Measurement*, vol. 63, no. 6, pp. 1583–1592, 2014.

[5] R. Szczepanik *et al.*, "Application of blade-tip sensors to blade-vibration monitoring in gas turbines," in *Thermal Power Plants*, InTech, 2012.

[6] S Heath and M Imregun, "An improved single-parameter tip-timing method for turbomachinery blade vibration measurements using optical laser probes," *International journal of mechanical sciences*, vol. 38, no. 10, pp. 1047–1058, 1996.

[7] O. Jousselin, *Blade tip timing uncertainty*, US Patent 9,494,491, 2016.

[8] C. P. Lawson and P. C. Ivey, "Tubomachinery blade vibration amplitude measurement through tip timing with capacitance tip clearance probes," *Sensors and Actuators A: Physical*, vol. 118, no. 1, pp. 14–24, 2005.

[9] M. Koeller, O. Magnor, and D. Reitebuch, *Device and method for reliably operating a compressor at the pump threshold*, US Patent App. 13/824,452, 2011.

[10] W. J. Bräunling, *Aircraft Engines, Flugzeugtriebwerke: Grundlagen, Aero-Thermodynamik, ideale und reale Kreisprozesse, Thermische Turbomaschinen, Komponenten, Emissionen und Systeme*. Springer-Verlag, 2015.

[11] H. Herwig, *Fluid Mechanics, Strömungsmechanik*. Springer Vieweg, 2016.

[12] H.-A. Schreiber, W. Steinert, T. Sonoda, and T. Arima, "Advanced high turning compressor airfoils for low reynolds number condition: Part 2-experimental and numerical analysis," in *ASME Turbo Expo 2003, collocated with the 2003 International Joint Power Generation Conference*, American Society of Mechanical Engineers, 2003, pp. 451–463.

[13] R Reinhardt, D Lancelle, O Hagendorf, O Magnor, and P Duenow, "Improved reference system for high precision blade tip timing on axial compressors," in *Optical Fiber Sensors Conference (OFS), 2017 25th*, IEEE, 2017.

[14] R. Reinhardt, O. Magnor, P. Duenow, O. Hagendorf, and A. Rohlfs, "Event detection methods for high resolution time measurements on an application example," in *AUTSYM 2014*, vol. 7, 2014.

Pose Identification and Updating in Autonomous Vehicles

Antoni Grau, Yolanda Bolea
Automatic Control Dept.
Technical University of Catalonia, UPC
Barcelona, Spain
e-mail: {antoni.grau;yolanda.bolea}@upc.edu

Rodrigo Munguia
Computer Science Dept.
University of Guadalajara
Guadalajara, Mexico
e-mail: rodrigo.munguia@upc.edu

Abstract—**In this paper, a novel algorithm to know the pose of any autonomous vehicle is described. Such a system (Attitude and Heading Reference System, AHRS) is essential for real time vehicle navigation, guidance and control applications. For low funded projects, with simple sensors, efficient and robust algorithms become necessary for an acceptable performance, and the well-known extended Kalman filter (EKF) fulfills those requirements. In this kind of applications, the use of the EKF in direct configuration has been much less explored than its counterpart, the EKF in indirect configuration. Specifically, in this paper a novel method based on an Extended Kalman Filter in direct configuration is proposed, where the filter is explicitly derived from both kinematic and errors models. Experiments with real data show that the proposed method is able to maintain an accurate and drift-free attitude and heading estimation.**

Keywords—Attitude Estimation; Sensor Fusion; Vehicle Navigation.

I. INTRODUCTION

Autonomous Vehicle applications (Unmanned Ground Vehicles, Micro-Air Vehicles, Unmanned Aerial Vehicles (UAV), and Marine Surface Vehicles) all require accurate position and attitude to be effective [1]. While navigation grade Inertial Measurement Units (IMU) have existed for many years, they remain very expensive, and out of reach both in terms of cost and payload for all but the best funded projects. Small UAVs, even if the can afford the cost, cannot supply the necessary power to these units. A combination of instruments capable of maintaining an accurate estimate of the vehicle attitude, while it maneuvers, is called Attitude and Heading Reference System (AHRS). The first AHRS implementations were based only in gyroscopes. Gyros are prone to bias, which could produce large errors after long periods of integration. Filtering techniques are often required if less reliable (low-cost) gyros are used. Using filtering techniques, other sensors (i.e., accelerometers and magnetometers) can be combined with gyros in order to limit the attitude errors in time. With the availability of hardware (i.e., MEMS sensors and microcontrollers) several approaches for AHRS systems in the literature have been appearing, especially in the last decade. Nowadays, AHRS are typically based on gyros that are updated by gravity sensors (i.e., accelerometers) for pitch and roll and by magnetic field sensors for yaw. Nevertheless, depending on the application, it is common to find approaches relying in alternative sensors for bounding attitude errors in time, [2]-[5].

Several estimation techniques have been used for attitude determination. Schemes presented in [2] and [3] use Linear Filtering and Iterated least-squares methods, respectively. The linear Kalman filter (KF), commonly used for estimating the system state variables and for suppressing the measurement noise has been recognized as one of the most powerful state estimation techniques. Some methods relying on linear Kalman Filtering are presented in [5][6].

There are two basic ways for implementing the EKF: total state space formulation (also referred to as the direct formulation) and error state space formulation (also referred as the indirect formulation).

EKF in indirect formulation estimates a state vector which represents the errors between the estimated state and the estimated nominal trajectory. The measurement in the error state space formulation is made up entirely of system errors and is almost independent of the kinematic model. Most of the approaches follow this kind of configuration [4][7][8]. The differences among those methods mainly consist of variations in the design of the error models.

In EKF, in direct configuration the vector state is updated implicitly with the predicted state and the measurement residual (the difference between the predicted and current measurement). In this kind of EKF configuration, the system is essentially derived from the system kinematics. One of the characteristics of the direct configuration is its conceptual clarity and simplicity. In addition, it is possible to found other methods which rely in variations of Kalman filtering as the Unscented Kalman filtering [9]. Another interesting family of methods for attitude estimation is the nonlinear observers [10], but unsuitable for this research due to high computation load and real time purposes.

In a previous work [11], an uncoupled approach is presented. In that method, an EKF in direct configuration derived from the kinematic model estimates the attitude of the device, whereas an extra KF derived from the error sensor model estimates the gyro bias. However, the main drawback for the previous architecture was not to use optimally the full information available in the system covariance matrix. These data are useful to make a finest estimation of the system errors. As a consequence, some parameters had to be artificially tuned in order to improve the performance of the method.

This paper describes a novel algorithm for implementing an Attitude and Heading Reference System based on an Extended Kalman Filter in direct configuration. In this approach, the filter is explicitly derived from both the kinematic and error models. One of the advantages of the proposed approach is due to the clarity and simplicity associated with the implementation of the EKF in direct configuration. Section II describes the proposed method and the novel system architecture. Results with real data are presented in Section III, and some conclusions and future work are presented at the end of the paper.

II. METHOD DESCRIPTION

A. Vector state and system specification

The goal of the proposed method is the estimation of the following system state $\hat{x}$:

$$\hat{\mathrm{x}} = \begin{bmatrix} q^{nb} & \omega^b & \mathrm{x}_g \end{bmatrix}' \tag{1}$$

where $q^{nb} = [q_1,q_2,q_3,q_4]$ is a unit quaternion representing the orientation (roll, pitch and yaw) of the body (device); $\omega^b = [\omega_x\ \omega_y\ \omega_z]$ is the bias-compensated velocity rotation of the body expressed in the body frame; $\mathrm{x}_g = [\mathrm{x}_{g\_x}\ \mathrm{x}_{g\_y}\ \mathrm{x}_{g\_z}]$ is the bias of gyros.

In this work, the axes of the coordinate systems follow the North, East, Down (NED) convention. For simplicity, the orientation of the body follows Euler angles α, β and γ denoting respectively roll, pitch and yaw, respectively. Euler angles can be computed from quaternion q^{nb}.

In order to estimate the system state $\hat{x}$, measurements obtained with an IMU of 9-DOF are considered. The IMU is formed by a 3-axis gyroscope, a 3-axis accelerometer, and a 3-axis magnetometer.

1) Gyroscope measurements

The angular rate ω^b of the vehicle, measured by the gyros (in the body frame) and indicated as y_g, can be modeled by:

$$y_g = \omega^b + \mathrm{x}_g + v_g \tag{2}$$

where x_g is an additive error (bias) and v_g is a Gaussian white noise with power spectral density (PSD) σ_g^2.

2) Accelerometer measurements

The acceleration of the device a^b, measured by the accelerometers (in the body frame) as y_a, can be modeled by:

$$y_a = a^b - g^b + \mathrm{x}_a + v_a \tag{3}$$

where g^b is the gravity vector expressed in the body frame, x_a is an additive error (bias), and v_a is a Gaussian white noise with PSD σ_a^2. Bias in accelerometers triads are often relatively small, thus in this work it is neglected.

Magnetometer measurements: The earth field m^b measured (in the body frame) as y_m can be modeled by:

$$y_m = m^b + \mathrm{x}_m + v_m \tag{4}$$

where v_m is a Gaussian white noise with PSD σ_m^2. Magnetometer bias x_m could be fairly large but extremely slow time varying; therefore in this work it is not considered for online estimation; instead a calibration technique, as the presented one in [10], could be used for setting its initial value.

B. Architecture of the system

Figure 1 shows the architecture of the system which is defined by the typical loop of prediction-update steps in the EKF in direct configuration:

System Prediction: Prediction equations propagate along the time the estimation of the system state, by means of the measurements obtained from gyroscopes. Prediction equations offer correct estimates at high frequency, but only for a short period of time.

System Update: The unavoidable small errors in gyro readings produce large errors in attitude estimation after long periods of integration. The use of aiding sensors capable of measuring external references becomes essential in order to limit the estimation error. In this work, the gravity vector g and the magnetic earth field m are used as external references for correcting roll, pitch and yaw estimations:

i) During the periods when the device is in a non-accelerating mode (variable rate), information about the attitude of the device-vehicle (roll and pitch) is incorporated into the system by means of the observation of the gravity vector.

ii) Information about the heading (yaw) of the device-vehicle is incorporated into the system (at a predefined constant rate) by means of the observation of the earth magnetic field.

System Prediction: At every step k, when gyroscope measurements are available, the system state $\hat{\mathrm{x}}$ is updated by the following (discrete) nonlinear model.

$$\begin{cases} q^{nb}_{(k+1)} = \left(\cos\left(\|\mathrm{w}\|\right) \mathrm{I}_{4\times 4} + \dfrac{\sin\left(\|\mathrm{w}\|\right)}{\|\mathrm{w}\|} \mathrm{W} \right) q^{nb}_{(k)} \\ \omega^b_{(k+1)} = -\left(y_{g(k)} - \mathrm{x}_{g(k)} \right) \\ \mathrm{x}_{g(k+1)} = (1-\lambda_{xg}\Delta t)\mathrm{x}_{g(k)} \end{cases} \tag{5}$$

In the model represented by (5), a closed form solution of $\dot{q} = 1/2(\mathrm{W})q$ is used for integrating the current bias-compensated velocity rotation ω^b over the quaternion q^{nb}. In this case $\mathrm{w} = [\omega^b_{(k+1)}\Delta t/2]'$ and:

$$\mathrm{W} = \begin{bmatrix} 0 & -\mathrm{w}_1 & -\mathrm{w}_2 & -\mathrm{w}_3 \\ \mathrm{w}_1 & 0 & -\mathrm{w}_3 & \mathrm{w}_2 \\ \mathrm{w}_2 & \mathrm{w}_3 & 0 & -\mathrm{w}_1 \\ \mathrm{w}_3 & -\mathrm{w}_2 & \mathrm{w}_1 & 0 \end{bmatrix} \tag{6}$$

Also an alternative kinematic model for modeling the orientation of a camera by a quaternion can be found in a previous authors' work, [12]. Parameter λ_{xg} is a correlation time factor which models how fast the bias of gyro is varying. Δt is the sampling time of the system.

The state covariance matrix P is taken a step forward by:

$$P_{(k+1)} = \nabla F_x P_{(k)} \nabla F_x' + \nabla F_u U \nabla F_u' \tag{7}$$

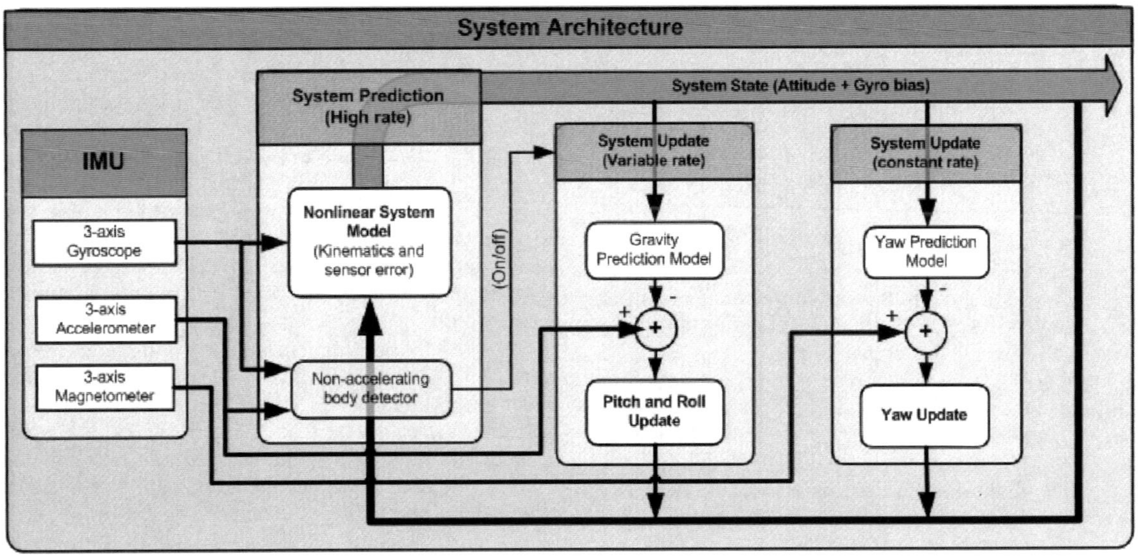

Figure 1. System architecture defined by an EKF in direct configuration.

The measurement noise of gyroscope v_g is incorporated into the system by means of the process' noise covariance matrix U, through parameter σ_g^2:

$$U = diag\left[\sigma_g^{\ 2} I_{3\times3} \quad \sigma_{xg}^{\ 2} I_{3\times3}\right] \tag{8}$$

The full model used for propagating the sensor bias error is: $bias_{k+1}=(1-\lambda\Delta t)bias_k + v_b$, where v_b models the uncertainty in the bias drift. The uncertainty in bias for gyro v_{xg} is incorporated into the system through the noise covariance matrix U via PSD parameter σ_{xg}^2.

$$\nabla F_x = \begin{bmatrix} \frac{\partial fq^{nb}}{\partial q^{nb}} & \frac{\partial fq^{nb}}{\partial \omega^b} & 0 \\ 0 & 0 & \frac{\partial f\omega^b}{\partial x_g} \\ 0 & 0 & \frac{\partial fx_g}{\partial x_g} \end{bmatrix} \quad \nabla F_u = \begin{bmatrix} 0 & 0 \\ \frac{\partial f\omega^b}{\partial y_g} & 0 \\ 0 & \frac{\partial fx_g}{\partial v_{xg}} \end{bmatrix} \tag{9}$$

The Jacobian ∇F_x is formed by the partial derivatives of the nonlinear prediction model, (5), with respect to the system state $\hat{x}$. In Jacobian notation, "$\partial fx/\partial y$" is used for partial derivatives and it must be read as the partial derivative of the function f (which estimates the state variable x) with respect to the variable y. Jacobian ∇F_u is formed by the partial derivatives of the nonlinear prediction model, (5), with respect to the system inputs.

A. *System Updates*

The filter can be updated as follows:

$$\hat{x}_k = \hat{x}_{k+1} + W(z_i - h_i) \tag{10}$$

$$P_k = P_{k+1} - WS_iW' \tag{11}$$

where z_i is the current measurement and $h_i = h(\hat{x})$ is the predicted measurement; W is the Kalman gain computed from:

$$W = P_{k+1}\nabla H_i' S_i^{-1} \tag{12}$$

S_i is the innovation covariance matrix:

$$S_i = \nabla H_i P_{k+1} \nabla H_i' + R_i \tag{13}$$

∇H_i is the Jacobian formed by the partial derivatives of the measurement prediction model $h(\hat{x})$ with respect to the system state $\hat{x}$. R_i is the measurement noise covariance matrix. Equations (10) to (13) will be used for system updates together with the proper definitions of z_i, h_i, ∇H_i and R_i.

1) Roll and pitch updates

If the device is not accelerating, (i.e., $a^b \approx 0$), then (3) can be approximated as $y_a \approx -g_b + v_a$ (x_a is neglected). In this situation, accelerometer measurements y_a provide noisy observations about the gravity vector (in the body frame). The gravity vector g is used as an external reference for correcting roll and pitch estimations.

In order to detect the time (corresponding to k instants) that the body is in a non-accelerating mode, the Stance Hypothesis Optimal Detector (SHOE) is used [13].

The gravity vector g is predicted to be measured by the accelerometers as h_g:

$$h_g = R^{nb} \begin{bmatrix} 0 \\ 0 \\ g_c \end{bmatrix} \tag{14}$$

where g_c is the gravity constant and R^{nb} is the navigation to body rotation matrix computed from the current quaternion q^{nb}.

If the device is not accelerating and a minimum period (corresponding to t_1 seconds) have elapsed since the last roll and pitch update, then the filter is updated (using (10) to (13)) with:

$$z_i = y_a \quad h_i = h_g \quad R_i = \mathrm{I}_{3\times3}\sigma_a^{\ 2} \quad \nabla H_i = \partial h_g / \partial \hat{\mathrm{x}} \qquad (15)$$

1) Yaw updates

The model h_γ used for predicting the heading (yaw) of the device is defined as:

$$h_\gamma = \mathrm{atan2}\left(2(q_2q_3 - q_1q_4), 1-2(q_3^{\ 2}+q_4^{\ 2})\right) \qquad (16)$$

where q^{nb}=[q_1,q_2,q_3,q_4] is the current quaternion; `atan2` is a two-argument function that computes the arctangent of y/x given y and x, within the range [-π, π].

As it can be observed in (16), the model does not predict the earth magnetic field to be measured. Instead, the model directly predicts the yaw angle to be measured. The idea of the selection of this measurement prediction model is due to the scalability of the system. In this sense, an alternative measurement device could be directly attached to the AHRS in order to correct the heading estimations.

In order to use the proposed measurement prediction model h_γ in the 3-axis magnetometer which is included in the 9-DOF IMU, a yaw measurement z_γ^n is obtained from the measured magnetic field y_m.

Due to the angle of inclination of the magnetic field vector, the measured magnetic vector is first projected to the north-east plane, by removing its z component:

$$m^n = R^{bn} y_m \qquad (17)$$

$$m_1^{\ n} = [m_x^{\ n} \quad m_y^{\ n} \quad 0] \qquad (18)$$

where m^n=[m_x^n, m_y^n, m_z^n] and R^{bn} is the body to navigation rotation matrix computed from the current quaternion q^{nb}. The magnetic field vector m^n_1 (expressed in the navigation frame), from which the z component has been removed, is projected back to the body frame by:

$$m^b = R^{nb} m^n_{\ 1} \qquad (19)$$

where m^b=[m_x^b, m_y^b, m_z^b] and R^{nb} is the navigation to body rotation matrix computed from the current quaternion q^{nb}. Finally, the measured yaw z_γ^n is obtained by:

$$z_\gamma^{\ n} = \mathrm{atan2}\left(-m_y^{\ b}, m_x^{\ b}\right) \qquad (20)$$

In this work it is assumed that the angle of declination of the magnetic field is ignored or is previously known. Measurements z_γ^n are assumed to be corrupted by Gaussian white noise v_γ with PSD σ_γ^2.

At constants intervals of t_2 seconds the filter is updated (using (10) to (13)) with:

$$z_i = z_\gamma^{\ n} \quad h_i = h_\gamma \quad R_i = \sigma_\gamma^{\ 2} \quad \nabla H_i = \partial h_\gamma / \hat{\mathrm{x}} \qquad (21)$$

III. Experimental Results

In order to validate the performance of the proposed method, a comparative study with real data is presented. In this case, the output estimated by the proposed algorithm (Direct method) is compared with the output obtained from the method described in [14], which is based in an EKF in indirect formulation (Indirect method). For the comparative study, the output obtained from a commercial 3DM-GX3®45 AHRS unit is considered as the ground truth. This unit can be easily mounted in any ground vehicle.

For each test the 3DM-GX3®45 was randomly gyrate while it was held in a hand. At the same time, raw data obtained from the accelerometers, gyroscopes and magnetometers included in the unit, along with the attitude computed by the same unit, were recorded in a plain text file at a frequency of 100 Hz. Several data captures were carried out trying to cover different dynamic circumstances like periodic and soft turns as well as random and strong shakes. Each capture lasts about 3 minutes.

A MATLAB© implementation of both, the proposed approach (Direct method), as well as the Indirect method were executed in off-line mode, using the raw sensor data stored in the plain text files as input signals. The execution time was: i) Direct method = 736 microseconds/step, ii) Indirect method = 586 microseconds/step. It is important to note that for the Indirect method the size of the system state is 6 (actual rotational velocity is not included), instead of 9. So (as is typical in EKF applications) difference in execution time should be mostly related with the size of the system state.

The outputs obtained with: i) the Direct method, ii) the Indirect method and iii) the 3DM-GX3®45 unit have been compared. In experiments the mean absolute error (MAE) was used for comparing the performance of both methods:

$$\mathrm{MAE} = \frac{1}{n}\sum_{k=1}^{n}\left\| f_k - y_k \right\|$$

where n is the number of samples, f_k is the angle measured by the 3DM-GX3®45 unit at instant k, and y_k is the angle estimated by a method at instant k. In experiments, for clarity purposes, Euler angles are obtained every time that they are needed from the current estimated quaternion q^{nb}.

For the comparative study two aspects were evaluated:

a) The performance of the methods for estimating the gyro bias x_g. That is, the ability of the filters to converge when the initial conditions differ considerably from the actual value, in order to minimize the error in estimations.

b) The performance of the methods when the frequency of operation is reduced (or the sample time is increased).

For the case (a), the methods were executed over the input signals stored in the plain text files. After that, the methods were run again over the same input signals, but artificially introducing a huge extra bias $\mathrm{x}_{g(a)}$ into each gyro measurement y_g, so that: $y_g = \omega^b + \mathrm{x}_g + v_g + \mathrm{x}_{g(a)}$, see (2). In experiments $\mathrm{x}_{g(a)}$ = [.05 -.05 .025] radians.

For the case (b), the methods were first executed over all the samples captured. After this operation, the methods were executed again but in this case periodically skipping samples in order to emulate different frequencies of operation. In this case, 100Hz, 50Hz and 25Hz were considered.

Table I shows the average MAE obtained with the Direct method and the Indirect method for several captures of data (considering all the conditions previously described). As it can be appreciated, the computed MAE is in general very similar for both methods. In a more detailed observation, the Direct method performs slightly better for converging (and thus minimizing the error in estimation) when an initial huge gyro bias is present. On the other hand, the Indirect method shows a slightly better response at very low frequency of operation.

Figure 2 shows the progression over time for the estimations obtained with the Direct and the Indirect methods, for a test with random turns and strong shakes. The plots correspond to the response of both methods when an extra gyro bias and a frequency of operation of 100Hz are considered. In Figure 2, at the beginning of the test (before second 30th) it can be clearly appreciated the adverse effect in the estimated roll, pitch and yaw due to the integration of the contaminated gyro measurements (observe the absolute error corresponding to this period). However, the estimated gyro bias rapidly converges to its actual value due to the system updates carried out in the filters. When the gyro bias is estimated then the absolute error is minimized. For this test, also it can be appreciated that the convergence of the Direct method is faster than the Indirect Method, thus accelerating the minimization of errors estimation.

TABLE I
MEAN ABSOLUTE ERROR (DEGREES)

No extra bias	**100Hz**	**50 Hz**	**25 Hz**
Roll (Direct)	0.65	0.84	2.62
Roll (Indirect)	0.66	0.83	2.50
Pitch (Direct)	0.36	0.58	1.80
Pitch (Direct)	0.35	0.56	1.74
Yaw (Direct)	0.68	0.96	2.42
Yaw (Indirect)	0.81	1.02	2.10
Extra Bias	**100Hz**	**50 Hz**	**25 Hz**
Roll (Direct)	1.12	1.28	3.01
Roll (Indirect)	1.39	1.54	2.92
Pitch (Direct)	0.87	1.07	2.30
Pitch (Direct)	0.98	1.19	2.33
Yaw (Direct)	2.52	3.52	5.76
Yaw (Indirect)	3.10	3.33	5.21

IV. CONCLUSION AND FUTURE WORK

This work presents a practical method for implementing an attitude and heading reference system that can applied to autonomous vehicles for an automatic navigation. The architecture of the system is based on an Extended Kalman filtering approach in direct configuration. Experiments with real data show that the proposed method is able to maintain an accurate and drift-free attitude and heading estimation. Moreover, it is capable of estimating the parameters of sensors error (i.e., gyro bias) in a robust manner, thereby improving the system estimations even when the quality of the measurements obtained from gyros is very poor. Therefore, the accuracy of the estimates is almost only limited by the pre-calibration of accelerometers and magnetometers. Based on the experimental results, it is considered that the method is enough robust for its use along with low-cost sensors. The modularity of the proposed architecture permits the scalability of the system. In such a case, an alternative measurement device could be easily attached to the system (replacing the magnetometers) in order to correct the heading estimations.

The EKF in general is not an optimal estimator (owned to its linearization nature). In addition, if the process is modeled incorrectly, the filter may quickly diverge. Also, it has been seen that the EKF tends to underestimate the true covariance matrix and therefore the filter could become inconsistent.

ACKNOWLEDGMENT

This work has been funded with project CICYT DPI2016-78957-R AEI/FEDER/UE.

REFERENCES

[1] G.H. Elkaim, "The Atlantis Project: A GPS-Guided Wing-Sailed Autonomous Catamaran", Journal of the Institute of Navigation, 53(4), 237–247, 2006.

[2] D. Gebre-Egziabher, R. C. Hayward, and J. D. Powell, "Design of multi-sensor attitude determination systems," IEEE Transactions on Aerospace and Electronic Systems 40(2), 627- 649, April 2004.

[3] F. L. Markley, "Attitude error representations for Kalman filtering", Journal of guidance control and dynamics 26, 311-317, 2003.

[4] J. F. G. Castellanos, S. Lesecq, N. Marchand, and J. Delamare, "A low-cost air data attitude heading reference system for the tourism airplane applications," IEEE Sensors, vol. 1, 44-47, 2005.

[5] M. Euston, P. Coote, R. Mahony, K. Jonghyuk, and T. Hamel, "A complementary filter for attitude estimation of a fixed-wing UAV," Intelligent Robots and Systems, 2008, 10.1109/IROS.2008.4650766.

[6] L. Wang, S. Xiong, Z. Zhou, and J. Lan, "Constrained Filtering Method for MAV Attitude Determination", IEEE IMTC Conf., 2005, 10.1109/IMTC.2005.1604397.

[7] Mei Wang, Yunchun Yang, R. R. Hatch, and Yanhua Zhang, "Adaptive filter for a miniature MEMS based attitude and heading reference system," Position Location and Navigation Symp. 2004, 10.1109/PLANS.2004.1308993

[8] Young Soo Suh, "Orientation Estimation Using a Quaternion-Based Indirect Kalman Filter With Adaptive Estimation of External Acceleration," IEEE Trans on Instrumentation and Measurement 59(12), 3296-3305, 2010.

[9] H.G. de Marina, F.J. Pereda, J.M. Giron-Sierra, and F. Espinosa, "UAV Attitude Estimation Using Uncented Kalman Filter and TRIAD", IEEE Trans on Ind. Electronics 59(11), 4465-4474, 2012.

[10] J. F. Vasconcelos, G. Elkaim, C. Silvestre, P. Oliveira, and B. Cardeira, "A Geometric Approach to Strapdown Magnetometer Calibration in Sensor Frame", IFAC Workshop Navigation, Guidance and Control of Underwater Vehicles, 2008, 10.1109/TAES.2011.5751259

[11] R. Munguia, and A. Grau, "An Attitude and Heading Reference System (AHRS) based on a Dual Filter", IEEE Conference on Emerging Technologies and Factory Automation ETFA 2011, 10.1109/ETFA.2011.6059089

[12] R. Munguia, and A. Grau, "Closing Loops With a Virtual Sensor Based on Monocular SLAM", IEEE Trans on Instrumentation and Measurement 58(8), 2377-2384, 2009.

[13] I. Skog, P. Handel, J. O. Nilsson, and J. Rantakokko, "Zero-Velocity Detection An Algorithm Evaluation," IEEE Trans on Biomedical Engineering 57(11), 2657-2666, 2010.

[14] J. Farrell, *Aided Navigation*, Mac Graw-Hill, 2008.

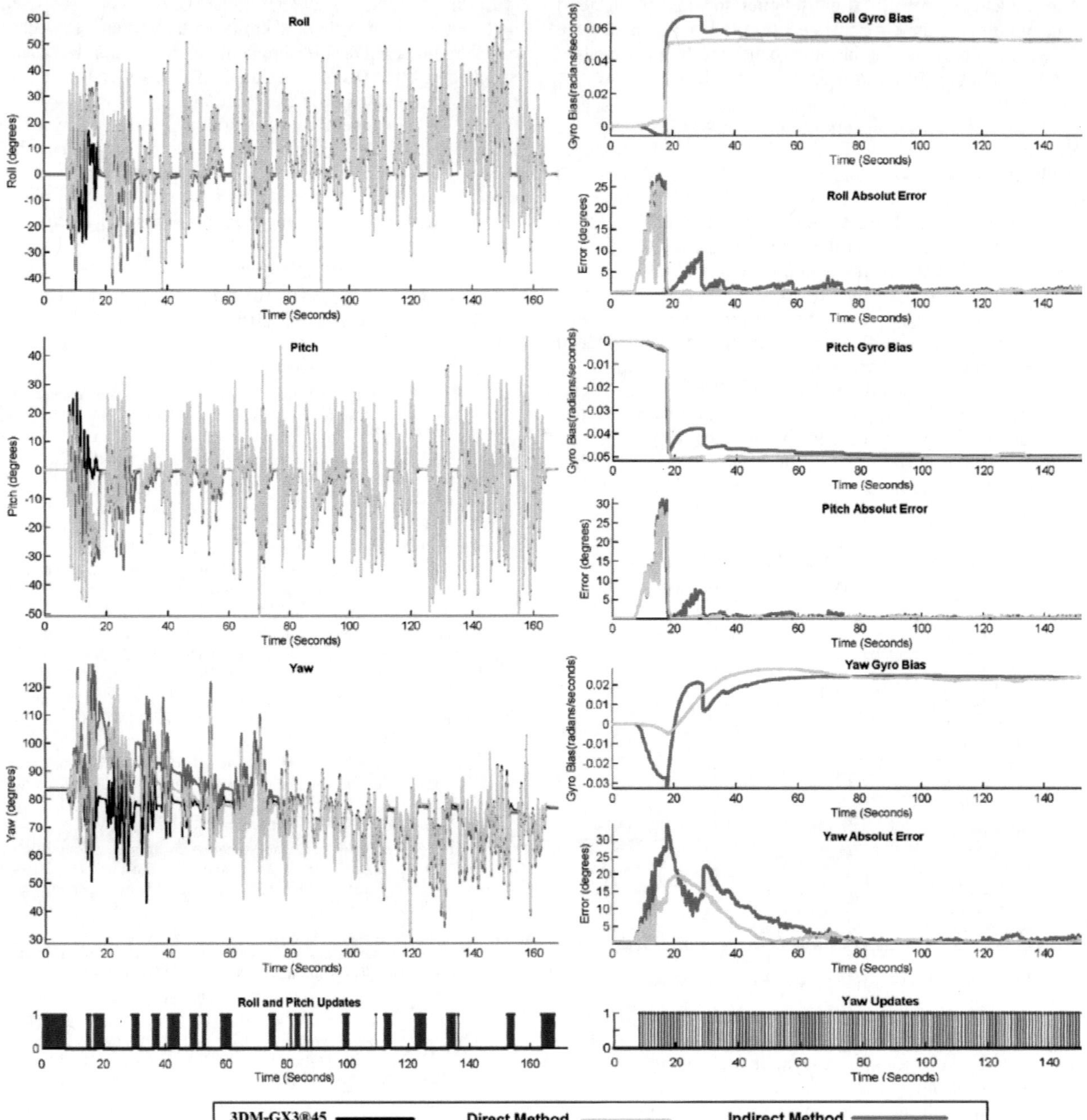

Figure 2. Estimation results for a test with random turns and strong shakes with a duration about 170 seconds.

A Portable Intelligent Bladder Irrigation Device for Long-Term Care Management Center Patients

Ming-Huang Chen, Ming-Chien Hung and Chen-Hsun Weng
Medical Device Innovation Center
National Cheng Kung University
Tainan, Taiwn
email: dearthund1@yahoo.com.tw, 9999lv@gmail.com, B88501113@gmail.com

***Abstract*—Urinary tract infection (UTI) is the most common nosocomial infection in many hospitals, accounting for 30% to 40% of all nosocomial infections. About 90% of them are related to long-term indwelling catheters, such as long-term care patients, diabetics, pregnant women, patients with Parkinson's disease, cortical stroke, brain tumors. Bacterial invasion of the human urinary system caused by inflammation of the bladder causes the bladder cells to induce cytokine secretion, including IL-1α、β、TNF-α, IL-6, IL-8 and IL-10, resulting in leukocyte aggregation, bleeding, and edema. This condition can lead to chronic nephritis, and severe cases can develop sepsis and even death. In this study, we developed a portable intelligent irrigation device based on activated carbon to assist the long-term use of urinary catheters in patients. Its principle works mainly through the activated carbon itself. The developed device has a large specific surface area and adsorption properties and can inhibit bacterial growth, while the adsorption of bacteria produced by internal and external toxins can slow down the pathogenicity of bacteria in organisms.**

Keywords-bladder irrigation; urinary tract infection; activated carbon.

I. INTRODUCTION

Bladder irrigation is a procedure in which sterile fluid is used to prevent clot retention/ infection by continuously irrigating the bladder via a catheter. Irrigation fluid management requires timely application of the right amount of detergent solutions. Competition for solutions, limited liquid resources and concerns for patients are making good irrigation management a challenge. In the world, Urinary Tract Infection (UTI) is the most common nosocomial infection in many hospitals [1][2]. Therefore, irrigation is a priority. However, poorly designed and planned irrigation management procedures and practices undermine the efforts to improve patients health and exposes people and the environment to risks. Many hospitals could benefit from having a proper irrigation schedule in place.

Just the right amount of irrigation needs to be determined. Too little irrigation can cause UTI; on the other hand, irrigation that is done too frequently can cause damage of the mucous membrane. There are many types of irrigation systems available on the market. The most common type is Continuous Bladder Irrigation (CBI) and it is a supplementary approach for irrigation management after surgery in order to prevent clot retention, cystospasm, and hemorrhage postoperatively. Although CBI is widely used to prevent clot retention and infection, it is not easy for nurses to transport the CBI device and bring it to each patient. Nurses are responsible for ensuring a continuous flow of prescribed solution during the whole procedure. Thus, it is imperative to assess the blocked catheter by checking the color of the drainage bag and controlling the flow rate. Currently, the flow rate of irrigation fluid is controlled manually by a nurse according to the color of drainage fluid. In this study, digital controllers using microcontrollers and analog controllers will be developed. These controllers are based on the measurement of the bladder tension. There are many types of sensors on the market that can be used to measure the tension, such as [3]. Some of these sensors are based on the resistance principle and some are based on the capacitance principle. Complementary Metal Oxide Semiconductor (CMOS) technology [3] is one of such technologies, which benefited from the communication and computing technologies. It should be pointed out that medical devices may themselves not require the sub-micron scaling of the CMOS technologies, but such developments, which generally serve in the first place for research purposes, can easily be translated into a medical device application. Further, claims of the field are shaped by biological media as novel resources. In this study, the integration of CMOS devices with various emerging sensing elements, utilizing techniques, such as surface activation by chemical means is quite promising in the field of research involving the development of CMOS-based sensors for bladder irrigation devices. The rest of the paper is structured as follows. In Section II, we present the materials and fabrication method. In Section III, we show the results and discussion. Finally, we conclude in Section IV.

II. MATERIALS AND FABRICATION METHODS

Bladder irrigation is one of the most effective measures to prevent urinary tract infection in patients with long-term indwelling catheter [4]. The operation of traditional artificial bladder irrigation is complicated and needs constant monitoring. Based on traditional artificial bladder irrigation technology, a kind of intelligent bladder irrigator and its control system are designed. The control system includes Programmable Logic Controller (PLC) and touch screen. By using a weighing sensor to monitor the weight of the infusion bag in real time, the irrigator control pinch valve can switch the infusion tube automatically. Bladder irrigation can be carried out automatically by using this intelligent bladder irrigator.

In order to assure a clean environment and to minimize the possible influence of environmental conditions in the experiments, a measurement cell was designed and fabricated. The use of this microfluidic chamber minimizes both the sample volume and the amount of reagents needed for detection, reducing thus the cost of the assay.

III. RESULTS AND DISCUSSION

The portable intelligent bladder irrigation device is the main part of the electronic system and its duty is to apply an electrical voltage and convert the electrochemical signal between the electrodes into an analog input. Figure 1 shows the device contains an analog digital converter ADS1256 from Texas Instruments (ADC), which turns the signal and sends it to the microcontroller composed of a FreeScale MC56F8037 commercial card (DSP, Digital Signal Processor). Finally, the data is sent to the control software by means of a USB connection.

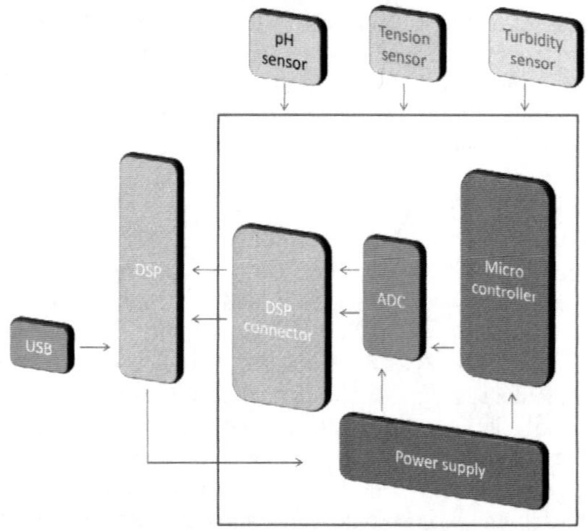

Figure 1. The electronic system

In order to integrate the intelligent bladder irrigation device with electrical connection pads, we have realized an integration scheme, in which the microchip is squeezed between a custom PolyMethylMethAcrylate (PMMA) fluidic adapter and a Printed Circuit Board (PCB), as shown in Figure 2. The electrical connections were realized between the electrical pads of the fabricated chip and the PCB, in which the conductive layers are oriented vertically in the thickness direction, making contact from top to bottom. These connectors prevent the use of fragile bond wires that may compromise fluidic integration, as well as the larger footprints that are required when using spring loaded connectors. Moreover, using the given integration scheme, the device replacement can easily be done within a minute.

For men or women, a bladder irrigation device measures the Escherichia Coli in the bladder, urethra, and abdomen. A catheter in the bladder fills the bladder with fluid and measures Escherichia Coli in urine. Another catheter, placed in the vagina for women or the rectum for men, reflects the Escherichia Coli in the abdomen. A bladder irrigation device can reveal detrusor over activity, stress incontinence from sphincter weakness, or weak pelvic floor muscles. Figure 3 shows the number of E.Coli could be reduced by the bladder irrigation device.

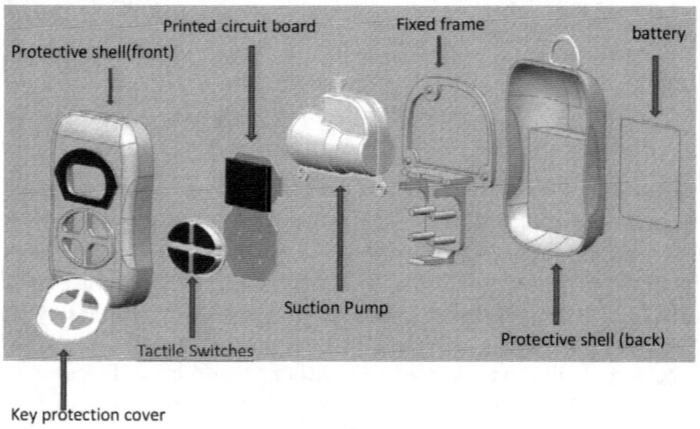

Figure 2. The bladder irrigation device

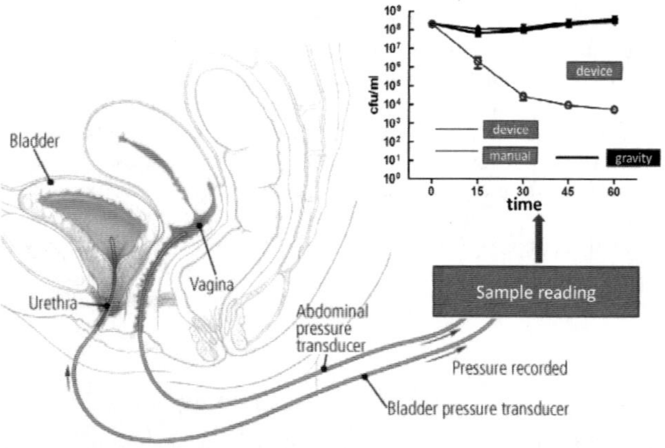

Figure 3. The bladder irrigation device measures the Escherichia coli in the bladder

IV. CONCLUSION

In this work, we have demonstrated an intelligent bladder irrigation device and a CMOS sensor to detect E. Coli in an artificial urinary bladder. It was capable of performing detection in an automated fashion while consuming fewer volumes of reagents using activated carbon.

REFERENCES

[1] J. A. Buitrago, S. C. Transplant, B. D.a Cruz, R. B., J. M. Estrella, Managing hemorrhagic cystitis in BMT patients using continuous bladder irrigation. Biol. Blood Marrow Transplant. vol.19, 2, pp.S357, 2013.

[2] V. T. Raup, A. M. Potretzke, B. J. Manley, J. A. Brockman, S. B. Bhayani, Hemorrhagic cystitis requiring bladder irrigation is associated with poor mortality in hospitalized stem cell transplant patients. Int. Braz. J. Urol. Off., no. 41, pp.1126–1131, 2015.

[3] M. N. Dakurah, C. Koo, W. Choi, and Y. H. Joung,

Implantable Bladder Sensors: A Methodological Review. Int Neurourol J. vol. 19, 3, pp. 133–141, 2015.
[4] J. Luo, Q. Zeng, J. Xiao, L. Huang, Recognition of drainage fluid color of continuous bladder irrigation for doctors and nurses of urological department. J. Nur. (China), vol.8, pp.18–20, 2010.

Self-monitoring the Breath for the Prevention of Cardio-metabolic Risk

Danila Germanese
Massimo Magrini,
Marco Righi and
Ovidio Salvetti

Institute of
Information Science and Technology,
ISTI-CNR, Pisa, Italy
mail: danila.germanese@isti.cnr.it
mail: massimo.magrini@isti.cnr.it
mail: marco.righi@isti.cnr.it
mail: ovidio.salvetti@isti.cnr.it

Mario D'Acunto

Biophysics Institute
IBF-CNR, Pisa, Italy
mail: mario.dacunto@cnr.it

***Abstract*—Breath analysis techniques offer a potential revolution in health care diagnostics because of their un-obtrusiveness and their inherent safety. However, while standard instrumentation such as mass spectrometers use laboratory settings to provide a correlation between exhaled substances and physical conditions, to fully realize the potential of breath analysis as a self-monitoring tool, its application must take place also in the clinics and at home and not only in a laboratory. This basic requirement has stimulated the necessity to develop cheap, portable, real time, easy-to-use devices for reliable breath tests and analysis. In this paper, we present the design of a portable breath analyzer, able to sense a set of breath volatile organic compounds (VOCs), to perform a processing of the data collected and to generate an output easily interpreted both by physicians and patients.**

Keywords–Breath analysis; Gas sensors; Self-monitoring; Home-care; Portable device; Signal processing.

I. INTRODUCTION

Breath analysis may play a key role in health care diagnostics [1]. This is because each breath contains fundamental information about the health status of an individual: breath molecules are the product of the composition of inspiratory air and the volatile substances in blood. In addition, also cells in the mouth, in the upper airways, in the gastrointestinal tract contribute volatile molecules to the exhaled breath. Consequently, the challenge is to extract from the breath meaningful data which can be correlated to subject's health.

On one hand, despite its great potential, breath analysis has not yet been employed in the ordinary diagnostic clinical trials. First of all, the main bottleneck is the lack of standardized protocol to collect breath sampling and to avoid all the confounding factors (such as inspired ambient air [2], breath flow rate, heart rate [3]). Moreover, the standard instrumentation (gas chromatography-mass spectrometry, for instance) is very expensive, time consuming and its use often requires highly qualified personnel. On the other hand, the main advantage of breath analysis is its un-obtrusiveness and safety. As a consequence, it may be a very suitable diagnostic tool, especially for those people who have to control a set of parameters daily.

These requirements have solicited the necessity to develop cheap, portable, real time, easy-to-use devices for breath analysis, in order to promote not only its purchase, but also its use in every type of setting (in home environment, for instance). In human breath, more than 200 volatile molecules have been identified and assessed. Some of such molecules were correlated to various diseases such as diabetes, oxidative stress, lung cancer, gastrointestinal diseases, etc. [4][5][6][7]. Due to such complex pattern of breath compounds, a design of a portable device for breath analysis should be based on selected chemical sensors able to sense specific VOCs. Generally, a long-term vision for breath analysis performed with a portable device should follow some basic requirements:

- the breath analysis device should be compact, easy to use, and able to follow, in real time, the breath molecules trend;
- the device should be able to transmit breath analysis results also to a remote personal computer (the family doctor's one, for instance);
- since it should be based on array of gas sensors, cross-correlation between sensors should be carefully taken in account to improve the sensitivity and the reliability of the overall device.

Recently, e-noses have gone in this direction. Formerly designed for broader applications (environmental gases monitoring, for instance), in recent years the idea of exploiting e-noses also for clinical applications has gained increased interest [8]. E-noses allow for performing breath analysis in a very short time, being quicker than a gas chromatograph. Since they are able to perform breath tests in real time, in many studies they have been employed to monitor volatile biomarkers related to cancer [9], for instance, in infectiology [10], and also to evaluate VOCs related to asthma [11]. Nevertheless, the majority of such e-noses exploit very expensive technology [12][13] or require complex circuitry [14][15].

In this paper, we describe how self-monitoring of someone's own well-being state could be done by means of a low cost device (called Wize Sniffer, WS) whose basic features have been described in [16][17]. In particular, the WS was designed to detect a set of breath molecules related to cardio-metabolic risk. Neverthless, its modular configuration allows for detecting a broader set of molecules, simply changing the gas sensors placed in gas samplig box. The WS is entirely based on low-cost technology: the semiconductor-based gas sensors are commercial, and breath signals are analyzed by a widely employed open source controller: Arduino Mega2560. In addition, it is programmed to also send breath analysis results also to a remote care center.

In the paper, Section II summarizes the detected VOCs; in Section III, the hardware/software architecture is described; Section IV reports the WS functionality tests and the different data analysis approaches. We conclude the paper in Section V.

II. CARDIO-METABOLIC RISK PREVENTION

The WS was conceived in the framework of SEMEOTICONS (SEMEiotic Oriented Technology for Individuals CardiOmetabolic risk self-assessmeNt and Self-monitoring, grant N. 611516) European Project [18], which aimed to develop a multi-sensory platform able to assess individuals well-being state by detecting in the human face all those signs related to cardio-metabolic risk [19]. Such multisensory, interactive platform included a sensorized Mirror (the *Wize Mirror*) and the WS. In particular, the WS was designed to help the user monitor his/her noxious habits for cardio-metabolic risk, by detecting the following VOCs:

- **Carbon monoxide** (CO). More than 5000 compounds in cigarette smoke are dangerous. CO, in particular, decreases the amount of oxygen that is carried in the red blood cells. It also increases the amount of cholesterol that is deposited into the arteries;
- **Ethanol** (C_2H_6O). Moderate ethanol consumption, in healthy subjects, reduces stress and increases feelings of happiness and well-being, and may reduce the risk of coronary heart disease. Heavy consumption of alcohol, instead, causes addiction and leads to an accumulation of free radicals into the cells, causing oxidative stress.

In addition, the device can also provide useful information about metabolism, user's carbohydrates adsorption and vascular status by detecting these other molecules:

- **Oxygen and carbon dioxide** (O_2 and CO_2): the amount of O_2, which is retained in the body, and the one of CO_2, which is produced as a by-product, can be considered as a measure of the metabolism;
- **Hydrogen** (H_2): it is related to the carbohydrates breakdown in the intestine and in the oral cavity by anaerobic bacteria;
- **Hydrogen sulfide** (H_2S): it is a vascular relax agent; for instance, it has a therapeutic effect in hypertension.

III. HARDWARE AND SOFTWARE ARCHITECTURE

A. *Wize Sniffer's sensor platform*

The core of a portable device designed to detect volatile molecules (wheather they derive from ambient air, for example, or human exhaled breath) is the gas sensors array. For this purpose, different technologies and sensors' transduction principles are exploited to assess the type and the concentration of the gases under investigation [8]. Regarding the WS, our aim was to find a trade off between good sensitivity, low cost and small dimension. As we mentioned in the previous section, the WS was developed to detect a set of molecules related to those noxious habits for cardio-metabolic risk; nevertheless, our aim was to design a modular sensor platform in order to detect a broader set of molecules, by simply changing the sensors according to the VOCs to be identified. As a consequence, the sensors' ease of integration in the circuitry was another requirement we needed.

On one hand, optical gas sensors, as well as quartz crystal microbalance (QCM)-based gas sensors and surface acoustic wave (SAW)-based gas sensors are very sensitive; on the other hand, they are expensive (especially in the case of optical gas sensors) and need complex circuitry (in the case of QCM and SAW gas sensors). Also, carbon nano-fiber (CNF) based gas sensors are very expensive, especially for their manufacturing. We chose metal oxide semiconductor (MOS)- based gas sensors: they are low cost and easy to integrate in the circuitry; they have very small dimension, long life and rapid recovery. In Table I, all the employed MOS-based gas sensors are listed.

TABLE I. SENSORS INTEGRATED IN THE WS SENSOR PLATFORM

Detected molecule	*Sensor*	*Best detection range*
Carbon monoxide	MQ7	20-200 ppm
	TGS2620	50-5000 ppm
Ethanol	TGS2602	1-10 ppm
	TGS2620	50-5000 ppm
Carbon dioxide	TGS4161	0-40000 ppm
Oxygen	MOX20	0-16%
Hydrogen sulfide	TGS2602	1-10 ppm
Hydrogen	TGS821	10-5000 ppm
	TGS2602	1-10 ppm
	TGS2620	50-5000 ppm
	MQ7	20-200 ppm

Unfortunately, humidity and cross-sensitivity strongly affect the behavior of MOS-based gas sensors [20]. In our case, humidity is a strong influencing parameter, as we deal with human breath. For this reason, we i)integrated a temperature and humidity sensor into the gas sampling box (Sensirion SHT11); ii)put a heat and moisture exchanger (HME) filter at the mouthpiece to reduce the contribution due to the water vapor from 90%RH to 65-70%RH; iii)investigated the behavior of Wize Sniffer's sensors both in response to a humidity variation and under precise measurement conditions: 30C+/-7% and 70%RH+/-5%, that are the ones that occur in the gases store chamber when a breath analysis is performed, as shown in Figure 1. Calculating the sensors' humidity drift is useful to potentially compensate it during the data processing. Figure 2 shows how the humidity strongly affects sensors' output (in this case, the one of MQ7 gas sensor). The relationship between humidity and sensors' output generally can be modeled by means of a power law:

$$V_{out} = f(hum) = a * (hum^b) + c \qquad (1)$$

where a and c are constant. In addition, we considered the entire range of humidity variation (for instance, 50%-55% Relative Humidity (RH) in the case of MQ7, as shown in Figure 2) and then, we calculated the slope of the curves. Based on the slope, drift coefficients were assessed (see Table II) as the decrease in sensors' output (Volt) per unit decrease in humidity, as given in (eq. 2):

$$S_d = \Delta V / \Delta hum \qquad (2)$$

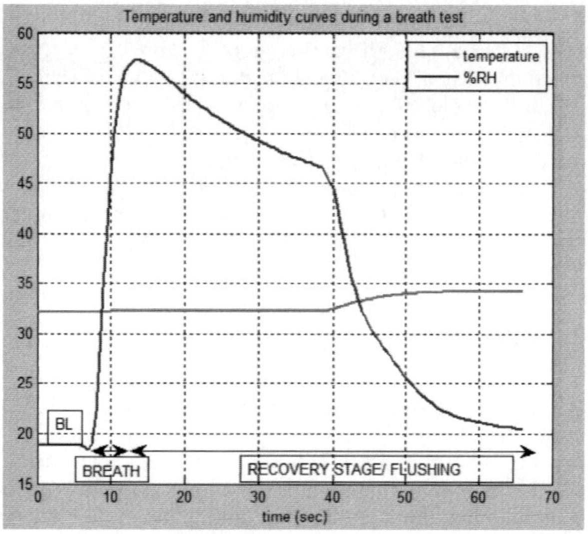

Figure 1. Temperature and relative humidity in the gas sampling box when a breath analysis is performed.

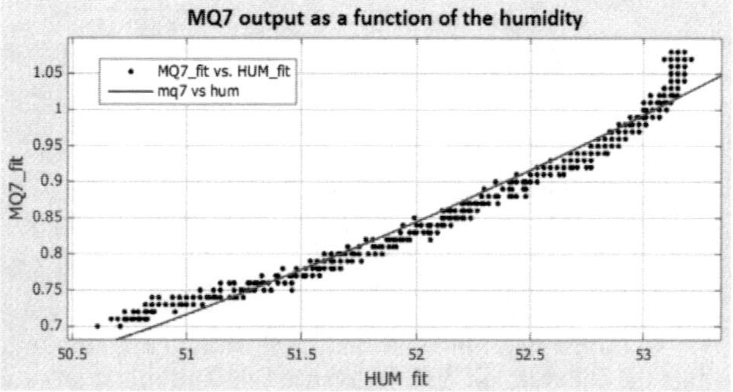

Figure 2. MQ7 output when a rise in humidity occurs.

TABLE II. SENSORS' DRIFT DUE TO HUMIDITY

Sensor	$\Delta V/\Delta hum$ *(mV)*
MQ7	296
TGS2620	60
TGS2602	82
TGS821	120
TGS2444	84

By keeping the humidity constant, sensors' output will depend on the gas concentration only. For this purpose, we investigated the sensors' output in response to a well-known gases concentration. The sensors were put into a vial. The humidity into the vial was kept at 70%RH+/-5% by means of a saturated solution of NaCl placed on the bottom; then, we injected well-known gases concentration and registered sensors' output. The raw sensors'output were read by an Arduino Mega2560 connected via serial port to a personal computer. The experimental data were displayed in real time on the computer screen and stored as text files for later processing. For example, in Figure 3, we can see TGS2620 output when well-known concentration of carbon monoxide, ethanol and hydrogen were separately injected into the vial. Also in this case, the relationship between sensors' output and gases concentration can be modeled by means of an equation similar to eq.1. Nevertheless, when a breath analysis is performed, a mix-

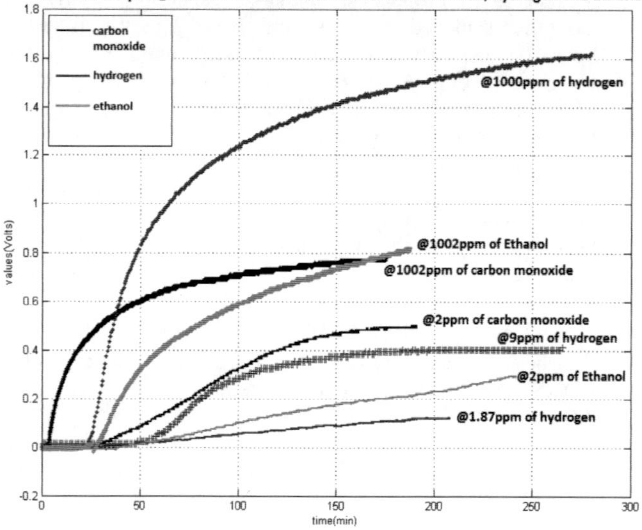

Figure 3. TGS2620 output when a well-known concentration of carbon monoxide, hydrogen and ethanol were injected into the vial.

ture of gases spreads into the gas sampling box and chemically interacts with the sensors. In this case, the phenomenon known as *cross sensitivity* makes these sensors non selective. Such behavior affects the method for data analysis, as described in Section IV.

Finally, the final set-up of the device is shown in Figure 4 and Figure 5. In the first one, the internal configuration of the device is reported: the gas sampling box, on the right, has a capacity of 600 ml according to the tidal volume [21]. The MOS-based gas sensors are placed within such box. Sensors' output is read and pre-processed by a widely used open source controller: an Arduino Mega2560. In Figure 5, the two configurations of the WS are shown: the WS can work both as a Wize Mirror tool and as a stand-alone device. In both cases, the user blows into a disposable mouthpiece, where a HME filter is placed. A flowmeter monitors the exhaled breath volume. Breath gases reach the gas sampling box by means of a corrugated tube. A fan is switched on between two breath tests to purge the gas sampling box with ambient air and to recovery sensors' steady state.

B. WS Software

Given its unobtrusiveness and its safety, breath analysis may be used as a daily monitoring analysis tool. To fully exploit its potential, its application must take place not only in laboratory settings, but also in the clinics.

In addition, our aim was to develop a device which could be used also in home environment and which could be able to send breath analysis results to a remote personal computer (for instance, to the one of the own family doctor) thus promoting independent living in community-based, home, and long-term care settings [22]. Arduino samples sensors' signals every 250 ms, saves raw vector data and extracts the maximum value of raw breath curve. Several parameters and features can be derived from breath curves [23] to fully characterize

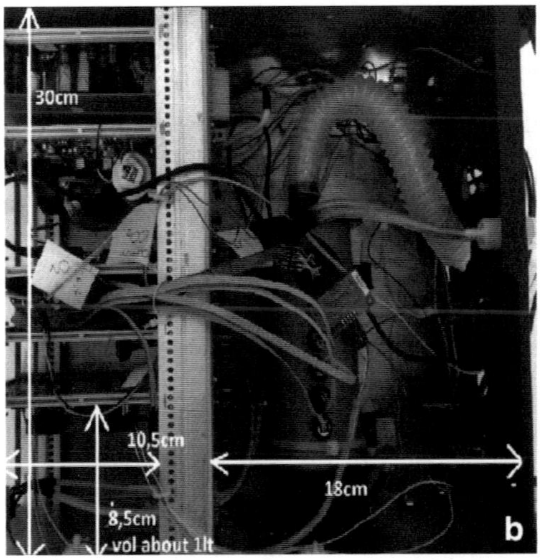

Figure 4. Final set-up of the Wize Sniffer. Internal configuration.

Figure 5. Final configuration of the Wize Sniffer. On the left, the WS is used a Wize Mirror tool. On the right, it is used in a stand-alone configuration.

them. We chose to calculate the value at curve plateau as it better describes the chemical balance between sensors'sensing element and target gases. Such data are then processed and analyzed, as described in Section IV.

In order to send breath analysis results also to a remote personal computer, we implemented a client-server architecture. It means that, after performing a test and processing the results, the device, by means of an internet connection and a TCP/IP communication protocol, can send the results to the physician, for instance. Arduino is programmed to execute a daemon on port 23. By implementing a Telnet server, it waits for a command line from the remote personal computer and then can provide the data. A measure is valid if the user's exhaled volume equals at least the one of gas sampling box.

IV. FUNCTIONALITY TESTS

The aim was to assess if the WS was able to monitor and evaluate the individuals' noxious habits for cardio-metabolic risk (smoke and alcohol intake in particular).

As described in [24], the WS underwent a clinical validation in three research centers: CNR in Pisa and Milan, CRNH (Centre de Recherche en Nutrition Humaine) in Lyon. The validation campaign involved 77 volunteers, with different habits and lifestyle. The subjects had to answer Audit test and Fagerstrom test, which respectively assessed the alcohol and smoke dependence, and other questionnaires about their lifestyle.

Taking into account the methodological issues about breath sampling [25], we outlined a measuring protocol, which considered mixed expiratory air sampling, since our interest was focused on both endogenous and exogenous biomarkers. The subjects took a deep breath in, held the breath for 10s, and then exhaled once into the corrugated tube trying to keep the expiratory flow constant and to completely empty their lungs. The study was approved by the Ethical Committee of the Azienda Ospedaliera Universitaria Pisana, protocol n.213/2014 approved on September 25th, 2014; all patients provided a signed informed consent before enrollment.

As mentioned before, MOS-based gas sensors are strongly affected by cross-sensitivity. It means that such type of sensors is not selective for one substance only, but they are sensitive for a set of VOCs. Such characteristic makes the quantitative analysis of the detected VOCs very difficult. As a consequence, we exploited another approach for data analysis, more classical, based on multivariate methods of pattern recognition. Pattern recognition exploits sensors' cross-correlation and helps to extract qualitative information contained in sensors' outputs ensemble. Then, first Principal Component Analysis (PCA) was performed, in order to provide a representation of the data in a space of dimensions lower than the original sensors' space. After assessing, by the PCA, the presence of clusters (see Figure 6), the data were processed with a K-nearest neighbor (KNN) classification algorithm, previously trained with the data coming from another acquisition campaign. The aim was to classify the subjects according to their habits: Healthy (that means, no cardio-metabolic risk), Light Smoker, Heavy Smoker, Social Drinker, Heavy Drinker, LsSd (Light smokers, Social drinker), LsHd (Light smokers, Heavy drinkers), HsSd (Heavy smokers, Social drinker), HsHd (Heavy smokers, Heavy drinker). The Audit and Fagerstrom questionnaires were our ground truth. The KNN classifier was able to correctly classify in 89,61% of cases. Errors were due to TGS2602 and TGS2620 cross-sensitivity for hydrogen. In fact, for instance, three no-risk subjects were classified as social drinker probably because of high hydrogen contribution, which caused a rise in these sensors voltage output.

Then, the population under study was increased, up to 169 subjects. Figure 7 provides a summary of subjects' habits and lifestyle in general. In particular, the subjects were divided into "low risk population", "medium risk population", "high risk population" basing on the sum of scores relative to Audit (AS), Fagerstom (FS) and lifestyle questionnaires, which were our ground truth also in this case. Also, the measuring protocol for breath sampling was the same, as well as data pre-processing: the parameter extracted from raw breath curve by Arduino was the value at the curve plateau, again. Given the significant

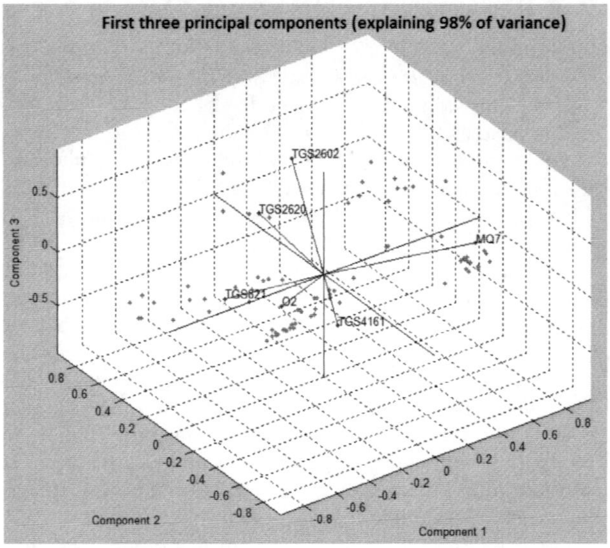

Figure 6. First three principal components.

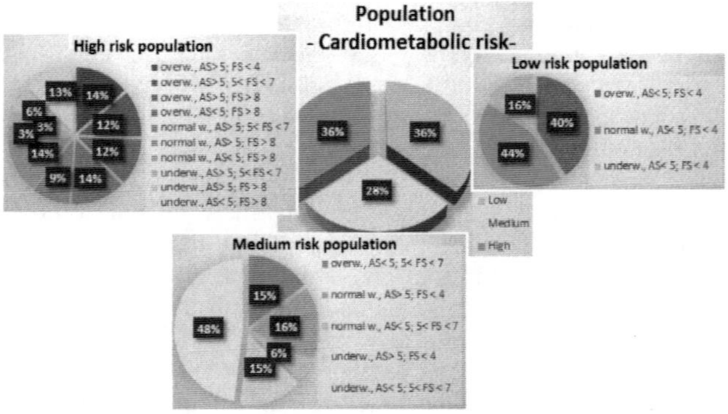

Figure 7. Population under study.

number of subjects, in this case we tried to implement a method of data analysis which was able to predict subjects' risk score (RS, it means, sum of Audit, Fagerstom and lifestyle questionnaires scores), based on the breath data.

Sensors' raw data first were zero-centered and normalized, thus putting in evidence the qualitative aspects of the data. Then, also in this case, the principal components were extracted and the PC scores were plotted against the subjects' RS (Figure 8). As can be deduced from the colours (green points derive from no-risk subjects, the blue ones from low-risk subjects, the yellow ones from medium risk subjects, the red ones from high risk subjects, the magenta ones from very high risk subjects), subjects' RS are arranged in ascending order.

Except for PC3, from a visual, exploratory analysis, we saw that the PC scores did not have a sharp increasing or decreasing linear trend with respect to RS, thus not having enough information to contribute to any prediction model. Such result matches the one reported in [26]. Being inspired by this study, we also implemented an Independent Component Analysis (ICA) on our data.

ICA is a high-order transformation method for data representation which extracts independent components from the

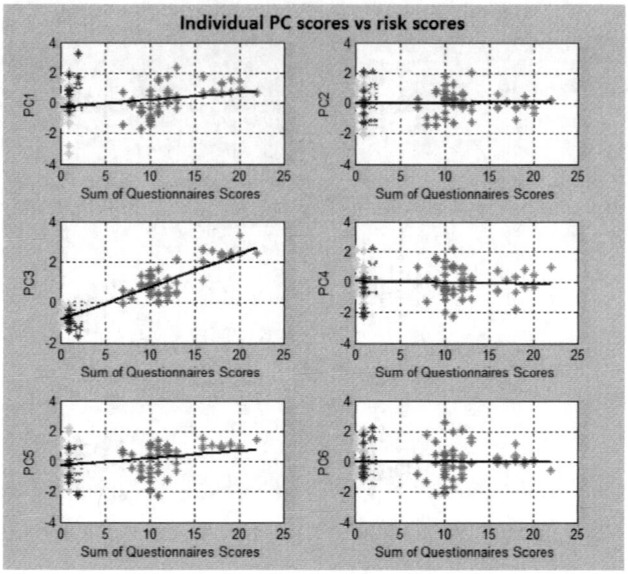

Figure 8. PC scores against subjects' risk scores.

data set. If, on one hand, PCA exploits the real sensors' cross-correlation, ICA originates from the assumption that the data has a non-Gaussian distribution, which often is a property of the gas sensors' array measurement data [27]. In our case, breath signals and the environmental ones (noise) get mixed with each other before the chemical interaction with the sensor array. As a consequence, each sensor's output is the result of a combination of different gaseous contributions.

We applied FastICA algorithm to our data set, and plotted individual independent components (IC) against subjects' RS. As shown in Figure 9, in this case, sharper linear trends emerge. Then, the data set was split into two data-sets (train

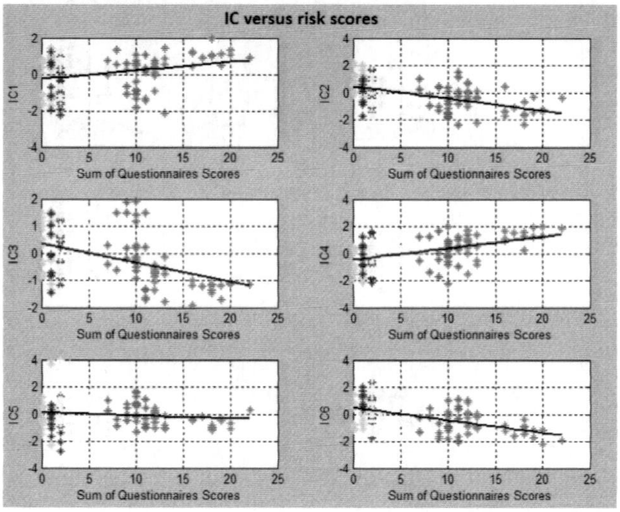

Figure 9. PC scores against subjects' risk scores arranged in ascending order.

data set and validation data set) to build the prediction model, which was developed by means of the Matlab LinearModel Tool. Indeed, by using the independent components, a linear regression model was built to establish a relationship between the risk score and the breath data pre-processed by ICA. Then, such model was validated by using the validation data set. In Figure 10, we can see that the correlation coefficient (r) between actual and estimated risk scores is 0.8976.

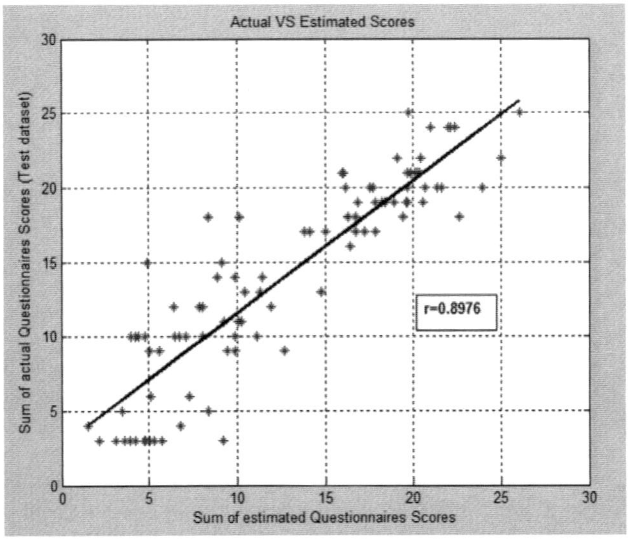

Figure 10. Actual risk scores against predicted ones.

V. Conclusion

In this paper, we describe how breath analysis could be exploited for daily self-monitoring by using a portable, low cost, very easy to use device that we developed and called Wize Sniffer. In the presented use case, the WS could help the user to monitor his/her habits and prevent the cardio-metabolic risk. Nevertheless, the WS modular configuration allows for changing the gas sensors according to the molecules (and then, to the related diseases) to be monitored. The core of such type of devices is the gas sensor array. We chose to use MOS-based gas sensors, because of their low cost, their ease to be integrated in the circuitry, their long life and rapid recovery time. Nonetheless, they are affected by humidity, which is, in our case, a parameter to be taken into account, as human breath is composed of 90% water vapor. As reported in Section 4, we faced this issue first by integrating a HME filter and then by calculating sensors' drift due to humidity in order to possibly compensate it. Another peculiarity of MOS-based sensors is the cross-sensitivity, which makes difficult any quantitative analysis approach. In this case, we faced this problem by using multivariate methods of analysis. In addition, our data analysis directly provides the user with him/her cardio-metabolic risk score. The safety and the unobtrusiveness of the device allow for a daily monitoring which, even if without a real diagnostic meaning yet, could represent a pre-screening, useful for an optimal selection of more standard medical analysis.

References

[1] W. Miekisch, J. Schubert, and G. Noeldge-Schomburg, "Diagnostic potential of breath analysis - focus on volatile organic compounds," Clinica Chimica Acta, Elsevier, vol. 347, 2004, pp. 25–39.

[2] F. Di Francesco and al., "Implementation of fowlers method for endtidal air sampling," J. of Breath Research, 2008, p. 037009(10pp.).

[3] J. Jones and S. Clarke, "Effect of expiratory flow rate on regional lung emptying," Clin. Sci., 1969, pp. 343–56.

[4] F. Di Francesco, R. Fuoco, M. Trivella, and A. Ceccarini, "Breath analysis: trends in techniques and clinical applications," Microchemical J., vol. 79, 2005, pp. 405–10.

[5] D. Guo, D. Zhang, N. Li, L. Zhang, and J. Yang, "A novel breath analysis system based on electronic olfaction," IEEE Transaction on Biomedical Engineering, vol. 57, 2010, pp. 2753 – 2763.

[6] D. Hill and R. Binions, "Breath analysis for medical diagnosis," Int. J. on smart sensing and intelligent system, vol. 5, 2012, pp. 401–440.

[7] J. Fenske and S. Paulson, "Human breath emission of vocs," J. of the Air and Waste Management Association, vol. 49, 1999, pp. 594–598.

[8] A. Wilson, "Recent progress in the design and clinical development of electronic-nose technologies," Nanobios.in Dis.Diagn., 2016, pp. 15–27.

[9] T. de Meij and al., "Electronic nose can discriminate colorectal carcinoma and advanced adenomas by fecal volatile biomarker analysis: proof of principle study," Int. J. Cancer, 2014, pp. 1132–1138.

[10] N. Yusuf and al., "In-vitro diagnosis of single and poly microbial species targeted for diabetic foot infection using e-nose technology," BMC Bionformatics, 2015, pp. 158–169.

[11] P. Montuschi, N. Mores, A. Trov, C. Mondino, and P. Barnes, "The electronic nose in respiratory medicine," Respiration, 2013, pp. 72–84.

[12] URL: http://www.bedfont.com/ [accessed: 2017-07-04].

[13] D. Walt and al., "Optical sensor array for odor recognition," Biosens. Bioelectron., 1998, pp. 697–699.

[14] F. Lai and H. Huang, "Fabrication of high frequency and low-cost surface-acustic wave filters using near field phase shift photolitography," Microelectronic Eng., 2006, pp. 1407–1409.

[15] L. Fan, H. Ge, S. Zhang, H. Zhang, and J. Zhu, "Optimization of sensitivity induced by surface conductivity and adsorbed mass in surface acoustic wave gas sensors," Sensor Act. B-Chem, 2012, pp. 114–123.

[16] D. Germanese and al., "A low cost, portable device for breath analysis and self-monitoring, the wize sniffer," De Gloria (eds) Applications in Electronics Pervading Industry, Environment and Society, ApplePies 2016, Lecture Notes in Electrical Engineering, vol. 349, 2017.

[17] D. Germanese, M. D'Acunto, and O. Salvetti, "Design of a breath analysis device for self-monitoring and remote health-care," in Proceedings of the 9th Intern. Joint Conf. on Biomedical Eng. Systems and Technologies (BIOSTEC 2016) February 21–23, 2016, Rome, Italy. SciTePress, 2016, pp. 9–14.

[18] URL: http://www.semeoticons.eu/ [accessed: 2017-07-04].

[19] S. Colantonio and al., "A smart mirror to promote a healthy lifestyle," Biosystems Eng., Special Issue: Innovations in Medicine and Healthcare. Elsevier, vol. 138, 2015, pp. 33–43.

[20] P. Clifford and D. Tuma, "Characteristics of semiconductors gas sensors i. steady state gas response," Sens. and Act., vol. 3, 1983, pp. 233–254.

[21] D. Shier, D. Butler, and R. Lewis, Holes Human Anatomy and Physiology, 11th ed. McGraw-Hill, 2007.

[22] A. Testa, M. Cinque, A. Coronato, and G. DePietro, "A formal approach for a dependability assessment of a mhealth monitoring system," Mob.Health, Springer S. in Bio-/Neuroinf., vol. 5, 2015, pp. 171–194.

[23] J. Yan and al., "Electronic nose feature extraction methods: A review," Sensors, vol. 15, 2015, pp. 2784–27 831.

[24] D. Germanese, M. Righi, M. Magrini, M. Guidi, M. D'Acunto, and O. Salvetti, "A device for self-monitoring breath analysis," in Proceedings of the 7th Intern. Conf. on Sensor Device Technologies and Applications (SENSORDEVICES2016) July 24–28, 2016, Nice, France. IARIA, 2016, pp. 77–82.

[25] W. Miekisch, S. Kischkel, A. Sawacki, T. Liebau, M. Mieth, and J. Schubert, "Impact of sampling procedures on the results of breath analysis," J. of Breath Research, 2008, p. 026007(7pp.).

[26] S. Balasubramanian, S. Paniraghi, C. Logue, C. Doetkott, M. Marchello, and J. Sherwood, "Independent component analysis- processed electronic nose data for predicting salmonella typhimurium populations in contaminated beef," Food Control, Elsevier, vol. 19, 2008, pp. 236–246.

[27] M. Kermit and O. Tomic, "Independent component analysis applied on gas sensor array measurement data," IEEE Sensors journal, 2003, pp. 500–511.

Estimating Emotion for Each Personality to Prevent School Dropout

Emi Takemoto
Graduate School of Information Science and Engineering
Ritsumeikan University, Shiga, Japan
Email: emi0403@de.ritsumei.ac.jp

Yusuke Kajiwara
College of Information Science and Engineering
Ritsumeikan University, Shiga, Japan
Email: kajiwara@fc.ritsumei.ac.jp

Hiromitsu Simakawa
College of Information Science and Engineering
Ritsumeikan University, Shiga, Japan
Email: simakawa@cs.ritsumei.ac.jp

Abstract—**This research estimates emotions of university students from their pulse waves. Negative emotion of university students causes school dropout, which is becoming a serious problem in Japan. It is indispensable for school staffs and counselors to know when and where students have negative emotion in the campus. Since pulse wave movement along with emotion changes varies with personality types, we build a model dependent on personality type, to estimate student emotion from characteristics of pulse wave movement. Experimental results show that the model for each personality type improves the accuracy of emotion estimation for new students. Positive or negative emotion estimated from pulse wave signals contributes to enhancement of campus environment by school counselors.**

Keywords–emotion; school dropout; pulse wave; personality

I. INTRODUCTION

University dropout is a serious social problem in Japan. According to a survey conducted by the Ministry of Education, Culture, Sports, Science and Technology, there are the rates of student dropout were 0.42% for elementary school, 2.83% for junior high school, 1.49% for high school and 2.9% for university [1] [2].

According to Kearney & Silverman, youths are considered to drop out of school for one or more of the following reasons (functional conditions):

- To avoid school-based stimuli that provoke a general sense of negative affectivity (anxiety and depression)
- To escape aversive school-based social and/or evaluative situations
- To pursue attention from significant others
- To pursue tangible reinforcers outside of school

The first two functional conditions refer to school dropout behavior maintained by negative reinforcement, or the reduction of unpleasant physical arousal or emotional states triggered by school-based stimuli [3]. This research focuses on these functional conditions. Students who drop out of school are assumed to not be able to deal well with negative emotions and situations causing them.

M.E.Pritchard and G.S.Wilson reported the combined influence of emotional health had a significant effect on intent to drop out [4]. Therefore, the university should aware of the emotional health condition of the students so that students can maintain a positive mood.

This research estimates when and where universities students have negative emotions leading them to school dropout. The estimation of the time and places causing negative emotion enables university staff to know what kind of events in campus activities bring them negative emotion. They can provide the students with mental care, such as emotional support and introduction of counseling agency, which prevents the students from dropping out.

Emotions are estimated through periodical inspection with questionnaires, behavior observation, and measurement of physiological responses. Since frequent questionnaires are a burden to students, they are not suitable to finely grasp emotions changing over time. Settlement of equipment, such as cameras is necessary to observe behaviors. However, it records the behavior of many students, which violates their privacy. On the other hand, physiological responses can be obtained through measurement of biological data using a wearable device. Biological data correlated with emotion enables us to estimate emotions online. The combination with positioning tools, such as GPS and WIFI identifies the place where negative emotions occur.

A classifier based on machine learning is a promising means for the estimation of emotion from measured biological data. However, the transition pattern of biological data for the occurrence of specific emotion varies with individuals [5]. If we want to estimate emotions from physiological responses, it is necessary to train a classifier with the biological data brought by emotions of each student in advance for a certain period of time [6]. In a classifier trained with biological data of any student, the estimation accuracy would be significantly low, while training of a classifier with biological data of each student is a big burden for the student. We need to overcome the problem to estimate emotion from a physiological response of students.

To solve this problem, this research trains a classifier with biological data collected from students of identical personality, because transition patterns of physiological response depend on personality types [7] [8]. Students of various kinds of personalities have diversity in patterns of the physiological response to the occurrence of a specific emotion. If we train a classifier using such physiological response, we cannot expect the classifier to extract the common patterns of physiological response. In this research, the emotion is estimated using classifiers trained with the physiological response of students similar in their personality type. Since a classifier is prepared for each personality type, the emotion of a new student can be estimated only with the student answering a quick personality test.

In this research, experimental results show classifiers for each personality type improved the accuracy of emotion estimation for new users. For each personality type, there was a difference in estimation accuracy, the pattern of the physiological response, and important variables. Among elements composing personality, the extroversion and the neuroticism seem to play a vital effect on the estimation accuracy. People strongly extroverted are likely to have positive emotion, while those who have high neuroticism are likely to be sensitive to stimulation. It is inferred that there was a difference in biological data and variables of importance because neuroticism certainly affects heart rate and Low-Frequency (LF) component/High-Frequency (HF) component of heart rate variablity, while extroversion, openness, and agreeableness certainly affect the natural log of LF.

A classifier for each personality type would tell the time and place for which university students have negative emotion in an on-line manner. For students who have negative emotions, such as anger and sorrow, it would be possible to provide support, such as keeping an eye on them, giving them a phone call, and introducing them to a counseling agency.

The rest of the paper is structured as follows. In Section 2, we show existing research about determinate emotions. In Section 3, we show the use case and method of my study. In Section 4, we show the experimental result. In section 5, we discuss from experimental result. Finally, we conclude in Section 6.

II. EXISTING RESEARCH

Section II describes the advantages and disadvantages of existing methods to determin emotions. A scale is necessary to determine emotions. The scale includes psychological scales to examine subjective emotional experiences, behavior scales based on external reactions, and biological scales based on internal responses.

The psychological scale includes the introspective method, the Likert scale, the rating scale method, the open-ended question method, the questionnaire method, and so on. Since these scale methods require students to answer big questionnaires, they have difficulties to obtain data of many university students.

The behavior scale needs permanent acquisition of various nonverbal behaviors, such as facial expression, posture, attitude, gesture, and voice. Although behavior data can be obtained through a lot of measuring equipment in many places, it causes privacy violation.

The biological scale uses both of autonomous reaction by activities of the autonomic nervous system and voluntary reactions by activities of the central nervous system. The former includes blood pressure, heart rate, skin electrical reflection, skin temperature, and blood flow rate, while the latter includes brain waves, electromyograms, and respiration. The wearable device for determination equipment enables to obtain those biological data all the time. Emotions can be estimated in an online manner from them.

However, physiological responses when each emotion occurs often do not match. The reason is that the physiological response patterns are different among individuals [5]. Leon has optimized classifiers with training using biological data for each person to eliminate individual differences in physiological response [6]. Since personalized classification method requires time for the training using individual biological data, new users cannot use it immediately.

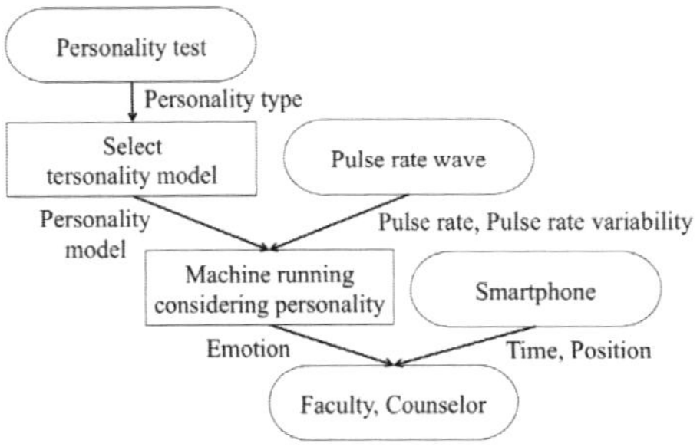

Figure 1. Estimating emotions considering personality

In order to obtain a practical solution to know the timing when each university student has a negative emotion, we need a method many users can use easily on the spot. These existing methods are not suitable for easy classification of student emotions.

III. EMOTION ESTIMATION WITH PERSONALITY

A. *Use Case*

This sections describes the method to estimate emotions in this research. Emotions are estimated from biological data considering personality. Students take a personality test to select a classifier according to their test result. The method estimates emotions from heart rate and its variability using a wearable pulse wave meter. Various wearable devices have been developed and operated in the field of health care and sports in recent years [9]. For students wearing a pulse wave meter, an application on a smartphone estimates negative emotions. Once it finds a student who often suffers from negative emotion, it notifies faculty and counselors of the information, to provide the mental care for the student. Figure 1 shows an operational diagram of the method.

B. *Estimating Personality*

In this section, a personality and the method to estimate personality are described. There are typology theory and property theory in the ways of grasping a personality. The typology theory applies a personality to a stereotype set based on psychological or biological characteristics. The typology theory is intuitively easy to understand, but the intermediate type is likely to be ignored in the theory. It is also difficult for one type to move to another. On the contrary, in the characteristic theory, the personality is composed of several characteristics. It expresses personality with multi-dimensions for quantitative comparison. The characteristic theory has the disadvantage that it is difficult to grasp the identity of personality. However, we can analyze personality statistically. It is also possible to grasp the personality in a typological way, if we classify subjects from a certain viewpoint.

The characteristic theory is used in this research. The Big Five test expressing personality with five factors is considered to be the most influential test in the characteristic theory. The five factors are neuroticism, extraversion, openness, agreeableness, and conscientiousness [10]. Neuroticism responds sensitively to external stimuli and shows emotional instability trend. Extroversion indicates a tendency to actively appeal to the outside world. People with high extroversion tend to have positive emotions. It means openness to experience. It shows a rich tendency for thought and images. Agreeableness shows a tendency to synchronize with other people in relationship with people. Conscientiousness shows a tendency to overcome things with clear purpose and intention.Conscientiousness is a dimension related to control of impulses.

Emotion is presumed to be affected by neuroticism related to anxiety causing emotional instability. It is also likely to be affected by extraversion leading to positive emotions.

C. Classifiers Based on Heart Rate

The students use the wearable device to measure biological data.We measure the heart rate and the heart rate variability. This section describes heart rate. The heart rate increases with anger, fear, and sadness, not with joy, surprise, and disgust [11]. The activity of the human autonomic nervous system changes when the emotion changes. The activity of the autonomic nervous system is measured from the frequency response of heart rate variability [12]. From the heart rate variability, the following components can be obtained; Very Low-Frequency (VLF) component (frequency is 0.0033 to 0.04 Hz), Low-Frequency (LF) component (frequency is 0.04 to 0.15 Hz), High-Frequency (HF) component (frequency is 0.15 to 0.5 Hz), Total Power (TP) component (the sum of the three frequency components), Standard Deviation (SD) of pulse record (PR) interval, RMssd (whose the deviation of the difference between adjacent PR intervals)

The value of HF indicates the enhancement of parasympathetic nervous system, while the value of LF/HF indicates the sympathetic nerve system. TP indicates the activity degree of autonomic nervous system. RMssd indicates the tension degree of the vagus nerve. This research uses a pulse wave meter attached to the earlobe.

D. Create Personality Model

This section describes how to classify personality. The estimation system in this research uses TIPI-J invented by Japanese as a scale of Big Five [13]. Since TIPI-J is a simple scale that can measure five personality traits with each of two items, the burden on students is small. The estimation system figures out personality vector on the basis of the five personality traits with TIPI-J. After it classifies them, it calculates the centroid vector of each cluster by the k-means method [14], to create a personality model. A new student is classified into the nearest cluster based on the distance from the personality vector of the student to the centroid vector of the cluster. The number of personality clusters is determined to the most appropriate one, trying from 2 to 6 clusters in the experiment.

E. Emotion Estimation along Personality Model

Supervised machine learning creates emotional classifiers. The emotional classifier is created for each personality model. The explanatory variable of the emotional classifier is heart rate and heart rate variability, while the objective variable specifies whether the student has negative or positive emotion.

To know the student has negative or positive emotion, we use the Circumplex Model and the Affect Grid proposed by Russell [15] [16].The Circumplex Model expresses all emotions in two dimensions of the pleasant-unpleasant one and the arousal-sleepiness one.The Affect Grid is an evaluation method of emotions, based on a Circumplex Model. It is formed in a square grid composed of 81 squares of 9×9.

It is considered that the accuracy to estimate emotion improves, if the biological data is classified into groups having common patterns. The personality is used as the scale for the classification. Section 3.2 shows that personality traits affect brain functions and body reactions. Some research reports that there is a difference in the balance of autonomic nervousness depending on personality [7] [8]. It is expected that common patterns of biological data can be extracted if students are classified according to personality models. The classifier for each personality model of the user would estimate the emotion more accurately than one ignoring the difference in personality.

IV. Recalling Experiment

A. Purpose and Method of Experiment

This section describes the experiment conducted in this research. Experimental results show that the personality model improves the accuracy of emotion estimation. Our subjects are 20 university students, 10 male and 10 female. Heart rate and heart rate variation were calculated from pulse wave signals obtained by a wireless earlobe pulse wave device, Vital Meter made by TAOS Institute [17].

Three types of emotions obtained through experiments were positive emotions, negative emotions, and emotion during relaxation. After the subject recalled one of pleasure events, anger events, and the others, we estimated their emotion. The recall time was 2 minutes. We conducted each of three types of emotion estimation after recalls five times.

We used the random forest to create classifiers. Explanatory variables are 17 variables in total. They include the average, the minimum, and the maximum of heart rate, beat count (heart rate at all measurement time), SDNN, RMssd, and the average of VLF, LF, HF, LF/HF and TP. It also includes the standard deviation of heart rate, VLF, LF, HF, LF/HF, and TP.

The objective variables are two variables; one means the student has positive emotion, while the other means negative emotion. To obtain the objective variable, the subject's emotion was attained with the Affect Grid. In the pleasant-unpleasant dimension of the Affect Grid, the center was set to 0. We regarded +1 to +4 as positive emotion, while -4 to 0 as negative emotion.

To show that the personality model works effectively, the classifier created from 20 subjects without classification by personality model was compared with the classifier trained for each personality model.

In the former, data of 20 subjects was divided into twenty pieces, one for each subject, and the 20-part cross-validation was carried out. In the latter, a classifier was created for each personality model resulting from clustering of the five personality traits of 20 subjects with the k-means method. After the data was divided into the number of subjects for each personality model, the cross validation for the number of subjects was carried out for each personality model.

B. Estimation Accuracy by Personality Model

We compared the estimation accuracy by the cross-validation of classifiers that do not classify personality models as well as classifiers for each of two to six personality models. The f-measure, a harmonic mean of the precision and the recall was used as an evaluation index of the estimation accuracy. When the personality is not classified, the F value is 0.501.

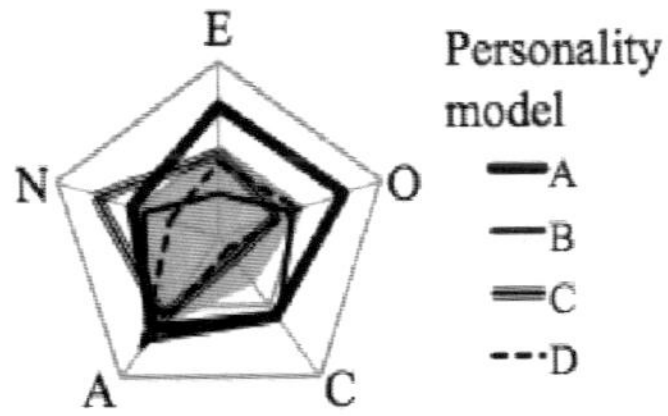

Figure 2. Personality Traits of Each Personality Model

TABLE I. P-VALUE ON EACH PERSONALITY MODEL

Compared	E	O	C	A	N
A:B	0.032	0.345	0.947	0.776	0.861
A:C	0.100	0.018	0.015	0.713	0.154
A:D	0.084	0.209	0.058	0.460	0.199
B:C	0.245	0.879	0.065	0.491	0.079
B:D	0.367	0.998	0.140	0.935	0.448
C:D	0.999	0.793	0.927	0.220	0.097

The best of estimation accuracy is 0.557 when the personality model is classified into four.

Figure 2 shows the codebook of each personality model when the personality model is classified into four. In the score of 5 personality traits by TIPI-J, the minimum is 2, while the maximum is 14. The gray marker shows the average values of all 20 subjects. Personality model A, B, C, and D involved 8, 5, 4, and 3 subjects, respectively. From Figure 2, personality model A is sociable, strong in outstanding curiosity and self-control, because of the high extraversion, openness, and conscientiousness. Personality model B is introverted, strong in intention and diligence, because of the low extraversion and high conscientiousness. Personality model C believes to be sensitive to the stimulus, has a solid idea, is unique, and accepts himself/herself as he/she is, because of the high neuroticism and low openness, agreeableness, and conscientiousness. Personality model D understands the psychological state of the others, is insensitive to stimulation, and has high impulsivity, because of high agreeableness, low neuroticism and conscientiousness.

We applied the Steel-Dwass test, which is a multiple comparison test [18], assuming that the score of personality traits of each character model can be described as "there is no difference between the average values of both groups". Table I shows the obtained p-value as a result of the Steel-Dwass test. The row of "A: B" in the column of "Compared" in Table I shows the result of comparing personality traits of personality model A and personality model B. The rejection region of p-value was set to 0.1. As a result, the personality models A and B showed the significant difference in extroversion, A and C showed it in openness and conscientiousness, A and D showed it in extraversion and conscientiousness, B and C showed it in conscientiousness and neuroticism, C and D showed it in neuroticism.

Next, Figures 3 to 5 show the comparison of the average values and dispersion of f-measures in each personality model when classified and not classified with the personality model. "Non" is the average value of the f-measure of persons belonging to each personality model when 20-part crossing verification was carried out without considering personality. "CP" is an abbreviation considering personality, which is the average of f-measure when cross-validation is carried out only

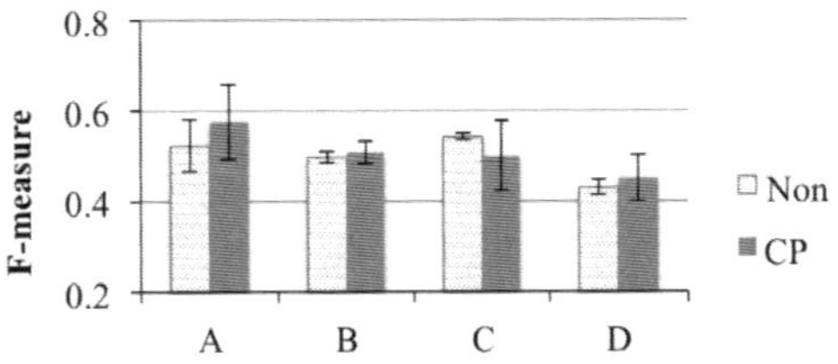

Figure 3. F-measures of Positive Emotion

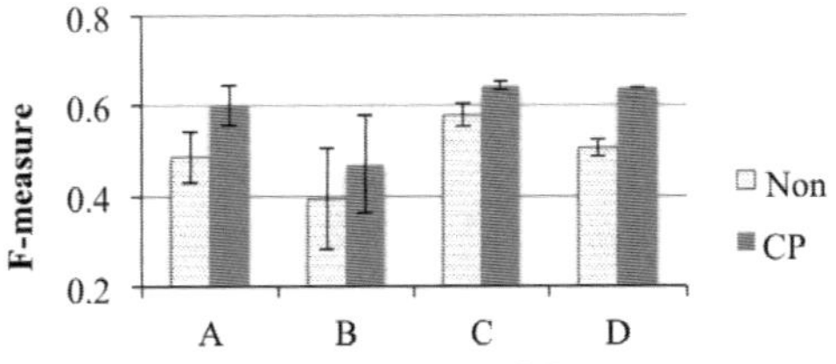

Figure 4. F-measures of Measures of Negative Emotion

for persons of each personality model when personality is considered.

The f-measure of positive emotion in personality model C decreased when personality was considered, but f-measure in the other personality model increased. Personality model C with high neuroticism had the greatest CP of negative emotion among other personality models, and D of low neuroticism is the greatest Non-CP of negative emotion. Moreover, personality model A with high extraversion had the greatest CP and Non-CP of positive emotion. Although dispersion of negative emotion decreased in all personality models, the dispersion of positive emotion, the average of dispersion of positive and negative emotion rose.

C. Emotions for Each Personality Model

Figure 6 shows a graph of biological data for each personality model. The Steel-Dwass test is applied assuming that there is no difference between the average values of both groups regarding biological data of each personality model. If the rejection area of the p-value is 0.1, a significant difference was observed in the average value and standard deviation of LF/HF of personality models A and D.

Table II shows the values of the questionnaire after recalling. The value is represented by the effect grid. Table II shows the range of positive emotion and negative emotion on the pleasant axis and the arousal axis for each personality model. On the pleasant axis, 1 to 4 corresponds to the positive emotion, while -4 to 0 to the negative emotion. Both of the emotions become stronger as the absolute value increases. Moreover, the range on the arousal axis is -4 to 4 for any emotion. As shown in Table II, personality model C seems to have a low arousal level. However, p-value with multiple comparison tests for the questionnaire after recalling presented no significant difference, if the rejection area is set to 0.1.

Table III shows the top 5 of the variable importance in each personality model in the random forest. It turned out that the importance of the explanatory variables is different depending on each personality model. In the comparison of personality model A with personality model D, A has at least 2.9, whereas D is less than 1 for every variable.

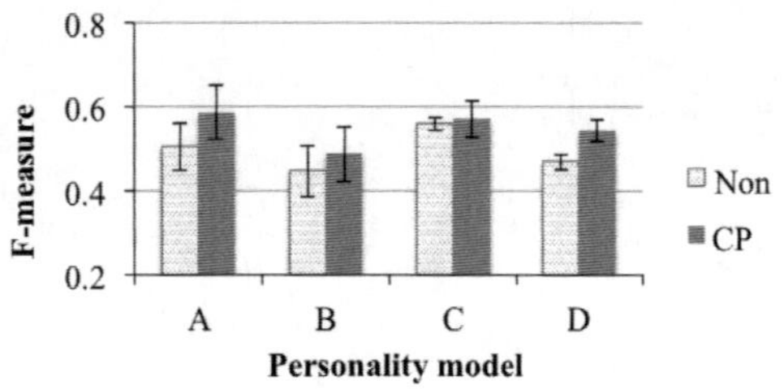

Figure 5. F-measures of Positive and Negative Emotion

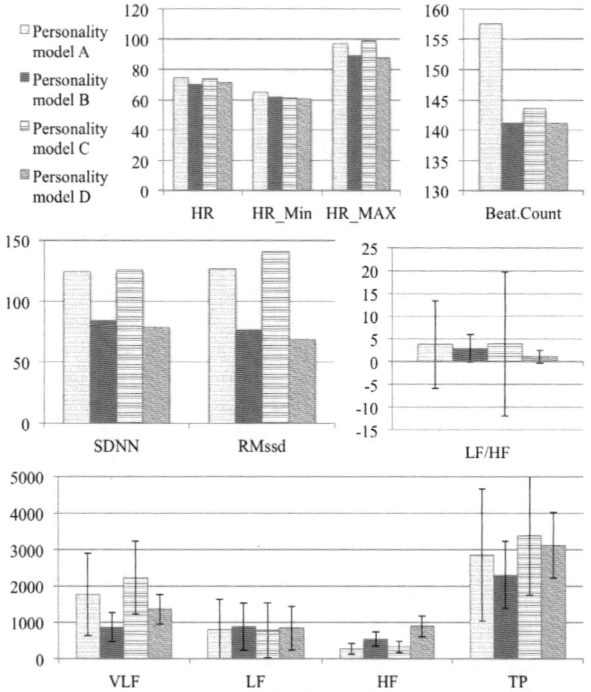

Figure 6. Biological Data of Each Personality Model

V. Discussion

A. *Personality and Estimation Accuracy*

For each personality model, we investigate the estimation accuracy of the classifiers incorporating the personality models and the classifier neglecting the personality models. Let us denote the estimation accuracy of the former with CP, while that of the latter with Non. The increasing rate of the difference of CP from Non for personality model A is the largest, 0.082, compared with other personality models. Personality model A is the highest in the extraversion. Those who are highly extroverted are said to feel positive emotions, which seem to increase the accuracy of positive emotion. Personality model B has low value both in Non and CP.

The activity of autonomic nerves was mild in personality model B, because the value of TP indicating the degree of activity of autonomic nerves was low. Personality model B is considered to be unlikely to change biological data because of its low extraversion as well as introverted and calm personality. In personality model C, CP of positive emotion decreased, while CP of negative emotion was 0.644, which was the largest

TABLE II. RANGES ON PLEASANT AND AROUSAL AXES

Emotion	Personality Model A Positive	Personality Model A Negative	Personality Model B Positive	Personality Model B Negative
pleasant axis	2.352	-1.439	1.786	-1.281
arousal axis	0.407	0.227	-0.179	-0.031

Emotion	Personality Model C Positive	Personality Model C Negative	Personality Model D Positive	Personality Model D Negative
pleasant axis	2.333	-1.167	1.696	-1.591
arousal axis	-0.667	-0.833	0.565	-0.273

TABLE III. TOP 5 VARIABLE IMPORTANCE

Rank	Personality Model A		Personality Model B	
1st	LF_AVG	5.002	VLF_AVG	1.820
2nd	HR_AVG	4.282	HF_SD	1.594
3rd	HR_Min	3.892	RMssd	1.341
4th	LF/HF_AVG	2.985	VLF_SD	1.330
5th	LF_SD	2.949	LF/HF_AVG	1.274

Rank	Personality Model C		Personality Model D	
1st	HF_AVG	2.604	LF_SD	0.908
2nd	HF_SD	2.310	SDNN	0.713
3rd	LF_AVG	2.205	RMssd	0.711
4th	HR_Min	1.958	LF/HF_AVG	0.650
5th	TP_AVG	1.542	LF_AVG	0.633

among all personality models. Since it has high TP, autonomic nervous activities are assumed to be intense in personality model C. Personality model C is sensitive to stimulation and feels anxiety because of its high neuroticism, which seems to affect the estimation accuracy of negative emotion. Since personality model D is introverted and has a low neuroticism, it is considered that its emotion is calm and stable. It is thought that the estimation accuracy of positive emotion was low. People with high agreeableness are reported to have high-stress values [19]. The estimation accuracy of negative emotion was good because of stress accumulation.

As a countermeasure to the personality model with low estimation accuracy, we can add behavior data, such as GPS logs and acceleration to explanatory variables. Since changes in biological data are unlikely to occur in low-accuracy models, it is considered that the accuracy can be improved with behavior data.

B. *Influence of Personality and Biological Data*

As a result of multiple comparisons of each biological data for each personality model, a significant difference was found in the average value and standard deviation of LF / HF of personality model A and personality model D. There was no significant difference in the questionnaire after a recall by each personality model. However, there was a significant difference in extraversion and conscientiousness in the personality traits of personality model A and personality model D. From the above, it is considered that extraversion and conscientiousness have influenced the average value and standard deviation of LF / HF with respect to personality model A and personality model D. Eysenck states that extroverts have a high level of restraint of the cerebral cortex caused by the reticular activating system, while introverts have a high arousal level [8]. Extroverts are insensitive to stimulation. Their cerebral cortex awakening is late, or the awakening falls quickly even if it gets awaken. On the other hand, introverts are sensitive to stimuli. Their cerebral cortex tends to awaken excessively even with a small stimulus. Therefore, the extrovert type is considered to have low physiological excitement. Buck, Miller&Caul [20] also showed that an extrovert person has a weak autonomic nervous system reaction. From the above, it is expected that the value of LF/HF will be low in personality model A who is high in the extraversion and insensitive to stimulation. On the contrary, the value of LF/HF would be high because personality model D is low in the extraversion and sensitive to simulation. However, the result was different. Personality model A with high extraversion had a high LF/HF value, while personality model D with low extraversion had a low LF/HF value. Although this research evaluates the extraversion as five factors in the Big Five, Eysenck evaluates it in the extrovert - introvert dimension. Because of it, the difference seems to have occurred.

The extrovert described by Eysenck has traits, such as sociability and impulsivity. On the other hand, extraversion by the Big Five is considered to be cautious with identifying it as sociability. In the Big Five, shyness is not extraversion. It considers the shyness corresponds to high anxiety and neuroticism in almost all cases [10]. In addition, the impulsivity of Eysenck's extrovert can be seen as conscientiousness of the Big Five. Therefore, although personality model A has high extraversion, it has high conscientiousness and low impulsivity. It is presumed to be different from extrovert described by Eysenck. The expectation that the value of LF/HF will be high is not adapted because personality model D with low extraversion is sensitive to stimulation.

Eysenck also states that people with high neuroticism are more likely to arouse the autonomic nervous system while people with low neuroticism are less likely to be aroused. Therefore, it seems that the value of the standard deviation of LF/HF was low because of the low neuroticism in personality model D.

Regarding the fact that explanatory variables emphasized in each personality model shown in Table III are different, it is presumed that biological data affected by personality are different. Kobayashi showed that the natural log of LF is correlated with openness and agreeableness during rest, while extraversion during calculation [21]. It is considered that the average value of LF is a variable of high importance for personality model A with high outgoingness and openness, while the standard deviation of LF is the variable of the highest importance for personality model D with agreeableness. Besides, Nagamine and Nakamura [22] show that there is a positive correlation between neuroticism and the degree of stress. They also state the degree of stress and the heart rate have a positive correlation. In the personality model C with a high neuroticism, it coincides with the fact that the average value and the maximum value of the heart rate are large, and the minimum value of the heart rate is the variable of the top importance.

VI. CONCLUSION

This paper addressed the school dropout problem of university students. As a method of estimating negative emotion, the paper proposed a method to estimate emotions considering personality.

From the experimental results, it was found that the estimation accuracy improves, if the classifier is trained for each personality model. Personality traits of each personality model were suggested to be related to biological data and variable importance. From the above, individual differences in physiological response differ from each personality type.

As future work, it is necessary to look at the correlation to see how the personality traits exactly affect biological data. The incorporation of gender difference could be one way to improve the accuracy. Linking time and location information to the estimated emotions, faculties and staffs can prevent school dropout of students with mental care, such as emotional support at a good timing.

ACKNOWLEDGEMENTS

This work was supported by JSPS KAKENHI Grant Number JP16K16471.

REFERENCES

[1] MEXT, "Survey results on problems related to student guidance such as problem behavior of student in 2015 (in japanese)," 2016.

[2] I. Mizuta, T. Kobayashi, S. Ishitani, N. Azumi, S. Ide, and Y. Taniguchi, "the research on grasping the actual condition of and supporting the school refusal and withdrawal of university students (in japanese)," Ministry of Health, Labour and Welfare, Tech. Rep., 2010.

[3] C. A. Kearney and W. K. Silberman, "The evolution and reconciliation of taxonomic strategies for school refusal behavior," Clinical Psycology: Science and Practice, vol. 3, 1996, pp. 339–354.

[4] M. E. Pritchard and G. S. Wilson, "Using emotional and social factors to predict student success," Journal of college student development, 2003.

[5] A. Hinz, R. Seibt, B. Hueber, and G. Schreinicke, "Response specificity in psychophysiology: A comparison of different approaches." Journal of Psychophysiology, vol. 14, 2000, p. 115122.

[6] E. Leon, G. Clarke, V. Callaghan, and F. Sepulveda, "A user-independent real-time emotion recognition system for software agents in domestic environments," Engineering applications of artificial intelligence, vol. 20, 2007, p. 337345.

[7] A. Crider and R. Lunn, "Electrodermal liability as a personality dimension," Journal of Experimental Research and Personalities,, vol. 5, 1971, pp. 145–150.

[8] H. J. Eysenck, The biological basis of personality. C.C Thomas, 1967.

[9] Ministry of Internal Affairs and Communications, WHITE PAPER Information and Communications in Japan. Nikkei Printing, 2016.

[10] N. Daniel, Personality: What Makes You the Way You Are. Oxford University, 2009.

[11] P. Ekman, R. W. Levenson, and W. V. Friesen, "Autonomic nervous system activity distinguishes among emotions," Science, vol. 221, 1983, pp. 1208–1210.

[12] G. G. Berntson, B.J.Thomas, D. L. Eckberg, P.Grossman, P.G.Kaufmann, M.Malik et al., "Heart rate variability: Origins, methods, and interpretive caveats," Psychophysiology, vol. 34, 1997, p. 623648.

[13] A. Oshio, S. Abe, and P. Cutrone, "Development, reliability, and validity of the japanese version of ten item personality inventory (tipi-j) (in japanese)," The Japanese journal of Personality, vol. 21, no. 1, 2012, pp. 40–52.

[14] K. Wagstaff, C. Cardie, S.Rogers, and S. Schroedl, "Constrained k-means clustering with background knowledge," in Proceedings of the Eighteenth International Conference on Machine Learning, 2001, pp. 577–584.

[15] J. A. Russell, A. Weiss, and G. A. Mendelsohn, "Affect grid: A single item scale of pleasure and arousal," Journal of Personality and Social Psychology, vol. 57, 1989, pp. 493–502.

[16] J. A. R. L. B. Feldman, "Core affect, prototypical emotional episodes, and other things called emotion: Dissecting the elephant," Journal of Personality and Social Psychology, vol. 76, 1999, pp. 805–819.

[17] T. I. Inc., "Vital meter." [Online]. Available: http://www.taos.tokyo/products/91.html

[18] C. E. Douglas and F. A. Michael, "On distribution-free multiple comparisons in the one-way analysis of variance," Communications in Statistics-Theory and Methods, vol. 20, 1991, pp. 127–139.

[19] H. Fukushima, T. Ohira, and M. Hirosaki, "Fundamental research on the subject's relationship between 5 factor traits and salivary cortisol value at the start of health classroom (in japanese)," Master's thesis, Tokai Gakuin University, 2011.

[20] R. W. Buck, R. E. Miller, and W. F. Caul, "Sex, personality, and physiological variables in the com munication of affect via facial expression," Journal of Personality and Social Psychology, vol. 30, 1974, pp. 587–596.

[21] H. Kobayashi, "Psychological determinants for short-term heart rat-evariablility (in japanese)," Report of the Grant-in-Aid for Scientific Research(no.19570233) by Ministry of Education, Science, Sports and Culture, Tech. Rep., 2010.

[22] M. Nagamine and N. Nakamura, "A study on stress processes for college students during semester-end examinations (in japanese)," The Japanese Journal of Psychology, vol. 70, 2000, pp. 455–461.

Mobile Sensor System AGaMon for Breath Control: Thermo-cyclic Operation and Numerical Signal Analysis of Ternary Gas Mixtures

Rolf Seifert and Hubert B. Keller
Institute of Applied Informatics (IAI)
Karlsruhe Institute of Technology
D-76344 Eggenstein-Leopoldshafen, Germany
e-mail: {rolf.seifert, hubert.keller}@kit.edu

Thorsten Conrad and Jens Peter
3S GmbH
D-66121 Saarbrücken
e-mail: {conrad, peter}@3S-ing.de

Abstract— **An innovative mobile sensor system for breath control in the exhaled air is introduced. In this paper, the application of alcohol control in the exhaled air is considered. This sensor system operates semiconducting gas sensor elements with respect to the application in a thermo-cyclic operation mode. This operation mode leads to so-called conductance-over-time-profiles (CTPs), which are fingerprints of the gas mixture under consideration and can be used for substance identification and concentration determination. Especially for the alcohol control in the exhaled air, ethanol is the leading gas component to be investigated. But, there are also other interfering gas components in the exhaled air, like H2 and acetone, which may influence the measurement results. Therefore, a ternary ethanol-H2-acetone gas mixture was investigated. The establishing of the mathematical calibration model and the data analysis was performed with a newly developed innovative calibration and evaluation procedure called ProSens 3.0. The analysis of ternary ethanol-H2-acetone gas samples with ProSens 3.0 shows a very good substance identification performance and a very good concentration determination of the leading ethanol component. The relative analysis errors for the leading component ethanol were in all considered samples less than 9%.**

Keywords--alcohol control; mobile sensor system; thermo-cyclic operation; data analysis; substance identification; concentration determination.

I. INTRODUCTION

There is a broad field of applications of breath monitoring in human health care, medical applications and alcohol control. In this context, several approaches are suggested [1]. In particular, metal oxide gas sensors (MOG) can be used as appropriate candidates for breath control. This is due to the fact that they are very sensitive, have good long-term stability and are low in price.

But, on the other hand, when these sensor devices are operated isothermally, they are not at all selective. That means that they cannot be used for sophisticated analysis of gas mixtures. Therefore, other approaches are necessary like a gas sensor array of MOGs [2][3] or by thermo-cyclic operation of the MOG and simultaneous sampling of the conductance, which leads to so-called "conduction over time profiles" (CTPs) [4]-[7].

These profiles give a fingerprint of the surface processes with the gas and represent the gas mixture under consideration. The gas specific features of the CTPs can be used for component identification and concentration determination. At the Karlsruhe Institute of Technology (KIT), many procedures were established to evaluate such signal patterns [8], for batch-wise calibration of sensor elements [9] and also for source localization [10].

In this paper, an innovative mobile sensor system AGaMon (AtemGasMonotor, Breath Control Monitor) for breath control in the exhaled air is introduced. Especially for alcohol control, which is the investigated application in this paper, ethanol is the leading component.

But, because other components like H2 and acetone may also occur in the breathing air and may influence the measurement results, ternary ethanol-H2-acetone gas mixtures are considered. This is an important update to the investigation performed in [11]. The analysis of these samples is performed with the calibration and evaluation program for ProSens 3.0, which is an integral component of the sensor system.

In Section II, the mobile sensor system AGaMon is described. A short outline of the calibration and evaluation procedure ProSens 3.0 is given in Section III. In Section IV, the data analysis for the application alcohol control with ternary ethanol-H2-acetone gas mixtures is given, including the calibration set up, substance identification and concentration determination of the leading component ethanol. Section V summarizes the results of this paper.

II. MOBILE SENSOR SYSTEM AGAMON

A. *Sensor System Platform and Adapter*

For breath control in the air we exhale, especially for alcohol control, an innovative sensor system platform AGaMon was developed. Based on this platform, an adapter for smartphones was developed for mobile monitoring of the breathing air.

This adapter consists of a combined and modular hardware- and software system, which runs an embedded metal oxide gas sensor in a thermo-cyclic mode and which determines the alcohol content on the basis of the measurement results via an innovative calibration- and evaluation procedure ProSens 3.0 in real time. The analysis results will then be displayed on the smartphone.

The following Figure 1 shows a pre-release version of the mobile sensor system.

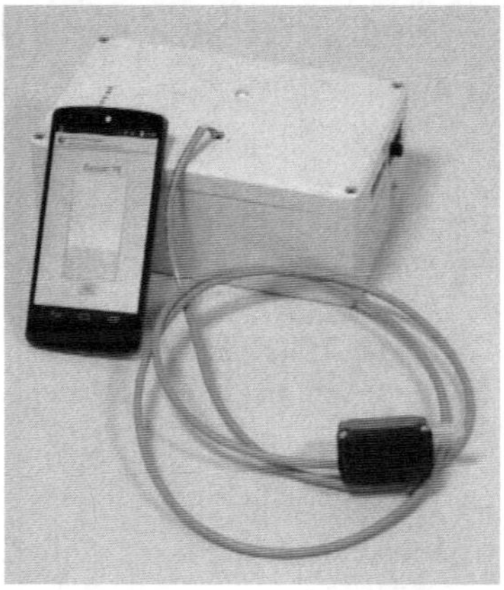

Figure 1. Pre-release Version of the Mobile Sensor System.

B. *Electronics for Heater Control and Data Acquisition*

In order to characterize and operate semiconducting gas sensor elements with respect to the application, a sensor platform was developed, which ensures a robust functioning of hard- and firmware. This platform supports a variety of commercially available metal oxide gas sensors. In this investigation, the sensor MLV (MultiLayer Varistor) from Applied Sensors [12] was used. Via its graphical user interface, different parametriseable temperature cycles can be configured.

Additionally, this system allows the sensors to be exposed to several interfering gases like: H2S (which is the leading component for halitosis), H2 (which is the leading component for dyspepsia and food intolerance), NO (which is the leading component for asthma) or Acetone (which is the leading component for diabetes), thus covering almost all significant aspects.

The core unit of the platform is a base-board with a powerful micro-controller communicating with external modules in a master-slave-configuration. The base-board is able to manage up to four gas sensor modules and features ambient condition monitoring.

The platform outputs the sensor raw data (basically the measured voltages), which can easily be transformed into resistances or conductances or pre-calculated values for a reduced data stream. Via USB, the platform is connected to a standard PC where the data live visualization and the storage is carried out. Via Bluetooth, the platform can be connected to mobile applications running on smart phones.

For the measurements in this paper, a platform with the following specifications was used:

- The temperature control allows a set-point accuracy of 2°C within an overall temperature range of 100 to 500 °C. The set-point can be updated every 10ms.
- The read-out circuit features a sampling time of better than 1ms.
- Measurement voltage accuracy is around of 5 mV (by using a 10-bit-ADC).
- The dynamic range of the read-out circuit is between 1k and 100M.

C. *Temperature Cycle*

Based on the above-explained electronics, several temperature cycles have been applied to the sensors while being exposed to the gas mixtures.

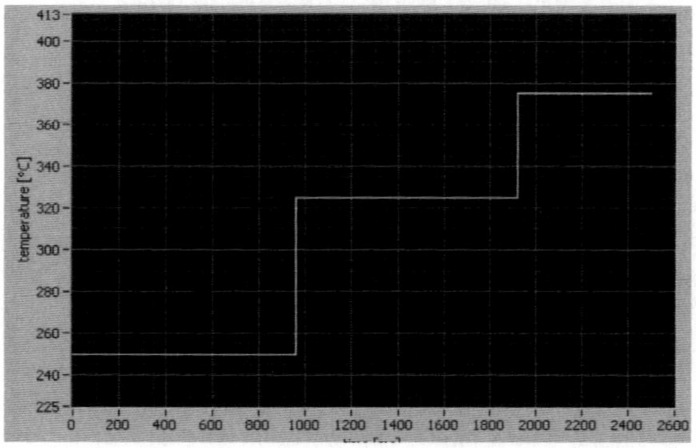

Figure 2. Thermo-cyclic (step-wise) temperature cycle.

For the experiments carried out in the scope of the publication, the temperature cycle in Figure 2 has been considered. It could be shown that this temperature cycle provides the best analysis results regarding the application under consideration.

III. Calibration- and Evaluation Procedure ProSens 3.0

As mentioned above, the calibration- and evaluation procedure ProSens 3.0 is included as an integral component in the mobile sensor system. ProSens 3.0 is an updated version of ProSens [13] to meet the requirements of this sensor system and to analyze ternary gas mixtures. Similar to ProSens, ProSens 3.0 consists of a calibration part and an evaluation part.

Using the calibration part of ProSens 3.0, the mathematical calibration model is calculated based on calibration measurements. The mathematical calibration model is a parametric model and only the parameters will be transferred to the evaluation part of ProSens 3.0. This is very important because all the time consuming calculations can be performed off-line.

If an unknown gas sample is measured, the evaluation part of ProSens 3.0 performs a substance identification and concentration determination of the sample, based on the calibration parameters. For substance identification, ProSens 3.0 determines a calculated CTP and compares this CTP with the real measured CTP. Only if the distance of calculated CTP and measured CTP is smaller than a pre-determined decision threshold, ProSens 3.0 identifies the unknown sample with the gas sample under consideration. In this case, the concentration determination will be performed.

Substance identification is very important to avoid misleading analysis results like false alarms.

IV. Application – Alcohol Control in the Exhaled Air

As mentioned in Section II-A and Section II-B, the mobile sensor system is suitable for a broad range of applications for breath monitoring.

In this application, we turn the focus to the investigation of the alcohol control in the exhaled air. In this context, ethanol is the leading component. But, there are also other interfering gas components in the air we exhale, like H2 and acetone, which may influence the measurement results. Therefore, ternary ethanol-H2-acetone gas mixtures are investigated.

The measurements were performed with the sensor system described in Section II using the cyclic variation of the working temperature in Figure 2. The determination of the mathematical calibration model and the data analysis were performed with the included program ProSens 3.0.

A. Calibration Set Up

In order to establish the mathematical calibration model using the calibration part of ProSens 3.0, calibration measurements with dosed concentrations of the ternary gas mixtures have to be performed. The following Table 1 shows the concentrations of the gas mixtures, which are used for calibration.

TABLE I. GAS SAMPLES USED FOR CALIBRATION

Ethanol-H_2-Aceton in ppm	Ethanol-H_2-Aceton in ppm	Ethanol-H_2-Aceton in ppm
50-10-0,5	50-10-1,0	50-10-2,0
100-10-0,5	100-10-1,0	100-10-2,0
175-10-0,5	175-10-1,0	175-10-2,0
50-20-0,5	50-20-1,0	50-20-2,0
100-20-0,5	100-20-1,0	100-20-2,0
175-20-0,5	175-20-1,0	175-20-2,0
50-30-0,5	50-30-1,0	50-30-2,0
100-30-0,5	100-30-1,0	100-30-2,0
175-30-0,5	175-30-1,0	175-30-2,0

It can be seen that only 27 samples were used for establishing the mathematical calibration model for the ternary mixture. This is a very good result, because calibration measurements are very time-consuming and expensive.

B. Data Analysis

To investigate the performance of the sensor system with the evaluation procedure ProSens 3.0, 9 further ternary ethanol-H2-acetone gas mixtures and a foreign substance were measured in the same manner as the samples for calibration and analyzed together with the samples of the calibration process. The samples are given in Table 2.

The red marked samples are additionally measured samples. The foreign substance is not listed in Table 2.

TABLE II. GAS SAMPLES USED FOR EVALUATION

Ethanol-H_2-Aceton in ppm	Ethanol-H_2-Aceton in ppm	Ethanol-H_2-Aceton in ppm	Ethanol-H_2-Aceton in ppm
50-10-0,5	175-10-0,5	135-20-0,5	100-30-0,5
50-10-1,0	175-10-1,0	135-20-1,0	100-30-1,0
50-10-2,0	175-10-2,0	135-20-2,0	100-30-2,0
100-10-0,5	50-20-0,5	175-20-0,5	135-30-0,5
100-10-1,0	50-20-1,0	175-20-1,0	135-30-1,0
100-10-2,0	50-20-2,0	175-20-2,0	135-30-2,0
135-10-0,5	100-20-0,5	50-30-0,5	175-30-0,5
135-10-1,0	100-20-1,0	50-30-1,0	175-30-1,0
135-10-2,0	100-20-2,0	50-30-2,0	175-30-2,0

C. Substance Identification

For substance identification, as already mentioned in Section III, the calibration and evaluation ProSens 3.0 calculates the so-called calculated CTP and compares this CTP with the real measured CTP.

Figures 3, 4 and 5 give a visual impression of calculated CTPs and measured CTPs.

In Figure 3 and Figure 4, the calculated CTP (green line) and measured CTP (red line) of ternary ethanol-H2-acetone samples are plotted. It can be clearly seen, that the difference between the two curves is in both cases very small. This means that ProSens 3.0 recognizes that these samples are the ternary gas mixtures under consideration.

Theoretical CTP and measured CTP for the foreign substance are shown in Figure 5. In this case, the calculated CTP is not so close to the measured CTP as in the case of the ternary ethanol-H2-acetone gas mixtures. So, the difference between the two curves is much larger. That means that ProSens 3.0 recognizes that this sample is not the calibrated ternary gas mixture.

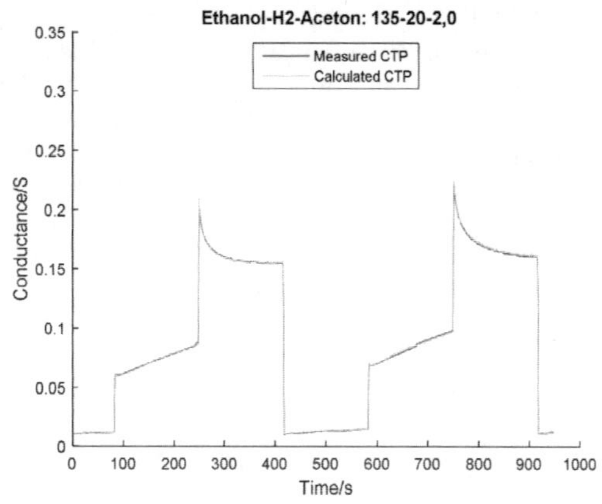

Figure 3. Comparison of measured CTP and calculated CTP: Ethanol 135ppm/H2 20ppm/Acetone 2ppm.

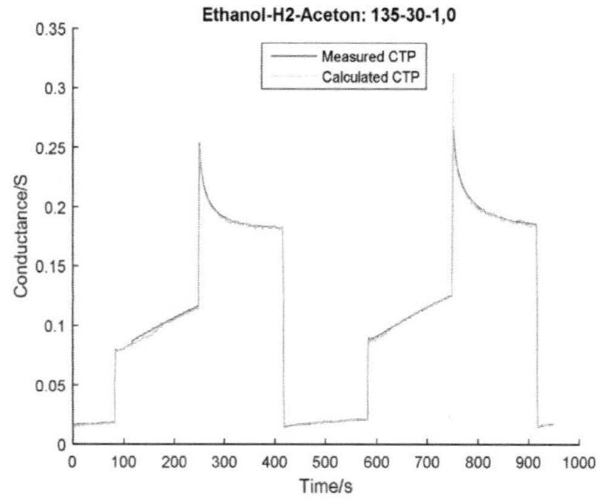

Figure 4. Comparison of measured CTP and calculated CTP: Ethanol 135ppm/H2 30ppm/Acetone 1ppm.

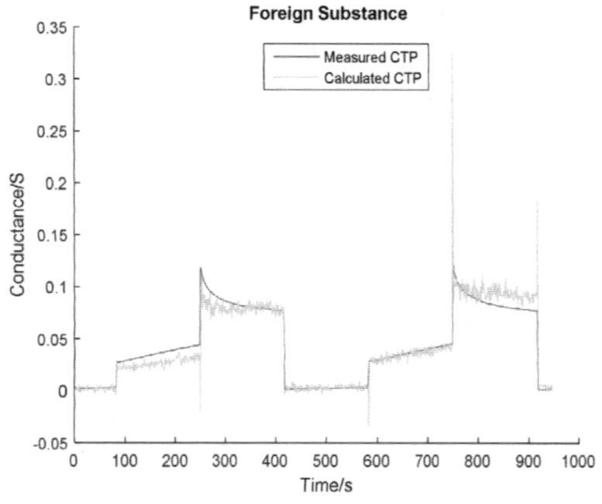

Figure 5. Comparison of measured CTP and calculated CTP of a Foreign Substance.

TABLE III. DIFFERENCE VALUES (BETWEEN MEASURED CTP AND CALCULATED CTP)

Ethanol/H2(*Aceton=0,5ppm)*	**10ppm**	**20ppm**	**30ppm**
50ppm	0,0000	0,0001	0,0001
100ppm	0,0001	0,0002	0,0001
135ppm	0,0000	0,0041	0,0001
175ppm	0,0000	0,0000	0,0000
Ethanol/H2(*Aceton=1,0ppm)*	**10ppm**	**20ppm**	**30ppm**
50ppm	0,0003	0,0000	0,0001
100ppm	0,0000	0,0000	0,0000
135ppm	0,0003	0,0027	0,0133
175ppm	0,0003	0,0000	0,0001
Ethanol/H2(*Aceton=2,0ppm)*	**10ppm**	**20ppm**	**30ppm**
50ppm	0,0001	0,0001	0,0001
100ppm	0,0000	0,0004	0,0000
135ppm	0,0022	0,0022	0,0035
175ppm	0,0001	0,0000	0,0000
Foreign Substance	0,5706		

Of course, the decision for substance identification is not based on the visual impression. Therefore, a "difference value" is calculated from the sum of quadratic differences of every sample point of the measured CTP and the theoretical CTP. Only if this difference value is smaller than a predetermined decision value, ProSens 3.0 identifies the unknown gas sample with the related calibrated gas mixture. Table 3 shows the difference value for the gas samples.

In Table 3, the green highlighted rows correspond to the difference values according to the ternary ethanol-H2-acetone mixtures, the dark green rows to ternary samples additionally measured for evaluation and the red row to the foreign substance. The difference value according to the foreign substance is 0.57 and much larger than the difference values according to the ternary gas mixtures, which are in all considered cases equal or smaller than 0.0035. Therefore, it is evident that the difference values in the green rows are smaller in dimensions than the difference value in the red row.

If the decision value is set, for example, to 0.1, there is good discrimination between the difference values of the ternary gas mixtures under consideration and the difference value of the foreign substance. That means that ProSens 3.0 is able to perform a very good substance identification.

D. Concentration Determination

After substance identification, ProSens 3.0 performs the concentration determination of the gas samples, which were identified as the ternary ethanol-H2-acetone gas mixtures. In the application under consideration, ethanol is the leading component. That means that only the concentrations of the ethanol components of the ternary mixtures are essential. The following Table 4 shows the calculated concentrations of the ethanol component in comparison to the dosed values of the ternary ethanol-H2-acetone gas mixtures.

TABLE IV. ANALYZED CONCENTRATION VALUES FOR ETHANOL IN PPM

Ethanol/H2(*Aceton=0,5ppm)*	**10ppm**	**20ppm**	**30ppm**
50ppm	49,6	49,1	51,2
100ppm	100,3	102,7	100,1
135ppm	131,5	141,0	133,8
175ppm	177,0	177,7	176,2
Ethanol/H2(*Aceton=1,0ppm)*	**10ppm**	**20ppm**	**30ppm**
50ppm	50,6	50,5	50,0
100ppm	102,1	99,0	99,8
135ppm	126,4	139,0	142,1
175ppm	174,7	174,0	172,7
Ethanol/H2(*Aceton=2,0ppm)*	**10ppm**	**20ppm**	**30ppm**
50ppm	49,7	49,9	49,0
100ppm	98,0	98,2	100,3
135ppm	128,0	136,2	123,5
175ppm	173,1	173,1	176,0

Next, Table 5 shows the relative analysis errors for the estimation of the ethanol concentration of the ternary gas mixture.

It can be seen that, in all cases, the relative analysis error for the ethanol concentration is smaller than 9%. This is a very good analysis result.

TABLE V. RELATIVE ANALYSIS ERRORS FOR THE ETHANOL DETERMINATION IN %

Ethanol/H2(*Aceton=0,5ppm)*	**10ppm**	**20ppm**	**30ppm**
50ppm	0,8	1,7	2,4
100ppm	0,2	2,7	0,0
135ppm	2,6	4,5	0,9
175ppm	1,1	1,6	0,7
Ethanol/H2(*Aceton=1,0ppm)*	**10ppm**	**20ppm**	**30ppm**
50ppm	1,2	1,0	0,0
100ppm	2,1	1,0	0,2
135ppm	6,4	2,9	5,3
175ppm	0,2	0,6	1,3
Ethanol/H2(*Aceton=2,0ppm)*	**10ppm**	**20ppm**	**30ppm**
50ppm	0,6	0,2	1,9
100ppm	2,0	1,8	0,3
135ppm	5,2	0,9	8,5
175ppm	1,1	1,1	0,6

Because ethanol is the leading component in this application, only the estimation of concentration of the ethanol concentration in this ternary gas mixture is important.

V. CONCLUSION AND FUTURE WORK

An innovative mobile sensor system is developed, which is able to run a variety of commercially available metal oxide gas sensors in different parametriseable thermo-cyclic modes and can be exposed to several gases in the exhaled air. Therefore, this sensor system can be applied to several applications. In the application under consideration in this paper, the alcohol control in the exhaled air, ethanol is the leading component. But, other interfering gases like H2 and acetone may occur in the air we exhale. Therefore, ternary ethanol-H2-acetone mixtures have to be considered and analysed. The sensor system, equipped with the metal oxide sensor MLV from Applied Sensors, operated in step-wise thermo-cyclic mode and with the incorporated advanced calibration and evaluation procedure ProSens 3.0, is an appropriated and powerful tool for this application. The analysis shows that very good substance identification can be achieved and the relative analysis errors of the concentration determination for the leading component ethanol is in all considered cases less than 9%, even in the presence of interfering gases like H2 and acetone.

The above obtained analysis results are based on measurements in the laboratory. In future work, the sensor system will be applied to field tests to prove the performance of the system not only to laboratory data. First tests in this area showed promising results.

Furthermore, the sensor system will be enhanced and adapted to further applications in the exhaled air like diabetes, asthma and halitosis. This would enable the sensor system to cover almost all significant aspects in human health care and medical applications.

ACKNOWLEDGMENT

This work is financially supported by the Central Innovation Program for small and medium-sized enterprises (SME) of the German Bundesministerium für Wirtschaft und Technologie (BMWi).

REFERENCES

[1] K. H. Kim, S. A. Jahan, and E. Kabir, "A review of breath analysis for diagnosis of human health", TrAC Trends in Analytical Chemistry, Volume 33, pp. 1–8, 2012.

[2] P. Althainz, J. Goschnick, S. Ehrmann, and H. J. Ache, "Multisensor Microsystem for Contaminants in Air", Sensors and Actuators B: Chemical, 33, 1-3, pp. 72-76, 1996.

[3] V. V. Sysoev, I. Kiselev, M. Frietsch, and J. Goschnick, "Discrimination Power of a Metal- Oxide Thin-Film Sensor Microarray", Sensors, 4, pp. 37-46, 2004.

[4] A. Jerger, H. Kohler, F. Becker, H. B. Keller, and R. Seifert, "New applications of tin oxide gas sensors II. Intelligent sensor system for reliable monitoring of ammonia leakages", Sensors and Actuators B: Chemical, 81, 2-3, pp. 301-307, 2002.

[5] K. Frank et al., "Metal oxide gas sensors for field analysis: Novel SnO2/La2O3 sensor element for analysis of dissolved toluene/ethanol binary mixtures", Sensor 2005: 12th Internat. Conf., Nürnberg, May, 2005, Proc. Vol. 2, AMA Service GmbH, Wunstorf, pp. 207–209, 2005.

[6] K. Frank et al., "Improving the analysis capability of tin oxide gas sensors by dynamic operation, appropriate additives and an advanced evaluation procedure", Sensor 2007: 13th Internat.Conf., Nürnberg, May, 2007, Proc. Vol. 1, AMA Service GmbH, Wunstorf, pp. 139–144, 2007.

[7] K. Frank et al., "Chemical Analysis with Tin Oxide Gas Sensors: Choice of Additives, Method of Operation and Analysis of Numerical Signal", Sensors Letters 6, pp. 908-911, 2008.

[8] R. Seifert, H. Keller, and J. Matthes, "A Review on Innovative Procedures for the Analysis of Data from Gas Sensor Systems and Gas Sensor Nets", Sensors & Transducers, Vol. 184, Issue 1, pp. 1-10, 2015.

[9] R. Seifert, H. B. Keller, K. Frank, and H. Kohler, "Batch-wise Mathematical Calibration of Thermo-Cyclically Operated Tin Oxide Gas Sensors", Sensor Letters, Vol. 9/2, pp. 621-624, 2011

[10] J. Matthes, L. Gröll, and H. B. Keller, "Source localization based on pointwise concentration measurements", Sensors and Actuators A 115, pp. 32–37, 2004.

[11] R. Seifert, H. B. Keller, T. Conrad, and J. Peter, "Alcohol Control: Mobile Sensor System and Numerical Signal Analysis", Sensors & Transducers, Vol. 205, Issue 10, pp. 10-15, 2016,

[12] https://ams.com/eng/Products/Environmental-Sensors/GasSensors/AS-MLV-P2 [retrieved: August, 2017]

[13] R. Seifert, H. B. Keller, K. Frank, and H. Kohler, "ProSens - an Efficient Mathematical Procedure for Calibration and Evaluation of Tin Oxide Gas Sensor Data", Sensor Letters, Vol. 9/1, pp. 7-10, 2011; doi: 10.1166/sl.2011.1408

Multichannel NDIR Methane Sensor for Soil Probes

Mariusz Duk, Andrzej Kociubiński, Tomasz Lizak
Institute of Electronics and Information Technology
Lublin University of Technology
Lublin, Poland
e-mail: m.duk@pollub.pl, akociub@semiconductor.pl,
tomasz@lizak.pl

Michał Borecki
Institute of Microelectronics and Optoelectronics
Warsaw University of Technology
Warsaw, Poland
e-mail: borecki@imio.pw.edu.pl

***Abstract*—The goal of this study was to examine a multichannel device using five commercial Non-Dispersive Infra-Red (NDIR) heads for the sensing of methane concentration changes in soil probe. The presented device consists also of a temperature and humidity sensing unit, a gas chamber equipped with a micro-fan, automated gas valves and a microcontroller that controls the measuring procedure. The temperature and humidity sensors are used to control working conditions. A redundant sensor unit is used to improve the measurement accuracy. The device worked in maintenance-free mode installed on soil probe for six hours. The main development of the proposed sensor included measurement procedures and proposition of errors corrections.**

***Keywords*- methane sensor; NDIR sensor.**

I. INTRODUCTION

The analysis of methane concentration in natural systems is becoming an important task for environmental research. Its leakage will result in explosion and fire disaster. Methane is the main constituent of natural gas, the fuel which is supplied to many domestic homes and industries. It is often released from the walls of coal mines and, when un-monitored, it can accumulate, causing dangerous explosions. The soil examination for methane emission is important from property owners' point of view, as well as from gas and oil field parameters investigation.

Several techniques have been successfully used to detect methane. Optical methods can produce very precise results [1][2]. But, at present, the main problem of methane measurement is reliability and precision of medium and long term detecting in maintenance-free mode [3]. In order to improve the available methane sensor, a new methane detection device based on a five non-dispersive infrared heads was set up and examined.

The paper consists of 4 sections. The first section is the introduction, where the problems of the methane measurement are discussed. The second section describes the measurement system construction. The experiment and the results of the methane concentration measurements are presented in section three. The conclusion is gathered in section four.

II. MEASUREMENT SYSTEM CONSTRUCTION

The measurement system (Fig. 1) consists of a methane sensing unit integrated in the gas chamber with humidity and temperature sensors, a micro-fan, a microprocessor controller and an RS485 transmitter. The measuring chamber is closed on both sides by shut-off servos [4]. The sensor head (Fig. 2) includes a set of five methane concentration units (TDS0034 type MSH-P/HC/5/V/P from Dynament Limited). The TDS0034 heads operate by using the non-dispersive (NDIR) principle. The concentration of the gas is obtained from the head output voltage using the equation:

$$C[ppm] = 25\cdot(S[mV] - V_0),$$

where: S is the output voltage, V_0 is the reference value of the concentration (0 ppm), under factory adjustment V_0=400 mV.

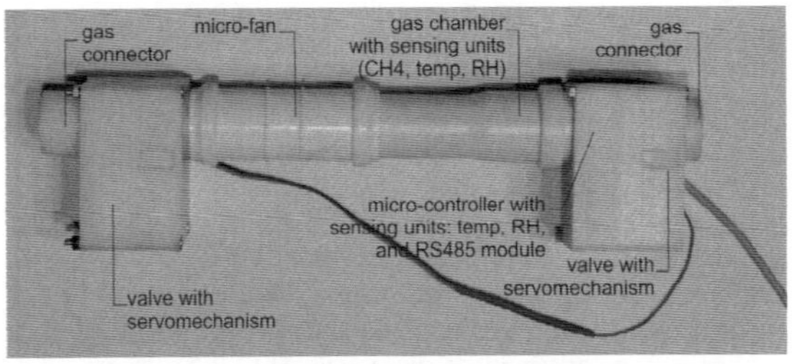

Figure 1. External view of sensor [4].

Figure 2. Sensor head: microprocessor unit, NDIR heads, and temperature plus humidity sensing unit.

The microprocessor module was built using the Texas Instruments MSP430F5529. The microprocessor controls the operation of the sensors, the air inlet and outlet and the micro-fan that can be used for equalization of concentration of gases in the chamber, gas chamber ventilation or gas pumping.

III. Experiment and Results

The developed measurement system was justified in horizontal position then installed on a soil probe in the village of Lublin.

A. System justification

System justification was performed with gas chamber positioned horizontally, with two ends gas valves open and with working micro-fan. The micro-fan enables movement of air compared to human breath speed. The indicative value of V_0 was 500 mV. The measured in 6 hours concentrations and temperature in gas chamber are presented in Figure 3.

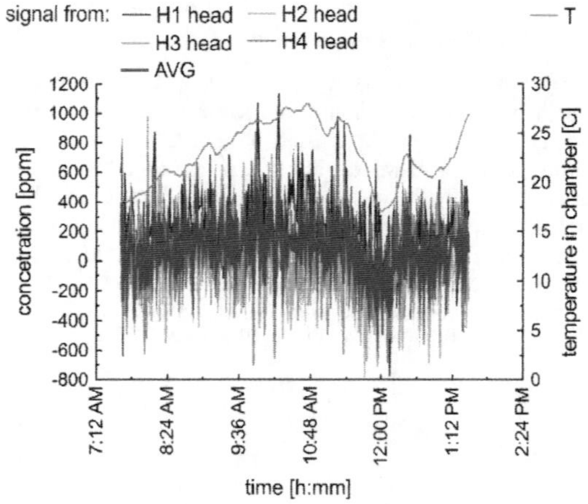

Figure 3. Results of system justification at free air where methane concentration is close to 0ppm.

The simple error concentration of correction measurement was performed using accepted results from 4 heads discarding the least likely one of a measurement result. The average signal was calculated for 5 heads. The calculated distance between each head in set and average signal was used to select 4 heads from which data are used for subsequent averaging and then for presentation. The raw data shows that heads are characterized with ±1000 ppm accuracy. The accuracy of the system with the proposed data analysis procedure is in ±400 ppm range. Because the range of humidity didn't exceed the permissible levels, the results of the measurement of the humidity was not used in the presentation data. The temperature compensation of the heads works well. But, the correlation of the signal concentration with temperature is visible.

B. System testing with forced air movement in soil probe

For system testing, the sensor was installed on a soil probe. The initial situation with open valve of the gas chamber to air and working micro-fan was used to set V_0 values of each sensor. Then, the valve to air was closed and the valve to soil was opened. The analysis of the results of this experiment (presented in Figure 4) shows that an initial dose of methane released into chamber at the beginning of the measurement was at a level of 130 ppm.

The increase of methane concentration in probe may be measurable on the interpolation base. In the presented case, the concentration is of 50 ppm during 6 hours.

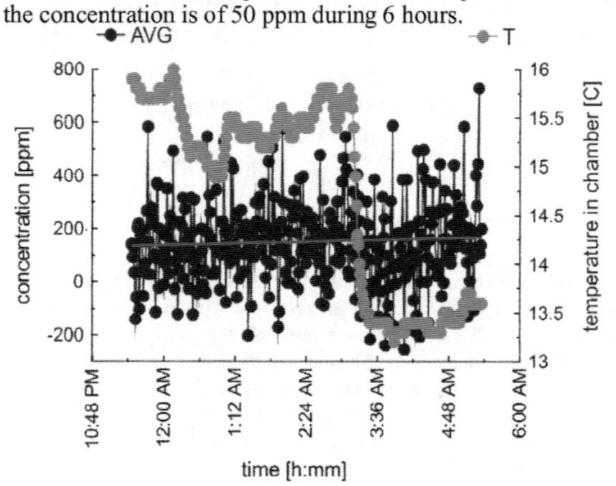

Figure 4. Results of system testing.

C. System testing with initial CH4 dose at air inlet system

The last system test was performed with initial methane dose given from the cloud at sensor air inlet. At the beginning of the procedure, the sensor valves were opened and the micro-fan was working. Next, the small methane cloud was generated at the small distance from soil probe. Then, the air inlet valve was closed and the micro-fan stopped. The registered values are presented in Figure 5.

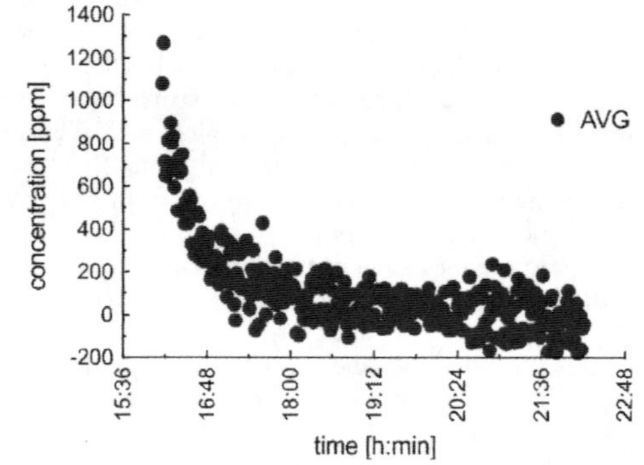

Figure 5. System testing with initial CH4 dose at air inlet system.

The classical exponential concentration damping is visible. Therefore, the examined soil can work as a gas absorber, what is quite usual phenomenon. The measured concentration dispersion increases when absolute value of the concentration decreases.

IV. Summary

The soil probe installation procedure may affect the examination of methane concentration in a short time. The correction of the initial value for data processing of the methane concentration (0 ppm) has to be confirmed before tracking of the environment concentration. The medium-term examination of the methane concentration is possible with a multichannel NDIR methane sensor when it is based on error correction procedures and data analysis.

ACKNOWLEDGMENT

This work was partially supported by the NCN grant 2012/06/A/ST700398 "Oxide nanostructures for electronic, optoelectronic and photovoltaic applications".

REFERENCES

[1] J.Y. Wong and R.L. Anderson, "Non-Dispersive Infrared Gas Measurement", IFSA Publishing, 2012.

[2] Z. Zhu, Y. Xu, and B. Jiang, "A one ppm NDIR methane gas sensor with single frequency filter denoising algorithm," Sensors, vol. 12, 2012, pp. 12729-12740.

[3] L. Jun, et al., "Miniature low-power ir monitor for methane detection," Measurement, vol. 44, 2011, pp. 823–831.

[4] M. Borecki, M. Duk, A. Kociubiński, and M.L. Korwin-Pawlowski, "Multiparametric methane sensor for environmental monitoring," Proc. SPIE, vol. 10175, 2016, pp. 101750M-1 - 101750M-9.

Printed Textile Touchpad

Josue Ferri, Jorge Moreno, Gabriel Martinez
Smart Textiles and ICT Solutions Research Group
Textile Research Institute (AITEX)-Alicante, Spain
e-mail: josue.ferri@aitex.es, jmoreno@aitex.es, gmartinez@aitex.es

Jose Vicente Lidón-Roger, Eduardo Garcia-Breijo
Instituto Interuniversitario de Investigación de Reconocimiento Molecular y Desarrollo Tecnológico (IDM), Universitat Politècnica de València, Universitat de València-Valencia, Spain
e-mail: jvlidon@eln.upv.es, egarciab@eln.upv.es

***Abstract*— The touchpad is a typical 2D gesture detection example of interface devices used on wearable technology. In this work, a textile touchpad based on a diamond pattern design has been developed by using screen-printing technology. In order to obtain the best configuration, two different architectures have been used. Prototypes have been tested by using a specific controller for projected capacitive (pro-cap) technologies. We show a simple device, inexpensive, easy to make and use with textile.**

Keywords-wearable sensing; touchpad; textile; screen-printing technology.

I. INTRODUCTION

Wearable devices are increasingly being developed due to their flexibility and portability. Among all wearable devices, the interface devices can be considered as essential tools for allowing the user to interact with other devices both external and wearable [1]. Buttons, touchpads, keyboards are example of interfaces. The common characteristics of all of them are the requirement of a large sensor area and a stretchable or flexible format; the first in order to detect the fingers [2] and the second in order to follow the movement of human body [3]. Several designs and techniques have been used but these can be divided into two main techniques: by using fibers and weaving the pattern or by using a printing technique for drawing the pattern on the fabric. Regarding fibers, in the last years, Jian Feng Gu *et al.* [4] presented a highly flexible capacitor fiber having a multilayer periodic structure of dielectric and conductive polymer composite films, fabricated by drawing technique; Stephan Gorgutsa *et al.* [5] reported on soft conductive-polymer-based capacitor fibers being used to build a fully woven 2D touchpad sensor and a 1D slide sensor. Regarding transfering a pattern on the textile, Seiichi Takamatsu *et al.* [1] present a stretchable keyboard based on capacitance sensors made of PEDOT:PSS electrodes patterned on a knitted textile by using spin-coat technique; Nur Al-huda Hamdan *et al.* [6] present Grabrics, a two-dimensional textile sensor that is manipulated by grabbing a fold and moving it between fingers by using sewing techniques; Dong-Ki Kim *et al.* [7] present the design and fabrication model of a touchpad based on a contact-resistance-type force sensor fabricated by using a simple screen printing technique.

The content of the paper is organized as follows: Section II presents the working principle of pro-cap sensors; Section III describes the textile touchpad design; Section IV presents the experimental results and discussion. Finally, Section V closes the paper with conclusion and future work.

II. DESIGN AND WORKING PRINCIPLE

Touchpad developed in this work is based on projected capacitive (pro-cap) technologies [8]. Projected capacitive technologies detect touch by measuring the capacitance at each addressable electrode. When a finger approaches an electrode, it disturbs the electromagnetic field and alters the capacitance. This change in capacitance can be measured by the electronics and then converted into X,Y locations that the system can use to detect touch. There are two main types of sensing methods, self-capacitance and mutual capacitance, where each has its own advantages and disadvantages.

There are several pro-cap controllers, many of which offer both self-capacitance and mutual-capacitance types. Microchip [9] uses a hardware sensing method called Capacitive Voltage Divider (CVD), which requires only an Analog-to-Digital Converter (ADC) to preform capacitive touch sensing. Microchip has a wide range of devices which have embedded a CVD acquisition engine as MTCH6102. This device is a turnkey projected capacitive touch controller which allows designers, through of self-capacitive scanning, to quickly and easily integrate projected capacitive touch into their cost-sensitive, low-power application. Capacitive sensors are connected directly to the device and the capacitance will be continuously polled for a significant shift to occur. The shift must be appreciably higher than the noise level in the worst-case conditions.

CVD is a charge/voltage-based technique to measure relative capacitance on a pin using only the ADC module. There are several benefits to use this technique: low temperature dependence, low power supply dependence, minimal hardware requirements and low-frequency noise rejection. Theory of operation is as follows: two capacitors are charged to opposite voltages, in a first phase on the sample A and the second on the sample B (Figure 1).

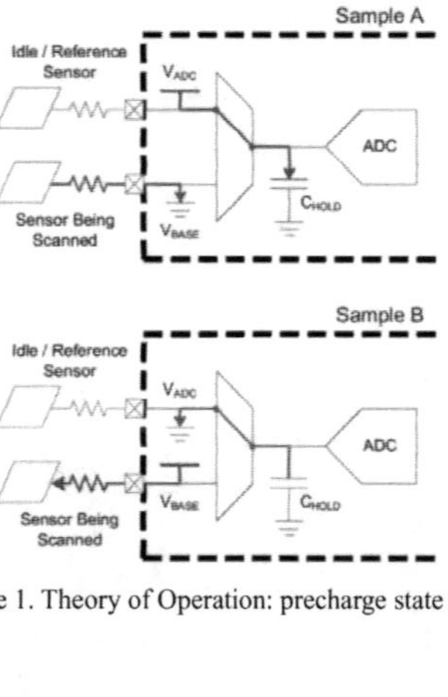

Figure 1. Theory of Operation: precharge state [9]

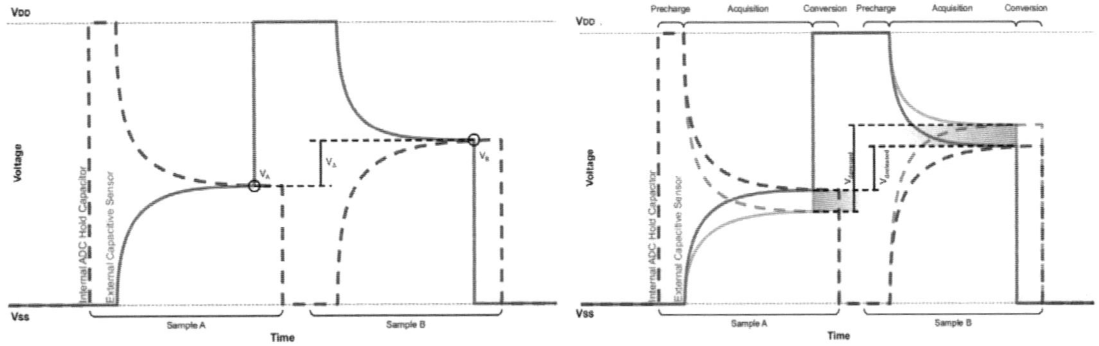

Figure 2. (Left) Differential CVD waveform; (Right) Difference between pressed and released differential values [9]

Then, the two capacitors are connected in parallel and the charges are allowed to settle. The final voltage on Chold is determined by the size of the external capacitance in relation to the size of internal capacitance. Finally, the operation is performed again, but this time the precharge voltages are reversed. The difference between the two results (V_B-V_A) is used as the currents sensor reading (Figure 2 left). If there is an user's finger capacitance, the analysis is the same but with an additional capacitor (Figure 2 right).

A. Sensor

The capacitance of touch is dependent on sensor design, namely, on front panel thickness, electrode geometry and pitch, X-Y layer-to-layer spacing and shielding. Therefore, sensor pattern is a very important aspect of capacitive sensor design. Linearity, accuracy and resolution of touch position are greatly dependent on the sensor pattern. Commonly the design consists of a set of electrodes in row and columns to form a matrix. Several touchpad-sensor pattern designs exist, commonly referred to by names that are indicative of the shape or construction of the pattern, such as triangles, diamonds, snowflakes, streets and alleys, and telephone poles.

Diamond pattern [10]-[13] is one of the most commonly used, it consists of diamonds interconnected with a narrow neck sections (Figure 3). The sensors nodes are formed by rhombus shaped electrodes. The construction consists of two layers and each having a multitude of conductive electrodes organized parallel to each other. An individual sensors node is formed by the region between the edges of the X and Y electrodes (Figure 3).

Diamond elements are used to maximize the exposure of sensor electrodes to a touch. The distance between the electrodes is referred to as the pitch (Figure 3). The pitch determines the range of finger sizes that can reliably be

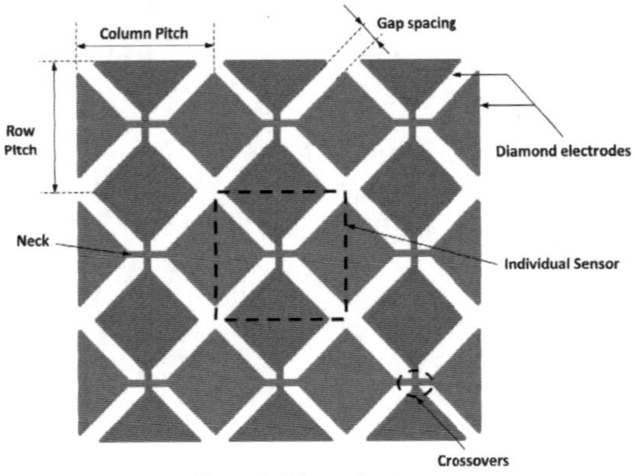

Figure 3. Diamond pattern.

detected; typical dimensions of the pitch are as minimum of 4 mm and maximum of 10 mm. The gap (Figure 3) between the X and Y electrodes determines how far a signal is projected as well as the level of noise in the measured signal. A sensor with a larger gap is able to detect a user further away but it will have more noise than a sensor with a smaller gap. A minimum of 0.1 mm and maximum of 0.5 mm have been reported.

The layers are distributed in close proximity to each other and electrically isolated from each other. The Y electrodes are arranged among rows on the top layer and the X electrodes are arranged along columns on the top layer or bottom layer (Figure 4), forming a two-dimensional array of sensors.

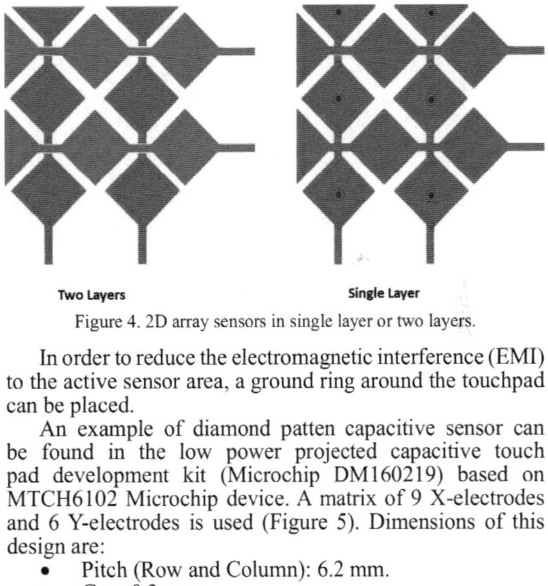

Figure 4. 2D array sensors in single layer or two layers.

In order to reduce the electromagnetic interference (EMI) to the active sensor area, a ground ring around the touchpad can be placed.

An example of diamond patten capacitive sensor can be found in the low power projected capacitive touch pad development kit (Microchip DM160219) based on MTCH6102 Microchip device. A matrix of 9 X-electrodes and 6 Y-electrodes is used (Figure 5). Dimensions of this design are:

- Pitch (Row and Column): 6.2 mm.
- Gap: 0.3 mm.

The capacity measure between electrodes is 20 pF [1 kHz] (Agilent U1731A LCR Meter).

The signal recorded on the R_{X0} line without finger touching (Figure 6 left) shows a difference of 60 mV and on the same line but touching (Figure 6 right) is 70 mV.

III. Textile Touchpad Design

A. Screen-printed Technology

Manufacturing technology used to implement this type of sensor was based on serigraphic technology of thick film. The screen printed process consists of forcing pastes of different characteristics over a substrate through some screens using scrapers. Openings in the screen define the

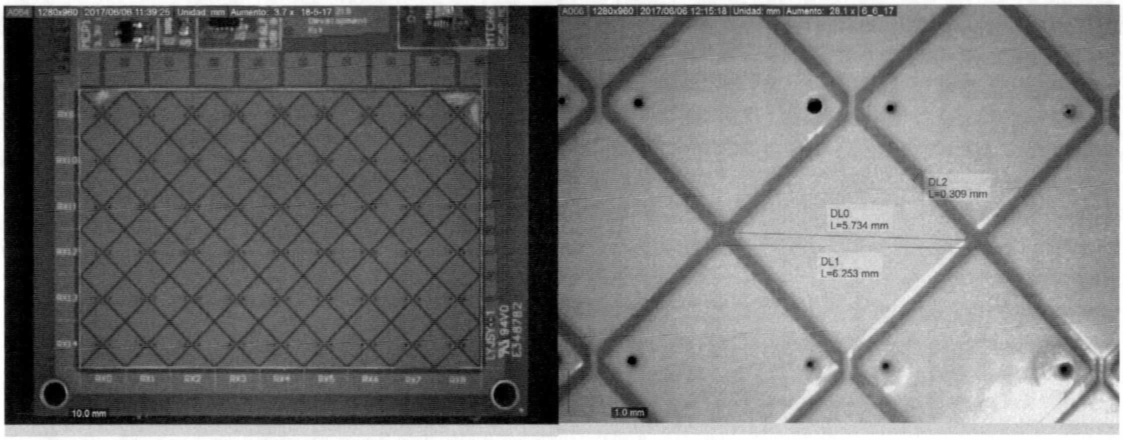

Figure 5. (Left) One layer PCB 9x6 sensor matrix; (Right) Gap and pitch size.

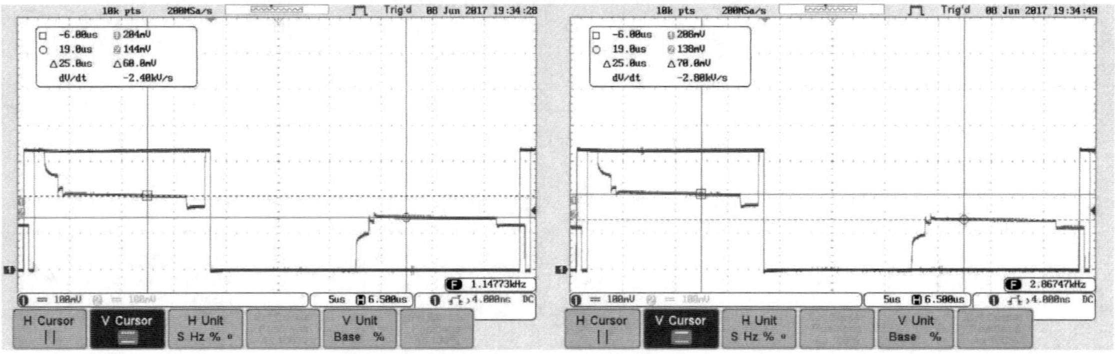

Figure 6. (Left) "released" signal ; (Right) "pressed" signal.

motif that will be printed on the substrate by serigraphy. The final thickness of the pastes can be adjusted by varying the thickness of the screens.

B. Two Layers Design [TLD]

A 9x6 sensor matrix has been designed developed with two layers of conductive tracks and one layer of dielectric. Figure 7 shows the three patterns: X layer (a), dielectric layer (b), Y layer (c) and the whole design (d).

The main dimensions of pattern are:

- Pitch (Row and Column): 8 mm.
- Gap: 0.4 mm.

C. One layer Design [OLD]

A 9x6 sensor matrix has been designed developed with one layer of X-Y conductive tracks and one layer of dielectric. Figure 8 shows the three patterns: Conductive shield and through hole layer (a), dielectric layer (b), X-Y layer (c) and the whole design (d).

The main dimensions of pattern are:

- Pitch (Row and Column): 8 mm.
- Gap: 0.5 mm.
- Through hole diameter: 1.6 mm

D. Development

In order to build the indicated sensors matrices, three screens were made, corresponding to the three defined layers in each design. The screen for the conductors was made with a polyester material of 230 mesh PET 1500 90/230-48 (Sefar) and the screen for dielectric layer was made with a polyester material of 137 mesh PET 1500 54/137-70 (Sefar). Next, a UV film Dirasol 132 (Fujifilm) was used with a final screen thickness of 10 μm for screen for conductors and 15 μm for screen for dielectric. The patterns were transferred to the screen by using photomaks UV light source.

The substrate used was the textile Mediatex TT ACQ 120 μm (Technohard).

The conductive paste used was the C2131014D3 Silver paste-58,85% (Gwent Group) and the dielectric paste was the D2081009D6 Polymer dielectric (Gwent Group)

Printing was carried out by using Ekra E2 XL screen-printer with a 75° shore squeegee hardness, 3.5 bar force, and 8 mm/s.

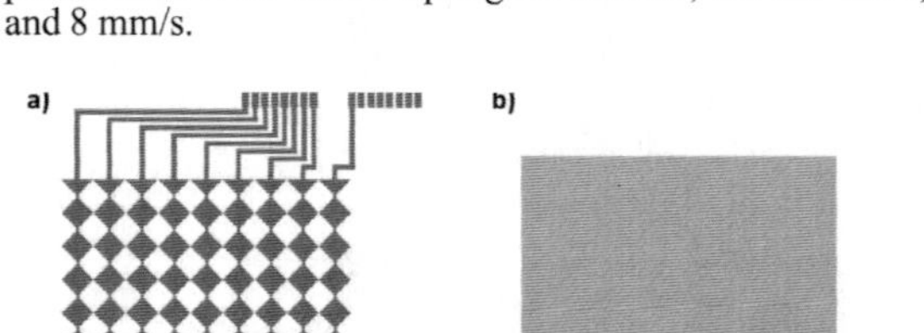

Figure 7. Two Layers Design: a) X Conductive layer ; b) Dielectric layer; c) Y Conductive layer; d) Complete Design.

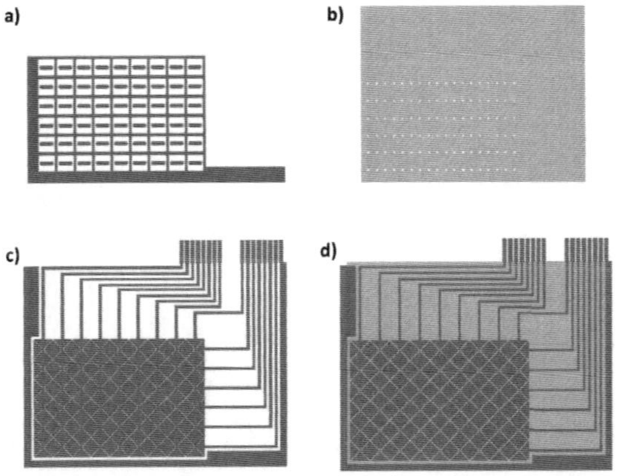

Figure 8. One Layer Design: a) Shield and through hole layer ; b) Dielectric layer; c) X-Y Conductive layer; d) Complete Design

Finally, the inks were cured in an air oven at 130ºC for 5 min.

To protect the surface, a new dielectric layer was added.

Short-circuits were detected between conductive layers due to the dielectric's thickness, to avoid this a total of three passes were made with dielectric ink in order to increment the dielectric's thickness.

E. Electronic System

A MTCH012 based system was designed, using PIC16LF1454 as master controller.

A Bluetooth module was used in order to make the system portable (Figure 9).

IV. Results and Discussion

A. Physical Parameters

Figure 10 shows the magnification view of the two designs with the dimension. Figure 10 left shows the TLD and figure 10 right the OLD.

B. Electrical Parameters

The capacitance of the sensors has been measured by using a RCL meter to 1 kHz (Agilent U1731A). Figures 11 and 12 show the capacitance distribution in each sensor. The TDL has an average of 13 pF and OLD of 50 pF.

Regarding TLD, the signal recorded on the R_{X0} line without finger touching (Figure 13 left) shows a difference of 54 mV and on the same line but touching (Figure 13 right) is 88 mV.

Respecting OLD, the signal recorded on the R_{X0} line without finger touching shows a difference of 160 mV and on the same line but touching is 168 mV.

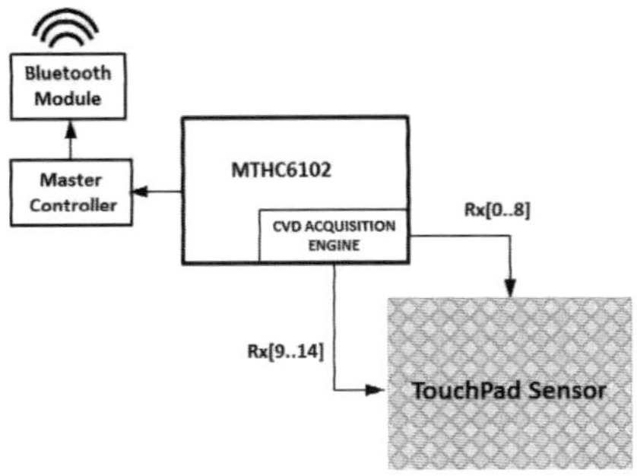

Figure 9. Electronic System Block Diagram.

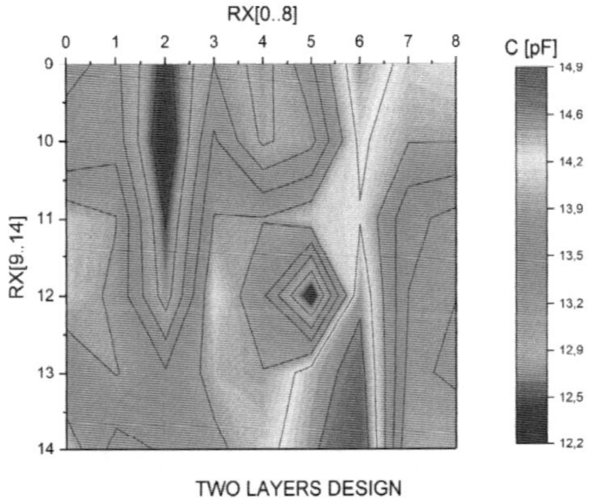

Figure 11. Capacitance distribution on TLD.

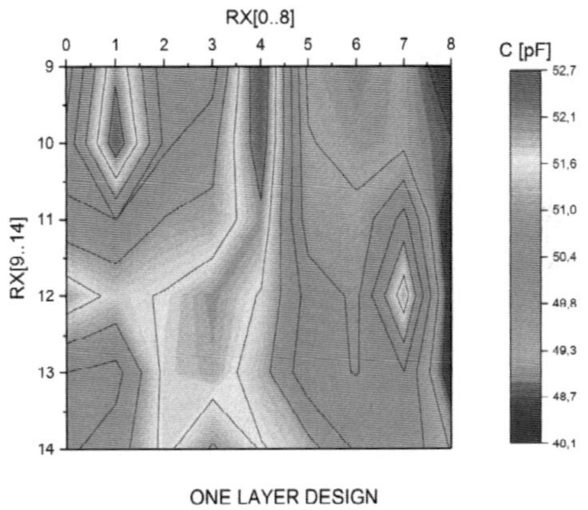

Figure 12. Capacitance distribution on OLD.

C. Operation

Both sensors were connected to the electronic system and tested with MTCH6102 utility, which allows to check all gesture detection of this device: Single Click, Click and Hold, Double Click, Right Swipe, Right Swipe and Hold, Left Swipe, Left Swipe and hold, Up Swipe, Up swipe and Hold, Down Swipe and Down Swipe and Hold. In both cases the operations were perfect and all possible gestures could be checked (Figure 14).

D. Discussion

The capacitance obtained in both cases was pretty similar to Microchip's PCB design, lower in the case of TLD. Capacitors in both cases have the same size, the difference lies in the dielectric; in TLD there is a dielectric layer between the two conductive layers whereas that in OLD there is not a dielectric layer. In spite of the technology used, the distribution of capacitance along the sensors is quite uniform. Due to its low capacitance, the differential voltage obtained with TLD is higher than that obtained with OLD even than Microchip's PCB design.

V. Conclusions and Future Work

A touchpad based on projected capacitive (pro-cap) technologies has been developed to be used with textile substrates and using techniques of low cost and habitual in the textile industry as the screen-printing. The system works on both flat and curved surfaces, which allows it to be used in parts of clothes, such as sleeves, trouser legs or textiles

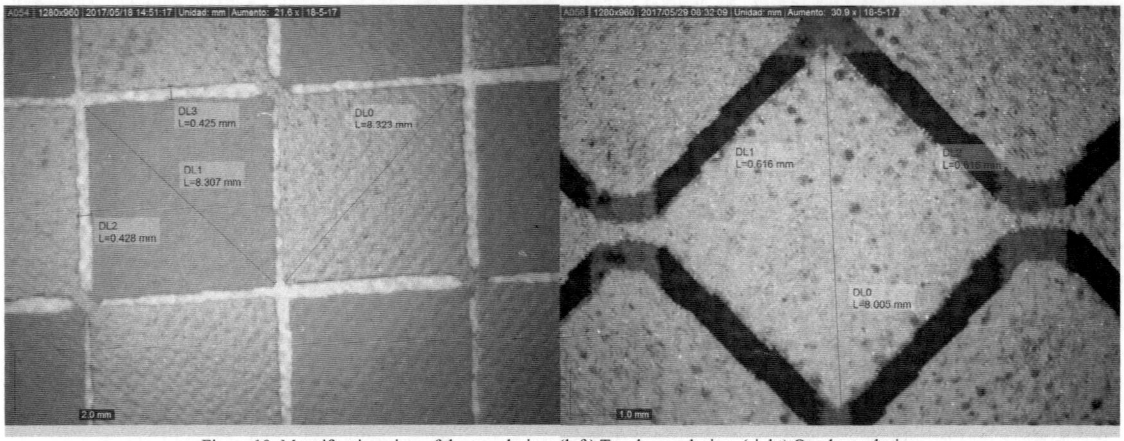

Figure 10. Magnification view of the two design: (left) Two layers design, (right) One layer design.

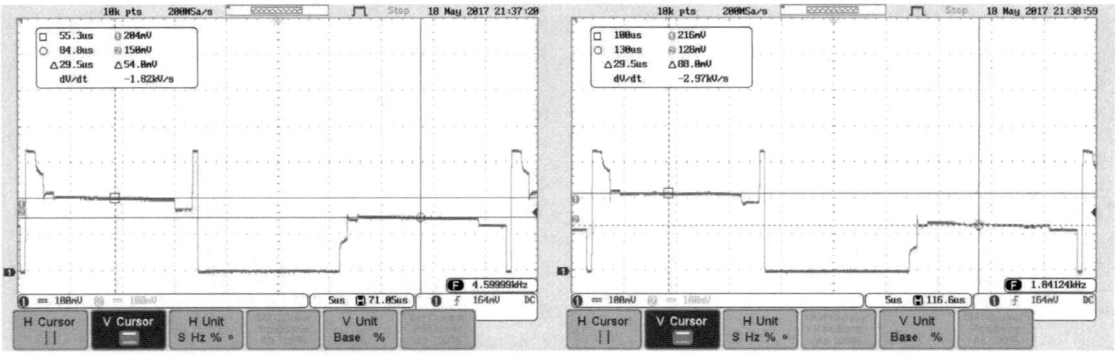

Figure 13. Two Layers Design: (Left) "released" signal ; (Right) "pressed" signal.

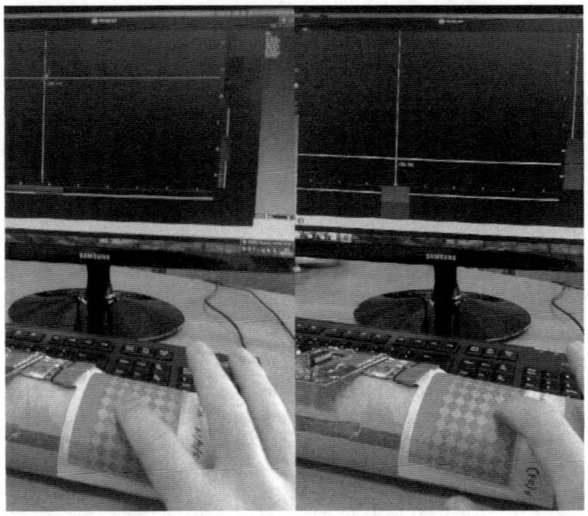

Figure 14. The function on a curved surface touching two different points.

for furniture such as sofas, armchairs, etc. When using the microchip MTCH6102 it is verified that the capacity should not be greater than hundreds of picofarad; the structure and type of dielectric have a great influence on the value of the capacity of the capacitive sensor used. An extension of this work should focus on the thickness and type of dielectric as well as the study for different types of fabrics.

ACKNOWLEDGMENT

This work was supported by Spanish Government/ FEDER funds (grant number MAT2015-64139-C4-3-R (Mineco/Feder)). The work presented is also funded by the Conselleria d'Economia Sostenible, Sectors Productius i Treball, through IVACE (Instituto Valenciano de Competitividad Empresarial) and co-funded by ERDF funding from the EU. Application no: IMAMCI/2017/1.

REFERENCES

[1] S. Takamatsu et al., "Wearable keyboard using conducting polymer electrodes on textiles," Advanced Materials, vol. 28, no. 22, pp. 4485-4488, 2015.

[2] J. A. Fan et al., "Fractal design concepts for stretchable electronics," Nature communications, vol. 5, pp. 3266, 2010.

[3] J. A. Rogers, T. Someya and Y. Huang, "Materials and mechanics for stretchable electronics," Science, vol. 327, no. 5973, pp. 1603-1607, 2010.

[4] J. F. Gu, S. Gorgutsa, and M. Skorobogatiy,"A fully woven touchpad sensor based on soft capacitor fibers," arXiv preprint arXiv:1106.3881.

[5] S. Gorgutsa, J. F. Gu, and M. Skorobogatiy, "A woven 2D touchpad sensor and a 1D slide sensor using soft capacitor fibers," Smart Materials and Structures, vol. 21, no. 1, pp. 015010, 2011.

[6] N. A. H. Hamdan, F. Heller, C. Wacharamanotham, J. Thar, and J. Borchers, "Grabrics: A foldable two-dimensional textile input controller," In Proceedings of the 2016 CHI Conference Extended Abstracts on Human Factors in Computing Systems, ACM, pp. 2497-2503, 2016.

[7] D. K. Kim, J. H. Kim and H. J. Kwon, "A touchpad for force and location sensing," ETRI journal, vol. 32, no. 5, pp. 722-728. 2010.

[8] G. Barrett and R.Omote, "Projected-capacitive touch technology," Information Display, vol. 26, no. 3, pp. 16-21, 2010

[9] Microchip Technology Inc., mTouch[tm] sensing solution acquisition methods capacitive voltage divider. Application note, AN1478. 2012.

[10] Atmel. Qtouch surface design guide. Application note, AT11849.

[11] Azoteq. A short guide on trackpad layout. Application note, AZD068. 2016

[12] Microchip Technology Inc. FAQs-Sensor design guidelines. Application note, AD120007-001. 2012.

[13] J. Lee, M. T. Cole, J. C. S. Lai and A. Nathan, "An analysis of electrode patterns in capacitive touch screen panels," Journal of Display Technology, vol. 10, no. 5, pp. 362-36, 2014.

Printed, Microwave-based, Transmission-line Sensor for Investigating the Electromagnetic Behavior of Pure Bacteria Culture and Algae in Water

Study the fresh water pathogens (algae and bacterial) electromagnetic behavior using transmission-line printed sensor

Mohammad Russel*, Li Xiaomeng, Qu Meixue
School of Food and Environment
Dalian University of Technology
Panjin 124221,P.R.China
e-mail: mrussel@dlut.edu.cn; 1875212201@qq.com; 2574348720@qq.com

Thomas Mascow
Department of Environmental Microbiology
UFZ, Helmholtz Centre for Environmental Research,
Permoserstr. 15,04318 Leipzig, Germany
e-mail: thomas.maskow@ufz.de

Abstract— **Freshwater ecosystem is playing a key role for maintaining a green environment. It is often subject to anthropogenic and natural hazards, which may adversely affect human health, natural resources and the general ecosystem. Therefore, it is a social urgency to protect the freshwater ecosystem by monitoring the quality of fresh water on regular time intervals. Available methods for monitoring the water quality are mostly laboratory-based, which is time-consuming, laborious and expensive. To solve this issue, we are proposing a printed, microwave-based, transmission-line sensor to better understand the electromagnetic behavior of pure culture of bacteria and algae cells in de-ionized water. This sensing technique is fast, robust, low-cost and requires a very simple sample preparation. We have designed a transmission-line, microstrip sensor that could be used for a wide frequency range. The sensor needs only 50µL of the sample and 60 seconds to analyze it. In this work, we have selected the fresh water algae *Chlorella vulgaris* GIEC-179 and the bacterium *Pseudomonas aeruginosa* to characterize their electromagnetic properties. We investigated their reflection coefficient (S11) resonance peak changes in both low (0.01GHz-1.0 GHz) and high (1.5-2.5 GHz) frequency ranges. The results shows that their S11 resonance peaks are identical with respect to the different concentrations of bacterial, algal and mixture of both in de-ionized water. We also have investigated their S11 parameters of their dead cells. The results indicated that for both alive and dead cells, the S11 peak shifts are significantly different from each other. This method could be a potential approach to real-time monitoring of the pathogenic detection of freshwater quality. Our proposed prototype sensor is able to detect bacterial cells in the range of 100 Cell/mL and algae 2.04 x 10^{-10} g/L, which is sensitive and selective enough for fresh water quality monitoring.**

Keywords- microstrip; transmission line; printed sensing probe; pathogens; microwaves.

I. INTRODUCTION

According to Dr. Tom Waller's quote "You only find what you are looking for and you only find it if it is in concentrations high enough to be detected by the method being used to analyze for it." [1]. To evaluate the quality of various surface water various water management programs, the term "water quality" should be different in terms of protection and restoration of lake, river and marine ecosystem. Water quality is rated with respect to chemical, physical and biological parameters in point-source pollutants (e.g., effluents), non-point-source pollutants (e.g., agricultural runoff, urban), and ambient surface waters [2]. The most common and widespread health-risks associated with drinking-water and infectious diseases are caused by water contamination with pathogenic bacteria, parasites and algae bloom. Therefore, on-line monitoring could assist to understand and manage the risks, especially those associated with waterborne diseases [3].

Surface water is contaminated by pathogens due to multifunctional anthropogenic activity like inadequately treated sewage, faulty or leaky septic systems, runoff from urban areas, boat and marina waste, combined sewer overflows, and waste from pets, farm animals, and wildlife. Therefore, human illnesses are transmitted by drinking or swimming in water that contains pathogens or from eating shellfish harvested from such waters. Sometimes, it is costly and impractical to directly test for pathogens because pathogens are rarely found in waterbodies. Indicator species are usually used to confirm pathogen presence in water that fecal contamination may have occurred. The four most common indicators used today for professional monitoring are total coliforms, fecal coliforms, *E. coli* and *enterococci*. Those are commonly found in the intestine and feces of warm-blooded animals, including wildlife, farm animals, pets, and humans [4].

Currently, available methods for water quality monitoring are plate counting and typical cell culture standards to confirm the presence of pathogens, while they are often costly and take approximately 24-48 hours [5] [6]. Based on this timeline, by the time the analysis results come in, the population may have been already exposed to a serious health hazard. Therefore, there is a need for fast and reliable detection of contaminants in a broad spectrum of water management situations. To face the current water management challenges, on-line monitoring seems to be the ideal approach for real time detection [7].

Electromagnetic wave sensing methods are gaining more popularity due to the study the materials dielectric properties (complex permittivity) and structural assessment. Materials' dielectric properties always correlate and, by comparing with other material characteristics, we can verify the materials properties, such as moisture content, bulk density, content of biological material, and chemical composition [8]. Electromagnetic wave sensing [9]-[11] has already been proven to be a pragmatic tool for the evaluation of the biomass concentrations of many different microbial strains [12] [13]. It is a straightforward method to measure the magnitude of all intact cells with their β-dielectric dispersion at radio-frequency range. In that case, the cells behave like a tiny capacitor and the signal correlates linearly with the volume fraction of biomass. At the very high levels of biomass concentrations they may lost the linearity. Therefore, the accumulation of lipid droplets, bioplastics, etc. was found to be one of the few exceptions to the rule [14] [15].

The fundamental electrical property through which the interactions are described is the complex relative permittivity of the material (ε_r'). It is mathematically expressed as:

$$\varepsilon_r = \varepsilon_r' + j\varepsilon_r'' \quad (1)$$

whereas the real part of relative permittivity (ε_r') describes how much energy can be stored by the material from the electromagnetic field and the imaginary part of the relative permittivity (ε_r'') shows how lossy the material is under the electromagnetic filed, both being functions of frequency ($\omega = 2\pi f$).

The volume fraction of biomass, the cell size and the membrane capacitance per unit area could be the possible reason to dielectric increment of a cell suspension from high to low frequencies. Also, the conductivity of the suspension has an effect on the permittivity measured at a particular frequency [16], but this effect can be minimized by choosing the right frequencies.

Correct detection and identification of waterborne pathogens based on conventional culturing techniques is very laborious, time-consuming, and must be completed in a microbiological laboratory. These factors make it unsuitable for water quality control if a timely response to possible risks is required.

In this work, a quantitative way is demonstrated, to measure the electromagnetic properties of algae and bacterial cultures by a microwave based, transmission-line, printed sensor, at microwave frequencies. For the exemplification of the method, *Chlorella vulgaris* GIEC-179 (fresh water algae) and *Pseudomonas aeruginosa* (gram negative bacteria) were chosen for our experiments.

II. BASIC THEORY OF THE S-PARAMETER

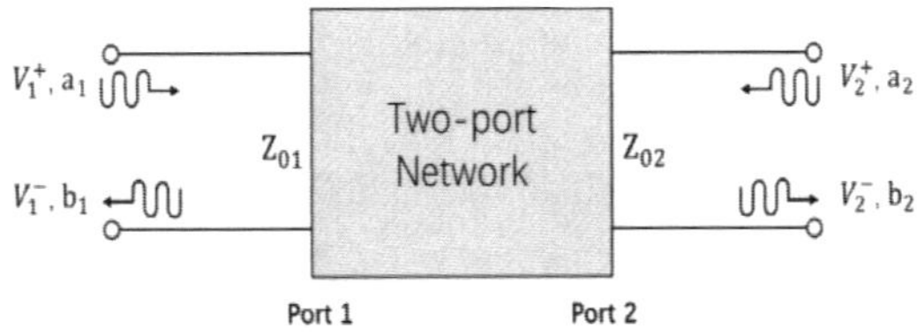

Figure 1. A two-port network with different characteristic impedance.

Measurement systems do not always work under the impedance match condition. Therefore, the general scattering parameter was introduced to describe an impedance mismatch system. A two-port network system is shown in Figure 1. The characteristic impedance at port 1 was Z_{01}, while the characteristic impedance at port 2 was Z_{02} and we assume that $Z_{01} \neq Z_{02}$. The incident power-wave amplitude at port 1 is a_1 and the reflected power-wave amplitude is b_1, while a_2 and b_2 are the incident and reflected power-wave amplitude at port 2, respectively. The incident power-wave amplitude a_1 and the reflected power-wave amplitude b_1 are defined as:

$$a_1 = V_1^+ / \sqrt{Z_{01}} \quad (2)$$

$$b_1 = V_1^- / \sqrt{Z_{01}} \quad (3)$$

The scattering parameter matrix connect the incident wave and reflected wave and are defined as:

$$[b] = [S][a] \quad (4)$$

where $[b] = \begin{bmatrix} b_1 \\ b_2 \end{bmatrix}$, $[a] = \begin{bmatrix} a_1 \\ a_2 \end{bmatrix}$ and $[S] = \begin{bmatrix} S_{11} & S_{12} \\ S_{21} & S_{22} \end{bmatrix}$

while the element in the scattering matrix can be defined as:

$$S_{ij} = \frac{b_i}{a_j} = \frac{V_i^- / \sqrt{Z_{0i}}}{V_j^+ / \sqrt{Z_{0j}}} \quad (5)$$

The generalized scattering parameter describes how the two-port network with the same impedance can be transformed to connect different impedance transmission-line networks [17].

III. FABRICATION OF TRANSMISSION LINE PRINTED PROBE

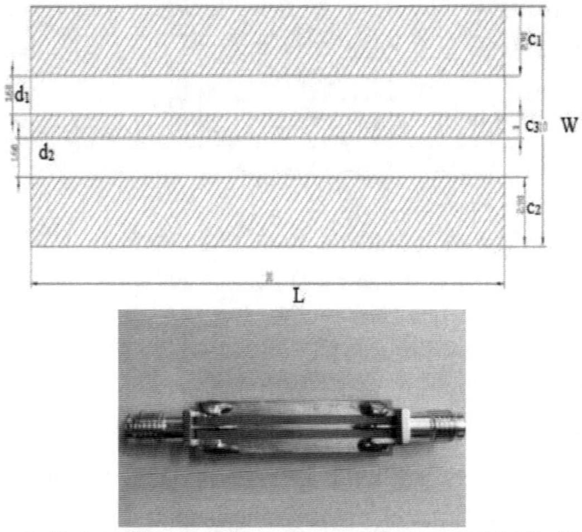

Figure 2. Design of the printed transmission-airline sensor (Up) (L=30mm, W=10mm, d1 & d2 =1.6mm and the copper conductors C1 & C2 = 2.9mm and C3 = 1mm printed on FR4 board). 50Ω SMA connector on both sides to connect to the VNA (Down).

The dual-port printed transmission-airline sensor was designed to be able to get the sample's full S-parameters. The design details are shown in Figure 2. This strip-line probe contains three main sections: one samples holder and two adapters (35 mm SMA connector) to connect the probe to vector network analyzer (VNA). We have used polar Si9000 PCB Transmission line field-solver to design the prototype probe. The length of the sample holder L=30mm, W=10mm is the width of the probe, d1 & d2 =1.6mm of sample holder and conductor C1& C2=2.9mm and C3=1mm of 35 μm thick layer of Cu printed on FR4 board platform. The size of the strip-line was designed to confirm only the transverse electromagnetic (TEM) mode electromagnetic wave translating through the sample under test. To meet the measurement system impedance, the sample holder's size was connected to a Teflon filled 50Ω transmission line section. A no-loss transmission line section can be described by two key parameters: inductance and capacitance [17].

IV. EXPERIMENTAL PROCEDURE

A. Measurement Setup

The measurement instrument VNA HP 8753D (Figure 3) was calibrated with the short, open, 50Ω load and through (SOLT Maury Microwave, model 8050CK11) calibration technique to move the measurement plane from the instrument's ports to the end of the test cables. The printed strip line probe was assembled with two SMA 35mm 50Ω connectors and the probe was connected with the test cables to get the air scattering parameters (Reflection S11 and transmission S12). The samples were carefully layered and compacted in the printed probe sample chamber. A full frequency range from 0.01 GHz to 3GHz was used to get the measurement data and the full two-port S-parameter, both in magnitude and phase form. 201 data points were acquired. A 32-point averaging factor was used to minimize the systematic measurement errors coming from noise.

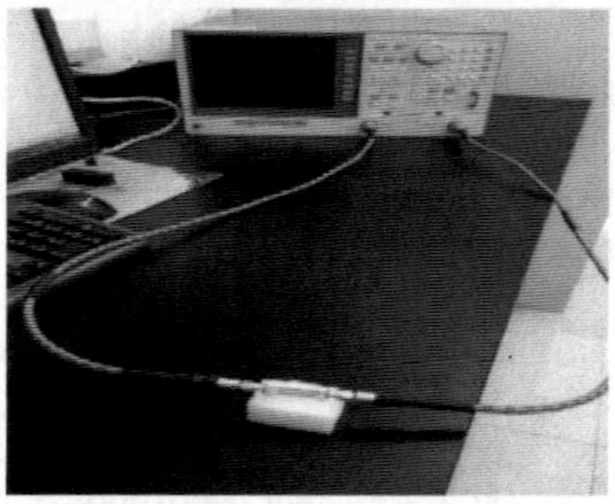

Figure 3. Measurement setup VNA HP 8753D connected to a microwave sensor via coaxial cable.

B. Sample preparation

1) Bacterial Cell sample:

Pseudomonas aeruginosa were inoculated in Luria–Bertani (LB) medium, culture in waterbath shock incubator at 30°C （ 150 rpm ） for 36h. After that, they were centrifuged under 8000 rpm for 5 min and the cell was diluted with de-ionized (DI) water until the absorbance reached approximately 0.5 (CFU is about 10^8/mL). The initial concentration selected was $1x10^8$ CFU/mL for preparing different concentrations of bacterial cell using dilution factor 1:10 with DI water.

2) Algal Cell sample:

The culture medium used for this Chlorella vulgaris GIEC-179 was BG11. The biomass concentration (dry weight per liter) of cultures were measured according to the method reported previously [18] [19]. Microalgae cells were collected, centrifuged and washed with de-ionized water. The washed microalgae pellet was dried at 105 °C for 10h and the dry weight was measured. The initial concentration selected was at 2.04 g/L for preparing different concentrations of algal cell using dilution factor 1:10 with DI water.

3) Dead Bacterial and Algal Cell preparation:

Live cells were heated in boiling water (100°C) for 5 minutes, then centrifuged at 8000 rpm for 5 min and washed with DI water.

V. RESULTS AND DISCUSSION

A. Different concentrations of Algae and Bacterial reflection spectra (S11)

Figure 4 illustrates the different concentrations of bacteria ($1x10^8$-$1x10^2$ CFU/mL) *Pseudomonas aeruginosa* and algal (2.04 - 2.04x 10^{-10} g/L) *Chlorella vulgaris* GIEC-179 cell reflection-spectral distribution in full frequency range of 0.01-3.0GHz, when they set into DI water using the microwave sensor. There were two types of reflection resonance observed. One in lower frequency range 0.01 GHz- 1.0 GHz and the other one in higher frequency range 1.5-3.0 GHz.

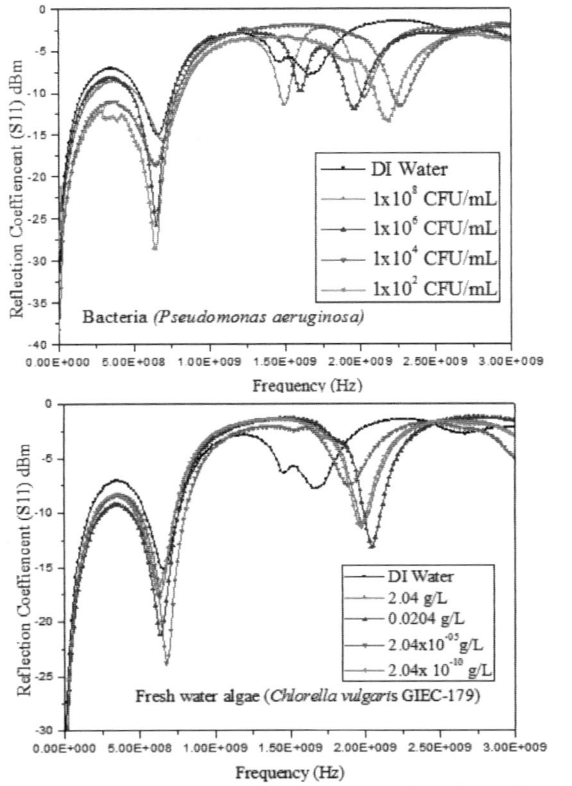

Figure 4. S11 spectra with different concentration of top Bacteria (*Pseudomonas aerugiosa*) and bottom fresh water algae (*Chlorella vulgaris* GIEC-179).

The shift of resonance peaks is quite distinguishable with respect to their different concentrations. If we look at around 0.6 GHz, there is a sharp magnitude drop of almost 30dBm for bacteria and 22dBm for algal cell. On the other hand, in higher frequency range their resonance peak shift is identical with respect to their concentration and the decrease in magnitude around 12dBm for bacteria and 15dBm for algae. It is clear that algae cells reflection resonance peak changes are more unique compared to bacterial cell both in high and low frequency range. Therefore, the microwave sensor is showing significant advantage to determine the bacteria or algae contamination in surface water. It could be a potential sensing method with greater sensitivity and selectivity for real-time monitoring of the water quality.

B. Mixture of both Algae and Bacterial reflection spectra (S11)

Figure 5 shows the sensor's response in a mixture of algae and bacterial cells. Here, the sensor's reflection spectra are behaving in a similar way with the single cell reflection spectra. Again, the resonance of reflection spectra appeared as higher peak changes at lower frequency range (around 45 dBm in 0.01-1.0 GHz) and as lower peak changes at higher frequency range (15dBm). The results show that the electromagnetic signals are dominated by 100% bacterial cell, 25% bacteria+75% algae and 75% bacteria+25% algae. However, it is difficult to understand the 100% algae and mixture of both (50% algae+50%bacteria) electromagnetic behavior. These results are leading us to a better understanding of the microwave sensor sensitivity and selectivity.

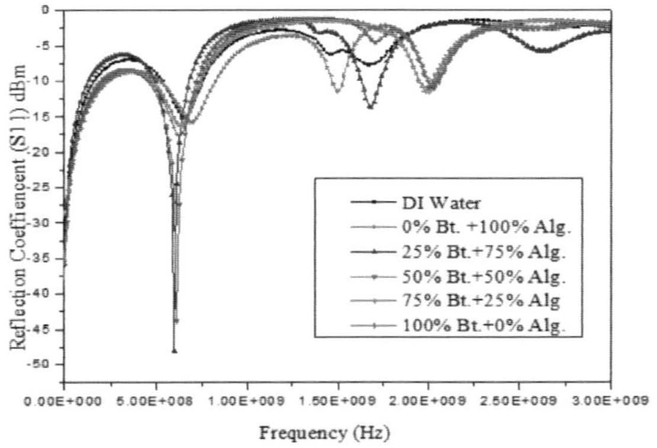

Figure 5. S11 spectra with different concentration of Mixture of both Bacteria (*Pseudomonas aerugiosa*) and fresh water algae (*Chlorella vulgaris* GIEC-179).

C. Dead and alive of Algae and Bacterial Cell reflection spectra (S11)

Another aspect of this work was to understand the differences in electromagnetic behavior of the dead and alive cells. The same experiment was ran with both dead and alive cells. Figure 6 shows the reflection spectra in the full frequency range. It is clearly depicted that there are major differences in the reflection spectra between dead and alive cells. There is a magnitude drop of 25 dBm at low frequency range and a 12 dBm at high frequency range. What is different between the dead and alive cells is the frequency where the magnitude drops at the higher frequency range. The peaks are shifted to lower frequencies for dead cells when compared to the living cells. These results show not only that the sensor can monitor concentration levels and distinguish between different pathogens, but also to assess whether the cells are alive or dead, something that is vital for water risk assessment for pathogen contamination.

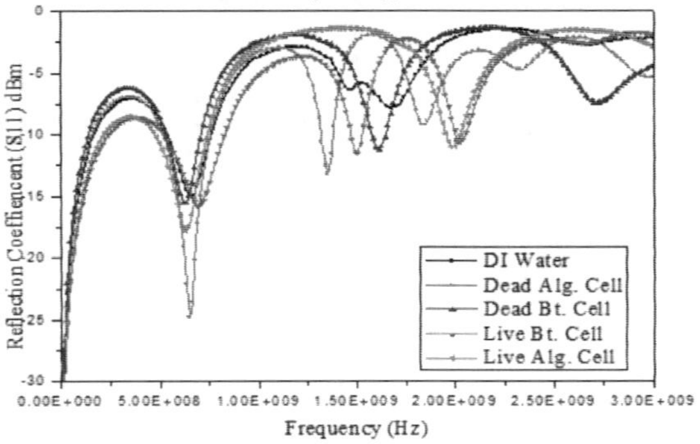

Figure 6. S11 spectral comparison with live and dead bacteria (Bt.)c& algae (Alg.) cells.

VI. CONCLUSIONS AND FUTURE WORK

This research was driven by the industrial need for a novel, real-time method of monitoring the presence of bacteria and algae in water. The printed, transmission-line, microwave-based sensor was developed and tested. The response of the sensor to bacteria and algae in various concentrations, mixture of both and dead & alive cells was investigated with respect to their reflected spectral (S11) analysis. The results clearly confirmed that the sensor is able to accurately determine the concentration of bacteria and algae in water, but to also distinguish between the two and whether the cells are dead or alive. Thus, our proposed method provides both superior sensitivity and selectivity compared to other existing methods. It is important to mention that, the sensor's response returned to its original position, namely air spectrum, after each water sample measurements, confirming that the developed printed, transmission-line sensor is reliable, re-usable and thus, a sustainable solution for water quality monitoring.

ACKNOWLEDGEMENTS

This work was supported by the National Natural Science Foundation of China (41603069) and the fundamental Research Funds for the Central Universities grants from Dalian University of Technology (Panjin campus) (DUT14QY48, DUT15QY54).

REFERENCES

[1] W. T. Waller and H. J. Allen, "Acute and chronic toxicity", In: Jorgensen SE., Fath BD, eds, Encyclopedia of Ecology, Elsevier, Oxford, UK, pp 32–43, 2008.

[2] W. B. Bryan, et al., "Are Harmful Algal Blooms Becoming the Greatest Inland Water Quality Threat to Public Health and Aquatic Ecosystems?" Environmental Toxicology and Chemistry, vol. 35, No. 1, pp. 6-13, January 2016.

[3] Guidelines for Drinking-water Quality,Fourth Edition, world health organization, "Microbial Aspects", Chapter 7, pp. 117, 2011.

[4] Chapter 17 of the Volunteer Estuary Monitoring Manual, A Methods Manual, Second Edition, EPA-842-B-06-003. The full document can be downloaded from: http://www.epa.gov/owow/estuaries/monitor/ July, 2017.

[5] Federal Register, Drinking water: National primary drinking water regulations; total coliform proposed rule. Federal Register vol. 54, pp. 27544, 1991.

[6] A. E. Greenberg, R. R. T. Russel, L. S. Clesceri, and M. A. H. Franson, "Standard Methods for the Examination of Water and Wastewater", American Public Health Association, Washington, DC, 1992.

[7] L. R. Ramon, T. Pol, C. Sophie, and L. C. Jose, "On-line bacteriological detection in water", Trends in Analytical Chemistry, vol. 44, pp. 46-57, March 2013.

[8] O. Büyüköztürk, T. Y. Yu, and J. A. Ortega, "A methodology for determining complex permittivity of construction materials based on transmission-only coherent, wide-bandwidth free-space measurements", Cement and Concrete Composites, vol. 28, No. 4, pp. 349-359, April 2006.

[9] C. Davey and D. B. Kell in M. O'Connor, RHC Bentall and JS Monahan (Eds.), Emerging Electromagnetic Medicine, Springer, Berlin, 1990.

[10] K. Foster and H. Schwan, CRC Handbook of Biological Effects of Electromagnetic Fields, 1986.

[11] K. R. Foster and H. P. Schwan, Dielectric properties of tissues, Handbook of biological effects of electromagnetic fields, vol. 2, pp. 25-102, 1995.

[12] C. Boulton, P. Maryan, D. Loveridge, and D. Kell, "The application of a novel biomass sensor to the control of yeast pitching rate", Proc 22nd Eur Brew Conv Zurich European Brewing Convention, Oxford University Press, pp. 653-661, 1989.

[13] C. L. Davey, D. B. Kell, R. B. Kemp, and R. J. Meredith, "On the audio-and radio-frequency dielectric behaviour of anchorage-independent, mouse L929-derived LS fibroblasts, Journal of Electroanalytical Chemistry and Interfacial Electrochemistry", vol. 254, pp. 83-98, 1988.

[14] G. Kedia, et al., "Addressing the challenge of optimum polyhydroxyalkanoate harvesting: Monitoring real time process kinetics and biopolymer accumulation using dielectric spectroscopy", Bioresource technology, vol. 134, pp. 143-150, 2013.

[15] T. Maskow, A. Röllich, I. Fetzer, J. U. Ackermann, and H. Harms, "On-line monitoring of lipid storage in yeasts using impedance spectroscopy", Journal of Biotechnology, vol. 135, pp. 64-70, 2008.

[16] C. M. Harris, et al., "Dielectric permittivity of microbial suspensions at radio frequencies: a novel method for the real-time estimation of microbial biomass", Enzyme and microbial technology, vol. 9, pp. 181-186, 1987.

[17] D. M. Pozar, "Microwave Engineering 3e." Transmission Lines and Waveguides, pp. 143-149, 2005.

[18] Y. J. Wang, J. He, Z. Li, and H. Y. Luo, "Determination of Chlorella pyrenoidosa biomass using optical density method", Journal of Northwest University (Natural Science Edition), vol. 42, No. 1, pp. 60-63, February 2012.

[19] S.F. Mohsenpour, B. Richards, and N. Willoughby, "Spectral conversion of light for enhanced microalgae growth rates and photosynthetic pigment production", Bioresource technology, vol. 125, pp. 75-81, 2012.

Thick Film Sensors for Soil Measurements

Gerardo Espindola Garcia, John Atkinson and Joel Smethurst
Faculty of Engineering and Environment
University of Southampton
Southampton, United Kingdom
Email: Gerardo.Espindola@soton.ac.uk, jka@soton.ac.uk, j.a.smethurst@soton.ac.uk

Abstract—**Water content has considerable influence on soil pore water pressure and shear strength, potentially leading to failure in earthworks. This research aims to develop novel sensors (employing Thick-Film electrodes) intended to detect changes in soil parameters such as resistivity, porosity and water content and determine if these are indicative of earthworks instability (potential slope failure). Using Thick Film electrodes to measure parameters could be a cost effective method for condition monitoring. The resistivity output of the sensors and how it relates to the soil water content needs to be understood, and a framework of working conditions for this sensing technology needs to be documented. In this study, the behaviour of the Thick Film cell developed by the University of Southampton was tested for a particular soil particle size by simulating heavy rainfall and rising of the water table within a soil column. Final results show a consistent response from Thick Film cell for the specific soil sample used, however, the direction of infiltration has created a very interesting difference in resistivity readings that need to be further investigated.**

Keywords- thick film; soil resistivity; water content.

I. INTRODUCTION

Landslides due to heavy rainfall have been a concern in the UK in recent times, particularly in 2012, when several incidents caused trains to derail, including Beaminster tunnel in Dorset, St Bees station in West Cumbria, and the West Highland line near Tulloch, among others. Not only is the safety of people a concern but also the cost of disruption to the rail transport system. As in most developed countries, the earthworks in the UK supporting the transport system are at risk due to ageing and a lack of maintenance and renovation due to the high costs involved [1].

However, predicting landslips has several difficulties. A significant part of the railway infrastructure dates from the Victorian age (the mid-nineteenth century), and this infrastructure does not comply with present design standards. In the period 1834 to 1841, around 1060km of railways were built in the UK following nine main lines. Pick and shovel excavations were used to build most of the soil cuttings and embankments, with the latter often poorly compacted, and heterogeneous in composition [2]. Vegetation and climate can modify the soil water content causing shrink and swell cycles, which will affect the strength of the soil. Natural weathering processes also occur and vary with rainfall, extreme temperatures and biological activity. Additionally, increases in the speed and weight of railway traffic affect applied loads and earthworks performance [3].

Railway earthwork failures can have impacts on railway operations, involving partial or total disruption of the rail network. Remediation implies significant cost, including the direct cost of reconstruction, and fines incurred by the track operator for unexpected line closure or delays to trains. Therefore, to prevent as much as possible reaching a state where they may fail and need to be remediated, a more effective and accurate condition monitoring of assets needs to be designed and developed, targeting smaller, low-cost and simpler sensing devices. Condition monitoring should enable more targeted interventions for earthworks. There is evidence that proactive maintenance can reduce the total cost of unplanned repairs considerably, reducing cost by about 60% per metre for London Underground Limited (LUL) [2].

This work tries to relate the water content of the soil with the soil resistivity/conductivity using printed Thick Film (TF) sensors, to develop a sensor device to infer changes in the soil structure due to water cycles using these parameters. Thick film sensing has been used for other applications such as water quality and other soil measurements [4]-[6].

The soil water content (θ) is defined as the amount of water that is removed when a soil sample is heated at over 100ºC until the maximum weight loss is reached. This parameter is commonly measured in the environmental field such as ecology and hydrology including agriculture [7]-[10], and along with electrical conductivity in many geotechnical applications [11]-[13].

The Electrical Conductivity (EC) of the soil is defined as the reciprocal of the soil's resistivity, which is linked to the electrical resistance that can be deduced between two electrodes in a conductive material on application of a known voltage. There are three possible ways that the current is able to flow in soils, and these are shown in Figure 1. The first path is a solid-liquid segment where an exchange of cations is associated with clay minerals.

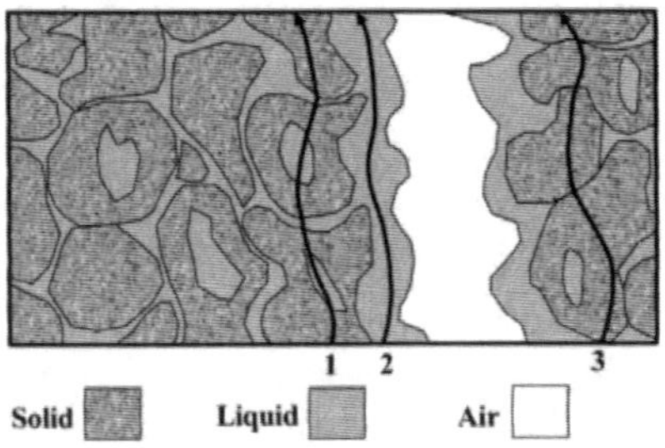

Figure 1. Soil sample cross section with pathways of EC [14].

The second is related to current flow in the liquids due to the presence of dissolved particles in the water, and the last is the flow in solids in direct contact with each other [14]. A key consideration for the TF sensor electrode arrangement is the potential heterogeneity of the soil, in terms of particle sizes and the way they pack around the sensor. A large spacing between electrodes is desirable to monitor larger and more representative volume of soil, but this can generate measurement noise due to the increase of the length of the electrical path between electrodes [15]. Soil resistivity/conductivity has been directly studied and linked to water content and used for measurement and assessment of seasonal water cycles on soil slope stability. A recent study using a clay soil performed by Hen-Jones et al. (2017) [3] showed an inverse relationship between soil resistivity and water content in both laboratory and field experiments which cycled water content (Figure 2) [3][16]. The instrumentation used included the Decagon 5TE sensor which uses a stainless steel electrode array to measure soil EC, temperature and water content directly. As the Decagon 5TE sensor requires good contact between the electrodes and the soil, the electrodes were coated with a layer of Nyogel 756 during the experiments.

The electrical resistivity in soil samples has also been investigated by McCarter (1984) [16] for compacted clay, including responses of different degrees of compaction and saturation. Figure 3a clearly shows that resistivity decreases quickly at high water contents and the rate of change almost flattens when water content exceeds 20%. Its reciprocal, the soil conductivity is shown in Figure 3b, in electrostatic units σ_{esu} ($\sigma_{esu}=1/\rho \cdot 9x10^9$).

The electrical conductivity of the soil (σ) is defined as the reciprocal of the soil's resistivity (ρ) which is linked to the electrical resistance (R) given by the equation:

$$\text{Resistance (R)} = V/I \quad (1)$$

The voltage (V) can be measured across a pair of electrodes by manipulation of the current, namely a drive current (I); this resistance generally is a function of the geometry of the electrodes (Cell), which includes the cross-sectional area (A) (of the electrical conductivity electrodes) and length (L) between the electrodes (of the material being measured).

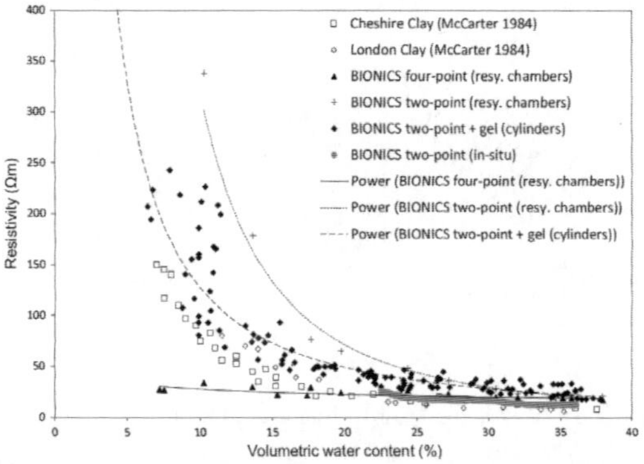

Figure 2. Water content - resistivity relationships [3]

With these known parameters a cell constant can be calculated by the following relationship:

$$\text{Cell Constant (K)} = A/L \quad (2)$$

Thus, the resistivity is expressed as follows:

$$\rho=R \cdot K \quad (3)$$

Conductivity is expressed as follows:

$$\sigma=1/(R \cdot K) \quad (4)$$

The apparatus, characteristics of the soil sample, TF cell parameters and the methodology used are described in Section 2. Table 1 lists the three different sets of experiments that were conducted. The results of each set of experiments are discussed in Section 3, including preliminary Tests used to obtain the initial set up. Finally, Section 4 gives some remarks and future work to follow given the results obtained.

II. METHODS

The general aim of the set of experiments included in this paper is to characterise the response of the Thick Film cell when used to determine the resistivity of a soil sample subjected to a simulation of seasonal wetting processes. The TF cell output voltage is used to calculate resistivity and conductivity of the soil sample over consecutive cycles of wetting and drying.

TABLE I. EXPERIMENT DATASETS DESCRIPTION

Name	Experiment Description		
	Drive Current	***Filling Direction***	***Draining Direction***
Preliminary 1 - 500	500 μA	Top → Bottom	Top → Bottom
Preliminary 2 - 250	250 μA	Top → Bottom	Top → Bottom
Test 1- Orientation	250 μA	Top → Bottom	Top → Bottom
Test 2- Location a	250 μA	Top → Bottom	Top → Bottom
Test 2- Location b	150 μA	Top → Bottom	Top → Bottom
Test 3- Wetting	150 μA	Bottom →Top	Top → Bottom

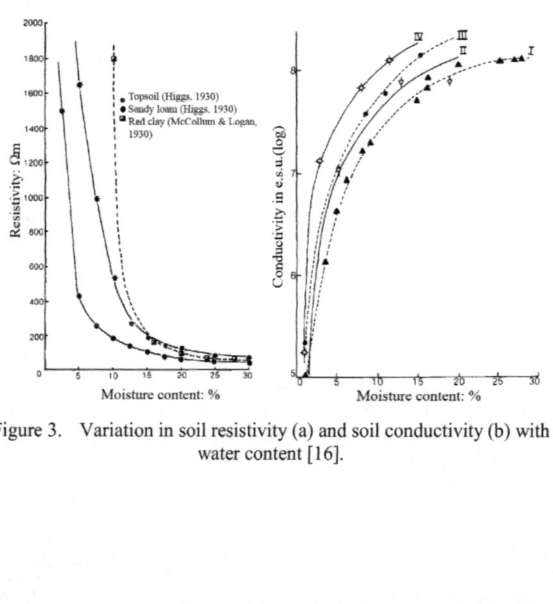

Figure 3. Variation in soil resistivity (a) and soil conductivity (b) with water content [16].

A. *Apparatus*

In order to achieve this goal, a series of laboratory experiments were conducted, using a column of 1.0m height and 0.255m diameter, with a geotextile and gravel filter layer at the base to avoid clogging of the drainage pipe. Following in part the methodology described by Sophocleous & Atkinson (2015) [15], the soil column was used to bury the Thick Film (TF) cell at the same depth as a soil water content probe (a Delta-T Devices ML2x Theta probe), at 0.20m above the geotextile filter in the bottom of the column. A schematic representation of this apparatus is shown in Figure 4. The GP1 Data Logger by Delta-T Devices™ was used as an instrumentation interface.

For all the laboratory experiments, the soil samples were subjected to complete cycles of water variation consisting of wetting (imbibition) phase followed by a draining phase. Measurements of water content and TF cell output voltage were recorded simultaneously, and full cycles are plotted and analysed.

One full cycle started when water was poured directly into the top of the column, and wetting continued until the Theta probe reached maximum water content and a column of water of 0.15m height had formed above the soil sample. The draining phase was continued for 24 hours after the bulk of the water in the column had drained out. Some water continued to drain until the water content reached about 10% after the first 4 ~ 6 hours. An average of 36% was recorded as maximum water content, with minimum values of the water content of 10-12%, as the soil retained some pore water that was not able to drain under gravity.

B. *Sample particle size*

The pluviation tube method was used to fill the column using fraction D of Leighton Buzzard quartz sand. This sand has particle sizes ranging from 150µm to 300µm. However, it was observed that after several consecutive cycles of wetting and drying the sand reorganised its particle size distribution, moving smaller particles to the bottom of the column. Therefore a particle size distribution test was made at the end of each set of experiments to determine sizes around the location of the sensors. The column was re-built after each test listed in Table 1.

C. *Thick Film cell and drive current*

The TF cell (Figure 5) used for the experiments compensates some of the drawbacks of an earlier conductivity sensor design used for soil monitoring by using the principle of ratio-metric symmetry (a balance between spacing and cross-sectional area) in the configuration of the electrodes [15]. The TF cell configuration is shown in Figure 5a. The screen printed electrodes are of gold isolated by a waterproofing layer, with two sets of electrodes placed parallel to one another using a custom 3D printed structure (Figure 5b). The structure allows space for the sample material to be inserted between the sets of electrodes.

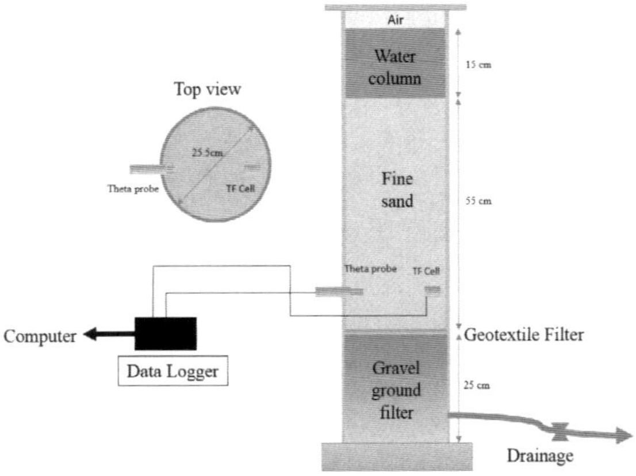

Figure 4. Schematic of apparatus used for experiments.

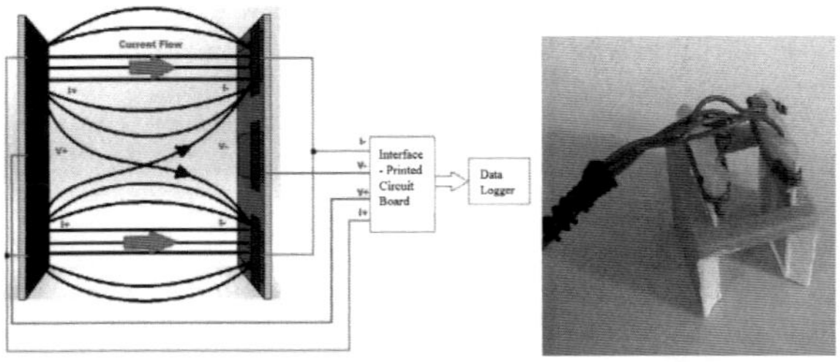

Figure 5. (a) TF Cell configuration [15] (b) TF cell 3D printed structure for the TF electrodes.

Each set is composed of 3 electrodes, where the outer electrodes are driving the current, and the potential of the cell is measured through the inner electrode on each set. The TF cell is interfaced by a low power electrical circuit designed to generate a voltage for conductivity, and the data logger easily reads this conductivity as a function of output voltage. This interface circuit allows the AC drive current amplitude to be varied up to 10mA.

D. *Experiments carried out*

For Test 1 and Test 2a, the drive current used to configure the Thick film cell was 250µA, while for Test 2b and 3 it was changed to 150µA, as this was found to be the lowest value giving a stable reading of the TF cell.

For Test 1, 2a and 2b the column was filled at the top of the apparatus allowing the water to drain at the bottom. Only in Test 3, the water was pumped upwards from the bottom, followed by draining at the base as in the rest of the tests (see Table 1).

For Test 1, the orientation of the Theta probe was changed to vertical. For the rest of the experiments, the Theta probe was restored to the original horizontal position. Both sensors, Theta probe and TF cell were physically closer together for Tests 2a, 2b and 3 than for the preliminary tests and Test1, which helped to give more consistent readings.

III. RESULTS

All water content values presented refer to volumetric water content, which corresponds to the parameter that is commonly used in literature and is therefore applicable for comparison purposes. Preliminary experiments used induced currents (drive current) of 500μA and 250μA respectively, and sensor responses were compared. These initial tests had the objective of providing the basic set-up of the TF cell.

The first set-up configuration using a drive current of 500μA proved to be inappropriate to obtain the full response during the wetting phases (labelled 1 on the graphs). As the soil sample reached maximum water content (~34%), the TF output voltage suddenly dropped, in addition, very inconsistent responses were recorded during the draining phases (labelled 2 on the graphs); the voltage data were converted to resistivity, and this is plotted in Figure 6. The range of operation for this configuration was recorded as resistivity from ~260Ωm to 360Ωm.

For the second set-up using a drive current of 250μA, the response for the wetting phases was improved, giving a complete set of measurements during wetting. Figure 7 shows the TF cell resistivity response, where it is evident that the response over consecutive cycles continued to be dispersed for both phases but more prominently in the wetting phases.

The improvement compared to the previous set-up is notable, but there is still a sharp change when the soil sample reaches a water content over 33%. Nonetheless, it is less variable than that of the response using 500μA. Therefore 250μA was chosen as the starting level of drive current to continue investigating the TF cell response, this time modifying other parameters.

For all cycles, the voltage (V) applied to the cell and the cell constant (K) were kept the same; 5V was the maximum valid output voltage for the interface circuit of the Thick film conductivity sensor, which also had a cell constant value of 1/15m. Readings from the Theta probe and TF cell were taken at intervals of 5 seconds. The first cycles of all tests were removed as the readings are considered outliers due to the initial dry condition of the sand (which gave a measured value of less than 0.1% water content).

Only three cycles are presented on each of the following plots for better visualisation, and in most cases, the re-wetting and re-draining cycles plotted are those that immediately followed cycle 1.

A. Test 1

Figure 8 shows the resistivity- water content curves of three of the five cycles made for Test 1. It can be observed that there is better repeatability over the draining phases than the wetting phases compared with the 250μA preliminary test. The sudden change in resistivity at higher water content (greater than 33%) was also no longer observed. Resistivity remains almost flat above 22% water content on all drying cycles and grows exponentially when the water content is below that value. Responses during wetting phases show an exponential decrease in resistivity, although the curves show significant variations between different cycles.

B. Test 2a

For Test 2a, the drive current was kept at 250μA, and the orientation of the Theta probe was restored as horizontal.

The location of both sensors was modified, moving them closer together. This was to try to obtain more consistent readings, as there was some concern that wetting of the sand was not occurring uniformly with time across the column. Figure 9 includes the resistivity-water content curves of three of the six cycles made for Test 2a. It can be seen that there is an improvement in the consistency and repeatability over the wetting phases compared with Test 1.

Resistivity continues to show an exponential trend, decreasing as water content increases over all the cycles. Responses during re-wetting decrease in resistivity as the water content increases up to 30%, then flatten up to 34%, while all draining cycles decrease exponentially from 34% to 12% water content. The re-wetting cycles still show some variability between successive cycles. The draining cycles seem to be missing readings at 33%, where there was an unexpected decrease in resistivity that was not recorded by the TF cell since it was outside of its working range.

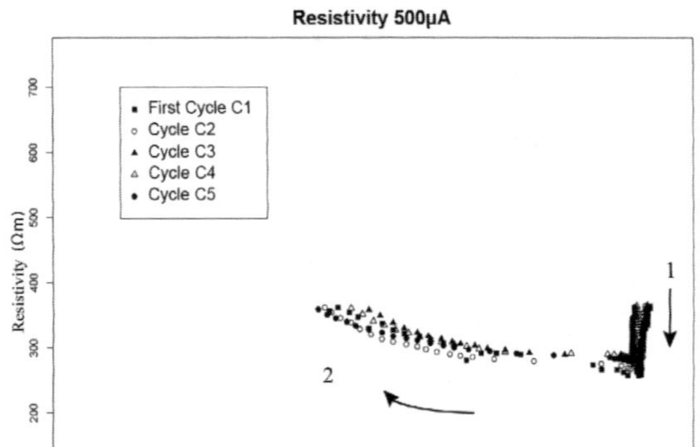

Figure 6. Water content - resistivity curves for all 500μA cycles.

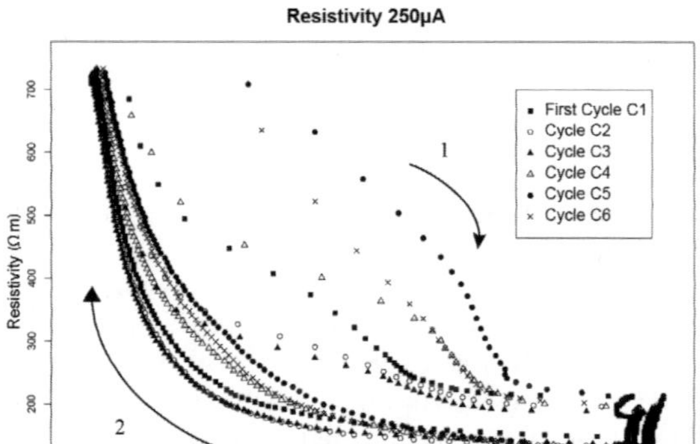

Figure 7. Water content - resistivity curves for all 250μA cycles.

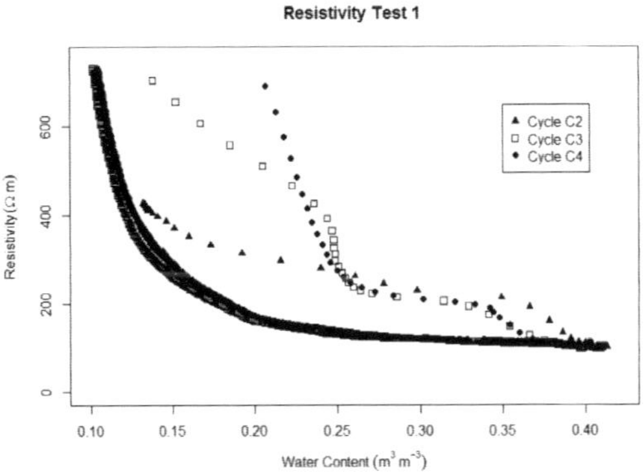

Figure 8. Water content - resistivity curves for Test 1 cycles.

C. Test 2b

Keeping the same configuration of Test 2a for the apparatus, Test 2b includes a change of drive current provided to the TF cell. As previously stated, the objectives of Test 2b were to use a drive current of 150μA to keep all readings within the range of the conductivity sensor output.

As can be seen in Figure 10, the range of the resistivity registered for all cycles is virtually double that of the previous experiments, preliminary and Test 1 (100Ωm-720Ωm) and almost triple that from Test 2a (50Ωm-480Ωm) ranging from 200Ωm to 1500Ωm. Re-wetting and re-drying phase's responses both follow the same trend with decreasing resistivity as water content is increasing.

However, re-drying phases again have lower resistivity readings compared to re-wetting readings. Measurements were taken at same 5-second intervals in both phases showing that the draining phase is much slower. The classic exponential trend is more explicit over the re-drying than re-wetting phases. There is an apparent hysteresis when responses of wetting and drying phases are compared in Figure 10; while there seems to be a good repeatability over consecutive cycles the responses follow different trends on each phase.

The TF cell gives different values of resistivity at the same water content being measured, e.g., in Figure 10 it is clearly seen that at 20% water content the value of resistivity is approximately 500Ωm and 900Ωm for wetting and draining phases respectively.

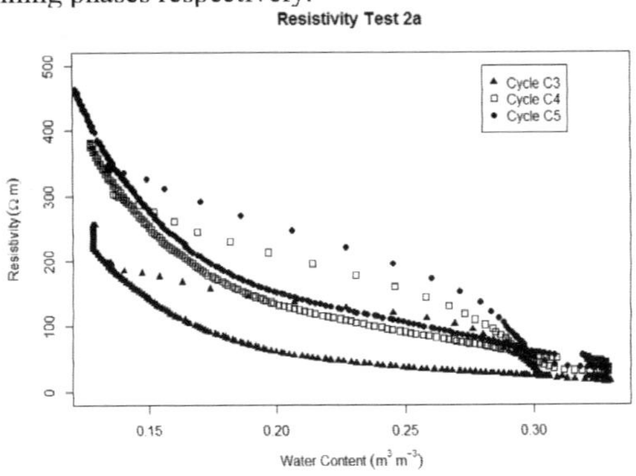

Figure 9. Water content - resistivity curves for Test 2a cycles.

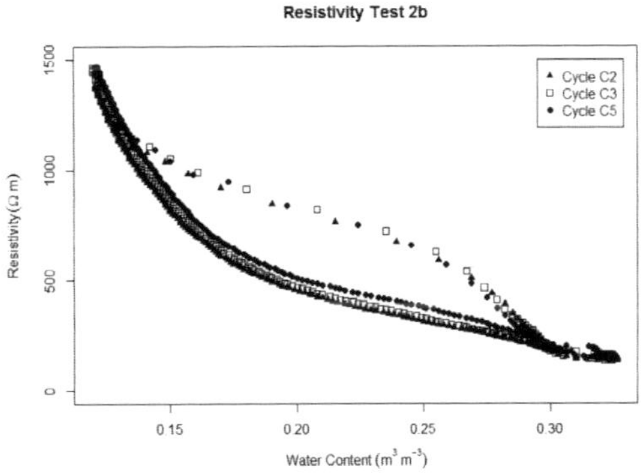

Figure 10. Water content - resistivity curves for Test 2b cycles.

A theory to explain this behaviour is shown in Figure 12a. Water is being added rapidly at the top of the column and allowed to drain at the bottom using only a small hose. Air trapped in the soil finds it difficult to escape, causing the water infiltration to be non-uniform. Figure 12b shows the sample between the electrodes of the TF cell when water is added at the top of the column, and Figure13b when water is added slowly from the bottom. The air that may stay trapped in the soil sample on rapid downward infiltration is the possible cause of the variation of the TF readings in the wetting phase, and this theory is supported by the results obtained on changing the direction of the water in the wetting phase of Test 3.

D. Test 3

For this test, the drive current was kept as 150μA, and the direction of filling was modified by adding water from the bottom, going up through the soil sample at an average flow rate of $7.68e^{-6}m^3/s$ until a water column of 0.15m height was formed at the top of the soil sample before draining started. The average drainage flow rate was a bit higher than filling with a value of $8.99e^{-6}m^3/s$.

Figure 11 shows water content-resistivity curves for three of the eight complete re-wetting and re-draining cycles. It can be seen that curves during wetting and drying phases both follow the same exponential trend of decrease in resistivity as soil water content increases.

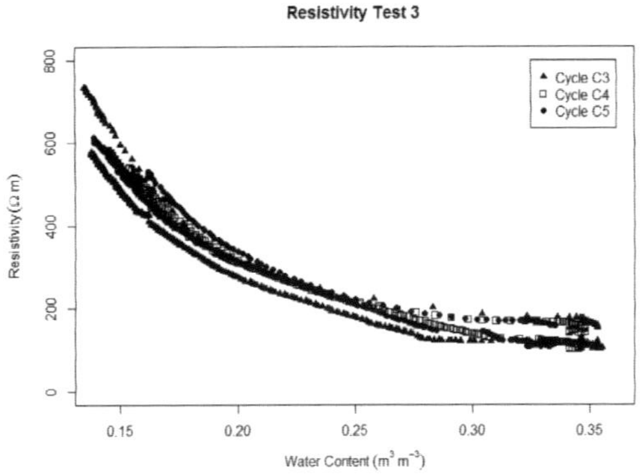

Figure 11. Water content - resistivity curves for Test 3 cycles.

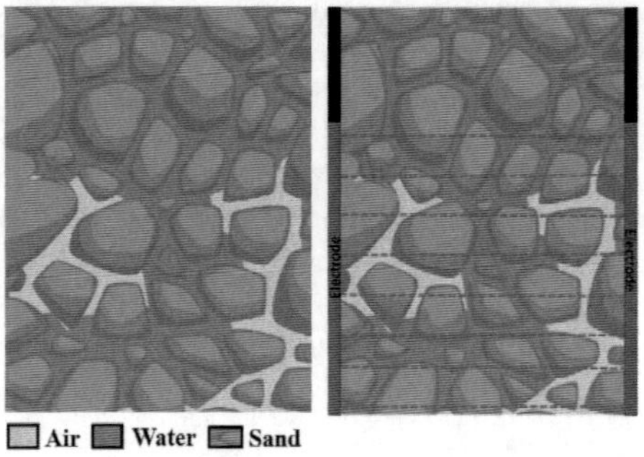

Figure 12. (a) Soil sample showing non-uniform downwards water infiltration, (b) non-uniform composition of soil/water between the TF electrodes.

However, the range of values over each phase are slightly different ranging from 200Ωm to 750Ωm for wetting, and 100Ωm to 600Ωm for drying. As explained previously, this may be because air is no longer trapped in the soil sample when the water is added from the bottom of the column, as is shown in Figure 13a. As the water surface moved upward, it pushed the air in the soil sample uniformly to the top of the open column.

IV. CONCLUSION

The Preliminary Test, along with Test 1 and 2a had the purpose of establishing the correct set-up of the experimental apparatus, including drive current and physical location of the sensors. The results from these have demonstrated the importance of setting the correct drive current for the TF cell. Test 2b and 3 compared the responses of the TF cell under two different water infiltration paths, downwards and upwards respectively, and this difference in the wetting method has created an interesting difference in the resistivity readings; the hypothesis of trapped air being the cause needs to be further investigated.

Resistivity measured using the output of the TF cell follows the trends in the available literature, including McCarter (1984) [16] and more recently Hen-Jones et al. (2017) [3], that show resistivity-water content trends for compacted clays. These can be seen in Figure 2 which summarises both works. The values of resistivity in Figure 2 are considerably lower than the values obtained in all experiments using TF cell. However, the soil samples used in this paper are sand instead of clay. Higher values were expected and correspond to soil resistivity generally having higher values in the sand than in clay soil samples.

Following the results presented, future work includes characterization of the response for different soil particle sizes and types (sand to clay), and relation to fundamental models including parameters of the soil such as density, porosity, saturation and compaction degrees.

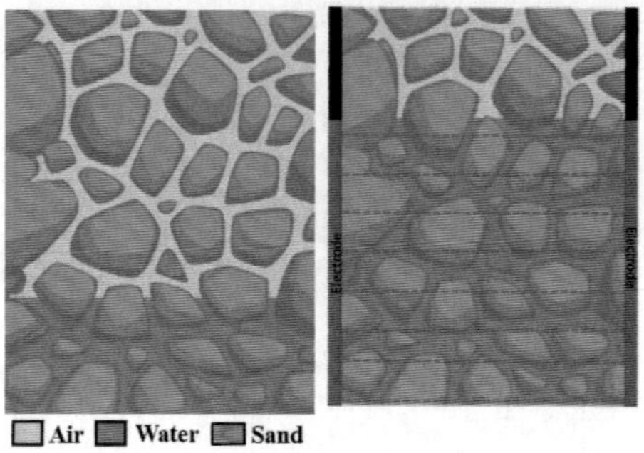

Figure 13. (a) Soil sample showing uniform upwards water infiltration, (b) uniform composition of soil/water between the TF electrodes.

ACKNOWLEDGMENT

Authors express their gratitude to the Mexican National Council for Science and Technology (CONACYT), the UK Engineering and Physical Sciences Research Council (EPSRC), and the Rail Safety and Standards Board (RSSB), who have all supported this work.

REFERENCES

[1] S. Glendinning, J. Hall, and L. Manning, "Asset-management strategies for infrastructure embankments," In Proceedings of the Institution of Civil Engineers-Engineering Sustainability, vol. 162, no. 2, pp. 111-120, 2009.

[2] J. Perry, M. Pedley, and M. Reid, "Infrastructure embankments: condition appraisal and remedial treatment," Construction Industry Research and Information Association. 2001.

[3] R. M. Hen-Jones, et al., "Seasonal effects on geophysical–geotechnical relationships and their implications for electrical resistivity tomography monitoring of slopes," Acta Geotechnica, pp. 1-15, 2017.

[4] J. K. Atkinson, A. W. J. Cranny, W. V. Glasspool, and J. A. Mihell, "An investigation of the performance characteristics and operational lifetimes of multi-element thick film sensor arrays used in the determination of water quality parameters," Sensors and Actuators B: Chemical, vol. 54, no. 3, pp. 215-231, 1999.

[5] J. K. Atkinson, et al., "Thick film screen printed environmental and chemical sensor array reference electrodes suitable for subterranean and subaqueous deployments," Microelectronics International, vol. 30, no. 2, pp. 92-98. 2013.

[6] A. Gac, J. K. Atkinson, Z. Zhang, and R.P. Sion, "A comparison of thick-film chemical sensor characteristics in laboratory and on-line industrial process applications," Measurement Science and Technology, vol. 13, no. 12, pp. 2062. 2002.

[7] C. M. Gardner, D. A. Robinson, K. Blyth, and J. D. Cooper, "Soil water content. Soil analysis: physical methods," pp. 1-74.

[8] R. D. Grisso, M. M. Alley, D. L. Holshouser, and W. E. Thomason, "Precision farming tools. Soil electrical conductivity," Available at https://pubs.ext.vt.edu/442/442-508/442-508_pdf.pdf (verified 2017.08.15), 2005.

[9] National Resources Conservation Service (NRCS), "Inherent factors affecting soil EC," Soil Electrical Conductivity, Available at

http://www.nrcs.usda.gov/Internet/FSE_DOCUMENTS/nrcs142p2_053280.pdf (verified 2017.08.15).

[10] J. D. Rhoades, N. A. Manteghi, P. J. Shouse, and W. J. Alves, "Soil electrical conductivity and soil salinity: new formulations and calibrations," Soil Science Society of America Journal, vol. 53, no. 2, pp. 433-439, 1989.

[11] V. Lapenna, et al., "High-resolution geoelectrical tomographies in the study of Giarrossa landslide (southern Italy)," Bulletin of Engineering Geology and the Environment, vol. 62, no. 3, pp. 259-268, 2003.

[12] Y. Mao, E. Romero, and A. Gens, "Exploring ice content on partially saturated frozen soils using dielectric permittivity and bulk electrical conductivity measurements," The third European Conference on Unsaturated Soil – E-UNSAT 2016 vol. 9, pp. 1-6, 2016.

[13] K. Suzuki and S. Higashi, "Groundwater flow after heavy rain in landslide-slope area from 2-D inversion of resistivity monitoring data," Geophysics, vol. 66, no. 3, pp. 733-743, 2001.

[14] D. L. Corwin and S. M. Lesch, "Apparent soil electrical conductivity measurements in agriculture," Computers and Electronics in Agriculture, vol. 46, no. 1, pp. 11-43, 2005.

[15] M. Sophocleous and J. K. Atkinson, "A novel thick-film electrical conductivity sensor suitable for liquid and soil conductivity measurements," Sensors and Actuators B: Chemical, vol. 213, pp. 417-422, 2015.

[16] W. J. McCarter, "The electrical resistivity characteristics of compacted clays," Géotechnique, vol. 34, no. 2, pp. 263-267, 1984.

International Academy, Research,
and Industry Association (IARIA)
412 Derby Way
Wilmington, DE 19810

ISBN 978-1-5108-5135-1

9 781510 851351

CURRAN ASSOCIATES INC.
proceedings.com

Eighteenth International Conference on Software Engineering Advances (ICSEA 2023)

Held at SoftNet 2023

Valencia, Spain
13-17 November 2023